Disorienting Fiction

Disorienting Fiction

THE AUTOETHNOGRAPHIC WORK OF NINETEENTH-CENTURY BRITISH NOVELS

JAMES BUZARD

PRINCETON UNIVERSITY PRESS

PRINCETON AND OXFORD

Library of Congress Cataloging-in-Publication Data

Buzard, James.
Disorienting fiction : the autoethnographic work of nineteenth-century British novels /
James Buzard.
p.   cm.
Includes bibliographical references and index.
ISBN 0-691-00232-0 (cl. : alk. paper) — ISBN 0-691-09555-8 (pbk. : alk. paper)
1. English fiction—19th century—History and criticism.   2. National characteristics,
British, in literature.   3. Alienation (Social psychology) in literature.   4. Difference
(Psychology) in literature. 5. Social isolation in literature. 6. Outsiders in literature.
7. Culture in literature.   8. Self in literature.   I. Title.
PR868.N356B89 2005
823′.809358—dc22
2004040127

British Library Cataloging-in-Publication Data is available
This book has been composed in Times Roman.
Printed on acid-free paper. ∞
pup.princeton.edu
Printed in the United States of America

1 2 3 4 5 6 7 8 9 10

CONTENTS

ACKNOWLEDGMENTS

MANY THANKS to James Eli Adams and Ian Duncan for their support, valuable criticisms, exemplary professionalism, and friendship. To Christopher Herbert, *il miglior fabbro,* I owe a special debt for his work and example. I would also like to thank Amanda Anderson, Joseph Childers, Jay Clayton, Penny Fielding, Eileen Gillooly, Tanya Holway, Michael Levenson, and Andrew Miller for many encouragements and enabling interventions. My department chair, Peter S. Donaldson, could write the book on how to nurture a colleague's developing career. The dean of my school, Philip S. Khoury, has afforded me every opportunity I could have asked for, and then some, in the form of leave time and research support. An NEH fellowship at the National Humanities Center was an invaluable stimulus in the early stages of my work on this project: at that time, Elizabeth Helsinger kindly read and commented on some early drafts. Lectures developing portions of my argument here have been delivered under the auspices of numerous organizations, including the MLA, NAVSA, the Dickens Project, the British Council, INCS, NVSA, the Victorians Institute, the Society for the Study of Narrative Literature, the Society for Utopian Studies, the Humanities Center at Harvard University, the CUNY Graduate Center, the History and Literature Workshop at MIT, the University of Exeter, the Literature Faculty of MIT, and the English Departments of the following universities or colleges: Edinburgh, Indiana, Duke, Salem State, Oregon, Tennessee, Harvard, and Fordham. I would like to thank all of these organizations for the opportunities they extended to me.

Mazviita, Tuku.

In a category of their own are Ina, the irrepressible Nathaniel, and the peerless Camilla. Camilla was born just after my previous book appeared and has had to wait far too long to be acknowledged in this one.

The following published essays represent early versions of parts of this book:

"'Anywhere's Nowhere': *Bleak House* as Autoethnography," *Yale Journal of Criticism* 12/1 (1999), 7–39.

"'Anywhere's Nowhere': Dickens on the Move," in Anny Sadrin, ed., *Dickens, Europe, and the New Worlds* (London: Macmillan, 1999), 113–27.

"Ethnography as Interruption: *News from Nowhere,* Narrative, and the Modern Romance of Authority," *Victorian Studies* 40/3 (Spring 1997), 445–74.

"Translation and Tourism: Scott's *Waverley* and the Rendering of Culture," *Yale Journal of Criticism,* 8/2 (1995), 31–59.

If everything is related to everything else, where does the description stop?
  —Raymond Firth

The concept of *Kultur* delimits.
  —Norbert Elias

"Where would you wish to go?" she asked.
"Anywhere, my dear," I replied.
"Anywhere's nowhere," said Miss Jellyby, stopping perversely.
"Let us go somewhere at any rate," said I.
  —Charles Dickens, *Bleak House*

I . . . have so much to do in unraveling certain human lots, and seeing how they were woven and interwoven, that all the light I can command must be concentrated on this particular web, and not dispersed over that tempting range of relevancies called the universe.
  —George Eliot, *Middlemarch*

PART ONE

Cultures and Autoethnography

CHAPTER ONE

Uneven Developments: "Culture," circa 2000 and 1900

[A]lthough it is still spoken of as "the science of culture," modern cultural
anthropology might be more accurately characterized as the "science of cultures."
—George W. Stocking Jr.[1]

AT THE END of the twentieth century, the anthropological concept of "culture,"
once heralded as a colossal advance in social thought, occupied an uncertain terrain. On the one hand, its usefulness and even indispensability were championed
in a series of ambitious studies of international economic and political relations,
including such works as Samuel P. Huntington's *The Clash of Civilizations* and
David S. Landes's *The Wealth and Poverty of Nations,* which sometimes treated
"cultural differences" as if they were capable of accounting for virtually every feature of contemporary geopolitics, and especially for every troubling feature. As the
title of a recent Landes essay puts it, "Culture Makes Almost All the Difference."[2]
Such books reflected the term's phenomenal success outside of academic discourse, where, on talk radio and in book groups, on editorial pages and elementary schools, it is scarcely an exaggeration to say that sustained conversation about
human affairs could hardly be carried on without almost constant recourse to the
idea that the world population is divisible into a number of discrete cultures, and
that these cultures determine or at least explain much of what goes on in the world.

At the same time, in progressive circles in the field that had developed and pro-
mulgated the concept, culture had become something of a pariah, an embarrassing
relic of early disciplinary formation and of anthropology's implication in colonial
institutions and agendas. Far from being an instrument encouraging sympathetic understanding of other peoples' ways of life, "culture" had been accused of functioning as an "essential tool for making other," corralling subjugated peoples into more
readily governable thought-packets and giving the differences, separations, and
inequities among groups of people "the specious air of the self-evident."[3] The anthropological concept of culture, it was said, "might never have been invented
without a colonial theater that . . . necessitated the knowledge of culture (for the

---

[1] Stocking, *Victorian Anthropology* (New York: Free Press, 1987), 302.

[2] In Lawrence E. Harrison and Samuel P. Huntington, eds., *Culture Matters: How Values Shape
Human Progress* (New York: Basic Books, 2000).

[3] Lila Abu-Lughod, "Writing Against Culture," in Richard G. Fox, ed., *Recapturing Anthropology:
Working in the Present* (Santa Fe: School of American Research Press, 1991), 143. For correction of
many charges leveled against anthropology, cf. Herbert S. Lewis, "The Misrepresentation of Anthropology and its Consequences," *American Anthropologist* 100/3 (1999), 716–31.

purposes of control and regulation)."[4] The "discourse of culture" was seen to operate "through [a] metaphor of totality [that] represses the reality of political differences and historical change."[5] Paul Rabinow had written of the "symbolic violence"
that turns real, encounterable-in-the-field people into nothing more than mouth-
pieces and mannequins for their cultures.[6] Arjun Appadurai had referred to the way
culture subjects living communities to "metonymic freezing," trapping them forever in (what James Clifford had called) that "ethnographic present" in which the
"common denominator people" of anthropological discourse ("the Nuer," "the Trobriander," et cetera) describe the same "typical" motions endlessly.[7] Anthropology
had been found (by Johannes Fabian) to produce an effect of "allochronicity," a "denial of coevalness" by which practitioners separate themselves from their objects,
whom they deny any such open-ended, living temporality as they and their Western, history-possessing and history-making cohorts enjoy.[8] The relativism extolled
by liberals of an earlier era had been sneeringly dismissed as "the bad faith of the
conqueror, who has become secure enough to become a tourist."[9] The best that
might be said from within the terms of this critique was perhaps, as Bernard S. Cohn
put it, that "[a]nthropologists developed practices through which they sought to
erase the colonial influence by describing what they took to be authentic indigenous
cultures," but that "[t]heir epistemological universe . . . was [ineluctably] part of the
European world of social theories and classificatory schema that were formed, in
part, by state projects to reshape the lives of their subjects at home and abroad."[10]

The multifaceted critique briefly surveyed here had tarnished the reputation of
concepts and conventions central to anthropology, leaving it in a position not unlike that of certain companies unlucky in civil litigation that go on existing solely
in order to pay off punitive damages to the plaintiffs ranged against them. Circa
2000 saw the publication of books considering *The Fate of "Culture"* and looking toward a future *Beyond the Cultural Turn.*[11] And anthropology's late-century

---

[4] Nicholas Dirks, "Introduction: Colonialism and Culture," in Dirks, ed., *Colonialism and Culture* (Ann Arbor: University of Michigan Press, 1992), 3.

[5] Daniel Cottom, *"Ethnographia Mundi,"* in *Text and Culture: The Politics of Interpretation* (Min-neapolis: University of Minnesota Press, 1989), 54; henceforth Cottom.

[6] "Symbolic violence": Paul Rabinow, *Reflections on Fieldwork in Morocco* (Berkeley: University of California Press, 1977), 129.

[7] "Metonymic freezing": Appadurai, "Putting Hierarchy in its Place," *Cultural Anthropology* 3/1 (Feb. 1988), 36. "Ethnographic present": Clifford, "On Ethnographic Authority," in *The Predicament of Culture: Twentieth-Century Ethnography, Literature, and Art* (Cambridge, Mass.: Harvard Univer-sity Press, 1988), 32. "Common denominator people": George E. Marcus and Dick Cushman, "Ethno-graphies as Texts," *Annual Review of Anthropology* 11 (1982), 32–33.

[8] "Allochronicity" and "denial of coevalness": cf. Johannes Fabian, *Time and the Other: How An-thropology Makes its Object* (New York: Columbia University Press, 1983), 25–69.

[9] Stanley Diamond, *In Search of the Primitive: A Critique of Civilization* (New Brunswick, N.J.: Transaction, 1993), 110.

[10] Cohn, *Colonialism and its Forms of Knowledge: The British in India* (Princeton: Princeton Uni-versity Press, 1996), 11.

[11] Cf. Sherry B. Ortner, ed., *The Fate of "Culture": Geertz and Beyond* (Berkeley: University of California Press, 1999) and Victoria E. Bonnell and Lynn Hunt, eds., *Beyond the Cultural Turn: New Directions in the Study of Society and Culture* (Berkeley: University of California Press, 1999).

onset of scruples about its foundational idea dovetailed with increasingly aggressive argumentation coming from evolutionary psychologists who strongly suggested that all talk of culture and of cultural difference would soon be giving way to a perspective that recognized every significant aspect of human behavior as an adaptive mechanism, restoring "human nature" to the throne from which mistaken ideas about the sway of culture had deposed it.[12]

Yet at the same time, and somewhat uncannily, there arose in a different corner of the Anglo-American academy a new post- or neo-Marxist interdiscipline or superdiscipline known as "cultural studies" that circumvented most of the questions raised about culture and mystified and frustrated more than a few of the critics of anthropology in doing so. "Why," Virginia Dominguez demanded, for example, "when the concept of culture has such an elitist history, would sympathetic antielitists [such as the practitioners of cultural studies] contribute to its discursive objectification by trying to argue *in terms of it?*"[13] She might have pointed as well to the so-called new historicism, prominent in literary studies since the 1980s, which sometimes reified units of time and space, such as the "culture of Early Modern England," in treating them as closed circulatory systems of meaning and value.

A hundred years earlier, the habit of putting an "s" to the word *culture* had not yet established itself in Anglo-American usage. The word *culture,* a German import, had of course been deployed and debated in works of social criticism arising out of the so-called condition-of-England question of the 1840s, when the polarizing pressures of intensified industrialization had driven essayists and novelists to wonder whether England was in fact one nation or two (rich and poor, capitalist and worker) and whether many celebrated "mechanical" advances from technology to politics did not degrade rather than cultivate humankind. In Matthew Arnold's famous polemic of the 1860s, *Culture and Anarchy,* a never-defined, singular culture had afforded an external standpoint from which to criticize the shortcomings and blindnesses of a self-congratulatory modern Britain. For the most part, Arnold used *culture* as a universal standard for judging the development of human faculties, but, like John Stuart Mill in *On Liberty,* like John Ruskin in "The Nature of Gothic," and like some other leading Victorian theorists of the social, he sometimes drew tantalizingly near the conceptual territory of the later anthropological concept of culture as the wholeness of a particular people's way of life.[14]

Yet the contemporaneous emergence of anthropology as a recognized academic subject—it earned its own section in the British Association for the Advancement of Science (BAAS) in 1874—seems to have discouraged further progress toward a *pluralizable* model of culture, for, as George W. Stocking Jr. has author-

[12] E.g. Steven Pinker, *The Blank Slate: The Modern Denial of Human Nature* (New York: Viking, 2002).

[13] Dominguez, "Invoking Culture: The Messy Side of 'Cultural Politics,'" *South Atlantic Quarterly* 91/1 (1992), 20. Cf. my "Notes on the Defenestration of Culture," in Amanda Anderson and Joseph Valente, eds., *Disciplinarity at the Fin-de-Siècle* (Princeton: Princeton University Press, 2002), 312–31.

[14] Cf. Christopher Herbert, *Culture and Anomie: Ethnographic Imagination in the Nineteenth Century* (Chicago: University of Chicago Press, 1991), 54–57; henceforth Herbert.

itatively demonstrated, mainstream Victorian anthropology, massively invested in the project of constructing one single narrative about the evolution of human social forms and technologies, was committed to dealing with levels of human Culture—frequently written with a capital C—from primitive to advanced, and not with separate, relatively autonomous "cultures," differently evolved under different environmental conditions. In a powerful essay published in 1968, Stocking demolished the myth, favored by many twentieth-century anthropological adherents of "cultures," that exalted Edward Burnett Tylor's 1871 study *Primitive Culture* as the sacred fount of the modern, relativistic culture-concept: contrary to this pious fiction, Stocking showed, Tylor had never treated culture "as an organized or functionally integrated or patterned way of life, nor did he use the word 'culture' in the plural form"; his method, rather, consistently "forced the fragmentation of whole human cultures into discrete elements which might be classified and compared out of any specific cultural context and then rearranged in stages of probable evolutionary development," and it "presupposed a hierarchical, evaluative approach to the elements thus abstracted and to the stages thus reconstructed."[15] The increasing institutional authority of an evolutionary, comparativist anthropology, unfolding during the period in which the extension and intensification of European imperialism put a premium upon certitudes about the supposedly fixed characteristics—moral, intellectual, and physical—of human races, granted an effective monopoly to the discourse that involved a single human Culture, with higher or lower levels thereof, and that retained the ideologically useful idea of savagery, or a state of human society apparently so unconstrained by morality or law that it could even be said to lie *outside* the reach or below the line of Culture altogether.

Even around 1900, among authors capable of considerable sympathy for the conditions, customs, and institutions of so-called primitives, one finds at most an inconsistent pluralization of *culture,* and frequently the persistent *avoidance* of it. The parallel cases of Joseph Conrad and Mary Kingsley, fin-de-siècle writers noted for their exploration of the geographical and epistemological frontiers between human groups, are illustrative here. Consultation of the concordances to his writings shows that Conrad, who is sometimes treated as a writer of "intercultural" contact, *always* operated within the evolutionist discourse that treats of a single human Culture, never in the one that treats of cultures. We read, for instance, of people who are "as innocent of culture as their own immense and gloomy forests" in *Almayer's Folly,* and of "Don Vincente Ribiera, a man of culture and of unblemished character" in *Nostromo.*[16] Nowhere in Conrad do we find anything comparable to the meaning in Mary Kingsley's statement, from the 1901 *West African Studies,* that the "Africans had a culture of their own—not a perfect one, but one that could be worked up towards perfection, just as European culture could

---

[15] Stocking, "Matthew Arnold, E. B. Tylor, and the Uses of Invention," in *Race, Culture, and Evolution: Essays in the History of Anthropology* (New York: Free Press, 1968), 81, 80.

[16] Sue M. Briggum and Todd K. Bender, *A Concordance to Conrad's* Almayer's Folly (New York & London: Garland, 1978), 118; James W. Parins, Robert J. Dilligan, and Todd K. Bender, *A Concordance to Conrad's* Nostromo (New York and London: Garland, 1984), 314.

be worked up"; and yet Kingsley herself would go on, in a chapter titled "The Clash of Cultures," to speak of "the African" as being "in a lower culture state."[17] Even the 1922 text often regarded as a (if not *the*) founding work of modern ethnographic pluralism—Bronislaw Malinowski's *Argonauts of the Western Pacific*— harbors both old and new, singular and plural senses of culture, and it is dedicated to one of the foremost comparativists, J. G. Frazer. The discourse of "cultures," from which we are now exhorted to liberate ourselves, was then struggling to liberate *itself* from the universalizing vision of ethnological comparativism.

One particularly revealing text from that cusp of the twentieth century when *culture* was still striving to acquire its "s" is William Morris's *News from Nowhere* (1896), a utopian narrative in which the hero, "William Guest," is sorely tempted to change his status if not his name, leaving behind his troubled nineteenth-century society once and for all and remaining in the (twenty-second-century) socialist paradise he has always longed for and finally dreamt himself into. In order to remain a dedicated late-Victorian socialist, and to avoid contaminating his dreamland by introducing into it the traces of an unjust society he bears with him from the past, he must subject this desire of his, to which he gives ardent testimony, to programmatic containment and disruption. The work is also a valedictory upon the Victorian (bourgeois) English novel, an "antinovel" holding a distorting yet strikingly illuminating mirror up to the major works of midcentury fiction.[18] As I shall return to argue in the fourth part of this work, Morris's text opposes its great bourgeois precursors not so much by departing from their methods as by intensifying or radicalizing them. In doing so, Morris opens a new pathway for us between the frequently dissociated Victorian and modernist narrative forms, because *News,* functioning as a kind of Minerva's owl for the nineteenth-century novel, suggests that narrative disjunction or interruption constitutes *the* unacknowledged novelistic principle, a vital element in fiction's treatment of—it is Morris's subject, too— the historical destinies of distinct peoples, nations, or cultures.

I am going to claim that thinking about the nineteenth-century novel as a determinedly *self-interrupting* form permits us to grasp its relation to twentieth-century cultural anthropology, with which it participates in a general system of cultural representation whose shape and coherence has been obscured for us by separate disciplinary agendas since the early 1900s. In this book, planned to be the first of two, narrative self-interruption will be read as the formal signature of British novels devoted to the performance of a "metropolitan autoethnography"—by which admittedly cumbersome term I mean a number of things that will be specified in this and the ensuing chapters. Regarding Morris's little book as an extreme or (as seems fitting for the 1890s) a "decadent" instance of metropolitan autoethnography offers both a way in and then a conclusion to this account of the great nineteenth-century novels' own status as leading precursors to modern anthropological "cultures."

---

[17] Kingsley, *West African Studies,* 2d ed. (London: Macmillan, 1901), xviii, 325.
[18] Patrick Brantlinger, "'News from Nowhere': Morris's Socialist Anti-Novel," *Victorian Studies* 19 (Sept. 1975), 35–49.

Yet an ethnographic perspective on a work like *News from Nowhere*—or the nineteenth-century "realist" novel, for that matter—might appear an unpromisingly obvious one, for if we take *ethnography* in the loose sense of the study of a people's ways, then what utopian work, with its detailing of (imaginary) social practices, *isn't* ethnographic? What realist *novel* isn't, with its "thick description" of social existence? It will be evident that I employ *ethnography* in a stricter sense than is conveyed by such questions: in the twentieth-century sense of a study of a people's way of life centering on the method of "immersion" in extensive fieldwork and raising the issue of how, and how far, the outsider can become a kind of honorary insider in other cultures. Texts to which we can apply the looser sense of *ethnographic* do not all warrant the label when the term is more narrowly construed. For Thomas More's Hythlodaeus, *becoming* a utopian is never as much of an issue as it is for Morris's William Guest. More wrote at a time when the perception of differences among human practices did not so readily usher in the idea that those differences composed separate "complex wholes," bounded life-worlds such as now go by the name of *cultures*. For writers working after that philological revolution of the late eighteenth and early nineteenth centuries, the borders between linguistically and territorially demarcated groups increasingly tended to become epistemological borders as well, so that the movements, literal and figurative, of an agent capable of crossing those borders generated increased interest and even urgency.[19]

William Morris envisioned his utopia at the start of a decade of crucial developments toward the ethnographic notion of cultures—developments such as the work of W. B. Spencer and Frank Gillen, whose field researches among the Arunta people, recorded in *The Native Tribes of Central Australia* (1899), regarded native life as a distinctive unity centered upon some "totalizing cultural performance."[20] The same decade saw the collapse of an ambitious campaign, undertaken by the Anthropology division of the BAAS, to organize a comprehensive Ethnographic Survey of the United Kingdom: the failure of this scheme cast light upon the fundamental differences of method and purpose between physical anthropologists and the forerunners of modern cultural or social anthropology, helping prepare the ground for the latter's emergence as a more or less autonomous discipline in the opening decades of the twentieth century.[21] It is only in regard to the more modern, more restrictive and reifying construction of differences in terms of cultures that navigating between the positions attributed to "insiders" and "outsiders" becomes a decisive feature in representations of human societies, producing images of the cultural authority as Participant Observer, capable of engagement and de-

[19] Cf. James Whitman, "From Philology to Anthropology in Mid-Nineteenth-Century Germany," in George W. Stocking Jr., ed., *Functionalism Historicized: Essays on British Social Anthropology* (Madison: University of Wisconsin Press, 1984), 214–29.

[20] George W. Stocking Jr., "The Ethnographer's Magic: Fieldwork in British Anthropology from Tylor to Malinowski," in Stocking, ed., *Observers Observed: Essays on Ethnographic Fieldwork* (Madison: University of Wisconsin Press, 1983), 70–120; see 79.

[21] See James Urry, "Englishmen, Celts, and Iberians: The Ethnographic Survey of the United Kingdom, 1892–1899," in Stocking, ed., *Functionalism Historicized*, 83–105.

tachment, each in proper measure. Such navigation forms no vital part of the interest in works like More's *Utopia* (1516), Swift's *Gulliver's Travels* (1726), or Johnson's *Rasselas* (1759). *Ethnography* acquires its modern, restrictive significance when it becomes definable, for all practical purposes, as the discourse in which "a culture" and a Participant Observer reciprocally define one another. A *culture* amounts to "that which it takes a Participant Observer to find."

It was not until the publication, in 1912, of the fourth edition of *Notes and Queries on Anthropology* that the model of the lone field ethnographer, "immersing" himself in "the natives'" way of life, acquired theoretical formulation and scientific license under the imprimatur of the BAAS; Malinowski's classic reflections on method, given in the first chapter of *Argonauts of the Western Pacific,* appeared a decade later. But it is important to place the emergence of these ideas in the context of a larger turn-of-the-century shift toward mobile forms of authority than can temporarily "become" their objects of study. This shift, it seems clear, reflects the intensification and heightened self-consciousness of late nineteenth-century imperialism. The modern fieldworker's displacing of the amateur "men on the spot" who provided data to university-based ethnologists, or of the fact-gathering teams such as those employed in the Torres Strait expedition or the United Kingdom survey of the 1890s, represents one crucial variant, but it shares the notion of a deliberate blurring of boundaries between investigator and object with a host of contemporaneous developments. "Transference" situations begin to figure in Freud's work from 1895, drawing the physician willy-nilly into the patient's treatment; in 1910 Freud argued that a rigorous *Selbstanalyse* would be indispensable if the analyst were to "recognize [the] counter-transference in himself and overcome it."[22] By 1922 the Congress of the International Psycho-Analytic Association had made submission to a training analysis a requirement for would-be analysts.[23] Earlier, Freud had subjected his own dreams to interpretation and himself to treatment with cocaine. The era includes as well Wilhelm Dilthey's notion of the "mysterious process of mental transfer" between interpreter and historical subject that distinguishes the *Geisteswissenschaften:* "We *explain* nature," Dilthey remarked; "*man* we must understand."[24] It's in this period that Sherlock Holmes characterizes his method by saying, "I put myself in the man's place, and . . . I try to imagine how I should myself have proceeded under the same circumstances."[25] During these years, the border-crossing subgenres of imperial travelogues, utopias, and tales of espionage flourish.[26] Fiction is peopled with scientists who experiment on them-

---

[22] Sigmund Freud, "The Future Prospects of Psycho-Analytic Therapy," *The Standard Edition of the Complete Psychological Works of Sigmund Freud,* trans. James Strachey et al. (London, 1954–74), XI: 139–51; quotation from 144–45.

[23] See J. Laplanche and J.-B. Pontalis, *The Language of Psycho-Analysis,* trans. Donald Nicholson-Smith (New York: Norton, 1973), 457, 454.

[24] Quoted in Richard E. Palmer, *Hermeneutics: Interpretation Theory in Schleiermacher, Dilthey, Heidegger, and Gadamer* (Evanston, Ill.: Northwestern University Press, 1969), 104, 115.

[25] Arthur Conan Doyle, "The Musgrave Ritual," in *The Complete Sherlock Holmes* (Garden City, N.Y.: Doubleday, n.d.), 395.

[26] In *The Culture of Time and Space, 1880–1918* (Cambridge, Mass.: Harvard University Press,

selves, detectives who mimic the criminals they pursue, imperial agents who merge with colonized peoples: Kipling's Kim "infiltrates a community by actually joining it."[27] In Conrad's *Lord Jim* (1900), the character Stein utters what may be read as the motto for the turn-of-the-century's authorizing metanarrative: "In the destructive element immerse"—to which we might add, "but make sure you get out again."[28]

For fin-de-siècle writers, the intensification of imperial rivalries, combined with numerous other factors political, technological, sexual, and aesthetic, gave new urgency and fascination to narratives about the danger that a frontier willingly but temporarily breached might vanish completely, stranding the explorer in the Other's place. These are, of course, the years of Jekyll and Hyde, of Kurtz. In Conan Doyle's "The Creeping Man" (1923), Professor Presbury, "the famous Camford physiologist," risks permanently transforming himself into an ape when he takes "serum of black-faced langur" in an attempt to recapture his youth.[29] Kipling's colonial policeman Strickland, who figures in several tales, has the holiday custom of disguising himself and "stepp[ing] down into the brown crowd [to be] swallowed up for a while," but he finds the habit dangerously addictive, as "the streets and the bazars, and the sounds in them . . . call[] to him to come back and take up his wanderings and his discoveries."[30] In this fraught context, an insistence upon the maintenance of the boundary, upon the final self-identity of the investigator, is indispensable to the desideratum of a controlled self-alienation. In crossing over, the mobile authority lays claim to the ability to set aside identity for a time, implying that such identity is there to begin with and that it will be recovered, rather than invented in defining contrast to, and engagement with, the visited (often the colonized and available-for-visiting) Other. In all these instances, authority derives from the demonstration not so much of some finally achieved "insideness" in the alien state, but rather from the demonstration of an *outsider's insideness*. Anthropology's Participant Observer, whose aim was a "simulated membership" or "membership without commitment to membership" in the visited culture, went on to become perhaps the most recognizable (and institutionally embedded) avatar of this distinctively modern variety of heroism and prestige.[31]

1983), Stephen Kern points to "an outburst of literary utopianism" between 1888 and 1900 (cf. 98, 332n9).

[27] Thomas Richards, *The Imperial Archive: Knowledge and the Fantasy of Empire* (London: Verso, 1993), 25.

[28] Conrad, *Lord Jim* (1900; New York: Signet, n.d.), 161. But cf. Vincent P. Pecora, "The Sorcerer's Apprentices: Romance, Anthropology, and Literary Theory," *Modern Language Quarterly* 55/4 (Dec. 1994), 345–82.

[29] Doyle, "The Creeping Man," in *The Complete Sherlock Holmes,* 1072, 1082.

[30] Kipling, "Miss Youghal's *Sais,*" in *Plain Tales from the Hills* (Oxford: Oxford University Press, 1991), 25, 29.

[31] Bernard McGrane, *Beyond Anthropology: Society and the Other* (New York: Columbia University Press, 1989), 125; henceforth McGrane. Cf. Susan Sontag, "The Anthropologist as Hero," in Nelson Hayes and Tanya Hayes, eds., *Claude Lévi-Strauss: The Anthropologist as Hero* (Cambridge, Mass.: MIT Press, 1970), 184–96; Nancy Bentley, *The Ethnography of Manners: Hawthorne, James, Wharton* (Cambridge: Cambridge University Press, 1995), esp. chap. 1.

This was the turn-of-the-century maelstrom from which the Participant Observer and the correspondingly plural and spatialized conception of culture arose into articulated form and commenced their careers at the heart of single discipline asserting primacy over all matters cultural.[32] Yet as Christopher Herbert has convincingly demonstrated, a more complete and complex understanding of "the culture idea" as an historical phenomenon requires that we approach the subject less as a discrete "idea" than as "a highly motivated discursive formation whose advent is registered, even before it has assumed distinct form, by the turbulence it generates within various nineteenth-century fields of thought" (Herbert 253). Like nationalism, as Benedict Anderson has famously handled it, culture, too, is not so much a kind of thought as a thing to think with, a "cultural artefact" in its own right, or what Kenneth Burke called a "scene word," denoting "not so much a clear concept as a cluster of interchangeable ideas and allusions open to mutual substitution and reciprocal definition."[33] Telling the story of its emergence thus requires us to look farther back than circa 1900, and it requires viewpoints different in kind from those of traditional histories of ideas, however expertly conducted they may be—as, for one splendid instance, Isaiah Berlin's *Vico and Herder: Two Studies in the History of Ideas* (1976) certainly was. Where Herbert charts "the ethnographic imagination" across a range of nineteenth-century discourses, this book concerns itself with a constellation of textual effects in British narrative fiction that I see as signs of an incipient *autoethnographic* imagination cutting against the grain of the self-universalizing mentality which critics have often imputed to elements of mainstream culture during Britain's long era of imperial expansion and consolidation. I contend that a self-delimiting (or, in narrative terms, a self-interrupting) autoethnographic project informs—that is, does not merely arise in but comes to preoccupy—the British novel after the 1801 Act of Parliament creating the United Kingdom of Great Britain and Ireland. In the immediate aftermath

[32] As with the first pluralization of *culture,* the first usage of *Participant Observer* is difficult to pin down. The OED's first documented use of the phrase dates from 1924 but points to some earlier source: cf. Eduard C. Lindeman, *Social Discovery* (New York: Republic, 1924), 191. Robert J. C. Young oversimplifies matters in asserting (in *Colonial Desire: Hybridity in Theory, Culture, and Race* [London and New York: Routledge, 1995], 49) that Anthony Trollope was the first to pluralize *culture* in an 1862 work. Cf. Stocking, *Victorian* 302–4, and Adam Kuper, *Culture: The Anthropologists' Account* (Cambridge, Mass.: Harvard University Press, 2000), 23–29, 59–72; henceforth Kuper.

[33] "Cultural artefact": Anderson, *Imagined Communities: Reflections on the Origin and Spread of Nationalism* (London: Verso, 1983), 13. "Not so much . . . ": David Simpson, *Situatedness: Or, Why We Keep Saying Where We're Coming From* (Durham, N.C.: Duke University Press, 2002), 95; cf. 39–41. Simpson's reference is to Burke, *A Grammar of Motives* (Berkeley and Los Angeles: University of California Press, 1969). Influential studies of culture focusing mainly on debates within anthropology include Alfred Kroeber and Clyde Kluckhohn's *Culture: A Critical Review of Concepts and Definitions* (1952), George W. Stocking Jr.'s magisterial *Victorian Anthropology* (1987) and other writings, and Adam Kuper's recent *Culture* (2000). Important nonanthropologists' accounts that argue for a broader view of culture's emergence include Raymond Williams's classic *Culture and Society, 1780–1950* (1958), Christopher Herbert's *Culture and Anomie* (1991), Susan Hegeman's *Patterns for America: Modernism and the Concept of Culture* (1999), Marc Manganaro's *Culture, 1922: The Emergence of a Concept* (2002), and Michael A. Elliott's *The Culture Concept: Writing and Difference in the Age of Realism* (2003).

of this nation-making legislation, Irish and Scottish practitioners of the National Tale and historical novel developed modes of fiction devoted to the representation of their own cultures—and to the self-conscious questioning of that task—but this book's major argument concerns the selective adaptation of such modes by some of the mid-century *English* novelists we have long identified as the masters of Victorian fiction.

This study treats important nineteenth-century novels for their constitutive linkages among three tropes: first, the "metaphorization [in Roy Wagner's phrase] of life into culture," whereby phenomena encountered serially in a particular society are "translated" and assigned value in terms of their position in the iconic space of that society's purported culture; second, the metaphorization of culture into *place,* whereby the iconic space of a culture is "mapped onto" the physical territory belonging to the people whose culture it is; and third, the metaphorization of a spatialized culture into the textual space of a novel.[34] The novelists I read practice upon their own people the fiction Roy Wagner has described as "the study of [humankind] *as if there were culture*": in their labors to invent and to represent their cultures as if they were things in space, they trope the textual space of their fictions as ethnogeographical space (Wagner 10, emphasis added).

As David Scott has argued, what "organizes the epistemological and geographical disposition of the anthropological gaze" is not so much the kind of knowledge delivered by the fieldworker as the "'constant dialectical tacking' across a field or fields of difference," the recurrent "movement . . . of going and returning."[35] Such a movement constitutes what Clifford Geertz has called anthropology's "inward conceptual rhythm."[36] It seems to me that the nineteenth-century British novel's contribution to the process that gave us the dyad of a culture and its Participant Observer has to be looked for in its reorientation and freighting with new significance of a fundamental aspect of narrative, the relationship between narrator and characters, or between what narratologists call *discourse-* and *story-spaces.*[37] As metropolitan autoethnography, the nineteenth-century novel anticipates modern fieldworking ethnography *in reverse,* by construing its narrator's (and many characters') desired position vis-à-vis the fictional world it depicts as that of an *insider's outsideness*—"outside enough" to apprehend the shape of the culture (and its possibilities of reform), yet insistently positioned as the outsideness of a *particular* inside, differentiating itself from the putatively unsituated outsideness of theory or cosmopolitanism as conventionally represented. This book's opening chapters spell out this claim in greater detail and explore some of the implications of making it.

---

[34] For Roy Wagner, see *The Invention of Culture* (1975; revised and expanded ed., Chicago and London: University of Chicago Press, 1981), 28; henceforth Wagner.

[35] Scott, "Locating the Anthropological Subject: Postcolonial Anthropologists in Other Places," *Inscriptions* 5 (1989), 78.

[36] Geertz, "'From the Native's Point of View': On the Nature of Anthropological Understanding," in *Local Knowledge: Further Essays in Interpretive Anthropology* (New York: Basic Books, 1983), 69.

[37] Cf. Seymour Chatman, *Story and Discourse: Narrative Structure in Fiction and Film* (Ithaca, N.Y.: Cornell University Press, 1978); also, on nineteenth-century fiction in particular, Harry E. Shaw, "Loose Narrators: Display, Engagement, and the Search for a Place in History in Realist Fiction," *Narrative* 3/2 (May 1995), 95–116.

Among the major benefits this argument seeks to accrue would be, first, a formally and historically richer way of understanding the English novel's transformation in the 1840s and 1850s from a loosely assembled entertainment to a self-reflexive "service delivery system" with aspirations to total formal integration: this commonly observed shift, which coincides with the novel's turn toward more ambitious social analysis, I want to construe as an important event in the story of culture's emergence. This effort, in turn, promises to adjust existing models for explaining the relationship between fictional form and imperial expansion during the nineteenth century. Most broadly, I suggest that the explicit formulation of culture as an anthropological category used mainly on remote, so-called underdeveloped societies actually follows and reverses a great deal of implicit reliance upon something operating discernibly *like* culture in novelistic representations of British society. A corollary of this thesis is that those strenuous critiques of anthropological representation that have so much occupied our attention and given shape to our assumptions in recent years have made it difficult to think about other motives for taking an "othering" or objectifying viewpoint on human affairs than those emanating from the desire to conquer and control. Once objectification gets limited to the kind of coercively reductive forms critics have found in anthropology, the obvious and correspondingly limited response is to promote the subjectification of everybody once anthropologically objectified. And that is what critics have limited themselves to doing, so far, with the concept of autoethnography.

In her *Imperial Eyes: Travel Writing and Transculturation* (1992), Mary Louise Pratt reasoned that "[i]f ethnographic texts are a means by which Europeans represent to themselves their (usually subjugated) others, autoethnographic texts are those the others construct in response to or in dialogue with those metropolitan representations."[38] Pratt influentially insisted upon the "transcultural" nature of the autoethnographic text, cautioning against simplistic views of it as an "authentic" or "autochthonous" expression of cultural essence. Yet what she called dialogue is not functionally distinct from "rebuttal": an erroneous and coercive representation of a culture, produced by hostile aliens, is counteracted by another that, however much it may appropriate the modes of the former for its own purposes, can be securely distinguished from it, and preferred to it, only by virtue of its author's indigenous status, which is taken to confer automatic authority to represent the culture. In the sense of "really proceeding from its reputed source or author," Pratt's model of autoethnography (only tentatively sketched to be sure) had everything to do with the cultural authenticity of the product.[39] In her tidy opposition, those who were once the direct objects of ethnographic depictions now "talk back" as the subjects of an inevitably self-referential discourse. Such an approach strikes me as having at least two major drawbacks. On the one hand, it makes no room for sustained consideration of how some individual member of a culture goes about *securing* the authority to represent or "speak on behalf of" the culture to which he

---

[38] Mary Louise Pratt, *Imperial Eyes: Travel Writing and Transculturation* (New York: Routledge, 1992), 7. Cf. my "On Auto-Ethnographic Authority," *Yale Journal of Criticism* (Spring 2003), 61–91.
[39] OED s.v. "authentic."

or she belongs. The logics, the narratives, the metaphors by means of which autoethnographers might need to explain to themselves and to others what they are up to remain analytical nonissues. In this book, I focus on the question James Clifford has raised in asking, "If, as I assume, no *inherent* authority can be accorded to 'native' ethnographies and histories, what constitutes their *differential* authority?"—for, as Clifford continues, "even when the ethnographer is positioned as an insider . . . in her or his community, some taking of distance and translating differences will be part of the research, analysis and writing."[40] I read important acts of narration in nineteenth-century British novels as enacting precisely such "taking of distance" and "translating [of] differences."

My second reason for being dissatisfied with Pratt's description of autoethnography is that, because Pratt accepts the meta-anthropological critique that virtually identifies an "ethnographic perspective" with the brutal "othering" powers and aims of colonization, she (along with others) is predisposed to conceive of autoethnography solely as reversing ethnography's presumed single tendency.[41] I do not believe that twentieth-century anthropology's widely held and vehemently professed relativism, even if it represents a utopian, ultimately unsustainable position, deserves to be wholly dismissed as the false consciousness of imperial dupes and stooges, however much the projects of anthropological fieldwork were constructed within and constrained by imperial power structures. Furthermore, it seems to me that any history of autoethnographic consciousness—the consciousness centered upon the notion of oneself as the product and possessor of a distinct culture—that accepts such preemptive bracketing of its subject matter renders itself both predictable and vitiated. When we remember that much passionate intellectual labor during the Victorian era was spent in coming to grips with the progressive invalidation of traditional theological underpinnings for society, and that numerous Victorian writers were much engaged in the effort to construct a vision of their way of life as *both* merely contingent *and* worthy of rededicated participation (cf. Carlyle's *Sartor Resartus,* for example), we should be prepared to insist upon a broader account of the emergence of autoethnography. Surely one definitive—and still ongoing—modern labor is that of finding that zone of productive ambivalence in which both the constructedness of and the undogmatic commitment to our systems of custom and value may be simultaneously affirmed.

The broader view of autoethnography which I recommend here might begin with a version of A. J. Greimas's "semiotic rectangle" illustrating the possibilities of ethnographic and autoethnographic representation within the global framework of imperial and postimperial history:[42]

---

[40] "Spatial Practices" in *Routes: Travel and Translation in the Late Twentieth Century* (Cambridge, Mass.: Harvard University Press, 1997), 79, 86.

[41] From such a viewpoint, the romantic strain in anthropology simply expresses that "imperialist nostalgia" which colonizers indulge in to bemoan the demise of their own victims: cf. Renato Rosaldo, *Culture and Truth: The Remaking of Social Analysis* (Boston: Beacon, 1993), 68–87.

[42] Cf. Greimas (with François Rastier), "Les Jeux des contraintes semiotiques," *Du Sens* (Paris: Seuil, 1970), 135–55, and Fredric Jameson, *The Prison-House of Language: A Critical Account of Structuralism and Russian Formalism* (Princeton: Princeton University Press, 1972), esp. 163–68.

WHO IS REPRESENTED

	Colonizable Periphery	Imperial Metropolis
Imperial Metropolis	Dominant mode of 20th-c. ethnography (Westerners study "traditional," "other" cultures)	"Metropolitan Autoethnography" (19th-c. British novel, cultural criticism, sociology)
Colonizable Periphery	Autoethnography as described by Pratt: colonized peoples speak of/for themselves (19th-c. romantic nationalisms; 20th-c. postcolonial nationalisms)	"Reverse Ethnography": representation of metropolitan societies by the formerly colonized (a product of "reverse colonization," esp. post-WWII)

WHO REPRESENTS

It is into just such an overarching structure for modernity that I wish to insert this book's readings in the English Victorian novel, that celebrated and, in recent years, suspect form whose relation to the British Empire has been the subject of considerable debate.

In seeking to rectify the systematic underdevelopment of autoethnographic thinking as it might apply to the imperial *center,* the next chapter will begin by taking up several inconsistencies that I construe as constitutive of, rather than simply flaws in, the ethnographic conceptualization of cultures.[43] These mainly have to do with the idea that the locations of ethnographic fieldwork "often come to be identified with the groups that inhabit them."[44] A common understanding of the discipline's history has been that a "spatial reorganization of human differences" was achieved when early twentieth-century figures like Malinowski and Franz Boas took to the field, breaking with their Victorian forebears in promoting a conception of plural, spatially distributed cultures.[45] As Margaret Mead succinctly put it, "we went to the field not to look for *earlier* forms of human life, but for forms that were *different.*"[46] Disciplinary "common sense" implicitly defined the "natives" of anthropology (to quote Appadurai) "not only [as] persons who are from certain places, and belong to those places," but as people "somehow incarcerated, or confined, in those places," whereas Western "explorers, administrators, mis-

[43] Cf. Ruth Behar, *The Vulnerable Observer: Anthropology that Breaks Your Heart* (Boston: Press, 1996), on the "deeply paradoxical" nature of anthropology, whose "methodology, defined by the oxymoron 'participant observation,'" is "split at the root" (5).

[44] Arjun Appadurai, "Introduction: Place and Voice in Anthropological Theory," *Cultural Anthropology* 3/1 (Feb. 1988), 16.

[45] Susan Hegeman, *Patterns for America: Modernism and the Concept of Culture* (Princeton: Princeton University Press, 1999), 32.

[46] Margaret Mead, *Blackberry Winter: My Earlier Years* (New York: William Morrow, 1972), 156.

sionaries, and eventually anthropologists," "regarded as quintessentially mobile . . . [,] are the movers, the seers, the knowers."[47]

Ethnography in its twentieth-century incarnation did not simply require travel, it depended upon the metaphor of knowledge *as* travel; conversely, the subject of ethnographic study, like the superceded model of nineteenth-century anthropological knowledge (the "armchair" scholar), was a stay-at-home. The ethnogeographical idea "that 'a culture' is naturally the property of a spatially localized people and that the way to study such a culture is to go 'there' ('among the so-and-so')" found its "clearest illustration . . . [in] the classic 'ethnographic maps' that purported to display the spatial distribution of peoples, tribes, and cultures," maps on which "space itself becomes a kind of neutral grid on which cultural difference . . . [is] inscribed."[48] What is more, the principle of native "incarceration [had] a moral and intellectual dimension," inasmuch as indigenous peoples were considered "confined by what they know, feel, and believe[,] . . . prisoners of their 'mode of thought' "—incapable, in other words, of thinking themselves "outside" the metaphorical "mental space" of their own culture to see it as historically produced and contingent rather than as natural or proper for all humankind.[49] Consequently, "all ethnography," as Michael Herzfeld has characterized it, "is in some sense an account of a social group's ethnocentrism."[50] The modern ethnographic imagination likened the physical territory inhabited by supposedly immobile natives to the iconic space of a cultural totality presumed to order and give meaning to every aspect of native life. In perhaps the tersest statement of this ethnogeographical doctrine, Malinowski proclaimed that "[w]ithin the boundaries of the tribe the writ of the same culture runs from end to end."[51]

A reexamination of this—in my view—only partly understood set of assumptions about the linkage between culture and place will prepare the foundation for my claim that English novels of the middle decades of the nineteenth century, under pressures specific to their era, began crafting fictions of metropolitan autoethnography. The chapters in part II of this study juxtapose two major metanovels produced in the early and middle nineteenth century, by writers self-consciously functioning as authoritative represeters of their peoples: Walter Scott

---

[47] Arjun Appadurai, "Putting Hierarchy in its Place," 37.

[48] "That 'a culture' . . . ": Akhil Gupta and James Ferguson, "Culture, Power, Place: Ethnography at the End of an Era," in Gupta and Ferguson, eds., *Culture, Power, Place: Explorations in Critical Anthropology* (Durham, N.C., and London: Duke University Press, 1997), 3. "Clearest illustration . . . ": Gupta and Ferguson, "Beyond 'Culture': Space, Identity, and the Politics of Difference," *Cultural Anthropology* 7/1 (Feb. 1992), 7. The authors have in mind such texts as George P. Murdock's various ethnographic atlases and the *Outline of World Cultures*, produced in several editions beginning in the 1950s. Cf. Liisa H. Malkki, "National Geographic: The Rooting of Peoples and the Territorialization of National Identity among Scholars and Refugees," in *Culture, Power, Place*, 52–74, and Karen Fog Olwig and Kirsten Harstrup, eds., *Siting Culture: The Shifting Anthropological Object* (London: Routledge, 1997).

[49] Appadurai, "Putting Hierarchy in its Place," 37.

[50] Herzfeld, *Anthropology through the Looking-Glass: Critical Ethnography in the Margins of Europe* (Cambridge: Cambridge University Press, 1987), 18.

[51] Malinowski, *A Scientific Theory of Culture and Other Essays* (Chapel Hill: University of North Carolina Press, 1944), 60.

and Charles Dickens. Scott writes *Waverley* in the decade between 1805 and 1814 as a self-critical performance of his own cicerone-like authority over a "Scottish culture" he knew to be a largely invented tradition; Dickens writes *Bleak House* in 1851–52 as an anti-Great Exhibition, to return British emotional investment to a domestic scene neglected by British men and women whose sights were too much fixed upon global perspectives. The chapters in part III then study all four of Charlotte Brontë's mature novels, considering the patterns employed and re-worked across her entire short career as elements in a sustained consideration of autoethnographic possibilities in local, national, and international frameworks. Part IV briefly discusses those self-delimiting, self-interrupting elements in the work of George Eliot—the premier English novelist whose career unfolds entirely after the formalization of the British Empire in India—that will be considered in greater depth in the sequel to this book. I then return to William Morris's anti-bourgeois antinovel *News from Nowhere* to frame the period to be explored in the sequel (roughly 1857–1900).

For Victorian case studies, I have chosen to emphasize Dickens, Charlotte Brontë, and Eliot, not only because I continue to find these the most lastingly stim-ulating of Victorian novelists, but because even an account limited for practical purposes to these three affords us a view of three quite different approaches to the question of an English autoethnographic fiction. I take their diversity as evidence that the autoethnographic turn in the mid-Victorian novel promised a general re-orientation of viewpoint—a promise largely forestalled and negated by official state epistemologies, as well as by the emergent sciences of society themselves. The readings in this book are extremely "close" and detailed ones because part of my burden is to show the depth of the English novel's preoccupation with its new proto- and autoethnographic labor. These readings are invitations for more.

This book attempts, then, to read the emergence of anthropological *culture* in the formal effects of British novels written after the Act of Union that formalized British control of Ireland and created the United Kingdom. I will be guided by the principle that historical explanations of the novel ought to be asked to substanti-ate their claims at a level of literary detail, and with a degree of nuance, we are not accustomed to seeing in some of the most influential historicist criticism. Only by so doing will we meet Katie Trumpener's recent challenge to make "lit-erary form . . . legible as a particularly rich and significant kind of historical evi-dence."[52] The risk involved in trying to meet this demand is that fewer novels, not to mention other kinds of documents, can be dealt with in a single work of criti-cism of manageable size, which means that the historical argument connected to the detailed readings will always be open to the charge that examples have been selected for their suitedness to the thesis, in other words that the thesis cannot stand the test of a broader view. I have decided to accept this risk and partially indem-nify myself against it by writing essays focused on some major reputations in the development of the British novel between 1800 and the late 1850s. By showing

[52] Trumpener, *Bardic Nationalism: The Romantic Novel and the British Empire* (Princeton: Prince-ton University Press, 1997), xv.

how works of recognized masters of the form during this period exhibit a preoccupation with the prospects and pitfalls of autoethnography—a preoccupation they testify to recurrently, variously, probingly in their use of the materials afforded by fictional narrative—I intend both to complement and to raise questions about more sweeping accounts that cover more examples more quickly.

A decade ago, in *Culture and Imperialism,* Edward Said wrote that his generative analysis of *Mansfield Park*'s marginalization of empire should be seen as "completing or complementing" other, more "mainstream interpretations" that, privileging the formal structure of Austen's text, mimicked rather than exposed its programmatic erasure of the imperial domain on which the Bertrams' English way of life was based. Said even went so far as to say "there is no way of doing such readings as mine . . . except by working through the novel," "reading it in full" so as to take full measure of the literary activation of the self-blinding imperialist mentality.[53] Ten years on, it is time to reverse the situation and offer detailed formal analyses of novels as completing or complementing, as well as challenging, some of the tendencies of decentering approaches.

[53] Said, *Culture and Imperialism* (New York: Knopf, 1993), 95.

CHAPTER TWO

≗

Ethnographic Locations and Dislocations

The anthropological relation is not simply with people who are different, but with
"a different society," "a different culture," and thus, inevitably, a relation
between "here" and "there."
   —Akhil Gupta and James Ferguson[1]

TWENTIETH-CENTURY anthropology repeatedly emphasized that the anthropology-
conducting nations of the West have cultures *of their own,* just as the peoples studied in the classic ethnographies do. Operating on a "culturalist" principle that "presupposes the universal value of [local] autonomy and proposes to apply it to every
particular group," the discipline worked toward a global vision in which no inhabited territory is *without* a culture of its own, a view of the world as divided up
into "equally significant, integrated systems of differences."[2] "Were we to take the
map of any continent," Malinowski wrote in *Freedom and Civilization* (1944), "we
would be able to divide it neatly into ethnographic tribal boundaries. Within each
such ethnographic area we would find people of the 'same' tribe. On the other side
of the boundary another tribe would be found, distinguishable from the first by a
different language, different technologies and material objects, different customs
and forms of grouping."[3] Culture was everywhere people were, in the particular
sense that every peopled region was under the governance of some culture. Yet
the principle that every human being lives as the member of some culture has
been shadowed by a romantic counternarrative holding that the type of collective
existence truly deserving the *name* of culture really belonged *only* to tradition-
bound, small-scale "face-to-face" kinds of societies—Ferdinand Tonnies's *Gemein-
schaften*—and not to the diverse, commerce-driven *Gesellschaften* of the West.
George W. Stocking Jr. has even claimed that "a romantic preservationism with
strong undertones of 'Noble Savagery' became the attitudinal norm of sociocul-

---

[1] Gupta and Ferguson, "Beyond 'Culture': Space, Identity, and the Politics of Difference," *Cultural Anthropology* 7/1 (Feb. 1992), 14.

[2] "Culturalist" and "presupposes": Pheng Cheah, "Given Culture: Rethinking Cosmopolitical Free-dom in Transnationalism," in Cheah and Robbins, eds., *Cosmopolitics: Thinking and Feeling Beyond the Nation* (Minneapolis: University of Minnesota Press, 1998), 308. "Equally": James Boon, *Other Tribes, Other Scribes: Symbolic Anthropology in the Comparative Study of Cultures, Histories, Religions, and Texts* (Cambridge: Cambridge University Press, 1982), 27.

[3] Malinowski, *Freedom and Civilization* (New York: Roy Publishers, 1944), 252–53. But cf. E. R. Leach, "The Epistemological Background to Malinowski's Empiricism," in Raymond Firth, ed., *Man and Culture: An Evaluation of the Work of Bronislaw Malinowski* (New York: Humanities Press, 1957), 126.

tural anthropology."[4] *Genuine* cultures were not everywhere; indeed, they appeared to be characterized by nothing so much as their disposition to turn away from the everywhere-encroaching forces of capitalist modernity.

Even if anthropologists rationalized their discipline's tendency (by no means as exclusive a one as has sometimes been suggested) to select "primitive" societies for research sites on the grounds that such comparatively simple societies afforded laboratories of cultural life wherein might be discovered with greater ease truths that held good for *all* societies, they permitted readers so inclined to conclude that their culture-seeking discipline was *exclusively* interested in the supposedly "untouched" kind. The fact that some of the classic early monographs conformed to literary conventions of romance in crafting visions of countermodern alterity and anthropological knight-errantry also enabled the view that the concept of culture was indeed a tool for making Other. Furthermore, the status of culture as a *conceptual reaction,* the fact that it has "always [been] defined in opposition to something else," lent support to the notion that the domain of culture could not be everywhere.[5] Whether culture has been invoked as "the authentic, local way of being different that resists an implacable enemy, a globalizing material civilization"; or "the realm of the spirit, embattled against materialism"; or "the human capacity for spiritual growth that overcomes our animal nature"; or, again, "the collective consciousness, as opposed to the individual psyche"; or "the ideological dimension of social life as against the mundane organization of government, factory, or family"—in any of these guises, culture has appeared as something whose essential geographical and/or epistemological *boundedness* and embattled condition made it possible to envision a world in which only some locations and peoples enjoyed the condition of culturehood, though for how much longer, in the modernizing world, theorists could not undertake to say (Kuper 14–15).

The ethnographic counternarrative—the very opposite of an ethnocentrism that believes only some "we" to possess universally applicable Civilization—has perhaps had its most eloquent champions in Edward Sapir and Claude Lévi-Strauss, the former for his famous essay "Culture, Genuine and Spurious" (1924), the latter for his denunciation of an aggressive Western "monoculture" of "mass civilization," in *Tristes Tropiques* (1955).[6] To call a culture spurious or to casti-

---

[4] George W. Stocking Jr., *Victorian Anthropology* (New York: Free Press, 1987), 289.

[5] Adam Kuper, *Culture: The Anthropologists' Account* (Cambridge, Mass.: Harvard University Press, 2000), 14; henceforth Kuper. Critics of Matthew Arnold's *Culture and Anarchy* have repeatedly made the point that the book really should be called *Culture or Anarchy:* cf., e.g. Williams, *Culture and Society,* 1780–1950 (1958; New York: Columbia University Press, 1983), 113, 60. Against various forms of Social Darwinism, German scholars of the 1880s and after (notably Rudolf Virchow, Adolph Bastian, and Franz Boas) conceived of culture "in opposition to biology" (Kuper 11). Alfred Kroeber built upon their foundations in designating "the Superorganic" as the proper subject matter of anthropology: A. L. Kroeber, "The Superorganic," *American Anthropologist,* n.s. 19 (1917), 163–213. Most salient for the present argument is culture's opposition to civilization, which has been influentially described by Norbert Elias (see *The Civilizing Process: The History of Manners and State Formation and Civilization,* trans. Edmund Jephcott [Oxford: Blackwell, 1994], ch. 1) and which I discuss in chap. 3, below.

[6] Lévi-Strauss, *Tristes Tropiques,* trans. John and Doreen Weightmann (New York: Atheneum, 1981), 38.

gate it as a monoculture is to accuse it of being not a culture at all, but rather a form of *anticulture* whose features define by opposition the ideals attributed to genuine cultures. The latter furnish a way of life "inherently harmonious, balanced, self-satisfactory," a totality "in which nothing is spiritually meaningless," comparable to "a sturdy plant growth, each remotest leaf and twig of which is organically fed by the sap at the core."[7] The "main virtue of any genuine culture," Rudolf Arnheim wrote, consisted in giving its members the "capacity to experience the practical activities of living as tangible manifestations of [its] basic principles."[8] In contrast, the commercialized "spurious" culture Sapir describes, at once entropic and bureaucratized, offers only a waste land's heap of broken images: the complex wholeness and semiotic plenitude of genuine cultures are sanctified by opposition to a social life manifestly *disconnected*. In Lévi-Strauss, on the other hand, monoculture lives up to its anticultural function in being *all too* unified, an airless prison of coercive social law to which all must finally conform. Anticulture appears here as a nightmarish *parody* of culture's positive integration, each of *its* remotest leaves and twigs infused with culture-killing poison from the metropolitan center.

This book does not attempt a full anatomy of the representational system or image-repertoire of "the anticultural," but argues that nineteenth-century British novels helped prepare for the arrival of the modern culture-concept by supplying a rich and varied archive of situations that turn out, in retrospect, to look like anticipatory travesties of the "genuine culture" for which nineteenth-century Britons lacked a term.[9] As Sapir and Lévi-Strauss were to do, these nineteenth-century texts tended to invoke their culture-catalyzing anticultures in complementary ways: either as a state of arid commodification and moral apartness existing among a people whose physical adjacency mocked real community (as in Sapir), or as a state of disastrous and inescapable *interconnection* (as in Lévi-Strauss). The former representations deliver versions of *pre-ethnographic* anticulture, since they emphasize the *absence* of any totality underlying the elements of a scene, whereas the latter describe a *protoethnographic* anticulture, since they involve a culture-like vision of social totality that is simply marked with a minus sign. Both varieties stimulate the ethnographic effort of "salvage," functioning within that mode of "ethnographic allegory" that responds to perceived threats to a way of life by offering to save an imperiled culture in textual form.[10] Nineteenth-century novel-

---

[7] Sapir, "Culture, Genuine and Spurious," in *Culture, Language, and Personality: Selected Essays,* ed. David G. Mandelbaum (Berkeley: University of California Press, 1960), 90–93.

[8] Arnheim, *Art and Visual Perception* (Berkeley: University of California Press, 1954), 106–7.

[9] Cf. Bentley, *The Ethnography of Manners: Hawthorne, James, Wharton* (Cambridge: Cambridge University Press, 1995), on how Malinowski regarded the novel as "antitype" to the ethnographic text, "embod[ying] the uncertain status of individual agency and the equivocal advances of civilization" (13). Kamala Visweswaran, in *Fictions of Feminist Ethnography* (Minneapolis: University of Minnesota Press, 1994), writes that ethnography established its authority by "self-consciously mark[ing] its narrative production against the novel" (4).

[10] James Clifford, "On Ethnographic Allegory," in Clifford and George E. Marcus, eds., *Writing Culture: The Poetics and Politics of Ethnography* (Berkeley: University of California Press, 1986), esp. 112–15. Cf. J. W. Gruber, "Ethnographic Salvage and the Shaping of Anthropology," *American Anthropologist* 72 (1970), 1289–99; George W. Stocking Jr., "The Ethnographic Sensibility of the 1920s

istic autoethnography was motivated by just such an effort, though the dangers it sought to head off are the self-incurred liabilities of a metropolitan anticulture. Post-Union British novels write into being the treasured substance of a nonuniversalizing, counterimperial (though by no means should we equate this with antiimperial) British or English culture which they present themselves, romance-style, as rescuing or recovering. In the process, the "way of life" they represent acquires an objective status, and a normative force, it has not hitherto possessed: behavior becomes custom, habits become rituals, ideas dogma, all of them together exhibiting a systematic interconnectedness not previously emphasized.

Applying the concept of autoethnography to literary works emanating from imperial Britain can substantially increase our understanding of the ways in which nineteenth-century Englishness or Britishness "was itself a product of the colonial culture that it . . . created elsewhere."[11] But I recognize that some will want to reserve autoethnography for contexts in which colonized peoples "talk back" to their masters and misrepresenters. Autoethnography, on this reasoning, arises when a people possesses a vision of itself as having "a culture of its own," which means not only that it tries to correct exogenous, ethnocentric characterizations of it as *lacking* in culture (and hence as needing the "improving" hand of colonialism), but that it acknowledges the contingent nature and limited scope of its social system and values, rather than trying to impose them on others. This self-limiting perspective colonizing nations are presumed to lack. As Perry Anderson put it in the course of a breathtaking survey of contemporary British culture, "*Omnia determinatio est negatio*—the very demarcation of a social totality places it under the sign of contingency." Anderson contended that Britain had "never produced a classical sociology largely because British society was never challenged as a whole from within": having successfully forestalled revolution throughout the nineteenth century, the British establishment had no interest in fostering a discipline designed to give the "'answer' to a question which to [its] ideological advantage remained unposed." Britain's liberal bourgeoisie, he thought, had devoted its energy to the task of *diverting* social-scientific attention from itself, "export[ing] its totalizations, on to its subject peoples. There, and there only, could it afford scientific study of the social whole. 'Primitive' societies became the surrogate object of the theory proscribed at home."[12]

---

and the Dualism of the Anthropological Tradition," in Stocking, ed., *Romantic Motives: Essays on Anthropological Sensibility* (Madison: University of Wisconsin Press, 1989), esp. 210–12.

[11] Simon Gikandi, *Maps of Englishness: Writing Identity in the Culture of Colonialism* (New York: Columbia University Press, 1996), x. Cf. Ian Baucom, *Out of Place: Englishness, Empire, and the Locations of Identity* (Princeton: Princeton University Press, 1999), 37. "English" and "British" have sometimes been too starkly opposed, with "English" applying to the insular, tradition-bound identity produced in reaction to the "British" imperial state's overseas entanglements. Victorian novels can make it quite difficult to enforce the distinction consistently because they so often draw upon Scottish or Celtic elements in crafting their visions of a recovered national culture. After 1801, an increasingly expansive sense of "Englishness" also complicates this simple opposition.

[12] Perry Anderson, "Components of the National Culture," in Alexander Cockburn and Robin Blackburn, eds., *Student Power: Problems, Diagnosis, Action* (Harmondsworth: Penguin, 1969), 264.

Leading scholars have tended to concur with Anderson's perspective if not with every aspect of his strong claim, regarding imperial Britain as, in effect, a culture fatally blind to its own culturehood and thoroughly devoted to a self-universalizing tendency that serves as both cause and effect in explanations of the British Empire. To Stuart Hall, for instance, the "English eye" of the imperial era thinks itself "coterminous with sight itself," systematically disregarding the fact that Englishness was always just as much a specific ethnicity or culture as any other, always just as much a particular location in the world and as little an Olympian vantage-point.[13] The bygone imperialists as Hall presents them appear to have believed in their own representations of Englishness as something "perfectly natural," something "condensed, homogeneous, unitary" (Hall 22). Hall speaks of the "large confidence with which the English have always occupied their own identities" (Hall 26).

In a complementary spirit, Edward Said's influential account of the English novel in the imperial era shows that form as carrying out an "ideological mapping" of the world, laying out "a slowly built up picture with England—socially, politically, morally charted and differentiated in immensely fine detail—at the center and a series of overseas territories connected to it at the peripheries." Said regards such spatial configuration as a powerful objective correlative for ethnocentrism, a sign of British "confidence" or "superiority" toward all those regions and peoples outside Britain that afforded the material basis for both the British way of life and its novelistic representation. The "departmental view" of the world that Said attributes to the novel aligns fiction too closely with the agendas of the state, as if fiction *were* a government department charged with the construction of tendentious geopolitical imaginings that exalt Britain and marginalize the rest.[14] Said's view of a self-centered English novel and Hall's account of an English eye that is blind to its own standpoint share the disposition to regard the imperial nation as almost unanimously expressing the arrogant belief that it is exempt from the universal law decreeing all cultures to be local and contingent. As Tom Nairn has put it, "the greater nations remain grandly unaware of their narrowness, because . . . their imagined centrality makes them identify with Humanity or Progress *tout court*."[15] I think that critical investment in the notion of imperial self-universalization should not be allowed to attain such a pitch that it discourages us from discerning all but the most obvious of counterhegemonic discourses. "Superiority" (an undeniable fact about nineteenth-century British power) needs to be divorced from "confidence" (an ascribed outlook) if we are to understand the culture-making labor of the British novel of this period.

This self-induced obtuseness about their own culturehood regularly ascribed to colonizing nations illustrates and Occidentalizes a canonical ethnographic princi-

---

[13] Stuart Hall, "The Local and the Global: Globalization and Ethnicity," in Anthony D. King, ed., *Culture, Globalization, and the World-System: Contemporary Conditions for the Representation of Identity* (Minneapolis: University of Minnesota Press, 1997), 20–21. Henceforth Hall.

[14] Said, *Culture and Imperialism* (New York: Knopf, 1993), 74.

[15] Nairn, *The Break-up of Britain* (London: New Left Books, 1977), 78.

ple long relied upon to demonstrate the power of anthropology's *culture*. For anthropology has tended to hold that life within cultures—wherever they are to be found—is *inherently* self-universalizing (hence Herzfeld's remark, quoted in chapter 1, that ethnography is the representation of a group's ethnocentrism). Twentieth-century anthropology made virtually axiomatic the belief that (as T. S. Eliot summarized it) a "people in isolation is not aware of having a 'culture' at all,"[16] since (in Roy Wagner's terms) "the culture in which one grows up is never really 'visible'—it is taken for granted, and its assumptions are felt to be self-evident."[17] Rather than seeing "their culture," the subjects of modern ethnography were supposed to see "how we do things," or even "the *way* to do things," since an attitude of "absoluteness" with regard to the customs of their own culture was deemed "a universal characteristic" of tradition-bound societies.[18] That is the reason, as R. R. Marett warned in the 1912 edition of *Notes and Queries on Anthropology,* fieldworkers should always ask their indigenous interlocutors the "what" question about their activities, never the "why," because members of cultures were presumed to "regard it as completely self-evident that theirs is the way in which the world of men as a whole wants to be viewed and judged."[19] In the critique of imperial self-universalization, the possessors of global dominance exhibit an ethnocentric complacency rivaled only by that manifested by ethnography's dominatable "natives." Anthropology's recent critics have helped us disbelieve the latter fiction.

The ethnographic topos of the native who inhabits a thoroughly naturalized cultural environment is bound up with assumptions about ethnographic place, for the site of ethnographic fieldwork typically presents itself as one whose "indigenous inhabitants . . . detect in it the traces of chthonian or celestial powers, ancestors or spirits which populate its private geography; as if the small fragment of humanity making them offerings and sacrifices in this place were also the quintessence of humanity, as if there were no humanity worthy of the name except in the very place of the cult devoted to them."[20] This is the best brief account I know of the linkage established in modern cultural anthropology between geographic and mental "locations": the native's physical territory and ideational domain virtually fuse into one imagined space "outside [of] which nothing"—from the indigene's point of view—"is really understandable" (Augé 44). Assumed indigenous ethnocentrism implies a geographical imagination whose fundamental distinction is not really between one "place" and another, but between place and placelessness, between the

[16] Eliot, *Notes Towards the Definition of Culture,* in *Christianity and Culture* (New York: Harcourt Brace Jovanovich, 1968), 165.

[17] Roy Wagner, *The Invention of Culture* (1975; revised and expanded ed., Chicago and London: University of Chicago Press, 1981), 4; henceforth Wagner.

[18] Bernard McGrane, *Beyond Anthropology: Society and the Other* (New York: Columbia University Press, 1989), 122.

[19] Marett, "The Study of Magico-Religious Facts," in BAAS, *Notes and Queries on Anthropology,* 4th edition (London: BAAS, 1912), 259. "Regard it . . . ": Norbert Elias, *The Civilizing Process,* 5.

[20] Marc Augé, *Non-Places: Introduction to an Anthropology of Supermodernity,* trans. John Howe (London: Verso, 1995), 42; henceforth Augé.

one place where it feels possible to make sense of things, and the nonplace ("out there") of non-sense, savagery, pointless behavior. Those presumed to operate according to such an ethnocentric geography face the question, not, "What distinguishes one culture from another?" but rather (as Leslie White phrased it), "[H]ow does one draw the line between . . . culture and not-culture?"[21] At the heart of ethnographic tradition lies this conflict between symmetrical and asymmetrical geographies, between an Enlightenment view of international space as rational, "empty," and homogeneous, on the one hand, and a purported "insider's" view that regards the boundary of one's own people's territory as somehow coextensive with the boundary of the *human,* or of the Cultural with a capital C.

Inasmuch as cultures have been so closely associated with different territories as to be representable as if they were places themselves ("cultural environment," "insider," "outsider"), then a fieldworker's physical traveling, necessary to get to that place on earth where an alien society was to be encountered, became very closely associated and virtually identified with the *mental* journey required to get the fieldworker "out" of his own customary thought-world and into that of his subjects. After all, the "main distinctive characteristic" of cultural anthropology was that it obliged fieldworkers to "go and live with the people under investigation."[22] In crossing the boundary dividing his familiar surroundings from the alien site of his research, the anthropologist also began the process of crossing the epistemological boundary demarcating the studied culture. And yet, like all things capable of being associated with each other, physical territory and cultural "space" had also, always, to be different: ethnography powerfully associated culture and place *in order to dissociate them* in the necessary second step of its self-authorizing logic. Because critics of anthropology have focused almost exclusively on the quasi-identification of cultures and places and on the concomitant "incarceration" of natives in their cultures, they have not been able to give due weight to the consideration of this second step, or to the overall inconsistency of the ethnographic model for thinking about what kinds of things cultures were and how one might go about acquiring authoritative knowledge of them. We need now to appreciate the fact that, as ethnography has represented them, cultures both were *and* were not "places," because, while you had to "go there" en route to locating one, it was not *in that place* that you would ultimately find it. Culture was always elsewhere.

A useful argument for thinking about this elsewhereness of culture is one that hardly uses the term at all: Elizabeth Ermarth's in *Realism and Consensus in the English Novel* (1983). Painting in broad strokes, Ermarth outlines a distinction between the typological or "vertical" interpretive framework characteristic of Medieval art and the "horizontal" one that began to displace it in the quattrocento. The former regards the field of human experience, the fallen world, as nothing but "a set of discrete instances that [have] no interesting relations to each other"; each

[21] White, quoted in Frederick Gamst and Edward Norbeck, eds., *Ideas of Culture: Sources and Uses* (New York: Holt, Rinehart and Winston, 1976), 69.

[22] Anthony Jackson, "Reflections on Ethnography at Home and the ASA," in Jackson, ed., *Anthropology at Home* (London: Tavistock, 1987), 13.

detail's only significant relation is to the typological code that links it to its figural counterpart. In contrast, the vision animating post-Renaissance realism is that of a field in which the details of human experience derive their meaning and value from relations among themselves, so that the identity of each phenomenon becomes "series-dependent," "discovered by comparing particular cases to each other" and by separating essential from accidental data. The discontinuous space and time of Medieval paintings gives way to a homogenized field in which identity "can be fully grasped only as an abstraction," experience yielding only "mere concretia that owe their significance to the invisible inner reality they register." "The implication of realist technique," Ermarth concludes, "is that proper distance will enable the subjective spectator . . . to see the multiple viewpoints and so to find the form of the whole in what looks from a closer vantage point like a discontinuous array of specific cases."[23] However we judge the historical accuracy of Ermarth's rough-and-ready distinction, it is clear that *culture* as ethnography has handled it constitutes just such an invisible, abstract identity, nowhere to be found among the myriad "concretia"—Malinowski's term was "imponderabilia"[24]—encountered in the course of fieldwork.

It is certainly true that anthropologist-authors have habitually "marshal[ed] . . . a very large number of highly specific cultural details" in the attempt to produce a "reality effect" that gives "the look of truth" to their accounts of field research.[25] By such means such authors attested to the experience of truly "Being There." Yet mere presence in a foreign territory, the mere surrounding of oneself with strange data, could never *in itself* become the criterion for authority over culture. As E. E. Evans-Pritchard put it, "[t]he fact that [the fieldworker] has been among a people for a long time proves nothing"; "what counts is the manner and mode of his residence among them."[26] The initial reality effect had to be matched by an *authenticity effect,* achievable by sorting the *ethnographically pertinent* from information that just happened to be gatherable in a place but bore no relevant relation to its culture.[27] E. B. Tylor had spoken of the "remarkable tacit consensus" that "induces

[23] Ermarth, *Realism and Consensus in the English Novel* (Princeton: Princeton University Press, 1983), 8, 18, 20, 35.

[24] Malinowski, *Argonauts of the Western Pacific* (1922; Prospect Heights, Ill.: Waveland Press, 1984), 18; henceforth *Argonauts*.

[25] Clifford Geertz, *Works and Lives: The Anthropologist as Author* (Stanford: Stanford University Press, 1988), 3.

[26] Evans-Pritchard, "Some Reminiscences and Reflections on Fieldwork," in *Witchcraft, Oracles, and Magic among the Azande* (Oxford: Clarendon Press, 1976), 249.

[27] On "authenticity effect," cf. my *The Beaten Track: European Tourism, Literature, and the Ways to "Culture," 1800–1918* (Oxford: Oxford University Press, 1993), 172–92. Franz Boas has been the major figure most commonly associated with the self-defeating disinclination to impose order on the plentiful data amassed in the field. Leslie White found Boas to be so "obsessed with particulars" that he ignored "general outlines or forms," leaving his followers "aghast before the multitude and complexity of facts" he had collected. White, quoted in George W. Stocking Jr., "Franz Boas and the Culture Concept in Historical Perspective," *Race, Culture, and Evolution: Essays in the History of Anthropology* (New York: Free Press, 1968), 212. Cf. John Van Mannen, *Tales of the Field: On Writing Ethnography* (Chicago: University of Chicago Press, 1988), 36n3.

whole populations to unite" in one set of customs as making it possible for the researcher "to ignore exceptional facts . . . [and] to represent immense masses of details by a few typical facts."[28] Ethnographic research required "a *cleared* place of work," one in which the researcher could "keep out distracting influences."[29] The concept of a people's culture thus invoked a double boundary running "through itself as well as around itself," delineating the culture from everything outside it, but also dividing that demarcated space into domains of the typical and deviant, the ethnographically relevant and the accidental or trivial.[30] In representations of the ethnographic process, this double boundary lent force to a narrative pattern of entrance (close association of culture and place) and withdrawal (dissociation of culture and place)—a pattern plainly amenable to masculinist romance (though, as I will suggest, by no means limited to it). The first movement focused on the geographical space of the tribe, the village, the region; the second on the iconic space of the culture, something "visible" only from a proper distance.

This constitutively divided attitude toward the relationship between culture and place can be traced back to its late eighteenth-century German origins, notwithstanding that tradition's heavy emphasis on the link between particular constellations of customs and their settings of origin. Many a text from this tradition—such as J. C. Adelung's *Versuch einer Geschichte der Kultur des menschlichen Geschlects* (1782)—stressed the degree to which "culture is produced by [distinctive] ecological pressures upon a population in a restricted territory": culture was the most site-specific of phenomena, its varieties corresponding to those of nature itself.[31] One famous English Victorian instance of this principle in action may be found in Ruskin's "The Nature of Gothic," where the sage invites us to imagine ourselves taking wing over Europe, noting the changes in climate and terrain as we range from South to North and thus preparing ourselves to appreciate the fitness of Gothic forms to their natural homelands.

At the same time, however, the culture of a people could not *finally* be "located in," still less equated with or seen as indivisible from, that people's territory. To be sure, the German autoethnographer, the folklorist or collector of ballads or *Märchen,* had to go about the territory of his people, gathering material from their very lips; yet this material did not become evidence of that people's culture *until* the researcher assembled, textualized, and presented it as such. The culture, in other words, was not the people's "beliefs, customs, moral values, and so forth, added together," but "the wholeness that their coexistence somehow creates or makes manifest," and the researcher's mobility enabled him to multiply instances of Germanness in a manner no homebound German speaker, holed up in one

[28] Tylor, *Primitive Culture: Researches into the Development of Mythology, Philosophy, Religion, Language, Art, and Custom* (1871; rpt. Boston: Estes and Lauriat, 1874), I: 10.

[29] James Clifford, "Spatial Practices," in *Routes: Travel and Translation in the Late Twentieth Century* (Cambridge, Mass.: Harvard University Press, 1997), 53.

[30] Daniel Cottom, "*Ethnographia Mundi,*" in *Text and Culture: The Politics of Interpretation* (Minneapolis: University of Minnesota Press, 1989), 72; henceforth Cottom.

[31] Adelung quoted in Gamst and Norbeck, 33.

provincial corner of the territory, could emulate.[32] Traveling through or among these many instances was to endow the researcher with a vantage point atop the inferential mountain from which things that people did, said, and believed transformed themselves, when assisted by selection, into signs of their peoplehood. The culture was, paradoxically, "given back"—re-presented—to its own people, who up to the moment they received it from the hands of the scholar had never possessed it.

For an early nineteenth-century work concisely enacting the pattern of the autoethnographic traveling authority in the context not of prenational Germany but of counterrevolutionary England, consider William Blake's celebrated "London," in which the "I" that "wander[s] through each charter'd street," surveying the conditions that obtain in a variety of circumstances, is distinguished from the denizens of those streets and given license to generalize about them by virtue of the differential between his mobility and their (presumed) incarceration in separate locations. "Charter'd" plays upon this opposition by evoking both "charted" or "mapped," on the one hand—the situation of the incarcerated native—and the great charter of liberty supposedly granted to the English at Runnymede, on the other. Blake's poem goes on to sketch out a metonymic vision of totality in the connections it traces between elements of the society that *immobile* inhabitants are positioned to view merely as so many discrete phenomena: Chimney-sweeper's cry and blackening Church, Soldier's sigh and Palace Walls, Harlot's curse, Infant's tear, Marriage hearse. The self-referential semiotic plenitude ascribed to cultures in later ethnographic theory is also visible in Blake's insistent "every": he sees "marks of weakness, marks of woe" in "every face" he meets, and hears "mind-forg'd manacles" in "every voice of every Man, / In every Infant's cry of fear, / In every voice, in every ban." As integrated totality, a culture *demands* this kind of hyperbole from those who would represent it; or, rather, there is no such thing *as* hyperbole when it comes to the representation of cultural totality. *Every* (selected) cultural detail is a typical detail; the demarcated space of the culture is ruled by "the presumption that the array of disparate-seeming elements . . . composes a significant whole, each factor of which is in some sense a corollary of, consubstantial with, implied, by, immanent in, all the others" (Herbert 5).[33] But of course what Blake presents in his excoriating verses is a terrible protoethnographic vision of British *anti*culture, an anticipatory travesty of genuine culturehood that can only wait, along with its stern poet, for utopian transformation into a nurturing way of life.[34]

---

[32] Christopher Herbert, *Culture and Anomie: Ethnographic Imagination in the Nineteenth Century* (Chicago: University of Chicago Press, 1991), 5; henceforth Herbert.

[33] Cf. Alan Liu, "Local Transcendence: Cultural Criticism, Postmodernism, and the Romanticism of Detail," *Representations* 32 (Fall 1990), 75–113, esp. 86–87 and 90.

[34] Similar to my use of "anticipatory travesty" is Saree Makdisi's argument that the romantic era's universal histories and "antihistories" "have the status of prophesy," being articulated before "the actual (and much more gradual) convergence of capitalist and imperialist practices within the process of modernization": *Romantic Imperialism: Universal Empire and the Culture of Modernity* (Cambridge: Cambridge University Press, 1998), 2–3.

Victorian social criticism and analysis often achieves this hyperbolic style when contemplating a variety of the anticultural—as, for example, when Henry Mayhew, in *London Labour and the London Poor,* furnishes a hellish burlesque of culture in his description of the costermongers' sordid "Penny Gaff," or cheap theater. In terms similar to twentieth-century accounts of the acculturation process, through which (as Ruth Benedict put it), "[b]y the time he can talk, [the individual] is the little creature of his culture, and by the time he is grown and able to take part in its activities, its habits are his habits, its beliefs his beliefs, its impossibilities his impossibilities," Mayhew writes of "these dens" as "the school-rooms where the guiding morals of a life are picked up": they "teach the cruelest debauchery" and "ring[] with applause at the performance of . . . scene[s] whose sole point turns upon the pantomimic imitation of the unrestrained indulgence of the most corrupt appetites of our nature."[35] In Mayhew's anticulture no less than in Edward Sapir's "genuine culture," "each remotest leaf and twig . . . is organically fed by the sap at the core"; only apparently lawless, the costermongers' life obeys E. B. Tylor's rule "that if law is anywhere, it is everywhere," even in the most seemingly "spontaneous and motiveless phenomena."[36] "[P]erfect in its wickedness," the depravity-factory of the Penny Gaff puts before its audience "[t]he most obscene thoughts, the most disgusting scenes": the performances testify that "ingenuity had been exerted to its utmost lest an obscene thought should be passed by." (Mayhew 41). The evening culminates with a charade in which "the most disgusting attitudes were struck, the most immoral acts represented, without one dissenting voice" being raised to protest the spectacle of "two ruffians degrading themselves each time they stirred a limb, and forcing into the brains of the childish audience before them thoughts that must embitter a lifetime, and descend from father to child like some bodily infirmity" (Mayhew 42).

Similar passages may be found in the social criticism of Carlyle, Ruskin, Arnold, and others, but it was in the novel, and especially, perhaps, in the later Dickensian novel, that the superlative-laden, hyperbolic rhetoric of anticulture became not simply a familiar stylistic element but the signature of a protoethnographic principle of structure. In no text is this more evident than in *Bleak House,* with its baleful "[f]og everywhere" and its way of describing the pervasive effects flowing outward from the slum neighborhood called (and here personified as) Tom-all-Alone's:

> There is not a drop of Tom's corrupted blood but propagates infection and contagion somewhere. It shall pollute, this very night, the choice stream (in which chemists on analysis would find the genuine nobility) of a Norman house, and his Grace shall not be able to say Nay to the infamous alliance. There is not an atom of Tom's slime, not a cubic inch of any pestilential gas in which he lives, not one obscenity or brutality of his committing, but shall work its retribution, through every order of society, up to the proudest of the proud, and to the highest of the high.[37]

---

[35] Benedict, *Patterns of Culture* (Boston: Houghton Mifflin, 1934), 3. "These dens . . . ": Mayhew, *London Labour and the London Poor* (1861–62; New York: Dover, 1968), I.40; henceforth Mayhew.

[36] Tylor, *Primitive Culture,* I.1.

[37] Dickens, *Bleak House* (1852–53; Oxford: Oxford University Press, 1996), 654–57.

In the very different *Jane Eyre,* Charlotte Brontë resorts to the hyperbolic vein when describing the heroine's initial situation with her horrid guardians as one in which the tyrannical scion of the family—Jane says—"bullied and punished me; not two or three times in the week, nor once or twice in the day, but continually: every nerve I had feared him, and every morsel of flesh on my bones shrank when he came near. . . . I had no appeal whatever against either his menaces or his in-flictions." Jane will wind up in a marriage as superlatively satisfying as her origi-nal circumstances are excruciating, a marriage deserving to be read by the light of those culminating allegorical unions found in the early nineteenth-century Na-tional Tale and historical novel, as pointing toward the utopia of a genuine English culture.[38]

Such protoethnographic varieties of Victorian anticulture have to be set along-side *pre*-ethnographic versions in which the desired condition of moral and cul-tural togetherness is evoked not by images of its nightmare double, as in Mayhew and Dickens, but by images of pervasive alienation, of relationships so utterly rei-fied that "society" dwindles to nothing more than an aggregate of bodies happen-ing, indifferently or rancorously, to occupy the same terrain. A classic instance oc-curs in Benjamin Disraeli's *Sybil* (1845), in which an authoritative stranger declares "there is no community in England; there is aggregation, but aggregation under circumstances which make it rather a dissociating, than an uniting, princi-ple." Without that "community of purpose that constitutes society," the stranger adds, "men may be drawn into contiguity, but they still continue virtually iso-lated."[39] Another noteworthy instance is Thackeray's *Vanity Fair* (1848), which has been well described as "imagin[ing] the fetishistic reduction of the material environment" to an array of "circulating, dispiriting objects in an oddly depthless space" in which "physical contiguity . . . is rendered insignificant."[40]

The crucial thing to ask about the relationship of culture and place turns out not to be, "When (or why) did people *start* associating the customs of different groups with the territories they inhabited?" but rather, "When did they start *dissociating* them?" Herodotus and Tacitus associate customs and location; Plato's Myth of the Cave gave the West one of its most influential metaphorizations of acculturated mentality as place; but ethnographic culture is an "occult" substance or network of relationships underlying or permeating or hovering above surface phenomena, inferable from everything one experiences in a place but not empirically detectable in it. Expressing a skepticism that would be echoed throughout the glory days of ethnography's discipline building, A. R. Radcliffe-Brown insisted, "We do not ob-serve a 'culture,' since that word denotes, not any concrete reality, but an abstrac-tion."[41] "No amount of individual particles of observed data will suffice to repre-

---

[38] Brontë, *Jane Eyre* (1847; Harmondsworth: Penguin, 1996), 16, 500.

[39] Disraeli, *Sybil* (1845; Harmondsworth: Penguin, 1985), 94–95.

[40] Andrew H. Miller, *Novels Behind Glass: Commodity Culture and Victorian Narrative* (Cam-bridge: Cambridge University Press, 1995), 9.

[41] Radcliffe-Brown, "On Social Structure," *Journal of the Royal Anthropological Institute* 70 (1940), 2. Cf. Ralph Linton in 1936 ("culture itself is intangible and cannot be directly apprehended

sent 'a culture' until one has a theory of their systematic interrelations," for—much as Ermarth argued in her different context—*"relationships are not observable phenomena"* (Herbert 10; emphasis in original). The fieldworker might probe a region's every nook and cranny and encounter every aspect of its institutions and behavior without ever running up against its culture.

If, following Ermarth's grand narrative about Medieval and Renaissance epistemologies, we are inclined to regard *culture* as one name that caught on for those horizontal interpretive frameworks which displaced typological verticality in the early Renaissance, then the objectification of cultures can in turn be regarded as a general effect of their use as instruments to think with—one that, to be sure, has sometimes taken the specific form of colonialist stereotypings but that should not be simply identified with that form. The concept of culture has performed the heuristic function of "draw[ing] the boundary of understanding . . . around the context proper to any work, event, or person" (Cottom 50). The idea that identities are to be sought at a "depth" or at a height of abstraction removed from the field of experience "dematerializes the surfaces of things," says Ermarth, since when "the real or essential qualities lie hidden, then what appears is factitious in some way, a mere façade hiding reality."[42] Just such an attitude animates Malinowski's reference to the "intense interest and suspense with which an Ethnographer enters for the first time the district that is to be the future scene of his fieldwork . . . on the lookout for symptoms of . . . hidden and mysterious ethnographic phenomena behind the commonplace aspect of things," as well as his admonition that "foolish indeed and short-sighted would be the man of science who would pass by a whole class of phenomena, ready to be garnered, and leave them to waste, even though he did not see at the moment to what theoretical use they might be put!" (*Argonauts* 51, 20). Trained by this master, a next generation of anthropologists took to its fields with the conviction that, as Hortense Powdermaker put it, "[n]othing [is] too small to escape my notebook": Malinowski, she remembered, "told us to note down everything we saw and heard, since in the beginning it is not possible to know what may or may not be significant."[43]

What Ermarth presents in terms of epistemology and aesthetics can be transposed into a sociopolitical key by observing that the concept of culture aims at an effect precisely the opposite of that of capitalist *reification* or commodity fetishism. Every culturally embedded object is, in fact, less an "object" than a node or point of intersection in a network, acting upon and acted upon by every other node, joined in one web: things looked at through the lens of culture dissolve into the social networks that explain them. Cultures are reputed to be wholes in which "[e]verything is somehow related to everything else" and "the problem of inves-

---

even by the individuals who participate in it"), Clyde Kluckhohn and William Kelley in 1945 ("has anyone ever seen 'culture'?"), Melford Spiro in 1951 ("culture has no ontological reality"), and Ralph Beals and Harry Hoijer in 1953 ("the anthropologist cannot observe culture directly"): quoted in Leslie A. White, "The Concept of Culture," orig. 1959, rpt. in Gamst and Norbeck, 55–71; see 56.

[42] Ermarth, *Realism and Consensus*, 20.

[43] Hortense Powdermaker, *Stranger and Friend: The Way of an Anthropologist* (New York: Norton, 1966), 61; henceforth Powdermaker.

tigation is that of finding the point of entrance in a circle."[44] But dereifying the "contents" of a culture increased the pressure to reify and concretize the culture *itself*, for unless we can envision the outer limit of this situation of total interconnectedness, judgment on the significance of details must await completion of a global survey. "If everything is related to everything else," Raymond Firth asked, "where does the description stop?"[45] The greater the inclination to treat the details of experience not as reified events or objects but as points of intersection, the more insistently we must impose the boundary between inside and out. To do any *work*, either epistemologically or affectively, "culture" cannot tolerate a porous border. This is why, while some early leaders in anthropological theory—Radcliffe-Brown, but also Robert Lowie and Edward Sapir himself—expressed misgivings about the reifying force of culture, its proponents could show time and again how, "in their procedures of study, explicit rejectors are often implicit acceptors" and how "[i]n the actual conduct of research and the presentation of interpretations . . . [both] idealists and realists [on the question of culture] . . . generally proceeded as if culture were indeed 'real.'"[46]

The ethnographic paradoxes about culture surveyed here find their match in the definitive instability of ethnography's accredited practitioner, the Participant Observer. Metaphorizing cultures as places aided in the self-authorizing efforts of a discipline bent on distinguishing its professionals from the "armchair" scholars of previous generations; recognizing, in turn, that cultures *were not* and *could not* be (like) places protected the new anthropological knowledge from claims advanceable by other people located in those places: "natives," primarily, but also those other figures referred to as "men on the spot," the colonial officials, traders, missionaries, or tourists who happened to be on site *without* managing to become honorary "insiders" in the culture surrounding them. Because of its mystique of self-transcendence and because it was so much stressed in the promotional writings of newly professionalizing anthropology of the early twentieth century, the "participant" side of the fieldwork method has received the lion's share of attention, with many pages by many hands devoted to the problems and rewards of establishing "rapport" with the studied people, of coming to feel like a member of their culture. And it is certainly true that, as Christopher Herbert writes, once culture is understood "as a discrete, self-contained whole, . . . there can be no substitute for a system of concentrated fieldwork designed to generate something resembling an insider's view of it" (Herbert 150–51).

Yet the cold, hard look of critique that has been directed at the manufactured "natives" of classic ethnographies makes it abundantly clear how partial, at best, was that crucial ethnographic injunction "to grasp the native's point of view, his

---

[44] Clyde Kluckhohn, "Cultural Anthropology: New Uses for 'Barbarians,'" in Lynn White, ed., *Frontiers of Knowledge in the Study of Man* (New York: Harper, 1956), 37. Cf. Susan Hegeman, "Imagining Totality: Rhetorics of and Versus 'Culture,'" *Common Knowledge* 6/3 (1997), 51–72.

[45] Firth, quoted in Kuper, *Anthropology and Anthropologists: The Modern British School*, (rev. ed., London: Routledge, 1983), 74.

[46] Gamst and Norbeck, *Ideas of Culture*, 35, 5.

relation to life, to realise *his* vision of *his* world" (*Argonauts* 25). By no means could this constitute, as Malinowski said it did, "the final goal" of ethnography; it ran contrary to his own principle that natives were "*of* [their culture] and *in* it" but have "no vision of the resulting integral action of the whole." "Not even the most intelligent native," the father of fieldworkers added, "has any clear idea of the Kula [gift-exchange cycle] as a big, organised social construction, still less of its soci-ological function and implications. If you were to ask him what the Kula is, he would answer by giving a few details, most likely by giving his personal experi-ences and subjective views. . . . For the integral picture does not exist in his mind; he is in it, and cannot see the whole from the outside" (*Argonauts* 83). Obedience to the drive toward insideness alone would place the fieldworker in the sort of po-sition William Foote Whyte found himself in during the course of his fieldwork for *Street Corner Society* (1943). "I began as a nonparticipating observer," wrote Whyte, but "[a]s I became accepted into the community, I found myself becoming almost a nonobserving participant. I got the feel of life in Cornerville, but that meant that I got to take for granted the same things that my Cornerville friends took for granted. I was immersed in it, but I could as yet make little sense out of it."[47] This was "going native," as "unprofitable from the standpoint of fieldwork as stay-ing at the airport or hotel and making up stories about the natives" (Wagner 9).

The alternation of celebrating and then discrediting the "native's point of view" corresponds to the sequence in which culture was likened and attached to place, then dissociated from it—the sequence structuring ethnographic narratives whose desideratum was the demonstrative achievement of an outsider's insideness vis-à-vis the object that reciprocally defined that stance, a culture. Malinowski playfully remarked to his English readers that his "Slavonic nature"—"more plastic and more naturally savage than that of Western Europeans"—gave him an advantage in the "participant" half of Participant Observation (*Argonauts* 21).[48] But the onus of producing ethnographic knowledge rather than reproductions of native ethno-centrism required the preemptive negation of any doubt that the Observer might be lost in the Participant: ethnography happened only insofar as fieldworkers could demonstrate that they had got back "outside" again or, uncannily, that they had somehow *remained* outside even while passing "in."[49] Such ethnographic self-portraiture could be achieved through narrative sequence (in, then out) or through the static image of a divided self (both in and out).

In ethnographic texts, this double duty could make itself felt in passages like the following, in which Malinowski's heavily qualified assertions about his status among the Trobriand Islanders function to remind us of the ultimately unbridge-

[47] Whyte, *Street Corner Society* (Chicago: University of Chicago Press, 1961), 321.

[48] Cf. Mary Kingsley's remark, quoted in Dea Birkett, *Mary Kingsley: Imperial Adventuress* (Lon-don: Macmillan, 1992): "I have a mind so nearly akin to that of the savage that I can enter into his thoughts and follow them" (99).

[49] "What we ordinarily mean by understanding of another people, of course," wrote T. S. Eliot, "is an approximation towards understanding which stops short at the point at which the student would begin to lose some essential of his own culture" (*Christianity and Culture,* 114). For Eliot as for many others, Conrad's *Heart of Darkness* was the classic cautionary tale.

able, the anthropologically necessary gap between indigene and visitor—as if the ethnographer's efforts at rapport might be so successful as to obliterate the saving difference: "Soon after I had established myself [in the Trobriands]," Malinowski writes, "I began to take part, *in a way,* in the village life, . . . to wake up every morning to a day, presenting itself to me *more or less* as it does to the native[;] . . . I had to learn how to behave, and *to a certain extent* I acquired the 'feeling' for native good and bad manners" (*Argonauts* 7–8; emphasis added). On larger levels of structure, the text might narrate the ethnographer's passage "inside" but also continually interrupt that narrative with portions of the text issuing from the detached perspective either retained or returned to by the claimant to ethnographic authority. Malinowski's own *Argonauts of the Western Pacific* sets out to narrate one typical cycle of the Kula system, linking this attempt (which occupies most of the book) to the ethnographer's quest for the "insider's" view. The narrative includes such reflections as, "As I sat there, looking towards the Southern mountains, . . . I realised what must be the feelings of the Trobrianders, desirous to reach the Koya, to meet the strange people, and to *kula* with them, a desire made perhaps even more acute by a mixture of fear." It relates various stages of the Kula journey as they would appear to a Trobriand participant, sometimes a novice participant—such as, in a sense, Malinowski was himself. In passages like the following, the visitor puts himself into the consciousness of the young native initiate: "Of all these marvels the young Trobriander hears tales, and sees samples brought back to his country, and there is no doubt that it is for him a wonderful experience to find himself amongst them for the first time." (*Argonauts* 220–21).

But the anthropologist breaks off his story in numerous places in order to explain what he is telling, to address the sociological embeddedness and ramifications of various details in his account, thereby showing, for all the insideness he has achieved, that he has not relinquished the scientist's proper distance on his material. What emerges from this dynamic is the possibility, not that narrative and ethnography are fundamentally at odds, but rather that a self-interrupting narrative may function as ethnography's textual analogue for its practitioner's dual role as Participant Observer and for its corresponding ambivalence about the association of culture and place. Self-interrupting narration may also set the temporal rhythm corresponding to ethnography's discrepant geographies, its asymmetrical pairing of a "culturalist" world order in which all inhabited space is broken up into separate, incommensurable, but functionally equivalent cultures, and the worldview ascribed to indigenous ethnocentrists, in which the only division that matters falls between the one place where everything is sensibly connected and the disorienting, unintelligible Outside.

Although the writings of many male culture-seekers certainly can be read for their expression of such romance fantasies and fears as the "penetration" of virgin territory and the castration anxiety that accompanies it, the trope of the self-interrupting narrative is by no means exclusive to male writers. Numerous women's texts also negotiate the double obligation to honor the Malinovskian prescription to "put aside camera, note book and pencil, and to join in . . . in what is going on" (*Argonauts* 21) while guaranteeing that they place in jeopardy no essential of the ethnographer's own acculturated identity. In tone, syntax, and larger structural elements, such texts reflect the constitutively unstable position of ethnographic authority, bound to disrupt and contain the "insideness claims" it advances. A distinctive topos of female ethnographic authority develops around the scene of the native dance, especially the sex-segregated women's dance. Frequently describing a circle, the women's dance functions as a handy metonym for the putatively closed circle of the native culture and occasions that necessary moment of crisis at which the ethnographer perceives that, though she has physically been in the territory of her studied people for some time, she has yet to step across that *epistemological* boundary dividing her internalized culture from theirs. Hortense Powdermaker recalls that, at the critical juncture when she stepped up to take her place in the dance, she was at first

> unable to pay much attention. Consumed with self-consciousness, I imagined my family and friends sitting in the background and muttering in disapproving tones, "Hortense, dancing with the savages!" How could I get up before all these people of the Stone Age and dance with them? . . . But there I was in my proper place in the circle; the drums began; I danced. Something happened. I forgot myself and was one with the dancers. Under the full moon and for the brief time of the dance, I ceased to be an anthropologist from a modern society. I danced. When it was over I realized that, for this short period, I had been emotionally part of the rite. Then out came my notebook. (Powdermaker 112)

What Powdermaker describes here in terms of the sequence "inside, then out again" she later revises to something like "inside, though *never not out*": the portrait of the ethnographer as chameleon, capable of transforming herself into another identity and then recovering her original one, gives way to a more secure self-portrayal in which that original identity was never relinquished, the ethnographer having the capacity to divide herself in two, with the detached observer's side plainly dominant: "Although I had enjoyed those brief moments of feeling at one with the women dancers at the initiation rites," she says, "and although I was fairly involved in this Stone-Age society, I never fooled myself that I had 'gone native.' I participated rather freely, but remained an anthropologist" (Powdermaker 115).

To take only one other example, we may turn to Laura Bohannon's "anthropological novel" *Return to Laughter* (1954), near the middle of which there occurs a similar sequence of the ethnographic process in miniature. It arises during the first wedding ceremonies to take place during the narrator's fieldwork in Africa, and the native wedding serves to suggest the deepening bond between the anthropologist and "her people." Again, the ethnographer faces the fateful choice: to dance, or not to dance?

> We reached Udama's hut. There the bride was handed to her mother-in-law. The women scrambled into the hut after them. I tried to follow. Udama herself stopped me. "You must make up your mind," she announced loudly, so all could hear, "whether you wish to be an important guest or one of the senior women of the homestead. If you are an important guest, we will again lead out the bride, so you may see her. If you are one of us, you may come inside, but then you must dance with us."

Of course she enters, subjecting herself to instruction and to the narrowed focus of the novice participant.

> If I were to dance at all, I had to concentrate on the music and my muscles, but while I danced, my anthropological conscience nagged that I was missing something. In response to my conscience, I craned my neck to watch the younger matrons decorate the bride. Whenever I looked, my feet subsided into an absent-minded shuffle, and then I was poked in the ribs by indignant old women: "Dance!"[50]

The perspective that opens up at such decisive moments in the ethnographic encounter is no more significant than the perspective that closes down, for the ethnographer-participant's need to attend to the details of her performance *blocks out* that larger view available to the researcher who "stands back" rather than plunging in. The ethnographic principle of native ethnocentrism mandates that being an insider means, above all, not seeing the *culture* of which one is a part, but rather only particular actions and particular individuals with whom one has specific relationships. It means knowing how and when to dance but not grasping the ethnographic significance of the dance. The native know-how, the "intimate and largely subconscious knowledge" of their culture's practices possessed by insiders, had to be distinguished from the knowledge of "how that culture is constituted," and only the latter could count as "anthropological knowledge."[51] If unchecked by its opposite, the ethnographer's movement inward from the outside would obliterate rather than secure the ultimate unit of ethnographic understanding.

[50] Bohannon, as Eleonore Smith Bowen, *Return to Laughter: An Anthropological Novel* (1954; New York: Doubleday, 1964), 123.

[51] Kirsten Harstrup, "The Native Voice in Anthropological Vision," *Social Anthropology* 1/2 (1993), 180.

CHAPTER THREE

The Fiction of Autoethnography

[N]othing seems more fictitious . . . than the classic monograph in which
a human group is drawn and quartered along the traditional categories
of social, economic, religious, and other so-called organizations, and
everything holds together.
    —Jean-Paul Dumont[1]

ANYONE NOW proposing to consider the nineteenth-century prehistory of the modern ethnographic imagination must be mightily indebted to Christopher Herbert's *Culture and Anomie,* a work that ranges broadly and brilliantly across a wide variety of Victorian discourses to take the measure of the "turbulence" caused by the nascent and then-nameless culture idea. This book could not have been written without that one. But Herbert's treatment of the novel seems to me the most questionable element in a powerful work. In a chapter on "The Novel of Cultural Symbolism," Anthony Trollope emerges as the solitary exception to the rule in nineteenth-century English fiction, that of "His Majesty the Ego," which regards most novels as antiethnographic in tendency by virtue of their supposed exalting of individual psyche over social "background." This singling out of a protoethnographic author runs contrary to Herbert's usual principle that culture represents "a widely disseminated 'thought style'" in the nineteenth century, and it blocks consideration of the possibility that the advent of anthropology's culture may have been furthered by the broad reorientation of a genre, rather than by the efforts of special individuals. Admiration for Herbert's deft reading of Trollope does not allay my feeling that such an exceptionalist argument (whether focused on this writer or on that) preempts broader historical and generic explanations.[2]

Herbert's isolation of Trollope as novelistic anomaly becomes all the more difficult to accept when we recall the tendency of much novel criticism to locate in nineteenth-century fiction precisely the kind of fine-grained analysis of social reality and logic of totality that Herbert identifies with the theory of culture as a "complex whole." Whether we think of Lukàcs (who champions the realist novel for its "ambition to portray a social whole" and to make that whole "constantly

---

[1] Dumont, *The Headman and I* (Austin: University of Texas Press, 1978), 12.

[2] Christopher Herbert, *Culture and Anomie: Ethnographic Imagination in the Nineteenth Century* (Chicago: University of Chicago Press, 1991), 253; henceforth Herbert. Cf. Richard Handler and Daniel Segal, *Jane Austen and the Fiction of Culture: An Essay on the Narration of Social Realities* (Tucson: University of Arizona Press, 1990).

present in [its] parts")[3] or Raymond Williams (who saw realism as furnishing "knowable communities,"[4] in which "neither the society nor the individual is there as a priority")[5] or Lionel Trilling (for whom the novel's "field of . . . research [is] always the social world," its subject the distinct textures of "manners and morals" constituting that world)[6] or Fredric Jameson (who writes of a novelistic "national allegory" in which "the telling of the individual story and the individual experience cannot but ultimately involve the whole laborious telling of the collectivity itself")[7]—whether we think of these or innumerable other critics across the ideological spectrum, it is more than plain that a view of the novel as performing holistic social analysis and as presenting what might appear to be protoethnographic conceptualizations of the relationship between totality and detail has occupied a far from marginal place in critical tradition.[8]

The novel has also figured prominently, and in much this way, in recent theories of nationalism such as Benedict Anderson's (for whom it bodies forth the "sociological solidity" of the nation through its handling of "general details" that are "representative (in their simultaneous, separate existence) of the [national whole]")[9] and Homi Bhabha's (which considers the process by which narratives turn "the scraps, patches, and rags of daily life . . . into the signs of a national culture").[10] It is perhaps the legacy of the disabling institutional schism between sociology (for "us") and anthropology (for others) that such hardly uncommon perspectives have still not led to the conceptualization, at any level deeper than the anecdotal, of the nineteenth-century novel as engaged in an (auto)ethnographic enterprise. Yet it was in the modern ethnographic discourse which Perry Anderson, in "Components of the National Culture," saw as "exporting" the category of totality away from Britain, and not in the more positivistic sociology, that the novel's constitutive internal division between narrator and characters, discourse- and story-spaces, got reworked into the central reciprocal relationship between object and authority, culture and Participant Observer; and it was anthropology and not (for the most part) sociology that inherited the nineteenth-century novel's habit of using the promised unity of a *book* to "vouch" for the unity of the social domain it represented (Her-

---

[3] "Critical Realism and Socialist Realism," in *The Meaning of Contemporary Realism,* trans. John and Necke Mander (London: Merlin Press, 1979), 99.

[4] Williams, *The Country and the City* (New York: Oxford University Press, 1973), 165.

[5] Williams, *The Long Revolution* (1961; Harmondsworth: Pelican, 1965), 304.

[6] Lionel Trilling, "Manners, Morals, and the Novel," in *The Liberal Imagination* (New York: Scribner's, 1950), 212.

[7] Jameson quoted in Homi Bhabha, "DissemiNation: Time, Narrative, and the Margins of the Modern Nation," in Bhabha, ed., *Nation and Narration* (London: Routledge, 1990), 292.

[8] Cf. Steven Marcus, "Literature and Social Theory: Starting in with George Eliot," in *Representations: Essays on Literature and Society* (New York: Random House, 1975): in Eliot's fiction, society and individuals constitute but the "collective and distributive aspects of the same circumstance or thing" (197). Cf. Morroe Berger, *Real and Imagined Worlds: The Novel and Social Science* (Cambridge, Mass.: Harvard University Press, 1977).

[9] Anderson, *Imagined Communities: Reflections on the Origin and Spread of Nationalism* (London: Verso, 1983), 35, 36.

[10] Bhabha, "DissemiNation," 297.

bert 7). Finally, it was ethnography that took up the novel's challenge of confronting the implications of the boundedness and plurality of culture by understanding itself to be, not the science of "society" or culture, but the "science of *cultures.*"[11]

Such anecdotes as exist linking novel and ethnography usually center on the two modes' commitment to "thick description" in their treatment of social life.[12] But establishing the connection on this basis alone overemphasizes realism and what texts show over the (frequently *romance*) patterns by which they show what they show.[13] As Jonathan Arac has argued, the novel's "search for continuity involved in trying to see society as a whole extended to the search for figurative techniques to integrate a book," since "[w]hat would be the point of arguing for an integrally related society in a book that fractured itself into formlessness in trying to bear the weight of that argument?"[14] In works like the ones I analyze in the following chapters, novelists learned how to produce what Clifford Geertz has called the "inward conceptual rhythm" of anthropology by endowing the intrinsic narrative feature of a discourse-space/story-space distinction with a new connotative force, making it stand for that unstable relationship between insideness and outsideness that brings a culture into view. They also evoked the distinct cultural "worlds of life" by using plot as the device for turning characters arrayed in the mere adjacency (or metonymic relation) of textual space into participants in a common, purportedly integrated—or at least prospectively integrateable—whole (Duncan 6).

[11] George W. Stocking Jr., *Victorian Anthropology* (New York: Free Press, 1987), 302; henceforth Stocking.

[12] Clifford Geertz, *The Interpretation of Cultures* (New York: Basic Books, 1973), chap. 1. Hortense Powdermaker recalls the pleasure of reading novels in the field for the "escape" they afforded her "from the endless details of life in Lesu into the multiplicity of details in another culture"—the one rendered in the pages of a novel (*Stranger and Friend: The Way of an Anthropologist* [New York: Norton, 1966], 100). Cf. Marcel Mauss, in *Manuel d'Ethnographie* (Paris: Payot, 1947): the anthropologist must "be also a novelist able to evoke the life of a whole society" (8). See also Edmund Leach, *Social Anthropology* (New York: Oxford University Press, 1982): anthropologists should stop thinking of themselves as "bad scientists" and start considering themselves "bad novelists" instead (52–54).

[13] On "the distracting taxonomic arguments about romance and novel, romance and realism" as marking "at the institutional level of genre a fruitful trouble and division at the core of national cultural identity," see Ian Duncan, *Modern Romance and Transformations of the Novel: The Gothic, Scott, Dickens* (Cambridge: Cambridge University Press, 1992), 6, and more generally 1–19 and 51–105; henceforth Duncan. Many recent literary-critical works on nationality or culture in nineteenth-century Britain have been so intent to cross generic boundaries that they downplay generically distinctive elements: this is true of Christopher Herbert's *Culture and Anomie* and also of Said's *Culture and Imperialism* (New York: Knopf, 1993); henceforth Said; Elizabeth K. Helsinger's *Rural Scenes and National Representation: Britain, 1815–1850* (Princeton: Princeton University Press, 1997); Mary Poovey's *Making a Social Body: British Cultural Formation, 1830–1864* (Chicago: University of Chicago Press, 1995); Ian Baucom's *Out of Place: Englishness, Empire, and the Locations of Identity* (Princeton: Princeton University Press, 1999). Notable exceptions are Nancy Bentley, *The Ethnography of Manners: Hawthorne, James, Wharton* (Cambridge: Cambridge University Press, 1995); Katie Trumpener, *Bardic Nationalism: The Romantic Novel and the British Empire* (Princeton: Princeton University Press, 1997); henceforth Trumpener; Eleni Coundouriotis, *Claiming History: Colonialism, Ethnography, and the Novel* (New York: Columbia University Press, 1999).

[14] Arac, *Commissioned Spirits: The Shaping of Social Motion in Dickens, Carlyle, Melville, and Hawthorne* (New York: Columbia University Press, 1989), 8.

Kamala Visweswaran has maintained that "the question of fiction and anthropology [is] not merely a question of genre, but one of history as well": this is true of the reorientation of novelistic equipment studied in this book.[15] Just as the way of life in imperial Britain depended upon processes elsewhere, the story of the English Victorian novel has to begin outside of England and before the Victorian era, in the early nineteenth-century narratives of cultural autonomy and United Kingdom consolidation produced by Irish, Anglo-Irish, and Scottish authors oriented primarily to the secondary capitals of the United Kingdom, Dublin and Edinburgh. It is in the hands of such writers that the novel first takes up the task of safeguarding, salvaging, or recovering cultural identities and territories, and it does so—a century before Malinowski's fieldworking science—through an increasingly self-conscious practice of self-interruption. Suvendrini Perera has noted how, in Edgeworth's *Castle Rackrent* (1800), arguably "the first significant English novel to speak in the voice of the colonized," the "narrative voice of the illiterate Irish peasant, Thady, is . . . heavily mediated by the obviously anglicised editor who interrupts and punctuates Thady's story on every page with textual annotations, learned interpolations, and ironic 'folk' anecdotes."[16] Intrusive scholarly apparatus and ironic consciousness also characterize the work of such novelists of the Other's voice as Sydney Owenson (Lady Morgan) and Walter Scott. In Owenson's *The Wild Irish Girl* (1806), disruption of the process by which we and the English leading man become immersed in the title character's perspective is mandated not only by these features but by the epistolary form, which forcefully reminds us of our situation within the English correspondent's viewpoint every time a new chapter begins. In Scott's self-reflexive *Waverley* (1814), the subject of the following chapter, interruption crosses into the narrative story-space to offer testimony about the paradoxical undertaking of cultural "translation." In the post-1801 period, when "for the first time, the novel becomes a prime genre for the dissemination of nationalist ideas" (Trumpener 13) and for representation of one's own (marginal) culture, the "pattern of "narrative + digression + narrative + digression" becomes the signature "feature of [ethnographic] narrative strategy."[17] Self-interruption comes to enact a novelistic meditation on the interplay of temporal and spatial or "configurational" features (story and plot, voice and print, narrative and picture) at the heart of both narrative and the embryonic unit of *a culture*.

The new model of autoethnographic fiction created in the United Kingdom's internal colonies during the first decades of the nineteenth century alternately tested and enforced Gayatri Spivak's useful distinction between *Darstellung* and *Vertretung,* mimetic and political representation.[18] "Interrupted" in its course, national-

[15] Visweswaran, *Fictions of Feminist Ethnography* (Minneapolis: University of Minnesota Press, 1994), 2.

[16] Perera, *Reaches of Empire: The English Novel from Edgeworth to Dickens* (New York: Columbia University Press, 1991), 15.

[17] Dan Rose, "Narrative Ethnography, Elite Cultures, and the Language of the Market," in E. Valentine Daniel and Jeffrey M. Peck, eds., *Culture/Contexture: Explorations in Anthropology and Literary Studies* (Berkeley: University of California Press, 1996), 111.

[18] Spivak, "Can the Subaltern Speak?" in Cary Nelson and Lawrence Grossberg, eds., *Marxism and the Interpretation of Culture* (Urbana: University of Illinois Press, 1988), esp. 275–78.

ist sentiment—now "separatist" sentiment—was generally referred to the aesthetic domain, where in condensing into artifactual form it became a symbol of reified culture itself. The category later to be headed "culture" begins to emerge in an English-language context as both a haven of differences from modern English power and as a commodity—the internal colony's most saleable one, other than cheap labor—for export to that power. As self-conscious or, in Schiller's sense, "sentimental" constructions, marginal British cultures-for-export are thus an effect or product of the London-centered United Kingdom, not its forerunners and victims.[19]

The internal-colonial autoethnographers of this period were also the first writers in English to establish the essential dislocatedness of culture through their awareness of their own necessarily unstable positions. In the context in which they worked, the idea that an autoethnographer's own culture was an abstraction visible only from the outside set a premium upon those Irish or Scottish figures most advantageously situated in relation to an English audience and able to look "back" at their own lands through English eyes. Keenly aware of themselves as creatures of a border between the new Kingdom's center and its peripheries, between its centralizing institutions and its populist movements, they present themselves as mediators, with varying degrees of self-promotion and self-criticism; and they aim at a condition of United Kingdom unity that is to be defined and not fractured by cultural diversity. Asserting cultural independence in texts that assented to and facilitated English political and economic predominance, novelistic autoethnography of the Celtic fringe took shape in differential relation to two other kinds of attempts to know the peoples of the United Kingdom: the prior campaigns, made in other genres, to locate and broadcast the popular voice (as in "Germanic" or populist approaches to the ballad and folktale, or in Macpherson's Ossian), and the state-sponsored efforts to survey and classify regions and their inhabitants (as in the Ordinance Survey, with which Edgeworth's father was associated). Reputed to have been born midway between Britain and Ireland on a ship crossing the Irish Sea, Sydney Owenson embodied one version of the mode's definitive betweenness; Walter Scott, friend of the Hanoverian heir (the future George IV), a fixture of the part-anglicized Lowland establishment, and almost single-handedly responsible for the modern mythology of the Highlands, incorporated another. Ambassadors without states to represent, these figures see themselves—in Homi Bhabha's terms—as occupying that "*in-between* space . . . that carries the burden of the meaning of culture."[20] It becomes a vital, repeatedly negotiated matter of concern for such figures to sort out in writing the relationship *between* the betweenness that enables their address to the metropolitan authorities and the insideness they consciously fabricate, which purports to authorize their accounts of "their own cultures." Scott in particular, where his own representations of Scottish culture are concerned, seems repeatedly to put readers in the position of avowal-and-disavowal that Slavoj Žižek has captured in the phrase "*Je sais bien que . . . mais quand même.*"[21]

It is in relation to characters and situations of knowingly invented insideness

---

[19] Cf. Robert Crawford, *Devolving English Literature* (Oxford: Clarendon, 1992).

[20] Homi Bhabha, *The Location of Culture* (London: Routledge, 1994), 38.

[21] Žižek, *The Sublime Object of Ideology* (London: Verso, 1989), 20–21.

that Scott's narrators can assert the authority that comes with getting "outside" their culture; yet this accrediting journey outward cannot be permitted to turn into any once-and-for-all escape: it too must be *interrupted,* its configurational powers of closure interfered with, lest the autoethnographer entirely forfeit his bond to the culture from which he departs. Autoethnographers of all peripheral culture regions know well the temptation to which their privileged positions expose them—that of kicking the dust of their cultures from their heels and joining the crowd of place-seekers (or "absentees" in the sense explored in Edgeworth's novel) in the metropolis. Resisting that urge, Scott and others stake out a position of *relative* distance from their cultures, not a stance of cosmopolitan exteriority to culture *tout court.* Through their movements, the *outside* of (a) culture becomes "culturally relative," reserved for the exercise of a *particular* insider's outsideness.[22] And just as later ethnographers represented their own authority in terms of either spatial or temporal arts—depicting themselves either as split selves simultaneously inside and out of the visited culture, or as going through a narrative of entrance into, then withdrawal from, that culture—nineteenth-century autoethnographers implied through their differential dealings with their characters either that they could both leave and *not* leave their own culture or that they could go out but would always return. Plots organized around the idea of return attain a new significance in the fiction of this period and after, as narrators explore the conditions of their own authority using characters as partial objectifications of themselves.

Moving on from early to mid-nineteenth century, a major question for the critic of the British novel then becomes, what could a mode of fiction that exported marginal United Kingdom cultures to the metropolis offer to a later fiction celebrated for its capacious and intensive scrutiny of *English* society and devoted to the location of *Englishness*? How might we understand the great achievements made by early and mid-Victorian writers as entailing an anglicization or centralization of autoethnography? Said's account of the nineteenth-century English novel in *Culture and Imperialism* does not necessarily point to a "departmental" mentality of imperialist hubris, and concluding that it does has serious consequences for the way we read, since if the novel's richly detailed portrayals of English society are regarded mainly as expansive efforts to *avoid* seeing steadily and whole the offshore basis of the English way of life, the critic's job then becomes that of "reading noncollusively," of focusing on "what is unsaid and occluded," on what gets pushed to and beyond the margins.[23] One commits oneself—in our shopworn metaphor—to "interrogating" the text. One *unreads* novels rather than reading them, supplying the information and perspectives they studiously neglect, unraveling their textures and averting one's eyes from their obfuscatory structures, fig-

[22] I regard this development as part of the move away from the structure of eighteenth-century Anglo-French literary relations, in which "the cross-Channel zone of literary culture produced a vision of the universally emotive human subject abstracted from national difference and historical specificity": Introduction to Margaret Cohen and Carolyn Dever, eds., *The Literary Channel: The International Invention of the Novel* (Princeton: Princeton University Press, 2002), 20.

[23] Perera, *Reaches of Empire,* 2.

ural strategies, and plots. One approaches novels the way Raymond Williams approached the country house poem, in *The Country and the City,* where all that is not included in the poem becomes the most important thing about the form. This has been a valuably defamiliarizing approach; but as I see it, accepting Said's claim that "the novel . . . and imperialism are unthinkable without each other" might *also* be taken as requiring us to pay *more* attention to what the novel presents as central, and how it does so, once we recognize the ways novels made themselves into the textual form *analogous to* the "knowable community," nominating their textual boundaries as stand-ins for the boundaries of the culture or nation, their plots and figural strategies as the centripetal force that laid down those boundaries, their narrators as the mobile authorities capable of apprehending the whole (Said 70–71). Not merely hypersensitive scrutiny of the novel's peripheries (and besides, *which* peripheries?), but detailed formal analysis of its central structures and language remains indispensable to a globally conscious novel criticism.

I hope it will be abundantly clear that the "return to the center" that I propose is not recidivist in nature; it stems from the desire to understand how English novels managed the pressures of imperial nationhood as well as of other economic, religious, and social factors more or less indirectly related to empire. I think we should ask not just, why *didn't* the preeminent genre of nineteenth-century Europe deal with the preeminent fact about Europe during this period: its empire? but also, why *did* Europe in its imperial heyday reconfigure the novel and elevate it to preeminence as a genre devoted to furnishing a more complete, more historicist account of modern Western societies than had yet been attempted? Putting the matter this way reorients our perspective on the ideological work of the novel, enabling us to think about it as defensive rather than smug. It encourages us, in other words, to approach the great masterpieces of Victorian fiction as attempts to comprehend and counteract a suspected by-product of British expansion, a moral evacuation or "meaning loss" at the imperial center—as if the exporting of British legal codes, school curricula, religious doctrines, investment capital, and personnel depleted the island nation's identity rather than aggrandized it.[24] Ironically, the approach to fiction that flows from Said's and other postcolonialist analyses actually outdoes the defensive nation-making efforts of the nineteenth-century English novel itself, by blotting out so completely all those fine differentiations (of class, of region, of religion, and so forth) observable *within* the imperial nation and regarding "England" or "Britain" (or even "the West") as one unanimous whole, poised against the whole it coercively constructs of its "Other." To make the novel's one-making labors *visible,* we have to emphasize the domestic diversities with which it had to contend but which it also had to mobilize—the internal differences that get obliterated under dichotomous schemes but that had to remain active in any convincing and culturally "thick" evocation of national unity.

To take only the three English novelists I examine in this work: consideration

---

[24] Cf. Jed Esty, *A Shrinking Island: Modernism and National Culture in England* (Princeton: Princeton University Press, 2003), 23–53, on this "meaning loss" as a phenomenon of "metropolitan perception."

of Charlotte Brontë, Dickens, and Eliot should quickly make very plain just how advisedly one needs to use the category of "the metropolitan" in applying it to the Anglican Yorkshirewoman of Cornish-Irish parentage (steeped in Byron, Scott, and *Blackwood's Edinburgh Magazine*), the peripatetic, Promethean Kentsman and Londoner (infused with the discourses of popular theater and public speaking), and the freethinking woman from the Midlands (saturated in Wordsworth and German scholarship and ultimately sympathetic to the religion she had spurned). (Adding into the mix Elizabeth Gaskell, Cheshire-born wife of the prominent Manchester Unitarian and the only mother among leading novelists of the 1840s and 1850s, would further complicate matters.) These English novelists operated in very different relationships to the institutions and energies of the metropolis: for Brontë and Eliot, gender and regional identifications and international contacts provided resources for the circumvention or deflection of nationalist appeals emanating from the capital; yet for both, class affiliations tended to encourage identification with the nation—in Brontë's case, through the Anglican clergy; in Eliot's, through the rural establishment forming the nation's traditional backbone. The result of these conflicting calls for imaginary investment encouraged each toward distinctive varieties of a displaced or decentered national culture. In Dickens, class *ressentiment* helped fuel a titanic ambition to master the metropolis, and the nation seen as radiating outward from it, as not even the state or its surrogates could do. Unlike the imperial state whose attention, he thought, was apt to wander everywhere but back to its own native land, Dickens's authorial persona is that of the metropolitan autoethnographer ideally capable of surveying, pervading, revealing the truth about, and discovering the interconnections among every last particle of British life.

In this book I try to show how the novel puts its own fictions of English or British culture *on* show, committing itself to the skeptical questioning and testing of its own nation-making and culture-making procedures. As Ian Duncan puts it, while the novel's "formal effects express a semiotic totality more purposive than that of 'the world'—the most influential contemporary term for it is 'culture'—at the same time . . . they chart the irregularity and accident and excess and privation that contradict any unity of purpose [and] unravel the order of culture" (Duncan 5–6). Novels assume this richly ambivalent shape precisely because they are not simply aligned with the interests of the state, or with the populist movements—especially Chartism—they view askance. On the one hand, the novel comes very self-consciously to assert a form of textual organization sharply distinguished from that of the catalogue, the list, the encyclopedia, the state-sponsored blue book or statistical table: it concurs with Carlyle's wish to see "not Redbook Lists, and Court Calendars, and Parliamentary Registers, but the LIFE of MAN in England."[25] All these positivistic forms provided defining opposites for the increasingly more coherent, less episodic novels of the later 1840s and after: they amounted to so many textual avatars of that anticultural scenario of mere adjacency, placing fact next to fact, event after event, but never making available the underlying connection

---

[25] Carlyle, *Works* (London: Chapman & Hall, 1899), 28.81.

among them. The same could be said about those seemingly exhaustive surveys of various nations' manners and customs that proliferated during the 1830s and 1840s (including, notably, Bulwer-Lytton's 1833 *England and the English*). Plenty of information about, but never the *culture of,* a given people could be rendered in these; it took a form equipped to realize and exploit the constitutive instabilities of the emergent ethnographic imagination to evoke a culture.

In her excellent study *Vanishing Points: Dickens, Narrative, and the Subject of Omniscience* (1991), Audrey Jaffe argued that the fiction of this period develops around a fantasy not incompatible with colonizing perspectives: that of an "unlimited knowledge and mobility" which can be imagined only "in relation to and at the expense of what it constructs as characters."[26] So described, narrative omniscience resembles Claude Lévi-Strauss's account of ethnography as involving "the subject's capacity for indefinite self-objectification (without ever abolishing itself as subject), for projecting outside itself ever-diminishing fragments of itself."[27] But it is precisely the novel's indication of a self-imposed *limit* on its fantasy, that parenthesis in Lévi-Strauss's sentence, that interests me here: it is not unlimited knowledge any more than boundless desire that the novel is after; it sets processes of knowing and desiring in motion in order to contain them within the national frame. The narrator's proliferation of partial or contrastive self-objectifications in the novel's dramatis personae has to stop short of the point at which all characters "become" (versions of) the narrator—no novelist confronts this possibility more forcefully than does George Eliot—and this principle is strikingly linked in Victorian novels to the idea that a grasp of the culture of England or Britain could be achieved only by the intelligence capable of recognizing that it must operate, as the narrator of a novel does, within the culturally relative outside of a *particular* bounded (iconic) space.

In Gaskell's *Mary Barton* (1848), for example, the narrator's own attempt to understand and unify the whole social system embracing the polarized classes of her industrial nation is reflected in the various characters who are either walkers of the city streets (as is the narrator herself) or, on the other hand, spokespersons for or representers of the industrial underclass (as she tries, through sympathetic exposure, to become). The narrator's self-subjection to the promiscuous contact of the streets, where she is "elbowed" into consciousness of the working class in the forced togetherness of the urban crowd, is the first step in what looks like an outside-in ethnographic process.[28] As not only the protagonist but numerous other characters will discover through a series of similar elbowings, those perilous streets are also full of redemptive possibilities that can be realized only by the figure who subjects herself to them: *in the destructive element immerse.*

---

[26] Jaffe, *Vanishing Points: Dickens, Narrative, and the Subject of Omniscience* (Berkeley: University of California Press, 1991), 13.

[27] Lévi-Strauss, *Introduction to the Work of Marcel Mauss,* trans. Felicity Baker (London: Routledge, 1987), 32.

[28] Gaskell, *Mary Barton* (Harmondsworth: Penguin, 1996), 3; henceforth Gaskell. Cf. Deborah Epstein Nord, *Walking the Victorian Streets: Women, Representation, and the City* (Ithaca: Cornell University Press, 1995), esp. chap. 5.

So far *Mary Barton* is aligned with fieldwork ethnography's pattern of entrance and withdrawal. But the woman novelist who riskily crosses the class divide is engaged in a larger project, that of a national, class-uniting autoethnography—*auto-*, because embracing the nation she shares with the workers—that is predicated on the discrediting of perspectives she sees as limited *to* class, perspectives that might generate a (possibly transnational) *working-class* autoethnography or worse, a working-class politics. Determined to "give some utterance to the agony which . . . convulses this dumb people" (Gaskell 3), she must truncate and silence attempts at indigenous working-class utterance, even while envying their authenticity.[29] Through elaborate contrasts among numerous characters brought forward as good or bad "voices" for the poor, Gaskell establishes her approval of working-class self-understanding and self-representation when it permits itself to be sublated in the more capacious (bourgeois) autoethnography of the shared nation. At the same time, the self-authorizing contrast which *Mary Barton* establishes between the (auto)ethnographer's pursuit of her working-class subjects and the coercive courtship of Mary by the mill owner's son occasionally appears liable to collapse, as if in acknowledgment of the necessary violence of Gaskell's endeavor. (Harry Carson's insulting caricature of the workers, and what becomes of it—crumpled and thrown to the floor, it is retrieved by their delegates and used to inflame the resentment against the employers that will ultimately result in the murder of Harry—is the most striking such instance. The nightmarish double of Gaskell's own goal—cross-class communication—appears in this piece of paper's transit from producer's into unintended recipients' hands, where it becomes the fuse of a violent retort upon that producer.)

It is worth noting that Charles Kingsley's contemporaneous *Alton Locke,* which works in a manner precisely the reverse of Gaskell's, is beset by a like insecurity. Where Gaskell's third-person narrator, ethnographer-style, confronts the difficulties of moving from the outside of working-class culture *in,* Kingsley's, the first-person Alton Locke himself, must cope with the perils of traffic in the opposite direction, from an initial position of entrenched class and sectarian identity to a capacious national vision. The stories told by these two novels eroticize the insistent question of narrative authority in complementary ways: in terms of the condescending desire felt by one who "slums," on the one hand (Harry Carson's, for Mary), and the unfulfillable desire felt by the upward-gazing idealist, on the other (Alton's, for the unattainable bourgeois Lillian). But in both outside-in and inside-out varieties, fictional ethnographies of the working classes, striving to apprehend the native's point of view and to demonstrate that the natives have "a culture of their own" must confront the conflict, and learn to exploit the tension, between their relativistic and their nationalistic impulses: they must pull up short of according to the workers *so* distinctive a culture that class-transcending national perspectives are preemptively negated (and class-specific international ones opened up); the workers in these novels must achieve not a culture of *their* own but some-

---

[29] Gaskell's character Margaret is reminiscent of the Corinnes and Glorvinas and Flora MacIvors who embody the essences of their peoples in romantic-era fiction.

thing like "a culture of *our* own," that "our" including both workers and bourgeois readers in the newly activated, positive cultural identity of the nation. To put it another way, these novels are all about the effort to turn ethnography into autoethnography. This happens, in *Mary Barton,* every time we encounter one of those Scott- and Owensen-like footnotes that not only explain the meaning of terms from Manchester laborers' dialect but also locate those terms in passages of Chaucer or Ben Jonson or other such fixtures in the English literary canon. The nation emerges as the ultimate horizon of cultural identity and the largest unit to which one can bear any meaningful moral responsibility. Gaskell makes nearly all her moral appeals on the grounds of a potentially universal Christian fellowship, yet she enjoins British workers to accept lower wages in order to keep British firms in business against foreign competitors; the question of what Christian duty British workers might owe to their French or German counterparts, upon whose lives they will place new pressure by agreeing, never arises. The operative principle seems precisely opposed to Josiah Tucker's declaration that "the love of country . . . has no place in the catalogue of Christian virtues";[30] here, nationality defines the *territory* (geographical and/or figurative) within which Christian virtues can be realized.

These examples give evidence of the same sort of ethnographic anxiety to which Scott's treatments of the Highlanders are systematically prone, and it is hardly surprising to see them arise in 1840s novels dealing with the Condition-of-England Question, though the seeming compulsion with which the narrators of these English Social-Problem Novels spin off versions or counterversions of themselves in the story-space of their fictions has never received a full appreciation. Further, the almost constant migration of questions about the narrator's authority from discourse- into story-space gets joined to a process which novels narrate, or imply, as taking an opposite course: in relation to a cultural field conceived as an array of more or less incarcerating, view-restricting positions, the novelistic narrator gains authority by traveling outward or upward from, or comprehensively among, those separate positions in order to grasp their structural and moral interdependence. We "know" that the narrator has made this dislocating, authorizing journey by the fact that he or she keeps demonstrating the ability and the inclination to *return* to the field in proxy forms. As we begin to read the particular story related in a novel, we are simultaneously presented with, or invited to infer, the story of its narrator's voyage out, the one that makes possible the authoritative returns. In this way do nineteenth-century English novels attest to the historicity of twentieth-century anthropology's governing tropes, giving formal embodiment to the same metaphors of spatial relation that later anthropologists employed about cultures and the fieldwork that gave access to them, but turning those metaphors inside out. Instead of a master narrative about the achievement of an outsider's insideness in another culture, they convey one about the attainment of an insider's outsideness with regard to one's own. Hyperbole, some instances of which I cited in chapter 2, is elevated from a stylistic feature to one signature trope of the autoethnographic labor Vic-

---

[30] See *Josiah Tucker: A Selection from his Economic and Political Writings,* ed. R. L. Schuyler (New York: Columbia University Press, 1931), 31.

torian novels perform, because that labor requires the vantage point of one who has been "thrown beyond" (*hyper-bole*) the omniexpressive totality in which the ordinary members of a culture dwell. Accordingly, evocations of the view "from above" make regular appearances in narrators' attempts to secure their authority: elevation and mobility are the leading tropes for an authority that conceives of cultural membership in tropes of being inside or down in a place.[31]

In his valedictory to the Victorian novel, *Tono-Bungay* (1909), H. G. Wells has his narrator recall "that English country-side of my boyhood [where] every human being had a 'place.' It belonged to you from your birth like the colour of your eyes, it was inextricably your destiny."[32] The figure who commemorates this attachment of identity and mentality to geographical and sociological place has grown up to be an amateur aviator, obviously a descendent of Dickens's many figures of comprehensive overview. Such self-reflexive imagery, pervasive in nineteenth-century fiction, is one way that fiction anticipates the aim of a reflexive social knowledge of "participant objectivation."[33] Yet in Wells, the desire to read flight from one's culture as *an element of one's participation in it,* a "moment" in one's relation *to* it, has been lost—whereas, in James Joyce, the desire of the Icarus-like hero, Stephen Dedalus, to fly free of suffocating Dublin inaugurates a career that never swerves from autoethnographizing the native land. In an early twentieth-century echo of the situation in the early *nineteenth* century, the Celtic fringe writer achieves a massively productive tension between the urges toward departure and return, while the English writer, Wells, knows *return* only as a backsliding that imperils the self made free through science. Unlike Jane Eyre or Pip, Wells's first-person narrator in *Tono-Bungay* makes a return to his past in the account he writes *without* ever making us feel that his critique of the culture that produced him partakes of his ongoing attachment *to* that culture; his liberation seems wholly negative, and we see him in the end driven only by a thoroughly unmoored curiosity, building destroyers to see how well he can build them, disturbingly disengaged from any question of what purpose they serve. In contrast, the Victorian style of detachment or dislocation I am interested in is typically envisioned as a distance taken on a culture that is the only way to find and serve that culture.

The *Edinburgh Review* signaled something like this when it remarked of Matthew Arnold that he "viewed his own country with continental eyes but with an English heart."[34] Arnold's own maddeningly vague, seemingly nonethnographic use of culture pertains to a perfection of the self that points forward not so much to the *object* of later ethnographic analysis (a small-c culture) as to the Participant Observer who apprehends that object. It does so in reverse: Arnold's ideal "best

---

[31] Cf. Bernard McGrane, *Beyond Anthropology: Society and the Other* (New York: Columbia University Press, 1989), 119–20; also Arac, *Commissioned,* for what remains the best account of the "comprehensive view" in nineteenth-century fiction and social criticism.

[32] Wells, *Tono-Bungay* (1909; Lincoln, Neb.: Bison, 1978), 15.

[33] Pierre Bourdieu, in Bourdieu and Loïc J.-D. Wacquant, *An Invitation to Reflexive Sociology* (Chicago: University of Chicago Press, 1992), 68.

[34] Quoted in Frederic E. Faverty, *Matthew Arnold the Ethnologist* (Evanston, Ill.: Northwestern University Press, 1951), 188.

self," "rising above" the plane of the class-determined "ordinary self," would be an objectifying participant, not a once-and-for-all, Enlightenment-fantasy escapee from the determining force of (ethnographic) culture into the Platonic domain of "the best that has been thought and said."[35]

To take another unlikely example, even John Stuart Mill, champion of individual freedoms, espouses in *On Liberty* a bearing toward one's own social environment that might *balance* the independence of the rational mind and the commitment to a particular community. Perhaps the most arresting sections of Mill's book are those in which the philosopher gives voice to his dread of what seems a creeping *dehistoricization* of the world, a sort of catching disease of enslavement to custom, to which he thinks the benighted Orient has long succumbed but which he now sees assailing the imperial center itself. Mill breathtakingly writes that "the greater part of the world has, properly speaking, no history, because [in it] the despotism of Custom is complete"; but he also describes an England shockingly prone to the same condition, and beseeches his compatriots to exert themselves to the utmost in the attempt to withstand this pandemic of the "magical influence of custom." Even if we confidently believe our own beliefs and habits to be the best in the world, he maintains, and even if science has shown them to *be* so, we must seek out all available opponents of them and, in the absence of any such, must resort to "some contrivance for making the difficulties of the question as present to the learner's consciousness as if they were pressed upon him by a dissentient champion, eager for his conversion." Such are the burdens of world domination: lacking actual challenges to their way of life, Britons must strenuously make believe such challenges exist, in order to preserve a lively rather than a merely "apelike" relation to their own customs. Mill does *not* imagine a state of civilization in which individual minds might be finally *free* of custom.[36]

If hyperbole constitutes one signature trope of Victorian autoethnography, another must be chiasmus, that figure of crossings. No novel gave this figure greater scope as a structural principle than Dickens's metafictional *Bleak House,* with its dazzling double narration involving third- and first-person voices that continually (fruitfully, magically) encroach upon each other's domains. Its operations are also discernible throughout the works of the other novelists I examine in this study: in the relationship between Jane Eyre the narrator and Jane the character, for example, or between Caroline Helstone and Shirley Keeldar in *Shirley,* or again between George Eliot's sympathy-promoting narrator and the numerous characters who attempt, as it were, to follow her example. The prevalence of such narrative transits in English Victorian fiction can be taken as one more sign of that fiction's commitment to the production or *location* of English culture by means of an "interactive travel," a spatial practice (as Michel de Certeau would call it) that transforms amorphous, unmapped space into a "discrete social space."[37] Employing estab-

---

[35] *Culture and Anarchy,* J. Dover Wilson, ed. (Cambridge: Cambridge University Press, 1990), 94–95. On Arnold and ethnography, cf. Herbert 54–57.

[36] John Stuart Mill, *On Liberty,* ed. Currin V. Shields (New York: Macmillan, 1956), 86, 8, 54.

[37] The wording here is from James Clifford, "Spatial Practices," in *Routes: Travel and Translation in the Late Twentieth Century* (Cambridge, Mass.: Harvard University Press, 1997), 54.

lished novelistic chronotopes of road and room—the loci of outsiderly "traveling" and an insiderly "dwelling"[38]—fiction around the middle of the nineteenth century works toward this view of culture by showing time and again that, where one side of this partnership exists without the other, it takes on the form of ruinous self-parody. The dialectic of potentially acculturating enclosures (domestic interiors in particular) and literal or figurative prisons is central to the cultural labor of many novels, as is the dialectic of a liberating mobility (such as the narrator's) and an aimless, corrosive vagrancy. In the first of these oppositions, the desired, "culturing" enclosure has to afford a means of egress; in the second, the favored image of motion has to guarantee a return to the site of departure. Recognizing this helps us appreciate anew the fact that *culture* as English novels develop it cannot properly be described as descending exclusively from *either* side of the great Liberal/Antiliberal antinomy of modern Europe: neither "French" free-ranging skeptical rationalism nor "German" rooted romantic nationalism, the evocations of English or British culture in the Victorian novel seek the utopian synthesis of these conditions. Toward that end, the novel comes to be, in a powerful sense, *all about* the narrator's movement outward and back, decades before Thomas Hardy's *The Return of the Native* (1878) gave this narrative dynamic an explicit and dark-toned thematization.

With that outward motion comes the dissociation of English culture from the place occupied by the merely existing English: the autoethnographic fictions I will examine in this book often represent their own procedures as involving the dislocation *of* British culture and identity from Britain to some position outside from which that culture might be repatriated, restored or "returned" to people who have never yet known it, being as they are mere insiders, the occupants and prisoners of *locations*. Sometimes the power of the returnee's viewpoint arose from biographical circumstances, as when Anthony Trollope returned from the South Pacific in 1872 and undertook *The Way We Live Now,* his most comprehensive portrayal of contemporary English anticulture. First-person narratives, like those of Jane Eyre or Pip or David Copperfield, enacted the therapeutic return to formative (or deforming) social environments and strove toward counterideals of a harmonious and nurturing togetherness, figured most often through the commonest of novelistic devices, the marriage plot. The narrator who flew above all the limited views available in the cultural field below, bringing her culture into being as she departed from it, would in the end (and perhaps many times before that) resume the guise of a character who, like the narrator of Brontë's *Shirley,* would show herself walking the landscape once peopled by the characters she had been describing from the third-person standpoint; or, like Arthur Clennam and his bride at the close of *Little Dorrit,* would go back "down into a modest life of usefulness and happiness," there no doubt, like Dorothea Ladislaw at the close of *Middlemarch,* to "live[] faithfully a hidden life," converting the power derived from a vision of interconnectedness into myriad "incalculably diffusive" acts of melioration.[39]

---

[38] Cf. James Clifford, "Traveling Cultures," in *Routes,* 17–46.

[39] "Went down . . . ": Dickens, *Little Dorrit* (1857; Harmondsworth: Penguin, 1985), 895; "live[]

Having become *visibly invisible* as an authority over his or her own culture, the narrator might then turn *invisibly visible* as the unheroic but rededicated protagonist, just in time to vanish altogether (until the next novel).

It is more than plain that the perspective I am recommending in this book would entail adjustment of some of our most influential models for "placing" Victorian literature in material history, just as it does for some established accounts of the evolution of the culture concept. Said's assertions that, witnessing throughout the century "a tremendous international display of British power virtually unchecked over the entire world," Victorian writers found it "both logical and easy to identify themselves in one way or another with this power" and that, in the nineteenth century, "[w]henever a cultural form or discourse aspired to wholeness and totality, most European writers, thinkers, politicians, and mercantilists tended to think in global terms"—these call for something more than an asterisked qualification to the effect that the English novelist's *way* of thinking in global terms was to hold the category of the global at bay by reinventing and focusing detail-rapt attention upon the *national*. That so-called Victorian ethic of duty for which Carlyle was the most eloquent advocate gave rise to the question for which, thanks to the novel, the nation became the obvious answer: what is the ultimate sphere of one's duty? If, as Dickens's *Bleak House* appeared to urge, readers were to construct their moral lives as a series of spreading concentric "circle[s] of duty," or if, as George Eliot's fiction repeatedly averred, they should learn by its offices to cultivate a broad, diffusive sympathy with their fellow men and women, such works also built a challenge into their form: how far should the circles spread, the sympathy extend? Self-conscious subjects of the one nation for which it had almost become a practical possibility to exercise "duty" and "sympathy" anywhere in the world, the leading midcentury novelists strategically exaggerated the self-interrupting capability of *all* narrative in an attempt to return British attention to the claims arising from the domestic totality, from (in George Eliot's phrase) a "particular web."

"Anywhere's nowhere": Dickens's phrase in *Bleak House* (see chap. 5) expresses the challenge of a subject yoked perforce to an empire of global reach, a subject for whom the very expansion of colonial holdings and international entanglements has brought on new anxieties about where and what Britishness or Englishness might be, if they could be, theoretically, anywhere. The midcentury novelists confronted a possible future in which British power might expand (in Marlon Ross's terms) "to the point of its own potential dissolution, losing its sense of oneness demarcated originally by the closeness of its geographical borders and loosening its bonds to that indigenous tradition that initially marked its sense of self-identity."[40] A nation for which it has become possible even just to *imagine* itself

---

. . ." and "incalculably . . .": George Eliot, *Middlemarch* (1871–72; Harmondsworth: Penguin, 1994), 838.

[40] Ross, "Romancing the Nation-State: The Poetics of Romantic Nationalism," in Jonathan Arac and Harriet Ritvo, eds., *Macropolitics of Nineteenth-Century Literature: Nationalism, Exoticism, Imperialism* (Philadelphia: University of Pennsylvania Press, 1991), 56.

endowed with the power to move about the world with the freedom of an omniscient narrator—"virtually unchecked"—seemed to require loyal subjects who might use the devices of their art to impose some sort of check, even just to *remind* Britons of the necessity for such a check, at a time when no foreign power seemed able to deliver one. A notable precursor was Edmund Burke, who had famously dreaded Britain's "being too much dreaded" and the ruin that might ensue "[i]f we should come to be . . . absolutely able, without the least control, to hold the commerce of other nations totally dependent upon our good pleasure."[41] One need not suggest that the novelists I study here were Burkean conservatives or anti-imperialists to be able to discern in their works a reaction-from-within to global power's self-induced vertigo. Constructing texts that raise the question of their own discursive unstoppability and then pointedly contain or disrupt the seemingly inexorable processes they have set in motion, these authors seek to manage the possibility that worldwide empire amounts not to a nation-expanding or nation-aggrandizing process, but to a nation-erasing one. Against the backdrop of the nation's increasingly visible entanglements elsewhere, which threatened to draw the nation out into (what Eliot called) "that tempting range of relevancies called the universe," metropolitan autoethnography could bring the national "imagined community" into view only through principled restriction *of* view.

To read midcentury English fiction this way is to extend backward by half a century or more the argument in which Fredric Jameson characterized *modernism* as the aesthetic of that phase in an imperial nation's career when daily life has come to feel "radically incomplete" because of its thorough dependence upon processes and places elsewhere. At such a point, Jameson has contended, the newly inscrutable metropolis seeks to see itself "by compensation . . . formed [in art] into a self-subsisting totality . . . a utopian glimpse of [itself as] an achieved community."[42] Yet with their enormously detailed and critically engaged analyses of English life, Victorian novels were attempting to redress that "systematic underdevelopment of Englishness" that issued from post-1801 British centralization. "To the degree that England becomes the center of the empire," Katie Trumpener writes, "its own internal sense of culture accordingly fails to develop," with the result that, in the romantic period, "the purely English novel comes to appear quite pallid (and indeed begins, in self-defense, to recast Englishness as a nationality or ethnicity whose complexity is comparable with that of the other cultures in Britain)" (Trumpener 15–16, 296n39).

One romantic-era text beginning to move in this direction is *Northanger Abbey,* in which Jane Austen apparently debunks but more deeply validates Gothic perception as a device for dislocating the self-congratulatory styling of England as the home of modern rationality and realism. Reflecting upon her interpretation of En-

[41] Burke, "Remarks on the Policy of the Allies," in *Empire and Community: Edmund Burke's Writings and Speeches on International Relations,* ed. David P. Fidler and Jennifer M. Welsh (Boulder, Colo.: Westview Press, 1999), 281–82.

[42] Jameson, "Modernism and Imperialism," in Terry Eagleton, Jameson, and Edward W. Said, *Nationalism, Colonialism, and Literature* (Minneapolis: University of Minnesota Press, 1990), 58.

glishmen's actions through the lens of the Gothic—the habit Henry Tilney admonishes her for, with his "Remember that we are English, that we are Christians"—Catherine Morland transposes into a comical key what otherwise might appear an alarming shrinking-island effect, with safe "English" space yielding ground to the sprawling realm of the alien where the Gothic mode can be taken as a reliable guide to human behavior. Catherine surrenders up the Continent and even "the northern and western extremities" of Britain itself to the rule of the Gothic, but wants desperately to believe "the central part of England" demarcatable and defensible against that rule.[43] For Tilney, to be English means merely to live by the light of reason and of God: this is no nationalism but the self-universalizing mentality that leeches that Englishness of positive cultural identity.

If Jameson's account of modernism's compensatory construction of imaginary totalities calls for such alteration, so too does Norbert Elias's stark opposition of *Civilization* and *Culture.* In his *History of Manners,* Elias famously argued that while the term *civilization* "giv[es] expression to the continuously expansionist tendency of colonizing groups," "*Kultur* mirrors the self-consciousness of a nation which had constantly to seek out and constitute its boundaries anew . . . and again and again had to ask itself: 'What is really our identity?'" According to Elias's etiology, or "sociogenesis," of the *Kultur* concept out of the "polemic of the stratum of German middle-class intelligentsia against the etiquette of the ruling courtly upper class," it was in a Germany lacking national unity, whose rulers spoke French, practicing the manners and espousing the values of courtly society elsewhere in Europe, that *Kultur* could emerge to oppose their Enlightenment cosmopolitanism with the unifying and delimiting spirit of a single people.[44] *Kultur* represented at its inception a kind of promissory note issued to a people without national statehood, expressing itself through the common language they spoke, the *Volkstimme* or "outward expression of the inner essence of a nation."[45] Yet recent work emphasizing how *continual* a process nation making is, how national identity must be secured, not once and for all by the actions of a state, but daily, through various technologies, imageries, and narratives, must discountenance Elias's contention that use of the term *Civilization* "expresses the self-assurance of peoples whose national boundaries and national identity have for centuries been so fully established that they have ceased to be the subject of any particular discussion." Elias's opposition of a self-universalizing *Civilization* that "emphasizes what is common to all human beings or—in the view of its bearers—should be" to a concept of *Kultur* that definitively "*delimits*" obstructs consideration of the appeal that

---

[43] Austen, *Northanger Abbey* (1817; Oxford: Oxford University Press, 1990), 159, 161. Cf. Claudia L. Johnson, *Jane Austen: Women, Politics, and the Novel* (Chicago: University of Chicago Press, 1988), chap. 2; See also Franco Moretti on Austen's novels as providing symbolic form for the transcendence of "local loyalties" by national ones, in *Atlas of the European Novel, 1800–1900* (London: Verso, 1998), 13–29.

[44] Norbert Elias, *The Civilizing Process: The History of Manners and State Formation and Civilization,* trans. Edmund Jephcott (Oxford: Blackwell, 1994), 5.

[45] Linda Dowling, *Language and Decadence in the Victorian Fin de Siècle* (Princeton: Princeton University Press, 1986), 15.

the delimiting force of culture may have held for segments *within* a nation of expanding reach and power; even if the development of *culture* as an English word took more or less the entire nineteenth century, there is little doubt that English Victorian writers found the question, "what is really our identity?" and the call to "seek out and constitute [their] boundaries anew" among their most pressing concerns.[46]

As Ian Baucom has recently maintained, extension of the territory lying under one nation's sovereignty may eventuate a corresponding contraction in "the territory of affect," true national identity coming to be seen as "isomorphic with either the 'original' boundaries of the nation or with certain revered and ultra-auratic locations within the nation."[47] This formulation of the relationship supplements other perspectives lately applying to the concept of national space Benedict Anderson's theory of national consciousness as operating through a medium of "homogeneous, empty time." Elizabeth Helsinger, for example, has read the late eighteenth-century Enclosure Acts as instituting a "bounded, emptied space of the national territory, subdivided into clearly demarcated units of private possession," a conceptualization of space that "functions very much like Anderson's 'simultaneous time' of the novel and the newspaper": Helsinger's space and Anderson's time are the media in which "individuals who do not know one another can imagine themselves to coexist, and hence to form a tenuous 'horizontal comradeship' in a national present and a national territory."[48] The blank horizontality of nation-space, instantiated through print media and discernible in a variety of nineteenth-century forms, adumbrates Malinowski's exaggeratedly homogeneous domains of culture, described for example in the dicta "Nationality *means* unity in culture" and "[W]ithin the boundaries of the tribe the writ of the same culture runs from end to end."[49] Helsinger's legalistic model (and Malinowski's)—according to which culture's "writ" covers every inch of national space like an evenly applied coat of paint—augments Baucom's emphasis on privileged "revered and ultra-auratic locations" or *lieux de memoire,* and vice versa: taken together they signal that asymmetrical pairing of geographic visions that I have described above as a constitutive feature of an (auto)ethnographic imagination. If, as Homi Bhabha has put it, the nation needs to be conceptualized in a "double-time," the authors treated in this study show that it needs to be thought of in a double-space as well.

The novelists I deal with here all give striking evidence of being conscious of their role in relation to an anonymous comradeship of Britons arrayed in functional equivalence across a "level" field of sovereign territory (and figured for them in the idea of their readerships), but they also show, to differing degrees, a counter-

---

[46] Elias, *The Civilizing Process,* 5. One might also adduce here recent work reading the phenomenon of "imperialist panic" back from the late nineteenth century to earlier decades. Cf. Ian Duncan, "*The Moonstone,* the Victorian Novel, and Imperialist Panic," *Modern Language Quarterly* 55/3 (Sept. 1994), 297–319.

[47] Baucom, *Out of Place,* 12.

[48] Helsinger, *Rural Scenes and National Representation,* 18–19.

[49] Malinowski, *A Scientific Theory of Culture and Other Essays* (Chapel Hill: University of North Carolina Press, 1944), 60.

vailing investment in alternative temporalities and discontinuous national landscapes containing special radiant sites. Dickens constructs a model of the nation
along the lines of a tellingly misheard remark in *Bleak House:* as uniformly "consequential ground." Both *Bleak House,* with its neglected Jo, one of the scores
"dying thus around us every day," and *Middlemarch,* with its closing vision of
"many Dorotheas," seem devoted to calling forth by means of such essentially interchangeable figures just the kind of anonymous nation-feeling Benedict Anderson found elicited by the 1924 Indonesian novel *Semarang Hitam* or the 1816 Latin
American *El Periquillo Sarniento.*[50] On the other hand, the powerfully regional-
ist imagination of Charlotte Brontë operates in the service of a national loyalty as
deeply committed to certain *vertical* (that is, region-specific) attachments as it is
to Andersonian "horizontal" ones, which in part means counterbalancing the
strong appeal of Brontë's own Wellington-worship and reverence for the nation-
blanketing Anglican church. Achievement of this proper equilibrium, which is
never final, turns out to rely—as does George Eliot's final effort to reinvigorate
English nationalism in *Daniel Deronda*—upon recourse to *international* perspectives, from which may be derived both strengthening forms of challenge *and* alternative forms of imagining collective identity. For both Brontë and Eliot, whose
very different Continental connections remained a major inspiration throughout
their careers, it would be absurd to hold that national imagining requires in any
simple fashion the opposition *and exclusion* of some alien Other; Brontë goes so
far in the direction of embracing a cultural Frenchness *as* an element of her Englishness that I have labeled this driving impulse in her work an "outlandish nationalism." Only in Dickens, among these major novelists, does the connection between nation and narration begin to resemble a cultural protectionism or "little
Englandism," and it does so with truly rigorous (but also self-parodying) severity
only, I think, in *Bleak House,* thanks to a combination of particular midcentury
pressures.

The historical factors encouraging English novelists to set to work salvaging
and/or fabricating their culture by securing its conceptual borders cannot be limited to those arising directly or exclusively from Britain's imperial involvements,
though to be sure there was little of significance in Victorian life that did not bear
a mediated relationship to empire. Conflict with France and Carlyle's *The French
Revolution* had helped make mistrust of universalist abstractions a reflex of British
self-identification. France was not simply that other nation against which Britain
defined and defended itself, but the nation that embodied an aggressive *transnationalism* in *both* its Catholic Church and its Enlightenment rationalism. This
battle-hardened distinction between the erstwhile imperial rivals was given the
patina of scientific authority toward midcentury, as varieties of "Teutomania"
began to assure Britons that they bore the (perhaps singularly undiluted) blood of
the hardy Germanic tribes in their veins, a legacy elevating them permanently
above Latin or Celtic races. The enormous prestige gained by the category of race

[50] Cf. *Imagined Communities,* 28–40.

in the second half of the nineteenth century may owe much to a *defensive* desire for sure boundaries between diverse peoples whose fates were becoming ever more entangled with each other.

The increasing physical and social mobility of Britons themselves, enabled by the harnessing of steam, threatened stable phenomenologies of spatial relation and must have added fuel to many a desire to resituate British identities in British ground. The advent of steam transport also had powerful repercussions that were not lost upon those charged with British territorial defense, exacerbating a situation in which "technological and international developments gravely undermined Britain's security" between 1814 and 1870. These authorities saw an England bereft in a generation of centuries of sceptered-isle separateness and confidence. "The Channel is no longer a barrier," declared Palmerston in 1845; "we can no longer be considered an island," lamented Admiral Sir Charles Napier; "our security exists no longer," Captain A. H. Frazier concluded, adding remorsefully, "we dare no longer promise ourselves exemption from the common lot of nations. The sea, once our chiefest safeguard, has become a highway to all who dread or envy our greatness; the barrier between us and the world is broken down, and England has become accessible and"—worst of all—"*Continental.*" Historian Michael Stephen Partridge writes that though many have "looked back on [the nineteenth century] as the age of the Pax Britannica," to those aware of England's new vulnerability "this comforting phrase would have meant nothing."[51] Nor would anxieties about British Isles security have been allayed by the recurrently debated schemes for a Channel Tunnel. The laying of the first submarine telegraph cable between Britain and France in 1851 had already elicited some nervously joking comment about the implications of this unprecedented linkage of the island and the continent it had always kept at a distance; after about 1860, with the French consistently enthusiastic (except when otherwise occupied by the Prussians), successive British governments entertained the idea of a passageway that might, in the view of its opponents, cause the unimaginable disaster of rendering the world-dominating British navy obsolete—for "of what avail will [our] fleet be if an enemy can go under the Channel?"[52]

The economic woes and Irish immigration of the 1840s constituted the nation's first *peacetime* crisis tending to stimulate positive specifications of British or English identity in defensive reaction against the dissolving or diluting forces of class and ethnicity. Britain's traditional identity as haven for exiles became burdensome as never before, and the fact that the nation possessed no policy on immigration—that "the ports of Britain were open to all"—generated controversy as never before, though it would take more than half a century and several more immigrant "waves" to stimulate the restrictive Aliens Act of 1905.[53] The "leveling" demands

[51] Michael Stephen Partridge, *Military Planning for the Defense of the United Kingdom* (New York: Greenwood Press, 1989), 9, 148.

[52] Quoted in Keith Wilson, *Channel Tunnel Visions* (London: Hambledon, 1994), 28.

[53] David Feldman, "The Importance of Being English," in Feldman and Gareth Stedman Jones, eds., *Metropolis: London Histories and Representations since 1800* (London: Routledge, 1989), 58; cf. 56–84.

of the Chartists surely incited some bourgeois counterimaginings of a *striated* national oneness, open to individual (self-helping), but not to *collective,* mobility. In the context of religion, the significant inroads made by Nonconformists in the late eighteenth and early nineteenth centuries, which had stimulated evangelical revival among alarmed factions in the Church of England, were followed up by the still more alarming incursions of the Church of Rome. Nationwide attention during 1850 was focused upon the campaign of "Papal Aggression" by which the Catholic Church had reinstated its British episcopal network for the first time since the Reformation. To Britons resenting the move as an act of cultural colonialism, the establishment of Cardinal Wiseman and his cohorts seemed a fitting insult to crown that dismal experiment, the Oxford Movement, which had aimed at revitalizing Anglicanism but had wound up by making Papists of some of its principal advocates.

Between the victory of the Anti-Corn-Law party in 1846 and the mounting of the Great Exhibition of the Works of Industry of All Nations in Hyde Park in 1851, Britons were also brought, quite quickly, to begin contemplating the prospect of a free-trade future in which national boundaries might cease to have the relevance they had once possessed. As George Stocking Jr. and others have noted, Prince Albert had even proposed, "[i]n an excess of the free trade spirit, . . . that [the] grouping [of objects displayed in the Great Exhibition] be without reference to national origin" (Stocking 2). A member of that small international elite placed above the commoner's relationship to nationality, the Consort had benignly intuited what late twentieth-century commentators have tirelessly reiterated about the global marketplace—that a truly free and international system of trade might put paid to the concept of nationhood, sweeping nations aside as capital sought markets wherever it could locate them, regardless of states and territories, of ethnic and religious ties. Then, as more recently, visions of the coming obsolescence of nations were greatly exaggerated, but they were influential nonetheless. There were logistical reasons for the Exhibition commissioners to reject Albert's design, but unease at the glimpse it afforded of a permanently dislocated future may also have played a part in making sure the floor-plan would be laid out along national lines, and that both visitors and national delegates would be encouraged to conceive of what was going on in the Crystal Palace as a competition among nations, not individual firms. And, at the same time when we can discern signs of Britons recoiling from a boundariless free-trade dystopia, we must also recognize certain complications arising from Britain's protected intraempire trade that had a decisive impact upon the ideological contours of the English Victorian novel. The crisis in Britain's balance of payments that led to the Opium Wars may have illustrated that crucial divagation of (British) culture from place that the novelists would seek to redress, in showing how "national defense" might require aggressive military action on the other side of the globe. So embroiled was the British economy in its far-flung investments of capital and personnel that *locating* the British or English "way of life"—did it not revolve around *tea,* after all?—might well have seemed a daunting project.

In his renowned *Principles of Political Economy* (1848), John Stuart Mill gave classic statement to the model of intraempire exchange that the British imperial state most wanted to believe in. The colonies, Mill wrote, were "hardly to be looked upon as countries, carrying on an exchange of commodities with other countries, but more properly as outlying agricultural or manufacturing estates belonging to a larger community[, . . . as] place[s] where England finds it convenient to carry on the production of sugar, coffee, and [other such] tropical commodities."[54] This comforting vision might not be shared, however, by those inclined to wonder where or what this "England" might be if, through imperial expansion, it put pressure on the border-defining distinction, fundamental to classical theories of trade, between "imports" and "exports." Besides, the first half of the nineteenth century, during which the discourse of political economy arrogated to itself an ever-greater authority to explain more and more aspects of social life, was also a time when British national prosperity might be seen to depend not so much upon a favorable imbalance between tangible exports and imports as upon forms of economic activity not involving the physical movement of objects across borders. As if in demonstration of political economy's fixation upon the bounded unit of the national market and upon quantifiable goods, these other forms, which included such "service" functions as shipping, insurance, foreign investment, and the hosting of tourists, would come to be known as "invisible exports"—a rather fantastic name suggestive of the notion that, in order to count on the national balance sheet, these intangibles had to be metaphorized as if they were just a ghostly copy of the true or real (that is, empirically observable) border-crossing trade in things. Pointing out that "at *no* time in the nineteenth century did Britain have an export surplus in goods, in spite of her monopoly, her marked export-orientation, and her modest domestic consumer market," Eric Hobsbawm has shown that it was the "invisibles" that "procured [for Britain] a large surplus and not a deficit with the rest of the world."[55]

Conditions in the second quarter of the century stood to furnish Britons with a powerful illustration of their dependence upon these invisibles, for between 1825 and 1850 the income from them did not quite cover the trading deficit in commodities, as it had previously done. The phrase *invisible export* does not appear to have entered the vocabulary of economics before 1882, but—as with the term *culture*—this would seem to be a case in which terminology follows the conceptual or representational operations it later comes to name.[56] As the label for an intangible, unquantifiable source of value indispensable to the national well-being, *invisible export* comes close to the conceptual territory of the emergent *culture,* and it does not seem too fanciful to regard the kind of English novel that arose around the middle of the nineteenth century as a species of *invisible import,* aiming to enrich Britain with a perspective upon its common life that could be gained only from

[54] John Stuart Mill, *Principles of Political Economy,* ed. J. M. Robson (Toronto: University of Toronto Press, 1965), 3.693.

[55] Hobsbawm, *Industry and Empire* (Harmondsworth: Penguin, 1982), 144–45.

[56] Sir Robert Giffen, assistant editor of the *Economist* and subsequently Chief of the Statistical Department of the Board of Trade, is credited with coining the phrase "invisible export" in "The Use of Import and Export Statistics," *Journal of the Royal Statistical Society* (June 1882), 181–94. Cf. Max J. Wasserman and Ray M. Ware, *The Balance of Payments: History, Methodology, Theory* (New York: Simmons-Boardman, 1965), 77–78.

outside the domain of actually existing Britons. As they devoted themselves more and more self-consciously to the formal integration of their works and to the redemptive possibilities of the self-estranged gaze, the great Victorian novelists came implicitly to suggest that novel writing had become a crucial service-sector activity, a profession that added value to British life by bringing into it, not any palpable "good," but the immaterial good of *its own culture.*

PART TWO

British Fictions of Autoethnography,

circa 1815 and 1851

CHAPTER FOUR

Translation and Tourism in Scott's *Waverley*

TO

HIS LOVING COUNTRYMEN

WHETHER THEY ARE DENOMINATED

MEN OF THE SOUTH,

GENTLEMEN OF THE NORTH,

PEOPLE OF THE WEST,

OR

FOLK OF FIFE;

THESE TALES,

ILLUSTRATIVE OF ANCIENT SCOTTISH MANNERS,

AND

OF THE TRADITIONS OF THEIR RESPECTIVE DISTRICTS

ARE RESPECTFULLY INSCRIBED,

BY THEIR FRIEND AND LIEGE FELLOW-SUBJECT,

JEDIDIAH CLEISHBOTHAM.

—Walter Scott, dedication, *Tales of My Landlord* (1816)[1]

What happens when the "other" that the anthropologist is studying is simultaneously constructed as, at least partially, a self?
　—Lila Abu-Lughod[2]

Is a translation meant for readers who do not understand the original?
　—Walter Benjamin[3]

I

THE CAREER of Walter Scott, Britain's leading man of letters in the years immediately following the Act of Union, pivots upon a much-noted transition from antiquarian anthology making and poetry to the novel, a shift marked by the 1814 anonymous publication of *Waverley*. I want to regard that shift as involving Scott's highly self-conscious and ambivalent performance of the role of autoethnographer on behalf of a "Scotland" he appears to have known himself to be fabricating to

---

[1] In Scott, *The Black Dwarf,* ed. Peter Garside (Edinburgh: Edinburgh University Press, 1993), 3.

[2] Abu-Lughod, "Writing Against Culture," in Richard G. Fox, ed., *Recapturing Anthropology: Working in the Present* (Santa Fe: School of American Research Press, 1991), 140.

[3] Benjamin, "The Task of the Translator," in *Illuminations,* trans. Harry Zohn (New York: Schocken, 1969), 69.

suit the touristic interests of English readers—a "Scotland" (a unit identified with Highland traditions and the Jacobite cause) to which he, evidently a "Scottish" writer, bore no simple relationship of indigenousness. Jedidiah Cleishbotham and the other avatars Scott employs in his fiction imply that they can apprehend and salute a "Scottish culture" entire only from a position "outside" or "above" any particular locality within Scotland or any mentality belonging to one of that nation's religious or political factions—whose bloody conflicts have constituted much of Scottish history. Looking back on the periods of crisis they narrate, they purport to have attained a detachment that enables them to put those periods in proper perspective: to emphasize the metaphor of spatial relationship once more, they claim to have got outside the imprisoning outlooks of the combatants and so to have attained a point of view from which both the nature and the good of Scotland as a whole can be gauged.

It is easy to attack this putative impartiality as being, in fact, a political position among others, and Scott has rightly been criticized along these lines, as well as for promulgating touristy stereotypes and currying favor with the House of Hanover.[4] Perhaps the most influential autoethnographer who ever wrote and the most *self-consciously* influential autoethnographer at work within the framework of United Kingdom internal colonialism, Scott compels us to confront head-on the embarrassments and discomforts intrinsic to a form whose producer must work his relationship to the central authorities for all he can get—both for himself and for "his people." What Scott makes abundantly clear is that, if the metaphorization of cultures as places gives rise to the question, what will one *find,* where will one *go,* if one goes "outside" one's own culture? then the internal-colony autoethnographer must authoritatively answer, "England." For internal colonialism suggests that the sole important, identity-making and prosperity-making relationship the erstwhile-nation-that-is-now-a-"region" *has* is with the center, not with other regions or nations. Each such identifiable region is to conceive of itself as a spoke on the wheel whose hub is London, a separate culture constellated around the Hanoverian sun. The center is the only relevant "outside"; interregional relationships are downplayed, and regions do not enter into relationships with the foreign that are not routed through the center.

In Scott this means deemphasizing the Irishness of Highland Celticism and turning it into a marker distinctive and applicable to Scotland as a whole. The ability to go outside of Scottishness and to recover it for Scots as what I have called (in the previous chapter) an "invisible import" *means* the ability to look at Scotland from the vantage point of England, to orient Scotland toward that vantage point, and to seek what gains are to be derived from accepting the arrangement. Scott's autoethnography appears to be of precisely the variety Mary Louise Pratt has described, one that "involves partial collaboration with and appropriation of the id-

---

[4] Cf. Hugh Trevor-Roper, "The Invention of Tradition: The Highland Tradition of Scotland," in Eric Hobsbawm and Terence Ranger, eds., *The Invention of Tradition* (Cambridge: Cambridge University Press, 1983), 15–42; Peter Womack, *Improvement and Romance: Constructing the Myth of the Highlands* (Basingstoke: Macmillan, 1988); Murray G. H. Pittock, *The Invention of Scotland: The Stuart Myth and the Scottish Identity, 1638 to the Present* (London: Routledge, 1991).

ioms of the conqueror,"[5] except that a member of the Lowland elite putting himself forward as the autoethnographer of a Highland-emphasizing Scottishness
raises much more troubling questions of position and allegiance than Pratt addressed. These arise from the kind of situation Marc Manganaro has described in
observing that the "fact that [an] ethnographer is of the same culture as the subject
may make the ethnographer more aware of the interpersonal liberties that [an outside ethnographer] takes for granted when conducting interviews and 'writing up'
the results."[6]

Scott's performance and exploration of autoethnography must be read as a response to the National Tales published about Ireland in the decade before *Waverley*'s appearance. Fiction in the United Kingdom had taken an autoethnographic
turn about as soon as that kingdom was founded, in these works by Anglo-Irish
writers like Sydney Owensen, Charles Maturin, and Maria Edgeworth; Edgeworth's 1800 *Castle Rackrent,* subtitled *An Hibernian Tale taken from facts and
from the manners of the Irish squires before the year 1782,* was an important precursor, though the genre came to self-conscious life only with the 1806 publication of Owensen's (Lady Morgan's) *The Wild Irish Girl,* whose subtitle was *A National Tale.* This fictional mode, recently the subject of increasing and excellent
critical commentary, represents "the first time[] the novel becomes a prime genre
for the dissemination of nationalist ideas," yet "within this literature, paradoxically, nationalist and unionist sentiments often appear side by side . . . and the per-
manence of national differences is recognized only to be overridden."[7] In each example appearing between 1806 and 1814, "an English character . . . travels to a
British periphery, expected to be devoid of culture" and "under the tutelage of an
aristocratic friend, . . . learns to appreciate its cultural plenitude and decides to settle there permanently. Each national tale ends with the traveler's marriage to his
or her native guide, in a wedding that unites [the] 'national characters'" of Saxon
and Celt (Trumpener 141). The National Tales insist that the new political order of
the United Kingdom must recognize itself as what we would now call a "multicultural" one, but they do so in plots supporting, or at least treating as incontro-
vertible fact, the concentration of power in London: "motivated by the desire to
make a case for the stigmatized nation . . . before the court of middle-class English
public opinion," they signal their acceptance of that "court's" jurisdiction (Ferris
289–90).[8]

[5] Pratt, *Imperial Eyes: Travel Writing and Transculturation* (New York: Routledge, 1992), 7.

[6] Manganaro, "Introduction: Textual Play, Power, and Cultural Critique: An Orientation to Modernist Anthropology," in Manganaro, ed., *Modernist Anthropology: From Fieldwork to Text* (Princeton: Princeton University Press, 1990), 29n14.

[7] Katie Trumpener, *Bardic Nationalism: The Romantic Novel and the British Empire* (Princeton:
Princeton University Press, 1997), 13; henceforth Trumpener. Cf. Ina Ferris, "Narrating Cultural Encounter: Lady Morgan and the Irish National Tale," *Nineteenth-Century Literature* 51/3 (Dec. 1996),
289–90; henceforth Ferris; Gary Kelly, *Women, Writing, and Revolution, 1790–1827* (Oxford: Clarendon Press, 1993), 178, 184–86; and Nicola J. Watson, *Revolution and the Form of the British Novel,
1790–1825: Intercepted Letters, Interrupted Seductions* (Oxford: Clarendon Press, 1994), chap. 3.

[8] On the trope of the "case," cf. James Chandler, *England in 1819: The Politics of Literary Culture
and the Case of Romantic Historicism* (Chicago: University of Chicago Press, 1998).

The authors of such works understand their position to be that of a mediator capable of both understanding Irishness "from the inside" and presenting it in terms likely to appeal to, though perhaps also to alter, English consciousness. As a sufficiently indigenous "translator" of her culture, the author of the National Tale makes the novel into a form in which a marginal people of the United Kingdom gets to "speak for itself" to the English powers-that-be through some glorified mouthpiece of Irishness (e.g., the Glorvina of *The Wild Irish Girl*) who asserts a cultural independence—that is to say, a qualified or *interrupted* independence, one that goes "only so far"—while assenting to or even facilitating English predominance. Like the officials now at work in virtually every nation on earth designing campaigns to solicit tourists, the National-Tale author seeks practical gains for her country at the cost of promoting a collection of cultural stereotypes about it for export to English reader-tourists. What will later be called a *culture* the National Tale implicitly defines as a nationality-without-statehood that is oriented in the direction of a nationality-*with*-statehood that controls it.

In *Bardic Nationalism,* Katie Trumpener has provided the thickest description so far of the literary context in which Walter Scott's turn to the novel took place, situating Scott's writing in relation to early and later phases of the National Tale and to narrative patterns set down in pro- and anti-Jacobin fiction of the 1790s. In this masterful survey of "the age of *Waverley,*" however, Scott and *Waverley* are so decentered as virtually to disappear, except when required to play the heavy for their "politically quietistic realism" (Trumpener 156). Trumpener's account of the literary background and surroundings of Scott's first novel, and especially her derivation of Scott's protagonist and of the novel's general tendency from two prior texts featuring a character named Waverl(e)y, recall old-fashioned source criticism in their propensity to dissolve a text in its sources. I want to reconstitute that text here, to consider it as a *reading* as well as an enactment of the issues raised by the culture-for-export model of fiction pioneered in National-Tale autoethnography, and to explore its development of narrative possibilities seized upon by later English writers when *they* began to push the English novel in an autoethnographic direction in the 1840s. It is true that aspects of Scott's fictional autoethnography were anticipated by the Anglo-Irish writers: both Edgeworth's *Castle Rackrent* and Owensen's genre-labeling National Tale *The Wild Irish Girl,* for example, exhibit the commitment to self-interrupting narration that I have characterized in the previous chapters as a distinguishing feature of fieldwork ethnographies: footnotes punctuate the peasant's monologue in the Edgeworth text, while in Owensen, as Ina Ferris points out, the frequent "disquisitions on Irish culture and history (both within the narrative and in the elaborate paratext accompanying it)" occasioned complaint from reviewers for "disrupt[ing] the pleasure of immersion in the fiction" (Ferris 289). And Owensen's novel, with its much-imitated allegorical marriage plot, certainly appears to work its English male protagonist toward a position foreshadowing that which Scott's Edward Waverley comes to occupy, both of them adumbrating the twentieth-century ethnographer's "outsider's insideness": as Ferris puts it, Owensen's book establishes for all its followers "the desire of the national tale . . . to turn the foreigner into the stranger-who-comes-nearer" (Ferris 297).

Yet in "reiterat[ing] and transform[ing] the national tale's generic premises by historicizing its allegorical framework" (Trumpener 141), Scott's *Waverley* goes beyond mere rehearsal of National-Tale patterns of autoethnography, becoming a forceful metafiction on the politics of cultural representation in the context of British internal colonialism. More than just producing a prettified version of Scottish culture (which it undoubtedly does), *Waverley* becomes a virtual primer on the aesthetics of internal colonialism. In the process, the longer-settled question of Scotland's place in the English-dominated order comes to appear as bestowing an advantage not yet enjoyed by the more recently incorporated Irish. A century removed from Scotland's formal unification with England and more than half a century after the paroxysms of the Jacobite Rebellion of 1745–46, the narrator of Scott's *Waverley* stakes out a position "outside" of the history he set himself to investigate—an end-of-history viewpoint unavailable to Irish writers working in the immediate aftermath of the 1798 rebellion, its suppression, and the Act of Union itself.[9]

In *Waverley*, Scott follows the National-Tale pattern of putting his English male protagonist through a narrative of ethnographic encounter that aims at the highest degree of sympathy and union achievable between culturally different and differently empowered peoples, but he simultaneously and conversely establishes the narrating persona of a Scot capable of moving beyond the limitations of his own culture to understand and present it to the English. That narrator's viewpoint cannot simply be regarded as one of abstract cosmopolitan or extracultural knowledge, common to all who have attained modernity; remaining distinctively, tenaciously Scottish, it deserves to be called an "end-of-*our*-history" viewpoint. With the end of "our history," Scott proposes, comes the beginning of "our culture," mastery of which entails (in Schiller's terms) a "sentimental" or semidetached perspective rather than unqualified commitment or unreflective immersion. For the Lowland Scot, the end of the Highlands as a distinct and viable society makes it possible to construct a Scottish culture associated mainly with Highland traditions but claimable by the Lowlander as "his," such that he can assert an *auto*ethnographic (and not merely an outsider's ethnographic) authority over it. No doubt the Lowlander's traditional *miorun mor nan Gall,* or enmity toward the Gaels, played some part in what could be described as Scott's act of cultural expropriation.[10] Yet in *Waverley* the preeminent Scottish author goes beyond performing such acts and constructs a text that insistently reflects upon them and on the conditions of their possibility.

"Both history and ethnography are concerned with societies other than the one in which we live," wrote Claude Lévi-Strauss.[11] *Waverley* gives evidence of

---

[9] As Saree Makdisi has noted, Scott's presentation of Culloden as the close of the premodern diverts attention away from the more recent violence of the Highland Clearances: cf. *Romantic Imperialism: Universal Empire and the Culture of Modernity* (Cambridge: Cambridge University Press, 1998), chap. 4.

[10] Cf. Fitzroy Maclean, *Highlanders: A History of the Scottish Clans* (New York: Penguin Studio, 1995), ix.

[11] Lévi-Strauss, *Structural Anthropology,* trans. C. Jacobson and B. Grundfest-Schoepf (New York: Doubleday, 1963), 17.

Scott's recognition that the same holds true for a Lowland portrayal of "Scotland." Scott's handling of the central relationship of narrator and protagonist renders Scottish autoethnography *unheimlich:* it does not simply emanate from the authentic heart or voice that awaits the English visitor, but avows itself a text mediated through, directed toward, and "translated into" England and English.

II

Not lastingly impressed by their artistry or convinced by their claims to authenticity, Walter Scott could nonetheless have found in James Macpherson's notorious Ossian texts a model of sorts for his own literary practice. Ironically, the very feature that convinced most British readers, Scott among them, to repudiate Macpherson—the fact that his texts were apparently "translations" without originals—may have been the hallmark of Scott's writings on Scotland, an identification that the writer appears self-consciously to have acknowledged when he embarked upon the new venture in prose fiction that commences with *Waverley.* During the period in which the term *authentic* was coming to acquire its modern meaning of "really proceeding from its reputed source or author; of undisputed origin, genuine,"[12] Macpherson's *Fragments of Ancient Poetry, Collected in the Highlands of Scotland, and Translated from the Gaelic or Erse Language,* and his more elaborate epics *Fingal* and *Temora,* had furnished a striking test case of the issues involved in guaranteeing the authenticity of cultural documents. It was a case Scott firmly believed closed, in spite of such late developments as the publication, in 1807, of an "original" (reconstructed) Gaelic text of Ossian by the Highland Society of London. In Scott's view, Doctor Johnson had cast down the unliftable gauntlet: where were the sources? Macpherson's failure to produce the manuscripts to which he had teasingly alluded for years had sealed the matter. Even the Highland Society's own researches, undertaken with the strong interest of validating the disputed works, "ha[d] only proved," Scott wrote, "that there *were* no originals[,] using that word as is commonly understood[,] to be found for them."[13]

For Scott, the Macpherson affair illustrated the equation *translation-without-original = fraud.* And yet he was keenly aware that the controversy over authorship had opened onto much broader concerns, the question of Ossian's genuineness having become something of a shibboleth of Gaelic, and even of "Scottish," identity.[14] His nuanced assessments of the putative aboriginal bard of Gael, offered in various forms in the first decade of the nineteenth century, provide a fulcrum for the great shift in his own career, from poetry to the novel. In a letter of 1806, Scott acceded to Anna Seward's suggestion that "the question of [the Oss-

---

[12] *Oxford English Dictionary,* s.v. "authentic" (first example 1790).

[13] H.J.C. Grierson, ed., *The Letters of Sir Walter Scott* (London: Constable, 1932), 1.322; emphasis added. Cf. Howard Gaskill, ed., *Ossian Revisited* (Edinburgh: Edinburgh University Press, 1991).

[14] See Robert Crawford, *Devolving English Literature* (Oxford: Clarendon, 1992), 122.

ian texts'] authenticity ought [not] to be confounded with that of their literary merit," but he added that "scepticism on that head takes away their claim for indulgence as the productions of a barbarous & remote age . . . [and] destroys that feeling of reality which we should otherwise combine with our sentiments of admiration." These reflections led directly to the declaration that Scott had himself long been planning "a Highland poem, somewhat in the style of the Lay [i.e., *The Lay of the Last Minstrel*]; giving as far as I can a real picture of what that enthusiastic race actually were before the destruction of their patriarchal government." He was forecasting *The Lady of the Lake,* published in 1810 to incredible acclaim. Yet before undertaking this work, Scott felt compelled to admit that "it is true I have not quite the same facilities as in describing border manners where I am as they say more at home." He owned to a "comparative deficiency in knowledge of Celtic manners": his next letter to Seward informed her that he had laid his Highland poem aside. Among other difficulties, Scott confessed himself "at a great loss . . . from not understanding the language of that enthusiastic [people]."[15]

He did, of course, write *The Lady of the Lake:* it promptly "shattered all records for the sale of poetry," sent scores of tourists to the Trossachs, everlastingly changed the image of "Scotland," and went a fair way towards earning Scott the Laureateship (offered and refused in 1813). But some evidence exists to suggest that he mistrusted his resounding triumph, that he thought the "real picture" yet unpainted, the voice of the Highlands yet unrendered, in large part because he remained unalterably alien to the culture he had attempted to represent and on whose behalf he had presumed to "speak." Taking a tour of the Highlands and Islands just after completing the poem, he recorded the ambiguous tribute paid him by his boatmen, who "solemnly christened a great stone at [the] mouth [of Fingal's Cave] the 'Clachan an Bairdh Sassenach more,' the stone of the great Saxon poet"; and when a bard made a lengthy Gaelic oration in his honor, Scott, unable to understand a word, was reduced to responding "as a silly beauty does [to] a fine-spun compliment—bow and say nothing."[16] The autoethnographer's standpoint of mediation between Celtic and metropolitan perspectives required the inside-outsideness of one who—as Anne Grant described herself in her contemporaneous travelogue on the Highlands—"is not absolutely a native, nor entirely a stranger" (quoted in Ferris 292); but such an experience, occurring so soon after Scott's first literary foray into the Highlands, raised the question of whether Scott could meet even this qualified criterion where a Scottish culture emphasizing Highland traditions was concerned.

The Lady of the Lake, Scott's nearly abandoned and then fabulously successful ethnographic tale in verse, has its prose companion and critique in *Waverley.* This novel, whose partial manuscript spent a decade (1805–14) lying in a drawer while

---

[15] *Letters* 1.320–21, 324, 347.

[16] "Shattered all records": Edgar Johnson, *Sir Walter Scott: The Great Unknown* (New York: Macmillan, 1970), 1.335; henceforth Johnson. For Fingal's Cave, cf. Johnson 1.333 and *Letters* 2.360. When, "at the height of the furore" over *The Lady of the Lake,* James Ballantyne asked Scott's daughter Sophia what she thought of the work, the girl responded, "I have not read it; papa says there is nothing so bad for young people as reading bad poetry" (Johnson 1.336).

its author built his reputation as Europe's preeminent narrative poet, offers both performance and exposure of the Macphersonian project of translation, a culture-making project Scott had also seen played out in the Ossian-influenced National Tales of 1806–14 and one that, in seeking to render "the Celtic voice," helped establish translation itself as a crucial ethnographic trope.[17] With *Waverley*, Scott commences building a body of work to place beside—or to unwrite—Macpherson's Ossianic texts, a body of work that, like those prior texts, both purports to represent or "speak for" Scotland and generates much public controversy over the question, who is the author? (It may not be entirely fanciful to see the Waverley Novels' anonymity as their subtlest allusion to the dilemmas of authenticity in cultural representation raised by Macpherson's Ossian.) But whereas the Macpherson case revealed the translator as (scandalously) an author, Scott's fiction of autoethnography in *Waverley* presents the author as translator-without-original, as if intent on making us recognize the crucial element of "*traduttore* in the *traditore*," the "lack of an equals sign [in ethnographic translation], the reality of what's missed and distorted in the very act of understanding, appreciating, describing."[18] Scott's implicit model for the National Tale's culture-for-export, his model for what we now call *culture* itself, is the "translation without original." The famous doubleness of Scott's fiction needs to be viewed in the context of that "broadly diffused movement of thought" by which, "always in self-divided forms," the anthropological culture-concept comes to articulation over the course of the nineteenth century.[19] Rendering a traditional "Scottish" way of life that by Scott's time had fallen into "almost total extinction," *Waverley* also translates Scotland *into culture,* in other emergent senses of the word—forecasting as it does so the entangled meanings and fuzzy nondefinitions of *culture* in the century and more to follow.[20] Scott's "Scotland" is, or furnishes: 1) a set of prized aesthetic objects and performances; 2) a process of cultivating or acculturating the self (for the protagonist Edward Waverley, but also for the imagined reader); and 3) an imaginary domain—a space that Raymond Williams labeled a "court of human appeal"—in which the compromises of modern social life might be redressed.[21]

In the "Dedicatory Epistle" to *Ivanhoe* (1817), Scott wrote that "[i]n the historical novel, it is necessary . . . that the subject assumed should be, as it were, translated into the manners, as well as the language, of the age in which we live."[22] A

---

[17] Cf. Talal Asad, "The Concept of Cultural Translation in British Social Anthropology," in James Clifford and George E. Marcus, eds., *Writing Culture: The Poetics and Politics of Ethnography* (Berkeley: University of California Press, 1986), 141–64; Tejaswini Niranjana, *Siting Translation: History, Post-Structuralism, and the Colonial Context* (Berkeley: University of California Press, 1992), 47–86.

[18] James Clifford, "Traveling Cultures," *Routes: Travel and Translation in the Late Twentieth Century* (Cambridge, Mass.: Harvard University Press, 1997), 42.

[19] Christopher Herbert, *Culture and Anomie: Ethnographic Imagination in the Nineteenth Century* (Chicago: University of Chicago Press, 1991), 24, 302; henceforth Herbert.

[20] Scott, *Waverley* (1814; New York: Penguin, 1988), 492–93; henceforth W.

[21] Williams, *Culture and Society, 1780–1950* (1958; New York: Columbia University Press, 1983), xviii.

[22] Ioan Williams, ed., *Sir Walter Scott on Novelists and Fiction* (New York: Barnes and Noble, 1968), 435.

writer second to none in his consciousness of the literary marketplace, Scott raised the point as a practical consideration. He had gleaned this lesson from the disappointing reception of Joseph Strutt's posthumous novel *Queen-Hoo Hall,* a work he had edited and completed for publication. Strutt's failing, he now saw, was to have overwhelmed readers with masses of historical detail and a dogged, monologic pursuit of "antique" idiom. Scott's reflections on the matter gave rise to two issues of considerable theoretical force.

One concerns the position of the reader, whose involvement Strutt's standoffish, self-contained narrative had done nothing to solicit: Strutt's fictional world was too much *en-soi* to afford the modern reader any purchase or point of entry. Subsequent historical novels must use deliberate devices to bring readers into relation with their material. Among Scott's solutions was to highlight the role of its translator, the genial, intrusive narrator, an anonymous Lowland Scot, firmly situated in the readers' present: the reflections of this Scottish inside-outsider frame the story in chapters called "Introductory" and "A Postscript, Which Should Have Been a Preface," but his presence is felt throughout. On the analogy with painting—not unwarranted for a work that dwells on the question of how a translation of a culture may be said to resemble a picture of it—*Waverley* thus furnishes its readers with a vantage point that is the novelistic equivalent of Renaissance vanishing-point perspective. Insisting on its contemporaneity, the novel records a past (the time of the Jacobite rebellion of 1745–46) that is held in steady relation to the reader as the *'Tis Sixty Years Since* of the subtitle. "We see the past from *here,*" the novel effectively says. The work's main title, on the other hand, names the character whose "wandering viewpoint" will be on loan to readers for the duration, and this availability of two positions—past and present, fixed and moving—structures the double perspective of Scott's work. The oppositions Wendy Steiner identifies as the legacy of Renaissance painterly perspective, which were enshrined in theory by Lessing's *Laokoön,* describe this doubleness very well: "Design versus narrative, essential versus unfolding identity, objectivity versus desire."[23] To the extent that we take up the position offered by Edward Waverley, we encounter a Scottish way of life that is heterogeneous, alive, forward-moving (like the narrative that is its medium), and, most of all, imperfectly understood; to the extent that we take up the narrator's position, we see a culture sealed off from history, susceptible to holistic representation, "finished." In the case of the Jacobite Highlands, "finished" suggests both "no longer capable of menace or surprise" and "possessing the 'finish' of a fine art object, packaged and ready for consumption." With its division between narrator and protagonist, Scott's novel puts into play both functions later contained in ethnography's compound labels for its practitioner: Participant Observer, fieldworker-theorist. Where the protagonist's participation in the culture being described purports to authenticate the description with the experiential density of "being there," the narrator's detachment from it guarantees proper apprehension of the whole.[24]

---

[23] Steiner, *Pictures of Romance: Form Against Content in Painting and Literature* (Chicago: University of Chicago Press, 1988), 3; henceforth Steiner.

[24] See Clifford Geertz, *Works and Lives: The Anthropologist as Author* (Stanford: Stanford Uni-

The second issue to stem from Scott's consideration of Joseph Strutt is that of selection. Influential readers of Scott from Lukàcs to Avrom Fleishman and Wolfgang Iser have emphasized the historical novel's need for consistency, urging that, as Lukàcs says, "faithfulness to the past" does not entail "a chronicle-like, naturalistic reproduction," an "extensively complete totality"—that is, a ponderous compilation of detail in the manner of Strutt.[25] To approach the past this way is to adopt the manner of the pedantic Baron of Bradwardine in *Waverley*, who "cumber[s] his memory with matters of fact—the cold, dry, hard outlines which history delineates"; better is the romantic protagonist's tendency "to fill up and round the sketch with the colouring of a warm and vivid imagination, which gives light and life to the actors and speakers in the drama of past ages" (W 109). To these critics, the "synthetic" historical imagination can arrive at a unified vision only through principled highlighting and exclusion. Traditional humanists presuppose what Scott called "that extensive neutral ground, the large proportion . . . of manners and sentiments which are common to us and to our ancestors" in seeking an Archimedean point from which to judge representations of the past.[26] Some accounts will answer to the notion of "man in general, conceived as a historical being who is subject to the forces of one historical age or another";[27] others, like Strutt's, will drown the general "man" in mere period detail, that thicket of imponderabilia that surrounds the mere insider or (in Anne Grant's terms) the "absolute native." Fleishman and Iser promulgate a "fiction-is-truer-than-fact" paradox, seeing artistic shaping as needed to transmute the formless lump of historical facticity into usable truth about humankind. For the Hegelian Marxist Lukàcs, the adjudicating principle on the selection of detail is derived from a presumptive knowledge of history's total plan, from the endpoint of which one may imagine oneself looking back to see which details will have mattered. Each included item should withstand the test of what Lukàcs calls *typicality* (or what Hegel called *concrete universality*). Needs must, writers will employ some "dramatic concentration and intensification" to bring these typical features to the fore, but the artist should be assured that the necessarily anachronistic view "can emerge organically from historical material, if the past is clearly recognized as the necessary prehistory of the present" (Lukàcs 61; cf. 41).

For both humanist and Marxist, we know one period from another, and we know which details of a period should count toward the definition of that period's distinctive identity, by virtue of the same kind of "double boundary" that Daniel Cot-

---

versity Press, 1988), esp. 1–24. Cf. Homer Obed Brown, *Institutions of the English Novel: From Defoe to Scott* (Philadelphia: University of Pennsylvania Press, 1997), 10–12, on the pertinent contrast Scott generates between Austen and eighteenth-century novelists like Fielding and Smollett.

[25] Georg Lukàcs, *The Historical Novel,* trans. Hannah and Stanley Mitchell (1962; rpt. Lincoln, Nebraska: University of Nebraska Press, 1983), 42; henceforth Lukàcs.

[26] Scott, *in Sir Walter Scott on Novelists and Fiction,* 436; quoted in Wolfgang Iser, "Fiction—the Filter of History: A Study of Walter Scott's *Waverley*" in *The Implied Reader: Patterns of Communication in Prose Fiction from Bunyan to Beckett* (Baltimore: Johns Hopkins University Press, 1974), 84.

[27] Fleishman, *The English Historical Novel: Walter Scott to Virginia Woolf* (Baltimore: Johns Hopkins University Press, 1971), 11.

tom has described as operating in the anthropological discourse of culture: one that runs both "around itself"—to sunder indigenous from alien—and "through itself"—to separate typical detail from deviant or trivial.[28] Period and culture, the objects of complementary temporal and spatial discourses, respectively, share "the presumption" that the "array of disparate-seeming elements [each mobilizes] . . . composes a significant *whole,* each factor of which is in some sense a corollary of, consubstantial with, implied by, immanent in, all the others": in each context, such a presumption "renders the various elements of a way of life systematically *readable*" (Herbert 5). It breaks history up into what Ernst Bloch called self-regarding "Gardens of Culture or . . . cultural monads . . . without windows, with no links among each other, yet full of mirrors facing inside,"[29] and it accordingly requires a perspective beyond that of the people standing inside such monads, who (as the ethnographers have seen it) are too much caught up in their own practices to observe the whole those practices describe, or who (as the historians have seen it) were too occupied with their period's *becoming* to appreciate what it was *coming to be.* In both historical and anthropological accounts, the translating scholar produces a discourse whose coherence and "unity," at odds with the variety and seeming haphazardness of lived experience, "vouches for the unity of the integrated cultural 'configuration' it claims to represent" (Herbert 7). The internal consistency of the ethnographic or historiographic text marks it as a translation without original, a "representation" of what wasn't empirically there to *be* represented, namely the wholeness, the "resident suchness," that has to be abstracted from the welter of details.[30] It was just such discursive unity or consistency of "voice" that Scott appears to have come to mistrust in his own early poetical triumphs and in Strutt, and then to have questioned even as he delivered it in his fiction.[31]

Scott's fiction shuttles across the point of presumed equivalence between the "discourse of chronology" and the "discourse of culture," configuring its own operations not only as exemplifying the translating work of the historian or the ethnographer but also as translating each of these discourses into the terms of the other.[32] In *Waverley,* travel in time and travel through space become narratable only to the degree that they become each other—refuting Lessing's dichotomy of temporal and spatial arts. Time is always on the verge of achieving spatial configuration, such as results from the posthistorical, retrospective "epoch-making" viewpoint; space, the visited space of Scotland, is always implying a temporal relation, such

---

[28] Daniel Cottom, "*Ethnographia Mundi,*" in *Text and Culture: The Politics of Interpretation* (Minneapolis: University of Minnesota Press, 1989), 72.

[29] Quoted in Johannes Fabian, *Time and the Other: How Anthropology Makes its Object* (New York: Columbia University Press, 1983), 44–45.

[30] Clifford Geertz, *After the Fact: Two Countries, Four Decades, One Anthropologist* (Cambridge, Mass.: Harvard University Press, 1995), 23.

[31] Cf. Ian Duncan, *Modern Romance and Transformations of the Novel: The Gothic, Scott, Dickens* (Cambridge: Cambridge University Press, 1992), on how Scott's fiction may be characterized by its "lack of voice" and its tendency to "display[] its character as composition rather than inspired invention" (93); henceforth Duncan.

[32] Cf. Chandler, *England in 1819,* 36.

as the evolutionary narratives of the Scottish "philosophical" historians supplied.[33] The translation of time (historical and narrative duration) into space (both geographical and iconic), and vice versa, is Scott's constant autoethnographic occupation, the means by which the presumed, the paired and self-contradictory, desires of his audience might be satisfied: on the one hand, the desire for insideness and participation; on the other, the desire for recoverable outsideness and observation. Scott seems to have understood acceptance of this labor of producing a "Scotland" framed in time and space as the terms on which any sort of Scottish distinctiveness could be maintained.

In his classic study of United Kingdom internal colonialism, Michael Hechter points out that, in the case of Scotland, "anglicization" of the Celtic fringe was "carried out extensively by lowland Scots who received . . . considerable help from the government in London."[34] Hechter's description admirably situates Walter Scott's authorial task of translating a Gaelic-oriented "Scotland" for an audience envisioned as either English or in the process of "Englishing"—that is, of translating themselves into agents conversant with English ways and idioms, as Lowlanders had been doing with increasing determination since the defeat of the Stuart party.[35] But to consider Scott's ethnographic translation as "anglicization" is not to suggest that it seeks the wholesale domestication of the alien, the production of a uniform "English" culture for Britain. On the contrary, the prospect of such uniformity filled Scott with dread and alarm. When, in 1807, the new Whig government in London proposed to bring Scotland's distinctive judicial system "into close conformity with the institutions of England," Scott felt the move to be "a violation . . . of the Act of Union of 1707, a deadly blow at Scotland's independence." He spoke passionately against the proposed changes before the Faculty of Advocates in Edinburgh and, when two reform-minded colleagues praised his eloquence but belittled his cause, replied even more passionately, "'tis no laughing matter; little by little, . . . you will destroy and undermine, until nothing of what makes Scotland Scotland shall remain" (Johnson 1.265). Seeing his nation's "manners and character . . . daily melting and dissolving into those of her sister and ally," Scott found the calling to resist the "lowering and grinding down" of "all those peculiarities which distinguished us as Scotsmen" all the more urgent.[36]

The fiction of *autoethnography* enacted in the Scottish Waverley Novels is the

---

[33] Cf. Peter D. Garside, "Scott and the 'Philosophical' Historians," in *The Journal of the History of Ideas* 36/3 (1975), 497–512.

[34] Hechter, *Internal Colonialism: The Celtic Fringe in British National Development, 1536–1966* (Berkeley: University of California Press, 1975), 112; cf. Linda Colley, *Britons: Forging the Nation, 1707–1837* (New Haven: Yale University Press, 1992), 386n9.

[35] Cf. Crawford, *Devolving*, 18, and Olivia Smith, *The Politics of Language, 1791–1819* (Oxford: Clarendon Press, 1984).

[36] "Manners and character . . . ": quoted in Penny Fielding, *Writing and Orality: Nationality, Culture, and Nineteenth-Century Scottish Fiction* (Oxford: Clarendon Press, 1996), 55. "Lowering . . . ": quoted in Alexander M. Ross, *The Imprint of the Picturesque on Nineteenth-Century Fiction* (Waterloo, Ontario: Wilfrid Laurier University Press, 1986), 59.

dialectical partner of what Scott regards as a regrettable but perhaps irreversible process of Lowland self-Englishing. The depopulating Highlands supply the elements of a new and intransigent *Scottish* cultural difference, and the Lowlander's cultural translation of "Scotland" strives for a double goal, an intelligible foreignness, for something at once alien and English. As I will explore later on, the objective correlatives of this intelligible foreignness that *Waverley* quite openly shows itself as producing to suit the tastes of romantic English readers are Fergus and Flora Mac-Ivor, the doomed Highland chieftain and his alluring sister, herself a translator of Gaelic into English. The Lowlander who submits the Highlands to a process of anglicization carried far enough to turn them into "Scotland" fends off the forces threatening to turn *him* into an Englishman and becomes instead a Briton—the label for that double allegiance to region and to multicultural state that is the foundation of Scott's autoethnographic authority.[37]

Scott sets about his translating work in the knowledge that, under the roomy auspices of "foreignness-to-the-English," all Scotland might appear one univocal substance. To the ear equally unpracticed in Scots and Gaelic, Lowlands and Highlands could seem united in alterity, even though the dialect of the first and the language of the second differ from each other much more profoundly than does Scots from standard English. Colonel Talbot, the militant Englishman of *Waverley,* takes the view that a common outlandishness unites Highlander and Lowlander more intimately than either may be united with its neighbors and betters south of the Tweed. Of the Highlanders, Talbot says, "Let them stay in their own barren mountains, and puff and swell, . . . but what business have they to come where people wear breeches, and speak an intelligible language? I mean intelligible in comparison with their gibberish, for even the Lowlanders talk a kind of English little better than the negroes in Jamaica" (W 387). Scott's novel rejects Talbot's bigotry, devoting considerable energy to the refutation of such views; but much of the work does seem to conform to Talbot's colonialist dualism.

Edward Waverley's first encounter with "Scotland" is a signal instance. Going north as an officer of the government's forces, Edward is the living embodiment of English power in Scotland—he wears his military uniform, of course, everywhere he goes—even though he neither comprehends nor endorses that power.[38] He moves through a landscape whose leading characteristic, for him, is its undifferentiated otherness. Scott's manner of exposition heightens the effect, for we see nothing of Edward's initial entry into Scotland, which takes him from his uncle's English estate to his regiment's post at Dundee; we see little of his time spent there, during which he scarcely takes note of his surroundings; but we get a long look at his first approach to Tully-Veolan, the seat of his uncle's friend the Baron of Bradwardine. The village and estate are situated "upon the braes," the border between Lowlands and Highlands, so we are already close to Gaelic Scotland when the

<hr />

[37] Cf. Crawford, *Devolving,* on Scott as "the greatest novelist of Britishness" (111–34). On Scott's *Minstrelsy of the Scottish Border,* cf. Fielding, *Writing and Orality,* 51.

[38] For Kim Ian Michasiw's different reading of this scene and my criticism, cf. my "Translation and Tourism: Scott's *Waverley* and the Rendering of Culture," *Yale Journal of Criticism* 8/2 (1995), 56n27.

novel begins to supply its protagonist with "Scottish" impressions. If the foreignness that is one side of Scott's double goal in translation is furnished, in part, by Highland details' being put forward as *Scottish* ones, intelligibility is secured, in part, by the contrivance of rendering the English dialogue spoken by Highlanders through the vehicle of the Scots dialect, which, with some tinkering, is capable of both sounding strange to English auditors and being understood by them. As Graham Tulloch points out in his survey of the many linguistic contrivances that show Walter Scott's devotion to "maintaining the interest of the non-Scot [reader]," Highlanders in fact "when they did not speak Gaelic spoke Standard English rather than Scots";[39] but in the linguistic arrangement of Walter Scott's novels, Scots mediates between Gaelic and English, not only reflecting as it does so the sociocultural map of Britain but reprising as well the internal colonialist dynamic wherein Lowlanders (such as *Waverley's* narrator) anglicize the Celtic fringe.

To complement its narrator's self-presentation as insider's outsider in relation to "Scotland," *Waverley* presents its protagonist as working toward the visiting ethnographer's outsider's insideness. In the sections relating Edward Waverley's journeys to Tully-Veolan and into the Highlands, Scott's novel seems intent on mobilizing its readers' identification with the protagonist by emphasizing his English bewilderment in the face of the semantic and syntactical mysteries of *both* Scots and Gaelic. Not only is *Waverley* full of language we are meant not to understand (single terms like "Duinhe-wassel," "taiglit," "curragh," and so forth, but also entire sentences); Edward's linguistic incompetence sometimes functions as a plot device. The most important instance occurs when the visitor is seriously injured on a Highland deer hunt because he cannot understand a shouted warning to get out of the way of the herd: "The word was given in Gaelic to fling themselves upon their faces," the novel tells us, "but Waverley, on whose English ears the signal was lost, had almost fallen a sacrifice to his ignorance of the ancient language in which it was communicated" (W 189). Rescuing him, the chieftain Fergus Mac-Ivor deftly exploits Edward's sense of obligation, using it as leverage in his effort to lure the young Englishman to the Jacobite cause. Furthermore, the recuperating Edward must be left behind when Fergus and the other chieftains ride off from the hunt on what turns out to have been their true errand all along, their meeting with the Young Pretender to plan the Rising. Because he remains outside of this conspiracy, Edward is the more easily pardonable at the novel's end.

Throughout, Waverley's experiences bear out and give political edge to Clifford Geertz's remark that, in fieldwork, "You don't exactly penetrate another culture, as the masculinist image would have it. You put yourself in its way and it bodies forth and enmeshes you."[40] Ethnographers' claims to successful enmeshment in a foreign culture have gained much support from representations of arrival scenes and other early stages in the fieldwork process, representations in which the visitor appears hopelessly lost and disoriented, the defining opposite of the authorita-

---

[39] Tulloch, *The Language of Walter Scott: A Study of his Scottish and Period Language* (London: André Deutsch, 1980), 319.

[40] Geertz, *After the Fact,* 44.

tive figure who writes the ethnography (cf. Herbert 11, 126). Readers are invited to conclude not only that such a figure has overcome his initially disabling outsideness and attained a degree of involvement permitting him to see how things look to the insider, but also that he has successfully held at bay the temptation to lose himself in meshes of *mere* insideness. Edward's progress over the course of Scott's novel describes precisely this pattern.

Related to the numerous instances in *Waverley* of the protagonist's incomprehension of Scottish languages are others emphasizing the baffling nature of Scottish social structure, itself a kind of language imperfectly translatable into forms familiar to English mentalities. At Tully-Veolan, the Jacobite Baron presides over a feudal "heritable jurisdiction"; in the Highlands, the logic and depth of clan loyalty defy English understanding. When, near the novel's end, Mac-Ivor is sentenced to death for treason, his right-hand man, Evan Dhu Maccombich, stuns the English courtroom audience by offering to redeem Fergus's offense with the lives of six substitutes, himself among them (W 465): unquestionably proper to Evan Dhu and utterly unthinkable to the courtroom audience, the gesture constitutes the ne plus ultra of cultural foreignness, its "culture-proving" effect comparable to those of cannibalism or clitoridectomy in twentieth-century ethnographic literature. Earlier in the narrative, Edward twice misapplies an English model of rural property relations, referring to Fergus Mac-Ivor as a "master": once to be gently corrected by Rose, the Baron's daughter ("he would consider *master* a sort of affront, only that you are an Englishman, and know no better" [W 128]); once to be met with the annoyance of Evan Dhu ("*My* master is in heaven" [W 149]). When Rose politely explains that Fergus is not to be referred to as "Mr Mac-Ivor" but that "the Lowlanders call him, like other gentlemen, by the name of his estate, Glennaquoich; and the Highlanders call him Vich Ian Vohr, that is, the son of John the Great; and we upon the braes call him by both names indifferently," Edward's response is, "I am afraid I shall never bring my English tongue to call him by either one or other" (W 128).

Classic pluralistic ethnography has been driven by a desire to respect the structural or semiotic autonomy of other cultures, to render, in Godfrey Lienhardt's words, "the coherence primitive thought has in the language it really lives in, as clear as possible in our own."[41] By showing that practices that, to the casual witness, seemed bizarre or "savage" made their own kind of sense in their own system, ethnographers expressed "an uncompromising rejection of any a priori 'standard of excellence'" or of civilization (Herbert 23). From the start of Edward Waverley's contact with Scotland, Walter Scott's historical novel bespeaks a similar urge to justify the phenomena it records, and such justification requires the shedding of ethnocentric blinders and the achievement of ethnographic rapport.[42] The condemnations Scott is concerned to refute are those of the Augustan-era John Bull, an outlook embodied within *Waverley* by Colonel Talbot and outside it, mem-

[41] Lienhardt, *The Institutions of Primitive Society* (Oxford: Basil Blackwell, 1961), 97.

[42] See Clifford Geertz, "Deep Play: Notes on the Balinese Cockfight," in *The Interpretation of Cultures* (New York: Basic Books, 1973), 412–17.

orably, by Doctor Johnson, who during his noted tour of the Highlands and Islands in 1773 mercilessly applied one self-universalizing English standard to all he saw. When, riding into the hamlet of Tully-Veolan, Edward gets his first real look, and ours, at Scotland, the impressions are all in the Johnsonian vein. "The houses seemed miserable in the extreme, especially to an eye accustomed to the smiling neatness of English cottages. They stood, without any respect for regularity, on each side of a straggling kind of unpaved street, where children, almost in a primitive state of nakedness, lay sprawling, as if to be crushed by the hoofs of the first passing horse." An occasional "grandma," "growling remonstrances," lurches into the road to snatch one of the children from violent death, only to "salute[] him with a sound cuff," the child "screaming all the while, from the very top of his lungs." To this duet is added "the incessant yelping of a score of idle useless curs, . . . snarling, barking, howling, and snapping at the horses' heels." The whole unedifying spectacle appears to indicate "at least a stagnation of industry, and perhaps of intellect" (W 74–75).

But we are yet in that uncomfortable prerapport phase of Edward Waverley's Scottish fieldwork, the phase during which the foreign has yet to reveal itself a system of "structural relativity" in which "each unit can only be defined in terms of the whole system."[43] Getting past this stage may involve, in contravention of relativistic principles, tactical recourse to cross-cultural comparisons. Thus *Waverley,* continuing its survey of the Scottish hamlet:

> Three or four village girls, . . . formed more pleasing objects; and . . . somewhat resembled Italian forms of landscape. Nor could a lover of the picturesque have challenged either the elegance of their costume, or the symmetry of their shape; although, to say the truth, a mere Englishman, in search of the *comfortable,* a word peculiar to his native tongue, might have wished the clothes less scanty, the feet and legs somewhat protected from the weather, the head and complexion shrouded from the sun, or perhaps might have thought the whole person and dress considerably improved, by a plentiful application of spring water, with a *quantum sufficit* of soap. (W 75)

Some critics have read this scene as undercutting Edward's addiction to romanticized or picturesque perspective,[44] but the references to picturesqueness and Italian scenes are unlikely to have come from *his* imagination. It is true that when Scott writes that the girls "formed more pleasing objects," the words appear to summarize *Edward's* pleasure upon seeing them as he rides through the village— they appear to situate us squarely inside Edward's point of view. A little farther on, however, it becomes difficult to maintain this position. Edward has never been in Italy, though he might well have seen representations of the Italian landscape; more significantly, the discourse of the picturesque was not yet available to the English visitor of 1745; it develops only in the 1780s and 1790s. We have gradually

---

[43] E. E. Evans-Pritchard, *The Nuer: A Description of the Modes of Livelihood and Political Institutions of a Nilotic People* (New York and Oxford: Oxford University Press, 1982), 135, 262.

[44] E.g. James Kerr, *Fiction Against History: Scott as Storyteller* (Cambridge: Cambridge University Press, 1989), 23.

shifted, in other words, from the character's present viewpoint to the narrator's retrospective one, and what this scene shows in miniature is the tendency of the novel
as a whole: to combine or to alternate positions of engagement and retrospective
detachment. Such combination (producing the uncanny effect of simultaneous insideness and outsideness) and alternation (producing a narrative about going inside, then getting out) are the elements of Scott's translation of events and phenomena encountered in the territory and story-space of old Scotland into Scottish
culture.

Both the instability built into the ethnographic model and that model's commitment to the wholeness or harmonious organization of cultures were anticipated
by the promulgators of picturesqueness in the travel writing of the Napoleonic and
immediate post-Napoleonic years. The passage just examined from Scott's novel
has obvious affinities with many from that literature on the competing attractions
of picturesqueness and modernization, all of which—like Anna Jameson's assertion that "civilization, cleanliness, and comfort are excellent things, but they
are sworn enemies to the picturesque"[45]—could have been written *only* by self-
conscious moderns seeking with one half of their hearts some haven of countermodern values. In Edward Sapir's classic essay "Culture, Genuine and Spurious"
(1924), Anna Jameson's claim finds a precise match, in a portion reflecting that
while "[i]t is excellent to keep one's hands spotlessly clean, to eliminate smallpox,
to administer anesthetics," "there can be no stranger illusion . . . than this, that because the tools of life are more specialized and more refined than ever before, . . .
it necessarily follows that we are . . . attaining to a profounder harmony of life, to
a deeper and more satisfying culture." A genuine culture would be "a sturdy plant
growth, the remotest leaf and twig of which is fed by the sap at the core."[46]

The scene of Waverley's arrival in Tully-Veolan shows the ethnographic process
that culminates in such a vision just getting underway. Whereas Edward's first
thought is that the village's depressing aspect argues for a "stagnation of industry,
and perhaps of intellect," the narrative goes on to point out that

> the physiognomy of the people . . . was far from exhibiting the indifference of stupidity:
> their features were rough, but remarkably intelligent; grave, but the very reverse of stu-
> pid; and from among the young women, an artist might have chosen more than one
> model, whose features and form resembled those of Minerva. . . . It seemed, upon the
> whole, as if poverty, and indolence, its too frequent companion, were combining to de-
> press the natural genius and acquired information of a hardy, intelligent, and reflecting
> peasantry. (W 76)

Edward's first impressions of a Scottish town are summed up in a way that illustrates how a defense of Scottish character and cultural autonomy goes hand in hand

[45] Jameson, *Diary of an Ennuyée* (1826; Boston: Ticknor & Fields, 1857), 321. Cf. my *The Beaten
Track: European Tourism, Literature, and the Ways to "Culture," 1800–1918* (Oxford: Clarendon,
1993), 172–215.

[46] Edward Sapir, "Culture, Genuine and Spurious," in *Culture, Language, and Personality: Selected
Essays,* ed. David G. Mandelbaum (Berkeley: University of California Press, 1960), 94, 93.

with a celebration of British Union. The conditions depicted in the Tully-Veolan of 1745 stand in implicit contrast to those described in the book's "Postscript, Which Should Have Been a Preface," which remarks upon the "gradual influx of wealth" and the "extension of commerce" that have followed the suppression of the '45 and effected a total reformation of Scottish society (W 492). The degenerate Scots whom Edward passes require only the encouragement of southern capital to improve their lot. Those children wallowing in the filthy street are the Glasgow factory operatives or the military rank and file of post-Culloden Britain.

Beginning in bewilderment and disgust, Edward Waverley undertakes the ethnographer's journey, undergoing immersion in the alien culture in order to achieve a greater and more valuable withdrawal from it, to that position from which one can assert authoritative apprehension of the whole. To frame matters in this way is to cast a new light on the question of *Waverley's* generic status as Bildungsroman. Much Scott criticism has followed the novel's own (qualified) claim that at the end of his Highland adventures Edward puts behind him "the romance of his life" and enters upon its "real history" (W 415), but the present reading would suggest that the *culturing* of Edward as a mature English landlord is inextricably bound up with the ethnographic romance of producing Scottish culture out of the most unprepossessing of materials. Waverley's (and *Waverley's*) progress is not from romantic fancy to sober fact, but rather from fragmented to unified visions, from ethnocentric first impressions to ethnographic total view.[47] The recognition that Scottish visions that might seem "imposing or sublime at a distance" come to appear "shabby or even ludicrous close at hand" can support the discourse of modernization and realism, but it can also sustain the countermodern discourse of culture by reminding us that ethnographic translation can take place only if we keep or recover our distance.[48]

Between Samuel Johnson's trip to Scotland and Walter Scott's *Waverley,* a number of travelers had headed north intending to counteract Johnson's negative images, which were seen as having rekindled enmities between South and North. The Sussex clergyman John Lettice wrote in 1794 that in repairing the damage done by Johnson, his travel book would have the effect "of rendering the *moral* as complete as the *civil union* betwixt the English and the Scots."[49] In the General Preface to the Waverley Novels (1829), Scott affirmed that his series had a strikingly similar goal. He championed the works of Edgeworth for helping to make the English "familiar with the character of their gay and kind-hearted neighbours of Ireland," to the point that "she may be truly said to have done more towards com-

---

[47] Cf. Jane Millgate, *Walter Scott: The Making of the Novelist* (Toronto: University of Toronto Press, 1984), 40; Duncan 1–19, 51–105; Joseph Valente, "Upon the Braes: History and Hermeneutics in *Waverley,*" *Studies in Romanticism* 25/2 (Summer 1986); and Franco Moretti, *The Way of the World: The Bildungsroman in European Culture* (London: Verso, 1988), on modern socialization as "the interiorization of contradiction" (10).

[48] Harry E. Shaw, *The Forms of Historical Fiction: Sir Walter Scott and his Successors* (Ithaca: Cornell University Press, 1983), 184–85.

[49] Quoted in Malcolm Andrews, *The Search for the Picturesque: Landscape Aesthetics and Tourism in Britain, 1760–1800* (Stanford: Stanford University Press, 1989), 198.

pleting the Union than perhaps all the legislative enactments by which it has been followed up." Inspired by her example, Scott says, he "felt that something might be achieved for my own country of the same kind with that which Miss Edgeworth so fortunately achieved for Ireland—something which might introduce her natives to those of her sister kingdom in a more favourable light than they had been placed hitherto, and tend to procure sympathy for their virtues and indulgence for their foibles (W 523)." Scott's novelistic project does not aim at a justification of English hegemony directed to Scottish readers, a "naturalization" of that hegemony attempting to sway them to a deeper acceptance; it does not *involve* any Scottish readers, only English or *Englished* ones. Again, Scott's fictional autoethnography, understood as the (self-) translation of Scottish culture, is the dialectical partner of, and perhaps the only effective check upon, Lowland self-Englishing. The labor to sustain a distinctive Scottish culture winds up looking like a British effort to make Scotland function *as* culture, in a different sense, *for* the English. And on this other form of translation Scott's *Waverley* also illuminatingly dwells.

III

The intelligible foreignness for which Scott's cultural translation self-consciously strives is designed for the satisfaction of an act of reading that *Waverley* as good as explicitly compares to tourism. Indeed, Scott sees little alternative to the cicerone's role for the autoethnographer of an erstwhile nation now incorporated as a "region" in the United Kingdom.[50] Professing his tale "an humble English post-chaise" that keeps to "his Majesty's highway," Scott's tour guide of a narrator undertakes to conduct his readers "into a more picturesque and romantic country" (W 63). He travels along roads not only belonging to the English monarch but lastingly testifying to the subjugation of Scotland by English armies for whom many of those roads were laid down. The familiar trope of the narrative as vehicle also describes the work's protagonist. Presented with the rare opportunity to review one of his own anonymous works of fiction in 1817, Scott took occasion to observe that the Waverley Novelist's tendency to depict his heroes "as foreigners to whom everything in Scotland is strange . . . serves as his apology for entering into many minute details which are reflectively, as it were, addressed to the reader through the medium of the hero."[51] That hero's relative colorlessness is licensed by the degree to which he is expected to function as a vessel for the fantasies of a host of unknown English (male) readers: the less marked his character, the better he can perform his function of offering conveyance to those readers, who seek along with him a rendition of a culture that must somehow appear both convincingly self-complete *and* duly solicitous of its

[50] Cf. Seamus Deane, *Strange Country: Modernity and Nationhood in Irish Writing since 1790* (Oxford: Clarendon, 1997), 148.

[51] Review of *Tales of My Landlord,* quoted in Alexander Welsh, *The Hero of the Waverley Novels* (New Haven: Yale University Press, 1963), 51–52.

visitor.[52] Satisfactory tourism requires this delicate balance, for the culture that, self-contained, truly turns its back on the outsider discourages imaginative investment, while the one that too openly courts him will seem a touristy fabrication. The touristic desideratum is an imagined relationship with the visited land that can feel antitouristic and yet meet the needs of a touristic romance: it aims at what I have elsewhere called an *authenticity effect*—a variant of *intelligible foreignness*.[53]

The critical commonplace of the passive Scott hero takes on a different aspect if we look back at it through the nineteenth century's extensive commentary on the stereotypical "tourist," a figure wholly the product and prisoner of the network of modern travel institutions regulating contact with the foreign. What was often castigated as a tourist's craven submission to the various authorities mandating schedules, routes, and even responses could from another point of view appear the act of surrender by which one gained entrance into a realm seemingly free of consequences, where imaginative faculties could be exercised at will. Those who entrusted Thomas Cook to deal with all the business of touring could devote their undivided attention to the undiluted *cultural* experience of the tour. During the years of the Waverley Novels, leisure travel was in the process of being redefined as an ameliorative vacation from modern life, the terms of that redefinition harking back to the German romantics and to Kant's idea of an aesthetic *purposiveness without purpose*. In traveling, Samuel Rogers would claim in 1830, we recompense ourselves for the boredom of a modern routine in which "the blood slumbers in the veins": we safely satisfy our lust for adventure and change; "we multiply events, but innocently."[54] *Waverley*'s interplay of narrator's and protagonist's perspectives offers a reading experience comparable to the form of picturesque sightseeing Malcolm Andrews labels "staged sublimity," in which tourists were afforded protected standpoints from which to view scenes truly perilous to enter. Readers can relish "the titillation of danger," perceived from what turns out to have been all along—what some part of them knew to have been all along—an absolutely safe position.[55]

It was this aspect of Scott's first novel that John Leycester Adolphus grasped in noting that its hero

> from the beginning to the end of his history, is scarcely ever left upon his own hands, but appears almost always in the situation of pupil, guest, patient, protege, or prisoner; engaged in a quarrel from which he is unconsciously extricated; half duped and half seduced into rebellion; ineffectually repenting; snatched away by accident from his sinking party; by accident preserved from justice; and restored by the exertions of his friends to safety, fortune and happiness.[56]

---

[52] Cf. Ina Ferris, *The Achievement of Literary Authority: Gender, History, and the Waverley Novels* (Ithaca: Cornell University Press, 1991), esp. 67, on Scott's masculinization of romance.

[53] Cf. *The Beaten Track*, 172–92.

[54] Rogers, *Italy: A Poem* (London: Cadell & Moxon, 1830), 170–72.

[55] Cf. Andrews, *The Search for the Picturesque*, 211, 216.

[56] Adolphus quoted in Welsh, *Hero of the Waverley Novels*, 46–47.

Edward actually joins the Jacobites, but there is also a sense in which, all the time he is with them, he remains encased in a protective bubble guaranteeing his security. He goes along for the ride; his martial adventures amount to a series of poses in fancy dress; he prevents the killing of a Hanoverian in battle rather than attempting any killings himself; in the end, he receives an unconditional pardon for his patent treason.[57] That "anticipation of retrospection" that Peter Brooks has characterized as narrative's master trope here takes on the specific function of vouching for the Englishman's sage passage through the history and culture of Scotland.[58] Like many a nation dependent on tourism today, Scott understands that outsiders' imaginative investment in his country has to be established as substantially risk-free *before* he can begin to work his relationship with visitors for whatever advantages he can secure through the alteration of their attitudes.

Waverley's illustration of its own labor to produce a Scottish space governed by authenticity effect can be traced in the contrasting opening and closing scenes at the manor house of Tully-Veolan. Since Edward's arrival at this spot is laden with the symbolic significance of entry into Scotland, it is striking to note that, having passed through the impoverished hamlet and reached the Baron's domicile, Scott's protagonist initially arouses no attention whatsoever. At the very door of Scotland, he knocks in vain. The butler is out digging in the garden: this official welcomer is not expecting any guests. When Edward begins to walk around the house in search of his hosts, he frightens away two washerwomen and encounters a ragged fool, Davie Gellatley, whose babblings are impenetrable to him. Scott's hero begins "to despair of gaining entrance into this solitary and seemingly enchanted mansion" (W 81). This is what it *means* to enter another culture, a distinct, self-regarding semiotic universe: one must expect to find it minding its own business, not holding itself in readiness for the visitor. As with the anthropological arrival scene, however, this one lays the foundation for the visitor's authority: the more closed and self-complete the visited culture appears on first sight, the greater the credit to be gained from acquiring ethnographic mastery over it.

Toward the end of the novel, Edward returns to Tully-Veolan, to find house and grounds thoroughly "sacked by the King's troops" (W 433) in vengeance for Bradwardine's insurgency. Later still, after he has been cleared for his own part in the Rising, he returns again, this time with Rose as his bride, to participate in the elaborate charade of restoring the estate to its dispossessed master. As the text importunately presses us to acknowledge, the destruction wrought by the occupiers has been magically undone. "Every mark of devastation [at Tully-Veolan], unless to an eye intimately acquainted with the spot, [is] ... totally obliterated"; "all seem[s] as much as possible restored to the state in which [the Baron] had left it when he assumed arms some months before." Even the talisman Bradwardine bears guarding the gate have been "renewed or restored with so much care, that

---

[57] Cf. John Sutherland's indignant questions along these lines in *The Life of Walter Scott: A Critical Biography* (Oxford: Blackwell, 1995), 172–75.

[58] Brooks, *Reading for the Plot: Design and Intention in Narrative* (Cambridge, Mass.: Harvard University Press, 1984), 23.

they bore no tokens of the violence which had been so lately descended upon them"; and "the house itself [has] been thoroughly repaired, as well as the gardens, with the strictest attention to maintain the original character of both, and to remove as far as possible, all appearance of the ravage they [have] sustained" (W 483–84). Scott's manner of exposition is again significant, for we see all this through the mystified eyes of the Baron himself, before we learn, a few pages farther on, that Colonel Talbot has overseen this painstaking reconstruction, with Waverley's assistance. The protagonist's collaboration with the bigoted "Southron" Talbot in reconstructing the Scottish estate images Scott's own position as autoethnographer and involves Scott's acknowledgment that the power to lay waste and the power to efface the signs of destruction, to build and map and represent culture, go hand in hand. Scott's own cultural re-presentation is bizarrely figured in the giving back of the Baron's estate, a translation-without-original if ever there was one.

The whole transaction can call to mind the joke about the man who returns home to discover that everything in his house has been stolen—and replaced with an exact replica.[59] All is the same, yet utterly different: Tully-Veolan is now a bought freehold, not a feudal estate;[60] English pounds have redeemed the Scottish house; the Baron, stripped of his title, is now merely "Cosmo Comyne Bradwardine, Esq."—though he *is* capable of bequeathing his property, in gratitude, to the second son of Edward and Rose (their first will inherit the English estate "Waverley-Honour"). Homi Bhabha's notion of colonial mimicry as "the desire for a re-formed, recognizable Other, *as a subject of a difference that is almost the same, but not quite*" is perhaps the flipside of the authenticity effect signaled here, which encodes the desire for a reformed, recognizable Other that is almost the same as its ("authentic") self, but not quite.[61] When we read that "every mark of devastation, unless to an eye intimately acquainted with the spot, was already totally obliterated," we should observe that the represented Tully-Veolan both is and is not addressed to eyes intimately acquainted with it (as the expository device of putting "us" English readers temporarily in the Baron's position indicates). On the one hand, the implied reader-tourist will not register evidence of a fall from a prior state he never knew, from an "authentic" condition that *necessarily* excludes him. On the other, the eyes of the former Baron, a finely calibrated register of such changes, will instruct him that he, too, has been "restored" as an antique among antiquities, reinstalled as a mediatized ruler, a figurehead. To describe this allegory of cultural re-presentation another way, Bradwardine becomes at the new Tully-Veolan the prisoner of a Scotland he is made to embody, just as, according to recent critics of anthropology, the subjects of classic ethnographies are "incarcerated" in their tradition-bound cultures.[62] Only on these terms, it seems, may the Scotsman receive the invisible import of his own culture.

---

[59] Steven Wright tells it on his recording *I Have a Pony* (WEA International).

[60] David Brown, *Walter Scott and the Historical Imagination* (London: Routledge & Kegan Paul, 1979), 24–25.

[61] Bhabha, *The Location of Culture* (London: Routledge, 1994), 86.

[62] Cf. Fabian, *Time and the Other;* Arjun Appadurai, "Putting Hierarchy in its Place," *Cultural An-*

If the space of the cultural exists in order to house the unsatisfied longings of the modern subject, then the significance of the gap between authenticity effect and the authenticity that is its central trope declines as those subjects' investment in culture increases. *Waverley*—and Scotland itself—tests the limits of reader-tourists' willingness to bracket evidence that the inward-looking culture of Scotland has turned aggressively outward-looking or touristy. What Ian Duncan identifies as "the text's excessive closure upon its own mechanisms" may be read as the recouping of a realism-versus-romance binarism (England/Scotland; modern society/traditional culture) that much of the novel labors to problematize—as a final, inescapable accommodation to presumed desires for symbols of Scotland (Duncan 61).

IV

The readerly tourism Scott sees himself as bound to gratify even as he exposes its operations shuttles between the domains of ethnography and history. It tends to regard time and space, respectively, under the signs of story (as processual narrative) and picture (as static image). Lessing and the tradition of Renaissance painterly perspective insist on the separation of the two, but Scott's autoethnography treats them as mutually translatable: geographical places are temporalized by becoming the sites of enthralling stories (in which the tourist might imagine himself acting a prominent role), but these are rendered "spatial" again by being treated as finished and available to the retrospective, totalizing gaze. The iconic space of a Scottish culture comes to substitute for any number of discrete physical locations within Scotland. Although *Waverley* establishes, through its narrator, a stable position for viewing the past that I have compared to the one structurally implied by vanishing-point perspective, it contradicts itself in a manner entirely characteristic of post-Renaissance tradition by also endorsing a principle of *ut pictura poesis.* The story opens with the reflection that "[p]ainters talk of the difficulty of expressing the existence of compound passions in the same features at the same moment: it would be no less difficult for the moralist to analyze the mixed motives which unite to form the impulse of our actions" (W 37). The translatability of painting and the storyteller's or "moralist's" art is presumed in this statement of their common representational dilemma. The kind of painting imagined here is a portrait, but the problem it raises implies a form defined, as is Renaissance landscape, by the strict exclusion of narrativity (Steiner 24).

Waverley's touristic translation of Scotland, then, temporalizes (narrativizes) space, only to spatialize (pictorialize) time in turn—or perhaps simultaneously. I will take the latter step first, because it—always already there in the text as the function of Scott's retrospective narrator—supplies that guarantee of safety for

thropology 3/1 (Feb. 1988), esp. 36–37; Bernard McGrane, *Beyond Anthropology: Society and the Other* (New York: Columbia University Press, 1989), esp. 119–120; James Clifford, "Traveling Cultures," in *Routes,* 17–46.

which the implied reader-tourist is looking. Spatialization of time involves the attempt to press diverse and even internally inconsistent elements of a living society into service as symbols for the purported whole of a culture.[63] The prevailing
form of such symbolization in nineteenth-century tourism, greatly influenced by
the works of Scott, took place, as I have suggested, under the hospitable aegis of
the picturesque.[64] The picturesqueness of a particular landscape could be grasped
only from a physical and imaginative distance: only to the detached observer could
the picturesque's pleasing arrangement of elements and, far more importantly, its
composed totality reveal itself. Coleridge defined picturesqueness as a mode in
which "parts only are seen and distinguished, but the whole is felt."[65] From experiential flux, picturesque perception would wrest an assortment of detail that typified and expressed in an instant the whatness of the particular scene. Nineteenth-
century tourism made this convention of viewing into its amateur ethnographic
principle: the achieved touristic moment secures an epiphany of cultural identity.
The great usefulness of the picturesque in this context was the result of the anti-
Laökoon latitude with which it had long been applied: even its theorists spoke not
only of picturesque scenery but of the picturesqueness of various *temporal* experiences or artistic forms. William Gilpin referred to the "picturesque memories and
associations" one might have of a particular place; Uvedale Price considered music
worthy of the label if it contained "sudden, unexpected, and abrupt transitions."[66]
Later applications absorbed poetry, Lessing's exemplary art of duration, as well.
In Scott, as critics have long remarked, history itself, "the record of time and
change, is viewed spatially and pictorially."[67] Like the iconic "successfully *poetic*
poem" that Murray Krieger has described, which in laying claim to "another order
than its own" reveals "the generic spatiality of literary form," the successful event
of the picturesque tour gestures toward the inescapable spatiality of culture.[68]

A seemingly satisfying moment in the course of Waverley's tour of Scotland occurs during another important arrival and welcome scene, this time at Mac-Ivor's
Highland house of Glennaquoich. The banquet in Waverley's honor seems to af-

---

[63] I use the phrase differently from the way critics have used it in debates surrounding Joseph
Frank's work on "spatial form" in literature: Wendy Steiner is right to say the proponents of the spatial-
form argument have tended to associate narrative more or less exclusively with pure sequence (Steiner
8). For another angle on the interrelationship of "spatialization of time" and "temporalization of space,"
cf. Georges Van Den Abbeele, *Travel as Metaphor from Montaigne to Rousseau* (Minneapolis: University of Minnesota Press, 1992), xviii–xix.

[64] Both William Gilpin and Uvedale Price located the pictureseque "in scenes that were essentially
either sublime or beautiful," making picturesqueness a category more "commodious" than the others
(Ross, *The Imprint of the Picturesque,* 9).

[65] Quoted in Martin Price, "The Picturesque Moment," in Frederick W. Hilles and Harold Bloom,
eds., *From Sensibility to Romance: Essays Presented to Frederick A. Pottle* (New York: Oxford University Press, 1965), 280.

[66] Cf. Ross, *The Imprint of the Picturesque,* 1–45.

[67] See Eric G. Walker, *Scott's Fiction and the Picturesque* (Salzburg: Institut für Anglistik und
Amerikanistik, 1982), 2–3.

[68] Krieger, *Ekphrasis: The Illusion of the Natural Sign* (Baltimore: Johns Hopkins University Press,
1992), 264–65.

ford a perfect illustration of the tight interdependence and harmonious integration of parts within the hierarchical "traditional culture":

> At the head of the table was the Chief himself, with Edward, and two or three Highland visitors of neighbouring clans; the elders of his own tribe, wadsetters and tacksmen, as they were called, . . . sat next in rank; beneath them, their sons, and nephews, and foster-brethren; then the officers of the Chief's household, according to their order; and, lowest of all, the tenants who actually cultivated the ground. Even beyond this long perspective, Edward might see upon the green, to which a pair of folding doors opened, a multitude of Highlanders of a yet inferior description, who, nevertheless, were considered as guests, and had their share both of the countenance of the entertainer, and of the cheer of the day. (W 162–63)

Each level of this meticulously striated social order is supplied with its appropriate food and drink: fish and game, along with "excellent claret and champagne" at the top of the table; "immense clumsy joints of mutton and beef" and a whole yearling lamb, with whisky and beer in the middle; while "broth, onions, and cheese, and the fragments of the feast," Scott writes, "regaled the sons of Ivor who feasted in the open air." He adds: "Nor did this inequality of distribution appear to give the least offense. Every one present understood that his taste was to be formed according to the rank which he held at table; and, consequently, the [elders] and their dependants [*sic*] always professed the wine was too cold for their stomachs, and called, apparently out of choice, for the liquor which was assigned to them from economy" (W 163–64).

Where the English visitor might expect undisciplined savagery, we see instead a vision of culture in frictionless operation: before our very eyes, "'savage' society is transformed from a void of institutional control . . . to a spectacle of controls exerted systematically upon the smallest details of life" (Herbert 65). The salient fact in the scene is that these controls are not exerted from without, but emanate from within the private heart of each banquet-guest: traditional Scottish culture seems to achieve a perfect concord of personal desire and social order, in which the interiority of the individual subject appears to exist for the sole purpose of pre-emptively ratifying its subjection.[69] The spectacle implies an identification of person and role so complete that unruly desire becomes an analytical nonissue—a comforting idea, to be sure, for the English time-traveler reading Scott's novel.

In order to maintain the "foreign" side of intelligible foreignness, the tourist-ethnographer on whose behalf Scott's novel does its work must be insulated against suspicions that this or that event, image, or impression has been "got up" solely for him, for he is prone to wonder, would they be doing this if I weren't here? Like a poem as understood by the New Criticism, the traditional culture should simply *be,* not labor to send messages to an audience; it should unself-consciously exhibit its characteristics, not engage in calculation about the rhetorical advantages of showing itself in certain ways to certain viewers. But it is every-

[69] See Louis Althusser, "Ideology and Ideological State Apparatuses," *Lenin and Philosophy,* trans. Ben Brewster (New York: Monthly Review Press, 1971), esp. 170–83.

where evident in Scott's novel that the figure at the center of this court is playing to *and on* the outsider's expectations. Fergus Mac-Ivor is a man who, grown aware of Edward's infatuation with Flora, shows his visitor Flora's poem on the Stuart loyalist Captain Wogan, implying that Edward may win her heart by stepping into Wogan's shoes (W 230–32). Once we recognize this tendency, the banquet scene we have just examined comes to appear a "spectacle" in another sense: Fergus's version of the state as a work of art, Schilleresque sentimental romance masquerading as naïve, or native, romance (Duncan 6–7). From his first meeting with Edward, the chieftain is already taking care about the impression he will create for the visitor: he decides to greet him without his customary entourage, "well aware that such an unnecessary attendance would seem to Edward rather ludicrous than respectable" (W 153). The word "unnecessary" shows Mac-Ivor alert to the utilitarian protocols belonging to the modern social formation that is supposed to have *superceded* his own. We read that "few men were more attached to the ideas of chieftainship and feudal power" than Fergus, but chieftainship and feudal power have clearly become manipulatable *ideas* for him, and he is "cautious of exhibiting external marks of dignity, unless at the time and in the manner when they were most likely to produce an imposing effect" (W 153).

Nothing like the indivisible compound of self-and-role imagined to thrive in feudal society, then, Fergus pointedly fails to conform to any desire for the kind of "coherent and transparent subject" of the successful translation or the "common-denominator" or "generalized" subject of ethnography, the kind that enables the ethnographer to "transform[] the research situation's ambiguities and diversities of meaning into an integrated portrait."[70] The novel distinguishes, repeatedly and in no uncertain terms, the ulterior personal aims driving the chieftain's Jacobitism from Flora's purer ardor for the cause (cf. W 158–59, 168–69). Indeed, as several critics have noted, Fergus actually comes to exemplify a modern selfhood corrosive of the feudalism he is supposed to represent. As the story goes on he appears more and more like a figure of anomie, subject to a rampant self-interest that, liberated from traditional culture's restraint, has become directionless and finally self-defeating. "Fergus's brain," we read, "was a perpetual workshop of scheme and intrigue of every possible kind and description[;] . . . he would often unexpectedly, and without any apparent motive, abandon one plan, and go earnestly to work upon another, which was either fresh from the forge of his imagination, or had at some former period been flung aside half-finished" (W 368; cf. Herbert 44–59).[71] And yet, after a whole novel's worth of evidence that this character "was

[70] "Coherent": Niranjana, *Siting Translation*, 3; "common denominator": George Marcus and Dick Cushman, "Ethnographies as Texts," *Annual Review of Anthropology* (1982), 32; "generalized subject": James Clifford, *The Predicament of Culture: Twentieth-Century Ethnography, Literature, and Art* (Cambridge, Mass.: Harvard University Press, 1988), 109.

[71] Saree Makdisi's stimulating reading of *Waverley* too simply identifies Fergus as a "perfect specimen of the [Highland] species" and aligns the narrator's perspective with Colonel Talbot's: cf. *Romantic Imperialism*, 87–88. Cf. Graham McMaster, *Scott and Society* (Cambridge: Cambridge University Press, 1981), for a view of Fergus as "exactly the type of man Adam Smith imagined in his account of the destruction of the feudal system by commerce" (68).

too thorough a politician, regarded his patriarchal influence too much as the means of accomplishing his own aggrandizement, that we should term him the model of a Highland Chieftain" (W 170); after being reminded that, half-French, he is not a "real" Highlander, his putatively indigenous Jacobitism actually an exogenous *Jacobinism;* after acknowledging how ill his opportunism comports with his sister's genuine devotion to restoring the Stuarts—after all this, we watch *this* unlikely figure go to his grisly execution shouting "God Save King James!" (W 476). And, at the novel's end, he is commemorated—ultimately *translated*—in an extraordinary ekphrasis that does indeed put him forward as a model Highlander and a soldier of the Stuart cause.

In the Tully-Veolan dining room, Colonel Talbot has made one crucial addition to the otherwise faithfully reconstructed estate: it is

> a large and spirited painting, representing Fergus Mac-Ivor and Waverley in their Highland dress; the scene a wild, rocky, and mountainous pass, down which the clan were descending in the background. It was taken from a spirited sketch, drawn while they were in Edinburgh by a young man of high genius, and had been painted on a full-length scale by an eminent London artist. Raeburn himself (whose Highland Chiefs do all but walk out of the canvas) could not have done more justice to the subject; and the ardent, fiery, and impetuous character of the unfortunate Chief of Glennaquoich was finely contrasted with the contemplative, fanciful, and enthusiastic expression of his happier friend. (W 489)

It is worth pausing at this juncture to consider something perfectly obvious, namely how utterly unlikely such an act of commemoration would have been in 1746, with Cumberland still afield on his campaign of retribution. Only a perspectival leap from the time of the narrative to the time of Scott, or from story-space to discourse-space, can account for the touristic pleasure everyone at Tully-Veolan takes in what would, in 1746, have been comparable to an incriminating surveillance photo showing Edward's collaboration with the enemy. Readers who have had the loan of Edward's "wandering viewpoint" throughout the narrative are invited in the end to rejoin the narrator in this instantaneous apprehension of a suddenly remote culture. Vanishing-point exclusion of narrativity and Johannes Fabian's critical ethnographic notion of "denial of coevalness" are fused here, as Scotland, in the unlikely figure of Fergus, is finally translated from time into space, from deliberative historical agent into static symbol: one could scarcely imagine a more forceful representation of what Arjun Appadurai has memorably labeled the "metonymic freezing" effect of the classic, stereotyping ethnography.[72] The Highlander's "ardent, fiery, and impetuous" features are easily confined in Lessing's arts of space—they are all of a piece, something Fergus never was—whereas Edward's "contemplative, fanciful, and enthusiastic" expression illustrates perfectly the painter's dilemma of capturing "the existence of compound passions in the same features at the same moment," to which *Waverley* adverts at the outset. But then, Edward is still among the living, is still capable of *having* passions, compound or otherwise; he is not captured by his own portrayal, but stands across the

---

[72] Appadurai, "Putting Hierarchy in its Place," 36.

room from it, the viewpoints of discourse- and story-space uncannily together. The English tourist-ethnographer here recovers the outsideness that completes and authorizes, that transcends and retains, his passage inside the alien culture.

What relation does the painting at Tully-Veolan bear to the "real picture" of Highland culture Scott had intended to deliver in *The Lady of the Lake?* We cannot read of the painting's "justice to the subject" without recalling Talbot's words to Edward on the irrevocability of Fergus's death sentence: "Justice, which demanded some penalty of those who had wrapped the whole nation in fear and mourning, could not have selected a fitter victim" (W 463).[73] Both Scott's nation and his novel turn the wayward and recalcitrant Highlander into a figure who all *but* walks out of the canvas. Tejaswini Niranjana's argument that "the notion of fidelity to the 'original' holds back translation theory from thinking the *force* of a translation" surely applies here.[74] The absence—actually, the judicial destruction and dismembering—of Fergus is the absolute precondition for an artwork that remembers him and the culture he is made to embody. In the nostalgic double portrait that concludes *Waverley,* Scott writes sentences that illustrate the aesthetic-judicial sentence he sees himself as bound to carry out.

Spatialization of time, then, as translation without original: a phenomenon *Waverley* enacts and displays not only through its highlighting of the painting's inauthenticity ("representing" a rocky pass, but sketched in Edinburgh and painted in London), but also in the figure of ekphrasis itself. Told the contents of a picture we can never see, we get "the illusion of an object marked by its own sensible absence," as Murray Krieger puts it, and "the object of imitation, as spatial work, becomes the metaphor for the temporal work which seeks to capture it in that temporality."[75] The three often dissociated senses of "culture" join in this figure: aesthetic, developmental, ethnographic. Like Scott's Lowland autoethnography of Scotland, a (British) artwork yokes the English inhabitant of open time, the representative of power and potentiality, with the Celtic prisoner of iconic space; it releases the former from youthful illusions while capturing the latter in an eternal present tense; it validates the "culturing" of its two male leads in the complementary modes of bildungsroman (in which the callow youth attains maturity) and ethnography (in which the traditional culture remains the same forever).

V

By "temporalization of space" I refer to tendencies visible in forms of tourism and historical fiction alike, involving the telling of a story that is attached to and distinguishes a particular spot of ground (however broadly or narrowly we define that "spot"). Coming upon a particular site, one fills in the associations that add value

[73] Cf. Bruce Beiderwell, *Power and Punishment in Scott's Novels* (Athens, Georgia: University of Georgia Press, 1992), esp. 17–18.

[74] Niranjana, *Siting Translation,* 58.

[75] Krieger, *Ekphrasis,* 28, 265.

to or justify it—justify our paying attention to it—by narrating what has made it what it is and made it worth seeing. These associations are a version of the "off-site markers" Dean MacCannell has described in his work on the semiotics of tourist attractions; they attain their formal apogee in the matchless Victorian guidebooks of Murray and Baedeker, and Scott the tourist was an adept in their deployment.[76] "But show me an old castle or a field of battle," he wrote in 1808, "and I [am] at home at once, fill[ing] it with its combatants in their proper costume and overwhelm[ing] my hearers by the enthusiasm of my description."[77] Coleridge confessed that whereas he could "walk over the plain of Marathon without taking more interest in it than in any other plain of similar features, Scott saw "every old ruin, hill, river or tree" saturated with "a host of historical or biographical associations."[78]

The justification of spaces by temporalizing or narrativizing them is particularly clear in the case of battlefield tourism, for this practice often provides only a blank piece of ground to which belated visitors must attach their explanations or elegies. *Waverley* offers a revealing example, in its account of Edward's visit to the field at Clifton where, he thinks, Fergus Mac-Ivor has fallen.

> "And this, then, was thy last field," said Waverley to himself, his eye filling at the recollection of the many splendid points of Fergus's character, and of their former intimacy, all his passions and imperfections forgotten.—"Here fell the last Vich Ian Vohr, on a nameless heath; and in an obscure night-skirmish was quenched that ardent spirit[;] . . . here ended all thy hopes for Flora, and the long and valued line which it was thy boast to raise yet more highly by thy adventurous valour!" (W 413)

In his haste to conduct the exequies over a comrade who, we later learn, has only been captured, Edward delivers a touristic memorial address rather more applicable to Marathon than to Clifton. For, taken in its narrative context, what ought to strike us is the fact that the skirmish at Clifton occurred only the previous night. The ground is still littered with "dead bodies of men and horses, and the usual companions of war—a number of carrion-crows, hawks, and ravens" (W 413). Instead of having to run through the battlefield tourist's usual reconstruction story of "the attack came from this hill; the enemy retreated to this wood," Edward can trace the events through the positions of the corpses still lying about. If his eulogy sounds appropriate for heroes dead and buried long ago, that is because Edward has, again, momentarily vaulted to that other perspective always available to the reader, the one from which the dead of "sixty years since" are no less dead than those of the last millennium.

As this instance makes clear, touristic temporalization of space operates *within* the confines of a spatializing imagination that both limits and enables it. It does

---

[76] MacCannell, *The Tourist: A New Theory of the Leisure Class* (New York: Schocken, 1989), 110–117.

[77] Quoted in Walker, *Scott's Fiction and the Picturesque,* 21.

[78] Quoted in James Reed, *Sir Walter Scott: Landscape and Locality* (London: Athlone Press, 1980), 9–10.

not free us from the fixed, vanishing-point-like perspective, or usher us into a condition of open metonymic flux. Quite the contrary: the storied associations of
tourism yield closed narratives telling of what transpired somewhere in a concluded past. If only implicitly, events tend to be assigned function and meaning
within a metanarrative that negotiates the passage from "history" to "now"—or,
in the terms of the Edinburgh philosophical historians whose metanarrative was
also Scott's, from "rude" to "civil society." From such a viewpoint, those in the
present enjoy the mobility of an unfolding modernity, but they stand still at the end
of a history whose finished movements have reached their goal in them. If we read
Waverley with that anticipation of retrospection that Peter Brooks emphasizes, we
can discern beneath its apparently rambling narrative, its appearance of being the
paradigmatic loose-and-baggy monster of a tale, an impressive array of devices
devoted to the assurance of an ultimate closure: framing chapters; a host of pro-
leptic and analeptic elements; various three-stage processes suggesting dialectical
progress. Edward makes three returns to Tully-Veolan; there are three strategically
placed passages on history as a stream; three women are put forward, fairy-tale
fashion, as candidates for the role of romantic heroine.[79] Even the Baron's fool,
Davie Gellatley, turns out to have been giving sage advice in his first, seemingly
nonsensical utterance in the novel, the song that urges its hearer to "turn again"
(W 82): for in the narrative that follows it, Edward's traitorous turn in the direction of Jacobitism and Flora Mac-Ivor must be followed up and canceled out by
his turning back again to the Hanoverian side and Rose Bradwardine.

It is within the limiting and enabling framework of Scott's ultimately "iconi-
cizing" narrative that the imputed romance desires of tourist-readers can be both
addressed and put on show. If one part of the complex and qualified satisfaction
on offer in *Waverley* centers on Fergus Mac-Ivor and culminates in figuring the
alien culture as a picture, another part centers on Fergus's sister Flora and attempts
to figure the foreign as a story. As important as the gesture of "standing back" and
asserting a total view is the complementary fiction of acting a part in, in some sense
belonging to, that culture. More than a merely spectatorial relation is necessary:
Scott's fiction acknowledges that it must address the kind of anticipation Edward
Waverley expresses when he thinks, "I am actually in the land of military and romantic adventures, and it only remains to be seen what will be my own share in
them!" (W 129). By the most demonstrative and formulaic of procedures is the
space cleared for Flora Mac-Ivor to occupy as the figure around whom a narrative
answering such a challenge might be organized.

As Edward proceeds into Scotland, he confronts in turn three candidates for the
role of romance heroine, three women to be held up against the "female forms of
exquisite grace and beauty . . . [that] mingle in his mental adventures" (W 55).
Rose Bradwardine, whom he meets first, "the Rose of Tully-Veolan," is found to
have "not precisely the sort of beauty or merit which captivates a romantic imagination in early youth," for she is "too frank, too confiding, too kind; amiable qual-

---

[79] On the returns to Tully-Veolan, see Millgate, *Walter Scott,* 43–44; on the "stream" passages, see
Brown, *Walter Scott and the Historical Imagination,* 25–27.

ities, undoubtedly, but destructive of the marvellous" (W 121). As Anthony Trollope once wrote in criticism of a disappointing piece of scenery, "a landscape
should always be partly veiled and display only half its charms."[80] Residing only
on the braes of the Highlands, not at their heart—and hence almost a Lowlander
herself—Rose holds insufficient mystery for the English visitor. She is fittingly
named for the English flower. Soon thereafter, a second figure is introduced to provide the dialectical opposite of this overly familiar and hence unsatisfactory object of romance. Alice Bean Lean, the daughter of the Highland cattle thief whose
depredations provide the motive for Edward's move northward, lavishes attention
upon the young Englishman during his brief stay at the robber's hideaway. Alice,
of course, represents a direction this novel has no intention of actually taking; like
the National Tales, *Waverley* will attach its hero to the daughter of a gentleman.
But her function within the unfolding dialectic becomes unmistakable when we
read that "[t]he smiles, displaying a row of teeth of exquisite whiteness, and the
laughing eyes, with which in dumb show, she gave Waverley that morning greeting which she wanted English words to express, might have been interpreted . . .
as meant to convey more than the courtesy of a hostess" (W 146). Too cold; too
hot: only by way of the overly English Rose and the overly alien, untranslatable
Alice do we make our way to the English-speaking yet exotic Flora, who possesses
"precisely the character to fascinate a youth of romantic imagination" (W 187).
She is perfectly suited to gratify the young man who is, as Fergus puts it, "a wor-
shipper of the Celtic muse; not the less so [because] he does not understand a word
of her language" (W 171). To be sure, Scott's protagonist, in keeping with Davie
Gellatley's advice, is always already going to turn his affections back to Rose
Bradwardine, but as George Levine has put it, "what Edward Waverley must dis-
miss, *Waverley* preserves."[81]

Scott's novel takes part in the rising convention of nineteenth-century travel
writing that depicts the male tourist's fantasy of participation in the foreign as a
courtship without consequences, an unfettered exercise in the domain of play.
Some decades after *Waverley,* Robert Browning would apostrophize Italy in terms
well suited to Flora and the feminized territory she represents, writing, "Oh
woman-country, wooed not wed, / Loved all the more by earth's male-lands, /
Laid to their hearts instead!"[82] Like Keats's urn, Scott's heroine of culture—
wooable, not weddable—is designed to sustain a desire that might remain untouched by the tristesse of consummation and domesticity. And, as with the feminized images of Italy, those of Scotland or the Highlands drew some strength from
selected associations of the place. Graham Tulloch notes an English and Lowland
tradition going back to the fifteenth century of using "*she* as a general-purpose pro-

---

[80] Trollope, *North America,* ed. Donald Smalley and Bradford Allen Booth (New York: Knopf,
1951), 144–45.

[81] George Levine, *The Realistic Imagination: English Fiction from Frankenstein to Lady Chatterly*
(Chicago: University of Chicago Press, 1981), 82.

[82] Browning, "By the Fire-Side," in *The Poems,* ed. John Pettigrew (New Haven: Yale University
Press, 1981), 1.553. Cf. *The Beaten Track,* 130–39.

noun for Highlanders," on account of the fact that "a Highlander was thought to refer to himself as *her nainsell,* 'her own self' . . . So well established was this as a literary convention," Tulloch writes, "that *Her Nainsell* became a jocular name for a Highlander."[83] What is more, for the English, thinking about entrance into Scotland could generate associations of precocious sexual license, inasmuch as Scottish law permitted eloping English couples to be married at Gretna Green and other border towns "without parental consent and within a few minutes of their arrival across the border." (Lydia Bennet, in *Pride and Prejudice,* makes off for Gretna Green with Wickham.) Thomas Pennant observed in 1774 that if the runaways should arrive with parents or their agents hot upon their trail, then "the frightened pair are advised to slip in bed, are shown to the pursuers who imagine that they are irrecoverably united, retire, and leave them 'to consummate their unfinished loves.'"[84]

John Brenkman's analysis of an "aesthetics of male fantasy" in *The Sorrows of Young Werther* can further assist us in historicizing Scott's figuration of Flora in *Waverley,* for here, as in the Goethe work, the sentimental hero casts his beloved as an "interiorized and heterosexualized" rendition of the bonds between feudal subject and lord.[85] Whereas Fergus, "accustomed to petty intrigue, and necessarily involved in a thousand paltry and selfish discussions," possesses a "political faith" that is "tinctured, at least, if not tainted, by the views of interest and advancement so easily combined with it" (W 168), Flora ironically resembles the "ideal type of the feudal nobleman" her brother so pointedly fails to embody. This figure "enjoys [a] unity between symbolic appearance and social being" that self-divided moderns cannot hope to emulate. In the transition out of feudalism, "the symbolic ties that feudalism embodies in the material relation of lord and vassal do not simply disappear," but are "reinscribed in the intimate sphere of the private individual," in the loved one's "[h]armony of being [and] self-presentation" (Brenkman 204–6). This seems exactly the framework in which to place the character of Flora in *Waverley,* she in whose bosom "the zeal of loyalty burn[s] pure and unmixed with any selfish feeling," whose "love of her clan . . . was, like her loyalty [to the Stuarts], a more pure passion than that of her brother," and whose attachment to "the music and poetical traditions of the Highlanders" was as sincere as Fergus's was "affected for the sake of popularity rather than actually experienced" (W 169).

Each of the women brought forward for the role Flora will occupy sings a song that helps secure her position in the dialectic of heroine-formation. The antithetical Alice's is the simplest: Edward awakes in the cave of the Highland extortionist Bean Lean to hear "the notes of a lively Gaelic song, guided by which . . . he [finds] the damsel of the cavern" arranging his breakfast outside (W 145). The situation is essentially that of Wordsworth's "solitary Highland Lass" in the 1805

---

[83] Tulloch, *The Language of Walter Scott,* 255.

[84] See Andrews, *The Search for the Picturesque,* 207.

[85] Cf. Brenkman, *Culture and Domination* (Ithaca: Cornell University Press, 1987), 204–6; henceforth Brenkman.

poem "The Solitary Reaper": like the figure in that verse, Alice sings entirely for her own satisfaction, in a language entirely unintelligible to the English visitor. (Wordsworth's third stanza begins, "Will no one tell me what she sings?")[86] Here, in Brenkman's terms, is a symbolic significance that the visitor from modernity lacks, but one whose stubborn unassimilability keeps it within the sphere of lyrical rather than narratable experience.[87]

In the more complex ballad of "St. Swithin's Chair," Rose Bradwardine raises issues related to her position as the figure of *British* nationality to whom Waverley and all the forgiven Jacobites must ultimately return. The "chair" is the name of a peak overlooking Tully-Veolan. If one is brave enough to stay atop it on the night of "Hallow-Mass Eve," one can stop the Night-Hag as she passes on her rounds and question her. A lady of the manor, left alone while her husband fought in the Highlands, accepts this challenge and demands to know from the witch if he will return. The song is only a fragment, though Rose comments after singing it, "I think there are some other verses, describing the return of the Baron from the wars, and how the lady was found 'clay-cold upon the groundsill ledge'" (W 113). This possible ending casts questions forward into the novel we are reading: will the current Baron return from his latest traitorous adventure in the Highlands? (He will, but not as "the Baron") Will Rose, figuratively speaking, be left out in the cold waiting for her husband (to be)? (She will do all she can to ensure Edward's safe return, bribing Bean Lean and beseeching the Pretender [cf. W 446–50].) Will the bewitching powers of Flora—Rose's close friend (W 170), but her adversary in this narrative—entrap the hero in the sphere of romance desire? (For Flora has the quasi-supernatural power Wendy Steiner describes in her analysis of romance: she "functions as a visual object with the peculiar combination of the passivity that every object has and the might that the beautiful object has over our senses" [Steiner 48].) Rose's fragmentary ballad prepares us for the secularized psychomachia to come, the struggle over the soul wavering between Flora and Rose, between the anticulture of Jacobite-Jacobin upheaval and the preserved culture of a British Scotland.

The dark lady in this struggle makes her appearance just after that initial banquet at Glennaquoich that so forcefully impressed its visitor with its spectacle of Highland social equilibrium. Like Scott, she is a mediator between two mutually uncomprehending peoples in an asymmetrical relationship of power; unlike him, she is fully identified with one of them, even though she knows how to address the other: she both performs and embodies autoethnographic translation, as he can never hope to do. As such, she represents the possibility of an indigenous, female Highland self-representation whose powers Scott must oppose or contain with his own.[88] "[E]mi-

[86] Wordsworth, *The Poems,* ed. John O. Hayden (New Haven: Yale University Press, 1981), 1.659–60.

[87] Ironically, Alice does later play an important role in the narrative, but it is scarcely the one romance requires: she saves Edward's skin by giving evidence that the young Englishman was ignorant of her father's treacheries (cf. W 447).

[88] One should acknowledge the fact that, raised abroad, Flora has had no childhood acculturation

nent as a translator of Highland poetry," she anticipates Macpherson in recognizing that if the bardic verse of the Gaels were "ever translated into any of the languages of civilized Europe," they could not fail "to produce a deep and general sensation" (W 173). Fergus's bard Mac-Murrough had sung at the banquet "a profusion of Celtic verses, which were received by the audience with all the applause of enthusiasm" (W 165); Flora follows and supercedes him, performing an English version of the same for Edward's private enjoyment. If Fergus makes his most lasting impression in the novel through the painting that "captures" him after his death, Flora makes hers through her rendition of Mac-Murrough's "Battle Song."

Scott's handling of *Flora's* handling of these verses provides a remarkable demonstration of the culture-making principle of translation-without-original in action. The monolingual Mac-Murrough (who, Fergus says, admires Flora's English translation of his lines "upon the same principal [*sic*] that Captain Waverley admires the original—because he does not comprehend them" [W 172]) expresses himself in Gaelic, but Scott's narrator naturally "omits" this purported original as meaningless to his imagined audience. Instead, we read a description of the recital's *effects* that actually serves to heighten the value of the missing poem. As with the novel's concluding ekphrasis—the portrait of Fergus and Edward that we readers cannot actually see—the literal absence of the rendered work makes the space Scott's fiction of Scottish autoethnography aims to fill. "As [the bard] advanced in his declamation," we read,

> his ardour seemed to increase. He had at first spoken with his eyes fixed on the ground; he now cast them around as if beseeching, and anon as if commanding, attention, and his tones rose into wild and impassioned notes, accompanied by appropriate gestures. He seemed to Edward, who attended to him with much interest, to recite many proper names, to lament the dead, to apostrophize the absent, to exhort, and entreat, and animate those who were present. Waverley thought he even discerned his own name, and was convinced his conjecture was right, from the eyes of the company being at that moment turned towards him simultaneously. (W 165)

The uncanny sensation that closes this passage marks the moment when events appear to promise a confirmation of the outsider's fantasy, that moment when the romance of the self-complete alien culture seems to open itself to grant the tourist a prominent role.

Introduced to Flora immediately after the stirring and mystifying experience of listening to Mac-Murrough, Edward is naturally "solicitous to know the meaning of that song which appeared to produce such effect upon the passions of the company," and especially concerned to learn, as he says, "what the Highland bard could find to say to such an unworthy Southron as myself" (W 166, 174). It appears that the poet's address to the English visitor was added extemporaneously onto a more or less regular text, so Flora promises to "engraft the meaning of these [added] lines upon a rude English translation" she has already made, and to meet

---

in Celtic literature or music but takes up the study of it when she comes to live at Glennaquoich, "to fill up the vacant time" (W 169).

Edward in her "Highland Parnassus" hard by Glennaquoich for the purpose of presenting to him what she modestly calls her "imperfect translation" in the very "seat of the Celtic muse" (W 177). Conducted to this spot, Scott's protagonist seems again to be crossing a crucial threshold, here between modern Britain and the Scottish "land of romance" (W 175) where impressions have been so organized as to balance the feelings of danger and safety, difference and expectedness. A "small path . . . ha[s] been rendered easy in many places" so that one may pass up the glen beside a "rapid and furious" brook, "issuing from between precipices, like a maniac from his confinement, all foam and uproar"—a brook that is the very image of Fergus and his atavistic rebellion, diverging from the larger national stream that is "placid, and even sullen in its course" (W 174). Flora, who shows herself to great advantage in this setting, seems to Edward at once completely strange and instantly referable to an established set of conventions: both "a figure of such exquisite and interesting loveliness" that he has "never, even in his wildest dreams, imagined," *and* "like one of those lovely forms which decorate the landscapes of Poussin" or "a fair enchantress of Boiardo or Ariosto, at whose nod the scenery around seemed to have been created" (W 176–77). Having altered nature in this place so as to "add to the grace, without diminishing the romantic wildness of the scene" (W 176), she rivals the Duke of Atholl with his notorious Ossian's Hall. To the accompaniment of a handy waterfall, she commences her reworking of the Gaelic voice.

Mac-Murrough's "Battle Song," it turns out, is an exhortation to the assembly at Glennaquoich to remember the ways of the ancestors and live up to tradition—by taking up arms in the Stuart cause. Flora's version, which, we are told, has "exchanged the measured and monotonous recitative of the bard for a lofty and uncommon Highland air," spans about a page and a half of Scott's text and runs through clan after clan in turn, recalling achievements and portending future glories. The *Waverley* narrator prefaces the excerpt by acknowledging that "the following verses convey but little idea of the feelings with which . . . they were heard by Waverley" (W 180). This untranslatable experience is then suddenly broken off when Fergus's greyhound comes bursting upon the scene, "interrupt[ing] [Flora's] music by his importunate caresses" (W 179). The rather absurd intrusion results in Flora's leaving the bard's particular addresses to both Fergus and Edward unsung. When the latter "expresse[s] his regret at the interruption," the translator replies,

> O you cannot guess how much you have lost! The bard, as in duty bound, has addressed three long stanzas to Vich Ian Vohr of the Banners, enumerating all his great properties, and not forgetting his being a cheerer of the harper and bard,—"a giver of bounteous gifts." Besides, you should have heard a practical admonition to the fair-haired son of the stranger, who lives in the land where the grass is always green—the rider on the shining pampered steed, whose hue is like the raven, and whose neigh is like the scream of the eagle for battle. This valiant horseman is affectionately conjured to remember that his ancestors were distinguished by their loyalty, as well as by their courage.—All this you have lost. (W 180)

Flora's shift to a perfunctory prose paraphrase ruptures the poem's discursive unity just at the point at which the English tourist was about to enter it. Fergus and Edward, the two figures foregrounded in the novel's closing ekphrasis, are here, long in advance, *elided* from the temporal form meant to be taken as a synecdoche of Highland culture—a catalogue of clans arrayed around a common purpose and implying a common nation-making narrative. Flora resumes her verse translation for three concluding stanzas addressed to the Highlanders in general.

"For what is it to be poetic?" Cleanth Brooks asks in "The Heresy of Paraphrase," an important work of modern literary theory dwelling on the question of translatability. His answer is that poeticity consists of a "positive unity," an "achieved harmony" of disparate elements, and that "the relation between all the elements must surely be an organic one." Brooks adds: "We can very properly use paraphrases as pointers and as short-hand references provided we know what we are doing. But it is highly important that we know what we are doing and that we see plainly that paraphrase is not the real core of meaning which constitutes the essence of the poem."[89] The emphatic stricture to "know what we are doing" approximates the tourists' advisory that implicitly accompanies *Waverley,* self-identified as a work of interrupted music and story, of spatialized Scottish time, self-reflexively translating Scotland into being at the same time that it forestalls any reader-tourist's desire to take that translation for an original that no longer exists, if it ever did.

VI

That the man who had so influentially tailored the representation of Scotland for English touristic consumption in his literary works should have taken up the task of organizing welcome festivities for the Royal Visit to Scotland of George IV in 1822 was, suffice it to say, ironically apt. Since well before his coronation in 1820, the Hanoverian had been prone to "Jacobitical" sentiments like Scott's own. Edgar Johnson writes of one

> long and gracious audience [during which] the Regent talked about the Stuarts with Scott. "Ah, Walter, if you had lived in those days," he teased, "you would have been a keen Jacobite." "If I had lived in those times," returned Scott, "I should not have had the honour to be known to your Royal Highness." But in the Regent's queer nature, too, there was a streak of romance which deeply sympathized with the unlucky dynasty that his own family had supplanted on the throne. [Scott later wrote of this audience that] "Baron Adam who was present says the impression upon his mind was a doubt whether the P. R. or I was the greater Jacobite." (Johnson 1.491)

In 1822, George, the perfect embodiment of "imperialist nostalgia," was now King, and in an act meant to symbolize a peaceably united Britain, he was rather

[89] Brooks, *The Well-Wrought Urn: Studies in the Structure of Poetry* (1947; New York: Harcourt Brace Jovanovich, n.d.), 193, 195, 200, 196–97. Cf. Manganaro, "Introduction," on the link between the "'pure aesthetic form' of modernism, represented in literature by the modernist poem or novel" and anthropology's "'society' or 'culture'" (10).

reluctantly becoming the first monarch of his line to set foot in his northern domain.[90] He would not visit the Highlands, would not even leave the vicinity of Edinburgh; the sojourn lasted but two weeks. For Scott, though, the opportunity to render the whole of Scottish culture in one city in a fortnight, for the delectation of one man symbolizing the whole of Britain, presented the translator's and tour-guide's challenge of a lifetime. "In charge of everything" related to the visit, he would choreograph all Scotland into one suave gesture of greeting: "Every trade and craft, every rank, profession, and public body, must play a part in the welcome, from Castle garrison to candlemakers, from peers to porters" (Johnson 2.790). His country's distinctive features, "all those peculiarities which distinguished us as Scotsmen," must come to the fore in this representation: and so we find Scott writing to one of the several clan chieftains whom he would contact, urging him to bring his "tail" of followers to Edinburgh, "so as to look like an island chief, as you are . . . [for] Highlanders are what [the King] will best like to see."[91] In constructing this grand fiction of autoethnography, Scott's "mind glowed with scenes like those he had conjured up in *Waverley:* the triumphal appearance of bonnie Prince Charlie at Holyrood, swirling visions of serried Highlanders, 'all plaided and plumed in their tartan array,' claymores, targes, bagpipes." The resulting extravaganza delighted the sovereign, though it had a few detractors. "Sir Walter Scott," wrote one, "has ridiculously made us appear to be a nation of Highlanders, and the bagpipe and the tartan are the order of the day" (Johnson 2.790, 794). "A great mistake was made by the Stage Managers," Elizabeth Grant recalled, "one that offended all the southron Scots; the King wore at the Levee the Highland dress. I daresay he thought the country all highland, expected no fertile plains, did not know the difference between the Saxon and the Celt."[92]

There is a moment in *Waverley* when the hero, having resolved to join the Pretender, is outfitted according to Fergus Mac-Ivor's precise instructions to his tailor:

> Get a plaid of Mac-Ivor tartan, and sash, . . . and a blue bonnet of the Prince's pattern, at Mr Mouat's in the Crames. My short green coat, with silver lace and silver buttons, will fit him exactly, and I have never worn it. Tell Ensign Maccombich to pick out a handsome target from among mine. The prince has given Mr Waverley broadsword and pistols, I will furnish him with a dirk and purse; add but a pair of low-heeled shoes, and then my dear Edward . . . you will be a complete son of Ivor. (W 300)

The clothes make the man—or do they? For the space of a reading, at least, the tourist's participation in the foreign seems as simply achieved as the dressing for a costume ball, and "Rose" may be translated into "Flora." In 1822, the Hanoverian King, showing himself a tourist who could not only apprehend, as a detached observer, an artful spectacle of Scottish culture, but could act his part in Scotland's

---

[90] Cf. Renato Rosaldo, "Imperialist Nostalgia," in *Culture and Truth: The Remaking of Social Analysis* (Boston: Beacon Press, 1993), 68–87.

[91] Quoted in Trevor-Roper, "The Invention of Tradition," 30.

[92] Elizabeth Grant of Rothiemurchus, *Memoirs of a Highland Lady,* ed. Andrew Tod (1898; Edinburgh: Canongate, 1988), 2.165–66.

story, made his historic entrance to Holyrood House, once the headquarters of Bonnie Prince Charlie, clad in the (inauthentic?) Stuart tartan.

VII

Ian Duncan has recently cautioned us against regarding *Waverley* as a template studiously adhered to in all Scott's subsequent fictions of Scotland: where the first novel "identifies the political movement of Jacobitism with a vanished Scottish cultural past . . . located especially in the Gaelic Highlands" and "aligns the perspective of [its] narrator and [its] reader with the temporality of . . . modernization," the 1817 *Rob Roy,* for example, "undoes both of these rhetorical moves" disconnecting Jacobitism from Celticism and "dissolv[ing] the teleological certainty" of the *Waverley* narrator's viewpoint of "sixty years since."[93] Similarly, as Katie Trumpener suggests, Scott's second novel, *Guy Mannering* (1815), refuses the comforts of the backward, end-of-history glance, exploring instead the "nonsynchronicity of historical development, as characters still held within the distinctly premodern political and cosmological worldview of early modern Scotland are shown to coexist with a Scottish Enlightenment culture" (Trumpener 192).

These readings are among the most prominent of recent attempts to question the "paradigmatic status" (Duncan, Introduction xv) accorded to Scott's inaugural work of fiction by earlier critics, and their arguments are compelling. Yet it was one of *Waverley*'s labors to showcase the processes by which Scott's text marked out spaces of alternate, nonmodern temporality that, even if they were consigned to the historical past and transmuted into aesthetic or cultural objects, remained available, and not *simply* for the untroubled gratification of English or Lowland-"Englished" tourists. Scotland as demonstratively translated into being in *Waverley* is certainly an aesthetic object, a collection of tourist attractions, but it is also a prime example of those "self-enclosed and self-referential enclaves of the antimodern" that Saree Makdisi reads as romanticism's preemptive defenses against a colossally dedifferentiating modern temporality glimpsed on the horizon: it makes a "distortion in the spatio-temporal fabric of the age of modernization."[94] Whatever capacity it possesses to produce any such "distortion" resides entirely *in* its performance of the touristic role nostalgic modern visitors expect it to play. Nowadays we can hardly imagine a more reprehensible figure than the man who *touristifies* his own country: such a figure seems to us the worst kind of traitor; but if it is Scott's evident alacrity in playing the cicerone that makes *Waverley* so deeply discomforting, it is also one of the features that now makes the novel so valuable. In its remorseless acknowledgment of the terms on which difference might be permitted to exist, it forecasts our era, in which governments everywhere devote huge sums to the development of "tourist infrastructure" and domestic pop-

---

[93] Cf. Duncan, introduction to *Rob Roy* (Oxford: Oxford University Press, 1998), xvi; henceforth Duncan, Introduction.

[94] Makdisi, *Romantic Imperialism,* 12–13.

ulations must be persuaded to accept, or at least not openly to reject, the prettified characterizations of their cultures made by those charged with the economically vital task of attracting visitors. Scott did not see a feasible alternative for the erstwhile nations of the United Kingdom than to convert what distinctive traditions and customs they possessed into the bases of a lucrative invisible export trade.

If, therefore, Scott's first novel operates according to a logic through which (as Joseph Valente has admirably put it), "[t]he Hanover ascendancy enshrines the Stuart cause; capitalism defines and aggrandizes feudalism" and "progress alone can engender tradition, the value of which lies precisely in its being not-progress," then the retrospectively manufactured culture, while it does have to answer for the violence that enabled its fabrication and the licenses taken in its construction, may appear to offer benefits difficult to refuse.[95] It may afford the only practicable means for retaining (an admittedly compromised) difference from metropolitan values, or at least for holding those values at a temporary and possibly profitable distance. It may also make available a space imaginatively "outside" of fierce local attachments or sectarian commitments, such as the kinds that furnish material for, and generate the conflicts in, most of Scott's novels on Scotland. For if Scotland after 1801 appeared to face the prospect of becoming nothing or no place distinctive in accommodating itself to English ways and expectations (and in exporting its troublesome surviving Celts), its history was marked, or so Scott thought, by the recurrent threat of devolution into *too many* things and places—too many regional or ideological "locations."

And some of what occupies Scott's attention in the subsequent novels is consistent with *Waverley*'s explorations in this direction. In *Guy Mannering,* for instance, we might find the obverse side of the touristic coin in the tempered and "sentimental" attachment to his own customs exemplified by the Edinburgh lawyer Pleydell, who identifies himself as follows to the visiting English officer Mannering: "I am a member of the suffering and Episcopal church of Scotland," he declares, "the shadow of a shade now, and fortunately so;—but I love to pray where my fathers prayed before me, without thinking the worse of the Presbyterian forms because they do not affect me with the same associations."[96] In his capacity to combine filial loyalty to inculcated traditions with deference toward other, often violently opposed traditions, and even with the consciousness that his own must accept a distinctly minority status, Pleydell, obviously modeled on Scott himself, offers a model *to* Scots, who have all too often shown themselves willing to go to the wall for their several creeds and clans. A Scottish culture might come into being through the influence of such men, the novel appears to suggest, men who can conceive of Scottish differences as elements in a larger Scottish identity. That ability is what Scott attempts to show in the dedication to the first series of *Tales of My Landlord* (used as an epigraph to this chapter), where the history of internecine bloodshed involving, for instance, those "Gentlemen of the North" (the Highland lairds) or those "People of the West" (Cameronians and political radicals) is set

---

[95] Cf. Valente, "Upon the Braes," 275.
[96] *Guy Mannering, or the Astrologer* (1815; London: Soho, 1987), 263.

safely in the past as a precondition for grasping the Scottishness that unifies them all. Scots from all points of the compass cannot really *become* Scottish, but must remain mired in parochial and factional loyalties, until they agree to bury their history and learn to look at themselves as (in T. S. Eliot's memorable phrase) "united by the strife that divide[d] them."[97]

In the later novel *The Heart of Mid-Lothian* (1818), the metaphoric outsideness necessary for a view of Scottish culture is literalized as Jeanie Deans makes her way south to London to beg mercy for her sister, condemned for infanticide. As in the Irish National Tale, Jeanie must "make her case" in London, and en route there she accepts the hospitality, near Durham, of a Mrs. Bickerton, a compatriot. The meeting of the two Scotswomen on the English side of the border triggers this reflection from the novel's narrator:

> The hostess . . . was her countrywoman, and the eagerness with which Scottish people meet, communicate, and, to the extent of their power, assist each other, although it is often objected to us, as a prejudice and narrowness of sentiment, seems, on the contrary, to arise from a most justifiable and honourable feeling of patriotism, combined with a conviction, which, if undeserved, would long since have been confuted by experience, that the habits and principles of the nation are a sort of guarantee for the character of the individual. At any rate, if the extensive influence of this national partiality be considered as an additional tie, binding man to man, and calling forth the good offices of such as can render them to the countryman who happens to need them, we think it must be found to exceed, as an active and efficient motive to generosity, that more impartial and wider principle of general benevolence, which we have sometimes seen pleaded as an excuse for assisting no individual whatever.[98]

In this manifestation of the "anywhere's nowhere" logic I trace throughout this book, the bond between two Scottish nationals defines by opposition an abstract humanist "principle of general benevolence" that too often yields no practical benefit at all. (Dickens's critique of "telescopic philanthropy" proceeds along these lines in the midcentury *Bleak House,* which I investigate in the next chapter.) The episode in Scott shows a benevolent pan-Scottish identification and allegiance being generated from a position *extraterritorial to* Scotland and in the land of the English overlords. That land, Mrs. Bickerton warns Jeanie, is "a more civilized, that is to say, a more roguish country than the north" (HM 288), so a Scot must be alert for highwaymen.

Scott's heroic avatar in the story-space of *The Heart of Mid-Lothian* is (controversially enough) the Duke of Argyle, who uses his connections in London to get Jeanie Deans the audience with Queen Caroline that is, at least in this fictionalized account, the only route to a pardon for her sister. Argyle is a kind of apotheosis of the Waverley Novelist, since, as a holder of both Scottish *and* English dukedoms, he is perfectly situated to serve as an efficacious intercessor for all Scots with a

---

[97] Eliot, "Little Gidding," from *Four Quartets,* in *The Complete Poems and Plays, 1909–1950* (New York: Harcourt, Brace and Company, 1958), 143.

[98] *The Heart of Mid-Lothian* (1818; Harmondsworth: Penguin, 1994), 287–88; henceforth HM.

grievance: not just a "representative" Scottish peer adorning the English House of Lords, but a man capable of *making* effectual representation on behalf of his entire people. His aid to Jeanie prompts the narrator to remark,

> [p]erhaps one ought to be actually a Scotchman to conceive how ardently, under all distinctions of rank and situation, they feel their mutual connexion with each other as natives of the same country. There are, I believe, more associations common to the inhabitants of a rude and wild, than of a well cultivated and fertile country; their ancestors have more seldom changed their place of residence; their mutual recollection of remarkable objects is more accurate; the high and the low are more interested in each other's welfare; the feelings of kindred and relationship are more widely extended, and, in a word, the bonds of patriotic affection, always honourable even when a little too exclusively strained, have more influence on men's feelings and actions. (HM 393)

As an account of the true state of affairs obtaining among Scotsmen at any period Walter Scott took as the subject of a historical novel, the above is no more or less utopian than is the characterization of the Duke of Argyle himself.

With the death of Jeanie Deans's father, Davie, the novel's leading exemplar of self-righteous and self-destructive Scottish factionalism, the way is supposed to be opened for leaders like Argyle, accommodationist-realists capable of "[s]oaring above petty distinctions of faction" (HM 360). This Scotsman of the future acts during a turbulent epoch as if endowed with the retrospective wisdom of a Scott narrator—he seems on both sides of the divide between discourse- and story-spaces—implying how much Scotland could have been spared if the posthistorical perspective had only been permitted to guide the enactment of Scottish history. He embodies that "anticipation of retrospection" I have referred to above, supremely valuable at a time when

> Scotland, his native country, stood . . . in a very precarious and doubtful situation. She was indeed united to England, but the cement had not had time to acquire consistence. The irritation of ancient wrongs still subsisted, and betwixt the fretful jealousy of the Scottish, and the supercilious disdain of the English, quarrels repeatedly occurred, in the course of which the national league, so important to the safety of both, was in the utmost danger of being dissolved. Scotland had, besides, the disadvantage of being divided into intestine factions, which hated each other bitterly, and waited but a signal to break forth into action. (HM 360)

By Scott's day, the cement of union seemed almost completely set—a dilemma complementary to the one Argyle faced, which found *its* nineteenth-century manifestation in the newly annexed condition of Ireland. Against the "consistence" of Scotland and England—the unilateral translation of Scotland into English form— that he dreaded as imminent, Scott devoted himself to shoring up the fiction of a self-consistent Scottishness, even if that undertaking meant setting his country in the cement of cultural stereotypes, and even if it could sometimes make his authorial persona resemble not so much the admirable Argyle as his retainer, Duncan of Knockdunder—a man

whose pleasure it was to unite in his own person the dress of the Highlands and Lowlands, wearing on his head a black tie-wig, surmounted by a fierce cocked-hat, deeply
guarded with gold lace, while the rest of his dress consisted of the plaid and philabeg.
Duncan superintended a district which was partly Highland, partly Lowland, and therefore might be supposed to combine their national habits, in order to show his impartiality to Trojan or Tyrian. The incongruity, however, had a whimsical and ludicrous effect,
as it made his head and body look as if belonging to different individuals; or, as some
one had said who had seen the executions of the insurgent prisoners in 1715, it seemed
as if some Jacobite enchanter, having recalled the sufferers to life, had clapped, in his
haste, an Englishman's head on a Highlander's body (HM 447).

CHAPTER FIVE

Anywhere's Nowhere: *Bleak House* as Metropolitan Autoethnography

The tendency of modern enquiry is more and more towards the conclusion that if law is anywhere, it is everywhere.
    —E. B. Tylor[1]

But if the field is everywhere, it is nowhere.
    —James Clifford[2]

"Where would you wish to go?" she asked.

"Anywhere, my dear," I replied.

"Anywhere's nowhere," said Miss Jellyby, stopping perversely.

"Let us go somewhere at any rate," said I.
    —Charles Dickens, *Bleak House*[3]

I

To TURN from Walter Scott and *Waverley* in 1814 to Charles Dickens and *Bleak House* in 1852 is to move from the early nineteenth century's most celebrated novelist at the United Kingdom's margin to the middle nineteenth century's most celebrated novelist at its absolute center, and to confront the implications of making that move for any account of the prehistory of *culture* and the (auto)ethnographic imagination. If Scott's fiction needs to be read as engaging with and self-consciously revising leading elements of the Irish National Tale, Dickens's unfolds alongside and seeks to outdo the so-called Social-Problem Novel of the 1840s, that bourgeois English mode stimulated by class polarization to attempt both a sympathetic analysis of working-class circumstances and a variety of imaginary solutions for the perceived breakdown of communication and commitment across class boundaries. As my brief discussion of Gaskell's *Mary Barton* and Kingsley's *Alton Locke* in chapter 3 suggests, such works tended to reflect on their autoethnographic

---

[1] Tylor, *Primitive Culture: Researches into the Development of Mythology, Philosophy, Religion, Language, Art and Custom* (1871; Boston: Estes & Lauriat, 1874), 1.24; henceforth Tylor.

[2] Clifford, *Routes: Travel and Translation in the Late Twentieth Century* (Cambridge, Mass.: Harvard University Press, 1997), 89.

[3] *Bleak House* (Oxford: Oxford University Press, 1996), 59; henceforth BH.

labors as they enacted them, questioning their procedures and perhaps also seeking to exorcise their self-suspected liabilities by depicting characters as engaged in boundary-crossing efforts both positively and negatively reminiscent of the narrators' own. In these works, the bourgeois novelist's ethnographic study of the manifestly alien domain of the workers had to be translatable into an *autoethnographic* study recognizing that domain as connected to and identified with the writer's and readers' own, a part and variety of one national whole.

No author, however, could approach Dickens of London in construing the novelist's task as rivaling that of the state in asserting a centralized and comprehensive mastery of the British way of life. By the time he came to write the mid-career masterpiece *Bleak House,* Dickens had already represented and aggrandized his own claims to comprehensive social knowledge in a series of memorable figures that includes the ghosts of *A Christmas Carol,* the "Good Spirit" who soars above the rooftops in *Dombey and Son,* and the "Shadow" presented as the presiding spirit of *Household Words*—this last a creature capable, Dickens wrote, of "go[ing] into any place, by sunlight, moonlight, starlight, firelight, candlelight and [of being] in all homes, and all nooks and corners, and [of being] supposed to be cognisant of everything and go[ing] everywhere, without the least difficulty."[4] Animating these and other objectifications of Dickens's narrative authority was something like that "lust to be a viewpoint and nothing more" that Michel de Certeau described in his essay "Walking in the City": all employ the spatial metaphors of getting outside or above the street-level of everyday practice.[5] But in Dickens, we must recognize this urge in a more particular way, as aiming for a view of a social field that comes *into* view as "one's own culture" through the very act of disengaging from it.[6] For him, "[t]he very condition of cultural knowledge is the alienation of the subject."[7] Audrey Jaffe's helpful identification of a "fantasy of [an] unlimited knowledge and mobility" in Dickens's fiction thus requires qualification, just as de Certeau's account does, for when the Dickensian narrator takes wing above the land of his compatriots, he does not fly off into some zone of permanently *dislocated* theory, some nonplace of relationless exteriority to all cultures or local knowledges whatever; on the contrary, he "maps" himself by his assertion of distance from the social field he lays bare.[8] In terms thematized with

---

[4] John Forster, *Life of Charles Dickens* (London: Chapman & Hall, 1872), 2.419–20.

[5] Michel de Certeau, *The Practice of Everyday Life,* trans. Steven Rendall (Berkeley: University of California Press, 1984), 92.

[6] Cf. M. M. Bakhtin, "Forms of Time and Chronotope in the Novel," in *The Dialogic Imagination: Four Essays,* ed. Michael Holquist, trans. Caryl Emerson and Holquist (Austin: University of Texas Press, 1981), on the carnival's rogue, clown, and fool personae as affording novelists the stance "of a man who is in life, but not of it, life's perpetual spy and reflector" (161).

[7] Homi Bhabha, "DissemiNation: Time, Narrative, and the Margins of the Modern Nation," in Bhabha, ed., *Nation and Narration* (London: Routledge, 1990), 301.

[8] Jaffe, *Vanishing Points: Dickens, Narrative, and the Subject of Omniscience* (Berkeley: University of California Press, 1991), 148. As Jaffe herself puts it, the double narrative of *Bleak House,* "constituting as it does a boundary omniscience cannot cross, raises a problem for the very notion of omniscience," for "what does it mean for omniscience to have a place?" (128).

special emphasis in *Bleak House,* the Dickensian narrator is very demonstratively a "nobody" who insists upon being recognized as one of us. The work's bold and perennially fascinating technique of double narration makes this celebrated (but never sufficiently celebrated) classic of Victorian fiction an extreme case in both the history of the novel and the prehistory of ethnographic representation, a supreme metafiction that burlesques elements of its form while implicitly defining that form as a leading variety of metropolitan autoethnography.

As I indicated in the opening chapters of this book, the term *metropolitan auto-ethnography* designates a species of romance devoted to the production, narratable as the *recovery,* of an Anglocentric cultural identity during a phase of intensive imperial, industrial, and commercial expansion. At a time when the designation *English* or *British* might have seemed drained of specific cultural content in becoming synonymous with imperial statehood, metropolitan autoethnography imagines into being a national culture represented as if it might be autarchic, autotelic, and, above all, *locatable.* If, as Simon Gikandi has written, "[t]o understand England in the nineteenth century, one must travel to the extremities of empire" and "explore . . . geographies that seem to be most removed from the imperial center," autoethnographic fiction responds by proliferating a series of discontinuous and seemingly irreconcilable spaces *within* Britain and setting in motion a narrative charged not only with the task of demonstratively connecting them but, more importantly, with that of *isolating* the single moral geography in which all these connections obtain against an expansive backdrop of other possible connections that must be disavowed if the former connections are to have any weight.[9] It is in this spirit that, surveying the horrors of the desperate slum known as Tom-all-Alone's, Dickens's third-person narrator in *Bleak House* says, "in truth it might be better for the national glory even that the sun should sometimes set upon the British dominions, than that it should ever rise upon so vile a wonder as Tom" (BH 657).

Rehearsing a deliberate, though conflicted, turning away from the boundariless world in which England's fortunes were so much embroiled, *Bleak House* offers its *iconic* space as an analogue for the space of the culture that might unify and demarcate the nation. In doing so, it exemplifies the way in which standards of textual and social integrity came to invoke and stand for each other in English fiction around the middle of the nineteenth century. No novel performs what Fredric Jameson has called the "'strategies of containment' whereby [novels] are able to project the illusion that their readings [of their own cultures] are somehow complete and self-sufficient" more studiously and self-reflexively than does *Bleak House.*[10] The work's famous self-referentiality has everything to do with its protoethnographic labor to redress the dissociative and evacuated character of imperial Britishness by evoking the culture of the the British as a domain "in which

---

[9] Gikandi, *Maps of Englishness: Writing Identity in the Culture of Colonialism* (New York: Columbia University Press, 1996), 89.

[10] Fredric Jameson, *The Political Unconscious: Narrative as a Socially Symbolic Act* (Ithaca: Cornell University Press, 1981), 10.

everything is intimately connected with everything else, . . . a vast interlocking system in which any action or change in one place will have a corresponding and reciprocal effect on every other place."[11]

But of course, as E. R. Leach trenchantly observed, the thesis "that cultures are functionally integrated . . . express[es] a Utopian state of affairs."[12] As perhaps *the* utopian idea of modern times, the notion of a social domain so densely interwoven as to both require and literalize hyperbole in describing it no sooner becomes operational than it induces a reaction: for what modern mind could ever find rest in this domain of its fantasy, where it would be "fettered at every turn by chains of custom," "bound by customs regulating the conduct of daily life in all its details"?[13] As Dickens appears to recognize, insofar as the fiction of cultural totality invokes a pervasive, inescapable social "law" that leaves nothing, not even the most seemingly "spontaneous and motiveless phenomena . . . untouched on the score of remoteness or complexity, of minuteness or triviality" (Tylor 1.24), the seeking of one's *own* culture must become an enterprise ambivalent to the core. Rigorous application of the culture idea to our own lives, as T. S. Eliot perceived in his 1947 *Notes toward the Definition of Culture,* gives "an importance to our most trivial pursuits, to the occupation of our every minute, which we cannot long contemplate without the horror of nightmare."[14] And so it is that, at the same time that Dickens's metanovel *Bleak House* may be seen to foreshadow the totality of culture, it may also be detected in the act of "chart[ing] the irregularity and accident and excess and privation that . . . unravel the order of culture."[15] Animated by that "desire to unmake as well as to make a whole" which James Clifford has discerned in Malinowski's founding ethnographic texts,[16] Dickens's great work of 1851–53 stimulates the urge for a national culture and frustrates it in turn.

Postcolonial criticism has tended to reserve the ambivalence I describe here to the "communities hitherto excluded from the major forms of cultural representation" and to regard the privileged practitioners of those major forms (which include the nineteenth-century novel) as wholeheartedly committed to propagating the myths and geographies of dominance.[17] Stuart Hall, for example, has argued

---

[11] J. Hillis Miller, *Charles Dickens: The World of His Novels* (1958; Cambridge, Mass.: Harvard University Press, 1965), 206.

[12] Leach, "The Epistemological Background to Malinowski's Empiricism," in Raymond Firth, ed., *Man and Culture: An Evaluation of the Work of Bronislaw Malinowski* (New York: Humanities Press, 1957), 121.

[13] "Fettered": E. B. Tylor, *Anthropology: An Introduction to the Study of Man and Civilization* (New York and London: Appleton, 1923), 409. "Bound": Franz Boas, *The Mind of Primitive Man* (revised ed. New York: Macmillan, 1938), 234.

[14] Eliot, in *Christianity and Culture* (New York: Harcourt Brace Jovanovich, 1949), 104.

[15] Ian Duncan, *Modern Romance and Transformation of the Novel* (Cambridge: Cambridge University Press, 1992), 6.

[16] Clifford, "On Ethnographic Self-Fashioning: Conrad and Malinowski," in *The Predicament of Culture* (Cambridge, Mass.: Harvard University Press, 1988), 104.

[17] Stuart Hall, "The Local and the Global: Globalization and Ethnicity," in Anthony D. King, ed., *Culture, Globalization, and the World-System: Contemporary Conditions for the Representation of Identity* (Minneapolis: University of Minnesota Press, 1997), 34; henceforth Hall.

that, for the newly vocal communities of twentieth-century globalization, the rediscovery of ethnicity and culture, of "the necessary place or space from which people speak," constituted an essential authorizing moment; but he went on to ask whether these newly empowered marginal voices had "to be *trapped* in the place from which they begin to speak" (Hall 36; emphasis added). *Two* voices, he insisted, arise from this one historical position: one that finds sustenance in local identities long denied expression, another impatient with traditional modes and with all pressure to speak as *nothing but* the representative of one's group. When Hall turned back to the nineteenth century and turned to the center, he could detect no comparable bifurcation, seeing only a colossally self-assured and monolithic Englishness that mistook its local viewpoint for "sight itself" and forgot that it *was* an ethnicity or culture—a "place"—like any other (Hall 22). The contrast was tendentious in the extreme, precisely reversing classic cultural anthropology's bad habit of attributing complexity to Western societies and unanimity to the tribal or traditional ones it studied. Yet a century and a half ago, in the stylistic experiment that has been called (and with much justice) "the most audacious and significant act of the novelistic imagination in England in the nineteenth century,"[18] Dickens put just such a pair of voices as Hall discerned in play against each other, when he divided the narrative of *Bleak House* between a faceless, masculine third-person voice, and the aggressively self-effacing first-person voice of Esther Summerson.

In chapter 3 I surveyed some leading historical factors that might have encouraged English fiction to take an autoethnographic turn around the middle of the nineteenth century. If there was one immediate cause, one spark that touched the tinder of all those many factors into the brilliant flame of *Bleak House,* it had to have been the inescapable British event of 1851, the grandiose "Great Exhibition of the Works of Industry of All Nations," which ran in Hyde Park for six months preceding Dickens's composition of the novel, and which consecrated, if it did not exactly inaugurate, a new era of global capitalism. Stuart Hall's characterization of contemporary globalization as a structure in which capital "works in and through the specificity of different cultures" (Hall 29) finds an uncanny match in Prince Albert's claim that the Crystal Palace exhibition demonstrated a "Unity of Mankind" that would not "break[] down the limits, and level[] the peculiar characteristics of the different nations of the Earth," but would be "the result and product of those very national varieties and antagonistic qualities."[19] The Crystal Palace gave Dickens the stimulus to produce a work in many respects more determinedly exclusive in its national focus than any of his others, and markedly opposed in tendency to his next major work, *Little Dorrit,* in which the advantages of certain cosmopolitan perspectives are inquired into and recommended.[20] In

---

[18] Steven Marcus, "Literature and Social Theory: Starting in with George Eliot," in *Representations: Essays on Literature and Society* (New York: Random House, 1975), 194.

[19] Quoted in John R. Davis, *The Great Exhibition* (London: Sutton, 1999), 67.

[20] Cf. Amanda Anderson's reading of *Little Dorrit* in *The Powers of Distance: Cosmopolitanism and the Cultivation of Detachment* (Princeton: Princeton University Press, 2001), chap. 2. Dickens's career ends with the return to hyperanxious nationalism in *The Mystery of Edwin Drood.*

Bleak House, the rigorous limitation of viewpoint and the interplay of voices enabled Dickens to furnish an incomparably thick description of contemporary British *anticulture,* designed both to stimulate utopian imaginings of a genuine national culture and to counterbalance the vision of Britain on offer in the Great Exhibition. Celebrating the "vast comprehensiveness" of the Crystal Palace exhibition, John Tallis wrote in his influential guidebook that

> Nothing was too stupendous, too rare, too costly for [the Exhibition's] acquisition; nothing too minute or apparently too insignificant for its consideration. Every possible invention and appliance for the service of man found a place within its embracing limits; every realization of human genius, every effort of human industry might be contemplated therein, from the most consummate elaboration of the profoundest intellect, to the simplest contrivance of uneducated thought.[21]

In *Bleak House,* Dickens rivaled such orgies of hyperbole by imagining a social domain, and its representing text, in which not even the most seemingly "spontaneous and motiveless phenomena" and the most apparently remote or minute or trivial of details might remain "untouched" by a ubiquitous and disastrous significance.

The anticulture of *Bleak House* is organized around a great nightmare likeness of ethnographic culture: the Court of Chancery and its crowning glory, the everlasting case of Jarndyce and Jarndyce. In these, Malinowski's ethnographic rule that "nationality means unity in culture" is scrupulously observed, in darkly parodic form.[22] At once enacting and symbolizing the collective life, the Chancery proceedings resemble some grand travesty of the rituals later studied by anthropologists as identifying features of the tribes that practice them. Chancery is precisely the kind of institution that "embraces a vast complex of activities, interconnected, and playing into one another, so as to form one organic whole": Durkheim's account of ritual as "above all the means by which the social group is periodically reaffirmed" could not find a better example.[23] Sir Leicester Dedlock esteems the court as "a slow, expensive, British, constitutional kind of thing" (BH 22); the solicitor Conversation Kenge celebrates the matter of Jarndyce and Jarndyce as "a cause that could not exist, out of this free and great country" (BH 29). The court itself draws into its web not only people from in or near the metropolis but those from "every shire." To illustrate the point, the novel gives us Mr. Gridley, "the man from Shropshire," no less blighted in his fortunes on the rural periphery of England than are the inhabitants of Tom-all-Alone's in the heart of the City.[24] The noxious fog of *Bleak House,* though called by the cockney Mr.

---

[21] Tallis, quoted in Jeffrey A. Auerbach, *The Great Exhibition of 1851: A Nation on Display* (New Haven: Yale University Press, 1999), 91.

[22] Malinowski, *A Scientific Theory of Culture and Other Essays* (Chapel Hill: University of North Carolina Press, 1944), 61.

[23] "Embraces": Malinowski, *Argonauts of the Western Pacific* (1922; Prospect Heights, Ill.: Waveland Press, 1984), 83–84; henceforth *Argonauts.* "Above all": Emile Durkheim, *The Elementary Forms of the Religious Life* (1915), trans. Joseph Ward Swain (New York: Free Press, 1965), 389.

[24] Gridley also brings into the novel the values associated with the humble yeoman farmer ideal-

Guppy "a London particular" (BH 37), is plainly *not* particular to London alone: center and source of the miasma, the Chancery Court "has its decaying houses and its blighted lands in every shire[,] . . . its worn-out lunatic in every madhouse, and its dead in every churchyard" (BH 13).

Like those of any central, definitive cultural institution, the operations of Chancery appear, from the outset of the novel, to have been always already in process, obeying a momentum of their own and compelling participation. Chancery is the envelope of custom within which the acculturated Briton comes to consciousness. "The little plaintiff or defendant, who was promised a new rocking-horse when Jarndyce and Jarndyce should be settled," we read, "has grown up, possessed himself of a real horse, and trotted away into the other world" (BH 14). As court of probate, Chancery determines degrees of relationship among contending claimants, functioning as guarantor of kinship structure and sorting out that structure's differential logic of personal identities. Participation in Chancery is just as little a matter of choice as is the identity of one's parents. John Jarndyce sums up his account of his family's entanglement in the court by saying, "And thus, through years and years, and lives and lives, everything goes on, constantly beginning all over again, and nothing ever ends. And we can't get out of the suit on any terms, for we are made parties to it, and *must be* parties to it, like it or not" (BH 109). Malinowski's Trobrianders put it more tersely: "Once in the Kula," they declare, "always in the Kula" (*Argonauts* 83). When *Bleak House* announces that "[t]he one great principle of the English law is, to make business for itself," that "[t]here is no other principle distinctly, certainly, and consistently maintained through all its narrow turnings," and that, "[v]iewed by this light it becomes a coherent scheme, and not the monstrous maze the laity are apt to think it" (BH 573), it provides a distorted mirror-image of later ethnography's vision of culture as self-reflexive whole and perpetual-motion machine. As J.G.A. Pocock put this simple and unremarkable ethnographic fact, "all societies are organized . . . to ensure their own continuity."[25]

II

Every reader of *Bleak House* will remember the scene in which, on her tour of Tom-all-Alone's, the shrouded Lady Dedlock gazes in horror through the gates of the decrepit graveyard where her lover lies buried. The particulars of the conversation she has with the miserable street-sweeper who is her reluctant guide may not come so readily to mind. Only Dickens could have concocted the mix of pathos and absurdity that makes up their exchange:

---

ized in Wordsworth's "Michael" and elsewhere as the very exemplum of British liberty and stability (see BH 229–31).

[25] "The Origins of the Study of the Past: A Comparative Approach," *Comparative Studies in Society and History* 4 (1962), 211.

"Is this place of abomination, consecrated ground?"

"I don't know nothink of consequential ground," says Jo, still staring.

"Is it blessed?"

"WHICH?" says Jo, in the last degree amazed.

"Is it blessed?"

"I'm blessed if I know," says Jo, staring more than ever. . . . (BH 243)

This bit of dialogue is one of those many passages in *Bleak House* in which narrative context appears to drop away for a moment and the language radiates outward to offer large implications about the novel we are reading. Jo mistakenly substitutes "consequential" for "consecrated" because he does not know what "consecrated" means, has perhaps never heard the word (though it is hard to imagine him having heard "consequential," either), and he is surely unfamiliar with the idea of something's being sacred or blessed. (A later passage considers that "the great Cross on the summit of St. Paul's Cathedral" might represent, for Jo, only "the crowning confusion of the great, confused, city," all of it devoid of meaningful or sympathetic associations for the homeless child [BH 290].) The substitution is an ironically apt one, for consecrated things are in a sense those considered especially consequential to God. What Jo says to Lady Dedlock amounts to, "I don't know of any place that matters," or even "no place where I am could matter." Someone who says he knows nothing of any consequential ground recognizes *his own* inconsequentiality to the world in which he lives. Yet in its handling of such forgotten people as Jo and the self-styled, opium-numbed "Nemo," *Bleak House* implies something like the lesson of Matthew 10:29–31, those verses assuring us of a Father in Heaven who numbers the very hairs of our heads and lets not even a sparrow fall without his willing it: the "Our Father" to whom, later on, the heroic doctor Allan Woodcourt instructs Jo to direct his last words (BH 677). The novel suggests, in other words, that it is impossible to be exiled from the sphere of things consequential to God, since nothing anywhere is beneath God's notice or beyond his care, and important characters in the novel seem to set examples of how to imitate the divine Rememberer. John Jarndyce is constantly gathering up human strays into his protection, among them the little girl called Esther Summerson; Esther herself attempts, though too late, to include Jo among that circle of protégés on whom she bestows her quiet acts of kindness, exactly the sort of unassuming yet *consequential* assistance Jo needed but never received from the self-satisfied preachers or "charity workers," the Mr. Chadbands or Mrs. Pardiggles, of the Dickens world.

The Dickens *world:* much of the most influential criticism on this novelist (from *The Dickens World* to *Charles Dickens: The World of his Novels* and beyond) has enabled readers to elide the phenomenological and the geographical senses of the term. Yet the argument of *Bleak House* is by no means simply or consistently or even more than occasionally the one I have characterized in the preceding paragraph. Whereas the Gospel of Matthew and nineteenth-century natural theology concur in envisioning a perspective from which everything everywhere, however trivial and base it appears, argues for design and invokes an all-encompassing view of the universe in which nothing is "lost" or overlooked, what seems to be going on in *Bleak House* is the appropriation of such comforting cosmologies for an implicit argument about the specific national community and its locale.[26] This transformation is an element in the novel's general repudiation of "the global" as an unmappably vague and destructive realm, lacking in coordinates and subject to the pitiless universal law of entropy (signaled on the novel's first page through Dickens's much-noted reference to "the death of the sun" [BH 11]). Opposed to this vast anomic landscape stands the demarcated space of the single nation, where identities both individual and collective may find their ground and sustenance. When it is not genuflecting toward the omniscient and omnibenevolent God of Christianity—which is to say, most of the time—*Bleak House* attempts to demonstrate that it is only and specifically *here,* within the domain of British culture, that nothing might fail to matter and there might be no *in*consequential ground.

That *Bleak House* performs an "anatomy of society," that it exercises the "sociological imagination" or provides "a model in little of English society"[27]—claims of this kind were established between the 1950s and 1970s as the very staples of criticism on this novel and, indeed, on much nineteenth-century fiction; they now appear to lack a forceful enough appreciation of the energies of *limitation* that structure Dickens's great metafiction. Readings that demonstrate the protosociological labors of *Bleak House* have shared the work's commitment to a movement of thought that stretches outward from particular elements (individual characters, locations, classes) and shows their unsuspected broader interconnection. They aim to answer the text's famously provocative questions, "What connexion can there be, between the [Dedlocks'] place in Lincolnshire, the house in town, the Mercury in powder, and the whereabouts of Jo the outlaw with the broom . . . ? What connexion can there have been between many people in the innumerable histories of the world, who, from opposite sides of great gulfs, have, nevertheless, been very curiously brought together!" (BH 235). In Marxist readings, the critic imitates or renders explicit Dickens's own efforts at connection in order to redress the reification of social reality, its devolution from a totality of relationships into an aggregate of inert things. Foucauldian treatments (D. A. Miller's is the best known[28]) exhibit the same widening tendency, with "disciplinarity" now the surprisingly expanding element that refuses confinement to its assigned localities (law courts, police stations, and so forth), instead pervading every corner of social life, down to the most seemingly private or individual ones. The centrifugal rigor of such read-

---

[26] Cf. Mary Poovey, *Making a Social Body: British Cultural Formation, 1830–1864* (Chicago: University of Chicago Press, 1995), on the uneven process by which vocabularies and protocols of reasoning developed in certain conceptual domains (such as the theological) are borrowed for use in emergent ones (such as "the social").

[27] "Anatomy of society": Edgar Johnson, *Charles Dickens: His Tragedy and Triumph* (New York: Simon & Schuster, 1952), 2.762–82; "sociological imagination": Barbara Hardy, *Dickens: The Later Novels* (London: Longmans, Green & Co., 1968), 14; "a model in little of . . . society": J. Hillis Miller, Introduction to Dickens, *Bleak House* (Harmondsworth: Penguin, 1971), 11.

[28] D. A. Miller, *The Novel and the Police* (Berkeley: University of California Press, 1988), chap. 3; henceforth D. A. Miller.

ings has led them to underplay *Bleak House*'s other, offsetting impulse to close off and secure the boundaries of the widening field, to deny its equivalence to "the world." Such everything-is-connected arguments have gone only half the distance necessary to comprehend a novel in whose form the trope of the unforeseen-but-now-revealed connection is matched by and even grounded in a trope of *dissociation* or disconnection. Another way to put this would be to say that the degree to which we are to be impressed by the novel's demonstration of more-than-local connections is contingent upon the degree to which we accept the tacit claim that transcendence of the local can be productive or meaningful *only* as actualization and delimitation of the national. So I want to consider not just how the novel occupies itself with "the social world," the "knowable community," or the "imagination of society,"[29] but how and why a rigorously *exclusive* evocation of Britain in particular, involving evocations of a wider world apparently for the sole purpose of demonstratively turning away from it, was a gesture that appealed to Dickens in 1851–53.

Writing in the aftermath of the "Papal Aggression" controversy that stimulated much defensive feeling and considerable jingoism among British Protestants, Dickens in *Bleak House* makes what Jo knows "nothink" about not so much the solacing doctrines of a globally applicable Christianity as the symbolic system constituting his particular nation's culture: what Jo fails to understand when he looks up at St. Paul's is not simply the Christian cross, but much more forcefully the sign of English self-determination in matters of religion. And Jo's inability to read, to recognize or ascribe significance to, such indicators of national specificity is clearly the result of his culture's failure to ascribe significance to *him,* or to inscribe it *in* him. "[U]nfamiliar with the shapes and in utter darkness as to the meaning, of those mysterious symbols" that mark his social milieu (BH 236), Jo is just as little known to or recognized by the institutions that govern and master those symbols. The clearest indication of this unrecognized condition comes when the Coroner investigating the death of Nemo refuses to hear Jo's testimony, in spite of the fact that the boy possesses privileged knowledge of the dead law-copyist: this is denial of recognition in the legal sense, justified by the Coroner because Jo is found to be ignorant of such basics of cultural literacy as his family name and the elementary principles of Christianity. As the self-declared occupant of inconsequential ground, Jo sees himself as he has been seen, and much more powerfully *not* seen, by the anticulture that bred him.

But Jo *moves:* this embodied principle of the-place-that-does-not-matter will not remain within its boundaries and eventually threatens all Britain with the same erasure of meaning and value that he has undergone. So, too, will the banished Nemo, though buried in obscurity, become "an avenging ghost" haunting his survivors (BH 165); just so will the whole of Tom-all-Alone's, that district "avoided by all decent people" (BH 235), reveal itself to be balefully consequential ground

---

[29] See, respectively: Lionel Trilling, "Manners, Morals, and the Novel," in *The Liberal Imagination* (New York: Scribner's, 1950), 212; Raymond Williams, *The Country and the City* (New York: Oxford University Press, 1973), chap. 16; Marcus, *Representations,* xiii–xvii.

after all. "There is not a drop of Tom's corrupted blood," the third-person narrator assures us,

> but propagates infection and contagion somewhere. It shall pollute, this very night, the choice stream (in which chemists on analysis would find the genuine nobility) of a Norman house, and his Grace shall not be able to say Nay to the infamous alliance. There is not an atom of Tom's slime, not a cubic inch of any pestilential gas in which he lives, not one obscenity or brutality of his committing, but shall work its retribution, through every order of society, up to the proudest of the proud, and to the highest of the high. (BH 654–57)

All the emphasis here is given to expanding the scope of the neglected place's influence, as the disregarded potency of the slum overrides distinctions once taken as crucial and determining but now shown to be illusory or merely secondary in relation to an undeniable unity. "[H]is Grace shall not be able to say Nay to the alliance," because the affliction can go "anywhere," can reach all levels. Those who people the so-called "world of fashion" (atop which Lady Dedlock sits enthroned) will find themselves yoked to their inferiors, and not just by the disease that proves their kinship, but by the activities of the narrator as well, who travels "as the crow flies" (BH 17) from scene to supposedly separate scene within the whole. A similar effect is achieved when the parodic double of the Lord Chancellor, the sinister Krook, inexplicably detonates in the middle of the novel and releases his criminal essence to the circulating air, to soil "everyone's" hands just as we see it soiling the hands of Mr. Guppy, the avid apprentice of Chancery law (BH 475–76).

And yet no matter how insubstantial and airborne this expanding and accusing cloud may be—blown by that "East Wind" that sends John Jarndyce skulking to his Growlery—it will halt at the shore, remaining a *British* infection: *Bleak House* treats the island-nation as an airtight container, like the street where Mrs. Jellyby lives, "an oblong cistern to hold the fog" (BH 46). Each particle of moral poison will carom off the inside surface of the outer boundary of the nation, to do its dreadful work throughout the interior. Hyperbole in describing the degree of interconnectedness in such an arrangement—every drop, every atom, every cubic inch— seems both rhetorically necessary and conceptually impossible. It cannot be safe to say something or someone does not matter or is not connected, if in a culture, as Thomas Carlyle famously wrote of history, "each atom is 'chained' and complected with all."[30] In such an arrangement, "if the relations between one [part] and another . . . are not beneficent, they will be harmful."[31]

Grasping the British anticulture as one unified landscape of consequential ground, Dickens presents the unit of the nation as the largest "place" there is, demarcating national place-hood not just against the functionally equivalent place-hood of another sovereign nation but, more fundamentally, against the backdrop of a world not credited with the same degree of "place-ness." Marc Augé's char-

---

[30] Carlyle, "On History," in Alan Shelstone, ed., *Selected Writings* (Harmondsworth: Penguin, 1980), 55.

[31] J. Hillis Miller, *Charles Dickens: The World of his Novels,* 206.

acterization of anthropological place (discussed in chapter 2) gets closer to Dickens's geographical imagination in *Bleak House* than do most accounts of the "contingent and relational" nature of national identity, envisioning as these latter do a more or less symmetrical opposition between "the collective self and its implicit negation, the other."[32] Augé and Dickens have in mind the discontinuous geography, the asymmetrical relation of place and surrounding space that belong to the anthropological "insider" and flow from a way of living "as if there were no humanity worthy of the name" except where that insider's culture is located.[33] Dickens handles the nation in *Bleak House* as the largest organizable space in an entropic universe, the sole guarantor of meaning and value, the most capacious and significant "somewhere" from which to withstand encroachment by the "anywhere" that is nowhere. Were we to require a name for these place-less, unrepresentable reaches of unmeaning or unvalue against which British consequential ground may locate itself, we might as well call it "Borrioboola-Gha," after the object of Mrs. Jellyby's "telescopic philanthropy"—as good a label as any for a nonsensical, boundariless, and inconsequential "rest of the world." Readers are not meant to object to Mrs. Jellyby's misdirected charity because it has deleterious effects "out there"—there *are* no effects out there; they are to protest its waste of resources needed in that bounded region where the production of effects is deemed *possible.*[34]

In *Bleak House,* this unit of one integrated national culture can appear the grand desideratum implied by "everything" the novel presents, even by—or especially by—such throwaway lines as the one about "consequential ground" or Caddy Jellyby's passing remark, "Anywhere's nowhere" (BH 59). The text containing these passages appears bent on giving the impression that it, too, is organized on the principle of "consequential ground" and that any little thing that occurs in *it* might matter enormously to the whole. The ideal both subscribed to and satirized by this novel is captured by Detective Bucket's description of a plot in which "the whole bileing of people was mixed up in the same business, and no other" (BH 840). More insistently than in any other work, Dickens suffuses his text with the aura of omnisignificance later to be found in the writings of anthropologists for whom "nothing was too small to escape [the] field notebook" because "[e]verything is somehow related to everything else."[35] *Bleak House* stimulates exactly the kind of interpretive paranoia Dickens makes a point of mocking in a character like Mrs. Snagsby, who converts every innocent datum of her husband's behavior into a proof of his guilt:

---

[32] Cf. Peter Sahlins, *Boundaries: The Making of France and Spain in the Pyrenees* (Berkeley: University of California Press, 1989), 271.

[33] Marc Augé, *Non-Places: Introduction to an Anthropology of Supermodernity,* trans. John Howe (London: Verso, 1995), 42; see discussion in chap. 2 above.

[34] Cf. J. Hillis Miller, *Charles Dickens,* 207.

[35] "Nothing": Hortense Powdermaker, *Stranger and Friend: The Way of an Anthropologist* (New York: Norton, 1966), 61; henceforth Powdermaker. "Everything": Clyde Kluckhohn, "Cultural Anthropology: New Uses for 'Barbarians,'" in Lynn White, ed., *Frontiers of Knowledge in the Study of Man* (New York: Harper, 1956), 37.

Mrs. Snagsby screws a watchful glance on Jo, as he is brought into the little drawing-room by Guster. He looks at Mr. Snagsby the moment he comes in. Aha! Why does he look at Mr. Snagsby? Mr. Snagsby looks at him. Why should he do that, but that Mrs. Snagsby sees it all? Why else should that look pass between them, why else should Mr. Snagsby be confused, and cough a signal cough behind his hand? It is clear as crystal that Mr. Snagsby is that boy's father. (BH 376–77)

What diligent reader of the later Dickens has not been prone to the interpretive excesses Mrs. Snagsby commits? (Or wondered whether, after all, she *does* commit excesses?) The fantasy of a closed and unfailingly efficient circulatory system in which nothing ever "gets lost" or fizzles out into inconsequentiality—the opposite of a universe suffering from incurable heat-loss—invites the reading practice represented and derided here.[36]

And not only does this maddening novel solicit and toy with our painstaking attention on behalf of "every" detail; it insinuates the significance of absent details as well. Suppressed fragments of the past have never really gone away, it suggests, but lie latent in the marks of their suppression. No buried moment or phase in the history of the self will be lost to interpretation. Thus it is, for instance, that when someone identified as "Mr. George" appears in the novel (actually George Rouncewell, concealing his identity in shame), readers are conducted through an account of his mannerisms that feels like a rehearsal for those numerous scenes in which Sherlock Holmes will read the past from the appearance of some fresh arrival at 221B Baker Street:

His sinewy and powerful hands, as sunburnt as his face, have evidently been used to a pretty rough life. What is curious about him, is that he sits forward on his chair as if he were, from long habit, allowing space for some dress or accoutrements that he has altogether laid aside. His step too is measured and heavy, and would go well with a weighty clash and jingle of spurs. He is close-shaven now, but his mouth is set as if his upper lip had been for years familiar with a great moustache; and his manner of occasionally laying the open palm of his broad brown hand upon it, is to the same effect. Altogether, one might guess Mr. George to have been a trooper once upon a time. (BH 314)

Like the neurotic, George reveals what he hides. He dimly recognizes Esther Summerson upon meeting her for the first time, though he does not know why. The reason is that she resembles her father, George's former officer; and George's unconscious behavior instantly makes the connection. Esther reports that, "He sat down, a little disconcerted by my presence, I thought; and, without looking at me drew his heavy sunburnt hand across and across his upper lip" (BH 362). Mr. George's military-moustache-that-isn't-there anticipates the dog-that-didn't-bark-in-the-night in Conan Doyle.

---

[36] For pertinent comments from contemporary reviews, see Philip Collins, ed., *Dickens: The Critical Heritage* (New York: Barnes & Noble, 1971), 278, 284, 291. Dickens is fully alert to the fact that the impression of omnisignificance calls for a practice of reading so paranoid as to bring narrative to a halt.

And the quirks of Mr. George are only local illustrations of what obtains in the novel's major plot lines concerned with the secrets in Esther's and her mother's pasts. Despite her studied self-control, Lady Dedlock cannot avoid alluding to her status as the mother of a child she presumes dead—even in that show of boredom that is so much identified with her persona and position "at the centre of the fashionable intelligence, and at the top of the fashionable tree" (BH 19):

> My Lady Dedlock (who is childless), looking out in the early twilight from her boudoir at a keeper's lodge, and seeing the light of a fire upon the latticed panes, and smoke rising from the chimney, and a child, chased by a woman, running out into the rain to meet the shining figure of a wrapped-up man coming through the gate, has been put quite out of temper. My Lady Dedlock says she has been "bored to death." (BH 18)

In all such instances—as Freud put it in his 1909 study of the "Rat Man"—"the thing which is meant to be warded off invariably finds its way into the very means which is being used for warding it off."[37]

In keeping with the models of society and text being tested out in *Bleak House,* and consistent with the novel's insistence upon the unburyable nature of the personal past, both the novel's heroine and her defining opposites are constructed as miniature leak-proof systems, too. Esther, the *moral* center of the novel and the harbinger of a beneficent and functionally integrated British culture, is driven by the resolution "to do some good to some one, and win some love to myself if I could" (BH 27). Out from Esther go good acts, back to her comes the love that is the consequence of those acts: she reaps what she sows, the recipients of her kindness being intermediate stations in a process essentially self-contained, like that of a perpetual-motion machine. At the *structural* center of the novel is a figure who might be taken as her very antithesis, the covetous drunkard Krook, who at the end of the tenth installment of this twenty-part serial fiction undergoes a death that is "inborn, inbred, engendered in the corrupted humours of the vicious body itself, and that only—Spontaneous Combustion, and none other of all the deaths that can be died" (BH 479). Krook's fate (to which I will return) represents perhaps the most sensational version of a destiny Dickens often metes out to his villains: bringing about their own destruction, sometimes with a tidy logic akin to Dante's *contrapasso,* Dickensian evildoers exhibit the tendency "to work no ruin half so surely as their own."[38]

Bleak House's capaciousness and seeming determination to include "everything" have led many readers to label it "encyclopedic," but it is important to recognize Dickens's privileging of a mobile, pragmatic, and engaged autoethnography over the Enlightenment ideal of the encyclopedia, which he tendentiously associates with the mere aggregation and listing of information. The encyclopedia, Dickens thinks, is liable to encourage mental activity like that of Mr. Pott's

[37] Freud, "Notes Upon a Case of Obsessional Neurosis," in Philip Rieff, ed. and intro., *Three Case Histories* (New York: Collier, 1963), 81.

[38] Dickens, *The Old Curiosity Shop* (1840–41; Harmondsworth: Penguin, 1985), 424; henceforth OCS.

critic on the *Eatanswill Gazette,* in *Pickwick Papers,* who has produced "a copious review of a work on Chinese metaphysics."

> "An abstruse subject I should conceive," said Mr. Pickwick.
>
> "Very, sir," responded Pott, looking intensely sage. "He *crammed* for it, to use a technical but expressive term; he read up for the subject, at my desire, in the *Encyclopedia Britannica.*"
>
> "Indeed!" said Mr. Pickwick; "I was not aware that that valuable work contained any information respecting Chinese metaphysics."
>
> "He read, sir," rejoined Pott, laying his hand on Mr. Pickwick's knee, and looking round with a smile of intellectual superiority, "he read for metaphysics under the letter M, and for China under the letter C, and combined his information, sir!"[39]

As lampooned by Dickens, the encyclopedia mistakes information for knowledge and goes about amassing data up to and even beyond the point at which readers will lose themselves in it. The form does not encourage a strenuous enough distinction between adventitious and meaningful *relationships* of data. Like the Parliamentary "Blue Books" and the Great Exhibition of 1851, the encyclopedia could be seen as based on the vulgar empiricist assumption that facts might magically speak for themselves and that more of them meant more knowledge.[40]

The progress of Dickens's novels away from episodic sequence toward tighter formal integration represents one leading instance of the arrival in English fiction of the totalizing urge Walter Scott and the authors of the National Tale had both satisfied and studied in their works upon the vanishing peripheral cultures of the United Kingdom. By the time we reach *Bleak House,* we confront the kind of text that hinges its claim to authority upon a demonstrative skirting of chaos, its tacit wager with its readers being that the heaps of facticity it seems determined to pile higher with every installment will eventually reveal themselves to be functioning components of form.[41] The novelist appears to say, along with that great waste-collector, Krook, "all's fish that comes to my net" (BH 63). Dickens evokes his textual and cultural ideals by means of two complementary strategies I have labeled (in chapter 2) *pre-ethnographic* and *protoethnographic* versions of anticulture—the former implying a universally applicable concept of Culture or Civilization, the latter the pluralistic, small-c cultures of modern anthropology.

In the very title of that diamond in the Chancery crown, "Jarndyce and Jarndyce," for instance, the echo of "jaundice" links up with the motif of the national

---

[39] Dickens, *Pickwick Papers* (Harmondsworth: Penguin, 1986), 815; henceforth PP.

[40] On knowledge versus information, cf. Thomas Richards, *The Imperial Archive: Knowledge and the Fantasy of Empire* (London: Routledge, 1993). Cf. William Johnston, *England As it Is; Political, Social, and Industrial, in the Middle of the Nineteenth Century* (London: John Murray, 1851), for the complaint that "the minds of our politicians in these days are too much engrossed by details" and that the getting of "the Blue Books by heart" is injurious to the mind's "discursive and soaring tendency" (1.142–43).

[41] Cf. D. A. Miller 90; Jonathan Arac, *Commissioned Spirits: The Shaping of Social Motion in Dickens, Carlyle, Melville, and Hawthorne* (1979; New York: Columbia University Press, 1989), 114–38.

disease, while the duplication of "Jarndyce" conveys a hostile togetherness, "the opposition of those whose interests ought to be identical."[42] The "and" mocks its own status as conjunction by really meaning "versus." Considered as the weightless "and" of parataxis, it may be taken as expressing the factitious nonrelationship of mere contiguity in space or coincidence in time—much as the encyclopedia sorts data only by "the accident of initial letters."[43] Protoethnographic harmful relationship (jaundice) or pre-ethnographic adjacency without relationship (parataxis) seem the Dickensian anticulture's only alternatives—the same ones discernible in the novel's opening scene, where we find "[f]oot passengers, jostling one another's umbrellas, in a general infection of ill temper, and losing their foothold at street corners, where tens of thousands of other foot passengers have been slipping and sliding since the day broke" (BH 11). Hobson's choice: either the general infection or the aleatory jostlings, the aggregate alonenesses, with each defending the meager space of one umbrella's shadow. This latter option is the intolerably senseless joint occupation of space, against which the utopias of genuine culture and integrated narrative stand out in relief. A text whose nonorganization matched that of the pre-ethnographic anticulture would resemble the wretched miscellany of Krook's shop, with its "quantity of packets of waste paper" (BH 68), and the Chancery suit itself, with its "great heaps, and piles and bags and bags-full of papers" (BH 366). Embodying a dream of total form, *Bleak House* also tacitly entertains the possibility that it might wind up the way Jarndyce and Jarndyce does when the contested estate is finally consumed in legal costs. When it is discovered there is nothing left to argue about, the lawyers and clerks in Chancery pile up the evidence of their case's pointlessness. "We stood aside," Esther says,

> and presently great bundles of paper began to be carried out—bundles in bags, bundles too large to be got into any bags, immense masses of papers of all shapes and no shapes, which the bearers staggered under, and threw down for the time being, anyhow, on the Hall pavement, while they went back to bring out more. Even these clerks were laughing. We glanced at the papers, and seeing Jarndyce and Jarndyce everywhere, asked an official-looking person who was standing in the midst of them, whether the cause was over. "Yes," he said; "it was all up with it at last!" and burst out laughing too. (BH 899)

III

The narrative of *Bleak House* does much to discredit the position of stable and disinterested overview that Dickens associated with the encyclopedia. The detective Mr. Bucket, when set upon the trail of the disgraced Lady Dedlock, "mounts a high tower in his mind, and looks out far and wide": he sees "everything," takes in fact after fact, but he cannot isolate the one figure he seeks (BH 798). Though credited

---

[42] Arac, *Commissioned Spirits,* 127.

[43] Coleridge, quoted in Alan Rauch, *Useful Knowledge: The Victorians, Morality, and the March of Intellect* (Durham, N.C.: Duke University Press, 2001), 36. On contiguity without common purpose, cf. *Pickwick Papers* on the system of "chummage" that assigns billets in the Fleet prison (PP 679).

by Jo with the ability to be, like the "Shadow" of *Household Words,* "in all manner of places, all at wunst" (BH 663), Bucket represents an ideal of knowledge
Dickens now holds at arm's length, according to which the perfect mind, like the
encyclopedia, would be a vast receptacle for facts, a glorified bucket capable of
containing all the world. Another evocation of lost possibilities of overview
comes with the original name for the Jarndyce house, "the Peaks," an eminence
from which Dickens's characters have irreversibly fallen into a pitiable em-
broilment "in Chancery," where they are subject to a social authority at once
peremptory and chance-like. The house first appears in the novel as "a light
sparkling on the top of a hill" (BH 75), but its function is mainly that of a threatened refuge for fugitive authenticity; it no longer affords any serene survey of its
social landscape.

Bleak House includes such evidence of an obsolete omniscience as part of its
effort to authorize the definitively unstable and shifting form of knowledge it
makes available through its division of the narrative between anonymous third-
person and identified first-person voices. Here the sociological template for readings of the novel proves most debilitating, because what Dickens's masterpiece is
most vitally "about" is the linkage between its ultimate object of representation
and its peculiar mechanism for representing it. Edgar Johnson's influential assertion that *Bleak House* presents an "anatomy of society," for instance, imports into
our thinking about the novel the inert *position* of an anatomist, a stance wholly at
odds with the book's central narrative effect, which W. J. Harvey memorably described as one "of pulsation, of constant expansion and contraction, radiation and
convergence."[44] To take a more recent example, D. A. Miller's brilliant but ex-
ceptionable reading in "Discipline in Different Voices" turns out—oddly enough,
for a chapter of that title—to have next to nothing to say about the double narration; and even though Miller interrupts his argument with some theoretical reflections on how "[p]henomenologically, the novel form includes the interruptions
that fracture the process of reading," he pays almost no attention to the technique
that makes this particular metanovel into a veritable self-interrupting machine
(D. A. Miller 83). In *Bleak House,* the necessity of alternating, often chapter by
chapter, between the two noncommunicating voices makes the effect of reading
the book nothing at all like that of reading works of nineteenth-century social
anatomy such as Tocqueville's *Democracy in America* or, more pertinently, Edward Bulwer Lytton's 1830 volume *England and the English.* The relationship between Dickens' impersonal narrator and Esther Summerson constitutes a sort of
hypertrophied specimen of the one intrinsic to narrative: Dickens has seized upon
and given exaggerated (that is to say, typically Dickensian) representation to the
discontinuity and incommensurability of narrative discourse- and story-spaces, as

---

[44] W. J. Harvey, "*Bleak House:* The Double Narrative," in A. E. Dyson, ed., *Dickens:* Bleak
House—*A Casebook* (London: Macmillan, 1969), 230. Cf. Robert Newsom, *Dickens on the Roman-
tic Side of Familiar Things: Bleak House and the Novel Tradition* (New York: Columbia University
Press, 1977), 14–15, and John Kucich, "Endings," in Harold Bloom, ed., *Charles Dickens's Bleak
House: Modern Critical Interpretations* (New York: Chelsea House, 1987), esp. 118.

a way of giving formal embodiment to the ambivalence residing in the conception of culture he reaches for. Each voice forestalls the possibility of the other's having free rein or gathering too much discursive momentum, much as, in the twentieth century, ethnographic Participant Observation will play the perspectives of outsider and putative insider off against each other and stake out the position of outsider's insideness in bringing a culture into view.

Bleak House appears to both presage and parody the ethnographic principle that once a culture is figured "as a discrete, self-contained whole, . . . there can be no substitute for a system of concentrated fieldwork designed to generate something resembling an insider's view of it."[45] Chancery is said to operate like some weird cult whose workings the outsider cannot fathom: at Lincoln's Inn Hall, scores of "the uninitiated" "peep in at the glass panes in the door" (BH 12); later on, Richard Carstone dismisses the opinion of his friend Woodcourt because the good doctor is "only an outsider" and "not in the mysteries" (BH 724). While elements such as these negatively foreshadow ethnography's exaltation of the participant's point of view and its recommendation that the fieldworker do all he can to achieve rapport, others gesture toward the flipside of anthropology's inconsistent rhetoric, discrediting *mere insideness* just as Malinowski would do in writing that the natives he studied were "*of* [their culture] and *in* it," but lacked any "vision of the resulting integral action of the whole" (*Argonauts* 11–12, 83).

In just this spirit does Dickens's novel make clear that the "parties" to Jarndyce and Jarndyce "understand it least"; even of the solicitors—the indigenous shamans of British anticulture—it must be said that "no two Chancery lawyers can talk about it for five minutes without coming to a total disagreement as to all the premises" (BH 14). At one point, Esther Summerson attends a session of the court and remarks, "I counted twenty-three gentlemen in wigs, who said they were 'in it;' and none of them appeared to understand it much better than I" (BH 366). Because ethnography ascribed to participants in a culture the pragmatic know-how and narrow perspective of mere insideness, even if an anthropologist attempted to see how things looked from every member's viewpoint, the result would be a multiplicity of partial views carried to the point of information overload, not a vision of culture. The fieldworker truly committed to considering everything and acquiring the native viewpoint runs the risk of drowning in minutiae, as seems to happen, in *Bleak House,* to Richard Carstone, who foolishly thinks he can get to the bottom of the Jarndyce case, or, to alter the metaphor, of being consumed by the voluminous data he attempts to consume, as seems to happen to the combustible Mr. Krook. Authoritative ethnographic representation, Dickens grasps in advance of the discipline, aims at a position of "membership without commitment to membership," at the paradoxical goal of acquiring a "place" within culture's consequential ground that does not take up any space: an anonymous participation, an invisible centrality.[46]

---

[45] Christopher Herbert, *Culture and Anomie: Ethnographic Imagination in the Nineteenth Century* (Chicago: University of Chicago Press, 1991), 150–51; henceforth Herbert.

[46] Bernard McGrane, *Beyond Anthropology: Society and the Other* (New York: Columbia University Press, 1989), 125.

This aspiration animates both narrators of *Bleak House:* both the third-person, notably demonstrative nonentity who can move at liberty over and through the social field of the novel, casting the "clear cold sunshine" of his detached judgment wherever he looks (BH 166); and the compulsively self-effacing Miss Summerson whose determined goodness sets a moral universe in orbit around her wherever she goes, "intent," as Harold Skimpole puts it, "upon the perfect working of the whole little orderly system of which [she is] the centre" (BH 558). Between them they describe a kind of "interactive travel," a spatial practice that transforms amorphous space, running off endlessly in all directions, into the "discrete social space" of a cultural field.[47] Raised in seclusion by her fanatical aunt—"set apart" (BH 26)—Esther becomes the novel's prime example of a buried life resurrected into efficacious action, the positive counterexample to those negative versions of unsuspected consequentiality we have already considered. The ethical principle enunciated and epitomized by her begins with a commitment to people personally known and reaches outward from there: Esther's resolution is "to be as useful as I could . . . to those immediately about me; and to try to let that circle of duty gradually and naturally expand itself" (BH 117). Esther's narrative does not explicitly take up the question of this circle's radius, the question of the point beyond which it may expand no further, though the matter is addressed in an insistent allegorical subtext I shall take up later.

Dickens's other narrator, however, works the other way around, invoking the most abstract, faceless, and "distant" national avatars and implying a unifying movement "inward" from there. We see this—to take only the most famous instance—when he pronounces poor Jo "[d]ead, your Majesty. Dead, my lords and gentlemen. Dead, Right Reverends and Wrong Reverends of every order. Dead, men and women, born with heavenly compassion in your hearts. And dying thus about us every day" (BH 677). Throne, Parliament, Church, readers: the *specific* moral community of the British is conjured up by reference not to known individuals who stand in for national qualities but to abstract institutions and their officials, as well as to a generalized British readership. Where Esther conceives of community from the inside out, as it were, this narrator imagines it from the outside in, intimating that each one of those men and women is addressed or "covered" by those institutions, just as each is held accountable in the matter of Jo. While Esther's narrative illustrates the thesis that only someone who is accorded a place within the consequential ground of culture can profitably *travel,* the anonymous narrator embodies the complementary principle that only the traveler can locate and measure the national ground on which each insider might *have* an "appointed place" (BH 17).

In the many works preceding *Bleak House,* Dickens had made ringing the changes upon figurations of mobility and immobility or placedness so recurrent a feature of his fiction that it can appear that fiction's very signature and motive force. In one quadrant of a semiotic rectangle devoted to these matters would belong those figures of moral beauty from the early novels, the kernels of goodness

---

[47] The wording here is from James Clifford, *Routes: Travel and Translation in the Late Twentieth Century* (Cambridge, Mass.: Harvard University Press, 1997), 54.

like Oliver Twist and Little Nell who are so plainly made to shine as beacons to the world. Oliver and Nell do not really act or move; they make their most forceful impressions when we watch them sleeping—and, of course, in Nell's case, lying dead. Dickens's handling of them is reminiscent of theologians' arguments about divine perfection, in which movement and change suggest imperfection or defilement (consider the wayward Alice Marwood of *Dombey and Son*). Plainly, such inert protagonists put a strain upon narrative's own movement; one way to incorporate them in narrative is to presuppose a fall, prior to the story's commencement, that has created a gap between actual and proper settings for the figure of moral beauty which it is the narrative's task to cross. And rather than being the volitional source of movement, these figures *are moved* on their narrative course by forces outside themselves—much as, in *The Old Curiosity Shop,* the flesh-and-blood Nell is carted through the streets alongside a waxen Brigand, to advertise the opening of Mrs. Jarley's exclusive wax-works exhibition (OCS 286). This narrative pattern, reserved for those characters marked as outside the reach of desire, is significantly extended in *Martin Chuzzlewit,* in which the steadfastly good Mark Tapley gets dragged along on selfish young Martin's ill-fated quest toward that Dickensian heart of darkness, Eden U.S.A. The cozy rural retreats where the heroes and heroines of most of Dickens's early novels wind up (self-parodied at the end of *Bleak House*) obviously belong here, while, in the opposing quadrant of negative stasis, we will find the many narrow incarcerating spaces represented in those novels (workhouse, prison, coffin, and so forth).

On the other hand, there is *Pickwick Papers,* in which perhaps the most powerful source of comic pleasure is to be found in the figure of the man self-invented on the move, free of determination by place and culture. Whatever the passing attractions of the "snug" Dingley Dell or of the fine new house Mr. Pickwick builds himself in the end at Dulwich (a telling name), the narrative of *Pickwick Papers* is mainly devoted to propelling itself through and past all way stations, up to the point at which narrative must cease. Bearing the surname of an actual coach proprietor, Pickwick signifies that he is less a "character" than an embodied commitment to keep moving; and Pickwick's nemesis Jingle speaks truth when he gives his address as "No Hall, Nowhere" (PP 584). In a famous set piece on a Fleet prisoner who has been beggared and brought to despair by Chancery, Dickens identifies the human body with ceaseless motion, as a "restless whirling mass of cares and anxieties, affections, hopes, and griefs, that make up the living man," whose tragedy it is to fall into the hands of incarcerating legal and other institutions (PP 734–35). Dickens's footloose males are always on the run from those man-traps of marriage, family, property, vocations, institutions, respectability and responsibility, all overseen by women seeking mates. The hero himself falls prey to Miss Witherfield, a sort of female minotaur at the center of the labyrinthine White Horse Inn, and he falls foul of the marriage-minded Mrs. Bardell and winds up in the Fleet. It is no coincidence that with his liberation from jail comes the reappearance of the uncontainable Bob Sawyer and a delirious return to the road. Phiz's illustration of "Mr. Bob Sawyer's mode of travelling" brilliantly captures the radical restlessness animating *Pickwick,* that vagabond appetite for which even the moving *vehicle* is too confining: Sawyer sits spread-legged atop the moving coach, a sandwich in one hand and a bottle in the other.[48] He would doubtless concur with the coachman Tony Weller's declaration that he "ain't safe anyveres but on the box" (PP 832). (Tony considers himself "a privileged indiwidual," for "a coachman may be on the wery amicablest terms with eighty miles o'females, and yet nobody think that he ever means to marry any vun among 'em" [PP 832].) The perfunctory punishment this book metes out to Jingle for his fraudulent self-fashionings pales in comparison with its animus toward the Law, represented by Dodson and Fogg, among others, but set in motion *only* at the behest of female characters. In sum, the novel's ultimate aim of safeguarding the inalienable mobility of men while acknowledging the most minimal claims of social order make it a veritable panegyric on that proverbial cornerstone of English liberty, the right of habeuas corpus: as Sam Weller memorably puts it, "[t]he have-his-carcase, next to the perpetual motion, is vun of the blessedest things as wos ever made" (PP 701).

What is more, male characters in Dickens may be chastised, as Marley's Ghost chastises Scrooge, for spurning their duty to "walk abroad among [their] fellow men, and travel far and wide"[49]—or, to alter the trope, for hoarding and refusing to "spend" themselves in society. Mobility here appears a style of philanthropy sharply distinguishable from Mrs. Jellyby's deskbound shuffling of papers, Mrs. Pardiggle's invasions of the poor, or Mr. Chadband's parlor orations. It signals the reconnection of the stagnant soul with its community. Some such commitment underpins the labors of the urban rambler who wrote *Sketches by Boz,* and it is to be seen in the nocturnal perambulations of Master Humphrey, as well—slow and serious researches into "the characters and occupations of those who fill the streets," forays that are explicitly contrasted to the erosive "pacing to and fro, [the] never-ending restlessness, [the] incessant tread of feet wearing the rough stones smooth" that constitutes workaday life (OCS 43). The ritual of the morally purposeful "tour" of one's territory endows space with conceptual and affective gravity, mapping that territory upon the mind.

Conversely, the travel of characters condemned for their selfishness *erases* the contours of community and reduces affectively charged "place" to empty, coordinateless space once again. Think of the murderer Bill Sikes's wanderings in *Oliver Twist,* which take a direction precisely opposite to that of the purposeful flow of traffic into London; or of the disorienting journeys of both Mr. Dombey and, later, the absconding Carker, in *Dombey and Son.* More generally, vagrancy—"travel" without a home to start from and return to—appears almost literally to decompose the individuals or groups who engage in it. The staccato bursts of almost syntax-free language Jingle uses to create himself on the fly are enchanting, but they devolve into mere futile sputterings when Jingle lands in the Fleet. In *Great Expectations,* the fugitive Magwitch is encountered in the cold, "clasping himself, as if

---

[48] The illustration appears in chap. 50. Phiz depicts the coach as pursued by a family of Irish beggars, figures who represented to English imaginations a more alarming version of mobility.

[49] Dickens, *A Christmas Carol,* in *The Christmas Books, Volume I* (Harmondsworth: Penguin, 1971), 61.

to hold himself together."[50] Most striking of all the threatened or realized erasures of identity by movement is *Bleak House*'s Jo, a figure whom the authorities relentlessly "move on" to his death. In this quadrant of the Dickensian rectangle, movement is inimical not only to personal identity but to the culture that is its ground and guarantor. The antisocial characters of Dickens's imagination seem ceaselessly and unpredictably on the move, driven by some evil perpetual-motion machine somewhere deep within. Fagin and Monks, of *Oliver Twist,* and Quilp, of *The Old Curiosity Shop,* share the alarming tendency suddenly to materialize wherever one happens to be, and to vanish just as inexplicably (as in the famous case of the missing footprints in *Oliver Twist*).[51] Quilp's misshapen body jerks and capers its way through every scene, "arms a-kimbo," impelled by "that taste for doing something fantastic and monkey-like, which on all occasions had strong possession of him" (OCS 124). Such a propensity to ceaseless, ultimately *self-canceling* movement is a symptom of a barbarous or bestial condition of existence "beyond culture," mere appetitiveness now appearing in its negative guise.[52] In such Dickensian villains, Iago's "motiveless malignancy" becomes malignant and seemingly aimless mobility. Multiplied, it manifests itself in the restless mob, for example in the "bands of unemployed labourers parad[ing] in the roads" in *The Old Curiosity Shop,* "maddened men, armed with sword and firebrand, spurning the tears and prayers of women who would restrain them, [rushing] forth on errands of terror and destruction, to work no ruin half so surely as their own" (OCS 424). Its terminus is that vision of cultural meltdown in the riot scenes of *Barnaby Rudge,* the image of people literally dissolving in the "liquid fire" of burning liquor in the street, consumed by their own unconstrained rage to consume: "the wretched victims of a senseless outcry" who "became themselves the dust and ashes of the flames they had kindled, and strewed the public streets of London."[53]

The conflicting drives toward motion and stasis reviewed here cohabit in the implicitly male and explicitly female narrators of *Bleak House*. Depending on where one stands (or in which direction one is moving), "traveling" can suggest the autonomy or the dissolution of the self, "dwelling" can seem like security or imprisonment, and each can recompense us for the other. A book of crossing and contradictory impulses, governed by the trope of chiasmus, *Bleak House* mobilizes all these alternatives, mapping its fictional space by their divergent itineraries and settlings. Each narrator embodies a tendency to pervade but is enclosed within rigid borders and so prevented from going just "anywhere": the customarily unplaceable, disembodied third-person narrator is, weirdly, *situated* in one half of the text, while Esther Summerson's "circle of duty" expands and expands, but not wider than the national community to which she is allegorically bound. The third-person voice's confinement to half the narrative renders the fiction of omniscience

---

[50] *Great Expectations* (Harmondsworth: Penguin, 1985), 38.

[51] *Oliver Twist* (Harmondsworth: Penguin, 1985), 309–13; henceforth OT.

[52] Cf. Herbert on representations of the anomic self as "prone to such volatility as to be wholly ineffectual until inscribed with the organizing principles of culture" (47).

[53] *Barnaby Rudge* (Harmondsworth: Penguin, 1986), 618.

strangely visible to us, raising the possibility of our learning to read the authorizing pre-text of omniscient narration, the unwritten story of how some self purports
to have attained a viewpoint beyond viewpoints, transcending the mechanisms of
acculturation and their product, the recognizable, socialized self. Exposure to the
contrasting narrative told by Esther "develops" this narrator's rhetoric of achieved
outsideness like a photographic negative.[54] Thanks to this contrast, we may locate
the anonymous narrator as a figure in flight from cultural location and identity,
while Esther's narrative establishes the heroine as a figure in transit *toward* them.
It would be a mistake to rest there, construing too final an opposition between a
masculine capacity for detachment from culture and a feminine passive situatedness, but it is important to explore the gendered division of labor Dickens insti-
tutes at the outset.

If one boundary invoked in the imagination of culture separates "consequential
ground" from the inconsequential, non-narratable backdrop of the world, another
works *inside,* segregating detail truly belonging to the culture from deviant elements that must be erased or expelled in a process capable of being represented as
a recovery or salvaging of coherence. The colossally obvious deviant in *Bleak
House* is Lady Dedlock's murderous French maid, Hortense, lone foreigner in the
cast of characters. The elements in her design are drawn from familiar stereotypes
of the passionate Southern European (Hortense is "from somewhere in the southern country about Avignon and Marseilles" [BH 171]), as well as from Carlyle's
portrayal of self-consuming Jacobin fury in *The French Revolution;* in *A Tale of
Two Cities,* Dickens would give full-dress treatment to these elements in the figure of Mme. Defarge. Looking at Hortense, Esther notices "a lowering energy in
her face . . . which seemed to bring visibly before me some woman from the streets
of Paris in the reign of terror" (BH 339–40). Lady Dedlock, the woman of im-
permissible sexuality, operates in a similar fashion. Helping to define both of the
novel's two narrators by opposition to them, demarcating their ground by being
expelled from it, this woman breaks out of the intolerably confining role of "My
Lady Dedlock" and flies off in search of oblivion. Her going literally astray toward
the close of the novel recapitulates her past sexual "waywardness" and makes her
the novel's most important rule-proving exception, the image of the woman in self-
propelled motion.[55] Her difference from her daughter is never more pointedly illustrated than when, in pursuit of her, Esther rides as the passenger of Mr. Bucket,
both "emissary" and foil of the third-person narrator in the story-space of the
novel.[56] In the logic of *Bleak House*'s dual narration, the final expulsion of the
wandering, desirous woman from the domain of reclaimed British culture must be
authored by the woman who permits herself to *be driven* by an eternally rest-less

---

[54] Cf. Christopher Herbert, *"The Occult in Bleak House,"* in Harold Bloom, ed., *Charles Dickens's
Bleak House,* 123.

[55] On Hortense and Lady Dedlock, cf. Michiel Heyns, *Expulsion and the Nineteenth-Century Novel:
The Scapegoat in English Realist Fiction* (Oxford: Clarendon Press, 1994), 111–12.

[56] Richard T. Gaughan, "'Their Places are a Blank': The Two Narrators in *Bleak House,"* *Dickens
Studies Annual* (New York: Arno Press, 1992), 86.

man (Bucket, John Jarndyce, the other narrator) whom "[t]ime and place cannot bind" (BH 742). Esther's is the story, in its first half, at least, of a *voyage in* to culture, defining a self that is rewarded, is given place and value, for differing from her mother's errant womanhood.[57] In turn, the male voice of *Bleak House*'s other chapters has Esther on hand, as the model of a defined selfhood it claims to have overcome.

The signs of this claim are many, and they include the third-person narrator's constant reliance on a verb tense of the nonprogressive present, a tense appropriate to the cultural outsider and inimical to the build-up of *memory*, which (as David Hume put it) "acquaints us with the succession of perceptions" and is thus "to be considered . . . the source of personal identity," since, "[h]ad we no memory, we never shou'd have any notion . . . of that chain of causes and effects, which constitute our self or person."[58] "It is in society that people normally acquire their memories," as Maurice Halbwachs would later contend, and memories may be "located" and coherently assembled only when "they are part of a totality of thoughts common to a group," when we "place ourselves in the perspective of this group[,] . . . adopt its interests and follow the slant of its reflections."[59] In contrast, the panoramic perspective sought by Dickens's nameless storyteller is solitary and instantaneous, requiring a durationless language. No cultural insider employs the "ethnographic present" tense.

From the opening page of *Bleak House,* two things are implicit in the fact that, of the two narrators, it should be this impersonal one who introduces us to the insufferable condition of being "in Chancery." The first is that the very reflex of locating oneself as subject to culture is the desire to get out, not to remain trapped (in Stuart Hall's phrase) in the place from which one speaks. This reflex is powerfully encoded for us, a bit later, in the arrangement of Krook's house, the travesty Chancery court. On the top floor lives a woman named Miss Flite with her caged birds; at the bottom dwells Krook, wallowing in drink and filth and paper; while in the middle resides a man known only as Nemo, a unit of anonymous humanity, a nobody-in-particular, torn between the desire to soar free and the weight of both social and bodily being. Dickens builds into this moral architecture of a British Everyman the cultural insider's ethnocentric conflation of the laws of his particular culture with the natural laws governing all material bodies. From such a perspective, pointedly opposed to the one being claimed by the anonymous narrator, the pervasive social law of this or that culture has become so thoroughly naturalized as to appear functionally indistinguishable from—no more and no sooner escapable than—corporeal existence itself. Nemo's predicament, here, is echoed by that of the petit bourgeois Mr. Snagsby, another man-in-between: caught or

---

[57] Cf. Virginia Blain, "Double Vision and the Double Standard in *Bleak House:* A Feminist Perspective," in Harold Bloom, ed., *Charles Dickens's Bleak House,* 139–56.

[58] Hume, *Treatise of Human Nature,* ed. L. A. Shelby-Bigge (2d ed. Oxford: Clarendon Press, 1978), 261–62.

[59] Halbwachs, *On Collective Memory,* ed., trans., and intro. Lewis Coser (Chicago: University of Chicago Press, 1992), 38.

"snagged" between the law and its truants, between the relentlessly hunting lawyer Mr. Tulkinghorn and his hapless quarries (Nemo, Jo), Snagsby lives oppressed by the sense of his complicity in nefarious networks beyond his comprehension or control. He fears "that he is a party to some dangerous secret without knowing what it is," a secret that might at any moment "explode, and blow up" (BH 374). After something like this does happen with Krook's spontaneous combustion, he "is not prepared positively to deny that he may have had something to do with it" (BH 483).

The second implication of the mode of address adopted at the very outset of *Bleak House* is that the voice speaking to us belongs to one who has indeed done what seems impossible from the vantage point of the ethnographic insider: somehow managed to place himself beyond the reach of his culture without ceasing to be. Consider, now, that famous opening passage:

> LONDON. Michaelmas term lately over, and the Lord Chancellor sitting in Lincoln's Inn Hall. Implacable November weather. As much mud in the streets, as if the waters had but newly retired from the face of the earth, and it would not be wonderful to meet a Megalosaurus, forty feet long or so, waddling like an elephantine lizard up Holborn Hill. Smoke lowering down from chimney-pots, making a soft black drizzle with flakes of soot in it as big as full-grown snowflakes—gone into mourning, one might imagine, for the death of the sun. Dogs, indistinguishable in mire. Horses, scarcely better, splashed to their very blinkers. Foot-passengers, jostling one another's umbrellas. . . . (BH 11)

The narrator here cannot be treated as simply "sight itself": he shows himself doing what none of those foot-passengers can do, namely rising out of that accumulating muck to range from the topical present of the mere insider scribbling in a diary to the grand vista bounded by the dawn and end of time (primeval mud and megalosaurus; death of the sun). The magical levitation of this narrator stands in stark contrast to that mock-hierarchy of the creatures presented in the London street (dogs, horses, people), where the much-vaunted ascendancy of humankind over the beasts seems held up for daily ridicule. A little later, in moving from the novel's first chapter to its second, from "In Chancery" to "In Fashion" (the latter focused on the Dedlocks' circle), the narrative voice displays its capacity to move "as the crow flies" (BH 17) between segments of the culture whose inhabitants do not perceive, or actively try not to perceive, their connection. With its importunate rhetorical questions asking in various ways, "What connexion can there be [?]" the voice flaunts its asserted privilege over the benighted prisoners of the British anti-culture and the fictional story-space that stands for it.

More than this, the narrator goes on to present himself as capable of almost unlimited *crossings-back* into the story-space and cultural order from which he has absconded—of reentries into the social field without the risk of entrapment. Like a ghost, or like the "man in the mackintosh" in Joyce's *Ulysses,* he seems to wander in and out of the fictional landscape as he pleases. His clear cold sunshine "looks in at the windows" at the Dedlocks' barricaded privacy at Chesney Wold, their Lincolnshire estate (BH 166); his are the "gaunt eyes" imaged by two holes in the shutters of the dead Nemo's room, peering in upon the man who is the narrator's unlucky counterpart, the man who "has established his pretensions to his name by becoming indeed No one" (BH 153). This narrator is Nemo with a plus sign, anonymity the condition of his unparalleled, nation-embracing mobility: the lamenting "Banshee" for the otherwise forgotten Nemo, he implicitly offers the same service to every unrecognized Briton. This commitment links him to the "dark young man" who suddenly appears, ghostlike, from the shadows by Nemo's bedside (BH 190): this is the young surgeon Woodcourt, a character whose nation-healing efficacy will turn out to depend, just as the narrator's does, on his getting *outside* of Britain so that he can all the more authoritatively come back again. (In Woodcourt's case, this means setting off as a ship's doctor, braving shipwreck in distant seas, and returning a hero.) When the doctor ministers to the dying Jo, he mimics the third-person narrator's deathwatch over Nemo, and in both situations, a *productively* "traveled" personage bears witness to the passing of someone whose identity has been erased by the *negative* travel of an aimless and homeless life.

One dazzling manifestation of the performative aspect of Dickensian limited omniscience occurs in chapter 10, when a crow darts back and forth across the line that imperfectly divides material *in* the story from the devices of its telling. The passage begins with Mr. Snagsby, who, "standing at his shop-door looking up at the clouds, sees a crow, who is out late, skim westward over the slice of sky belonging to Cook's Court. The crow flies straight across Chancery Lane and Lincoln's Inn Garden, into Lincoln's Inn Fields. Here, in a large house . . . lives Mr. Tulkinghorn" (BH 145). At this point, the narrative shifts its attention from Snagsby to Tulkinghorn—flying with the crow, as it were—and follows the latter as he makes his way to Snagsby's, moving "as the crow came" and exhibiting other crow-like features (the glossy black clothes, the "scavenging" for information). We then vault back to Snagsby's point of view, just in time, for "Mr. Snagsby was about to descend into the subterranean regions to take tea, when he looked out of his door just now, and saw the crow who was out late. 'Master at home?' [Mr. Tulkinghorn asks]." The bird that began its life in this novel as part of the figure of speech for describing the narrator's freedom of movement from setting to setting has here become a creature visible to characters in the narrative and has even "become" one of those characters, Tulkinghorn—who, as one so obviously bent upon making connections among disparate social spheres (though for harmful, not for beneficent, ends), is after all one of the novel's partial objectifications of its nameless teller.[60]

We ought also to note the narrator's sudden, momentary incursion into the arena of characters at the crucial instant, just at the novel's midpoint, when the hapless duo of Guppy and Jobling come upon the charred remains of the spontaneously combusted Krook. The crossover occurs just at the point of discovery.

> They advanced slowly, looking at all these things. The cat remains where they found her, still snarling at the something on the ground, before the fire and between the two chairs. What is it? Hold up the light.

[60] Cf. Harry E. Shaw, "Loose Narrators: Display, Engagement, and the Search for a Place in History in Realist Fiction," *Narrative* 3/2 (May 1995), 95–116.

Here is a small burnt patch of flooring; here is the tinder from a little bundle of burnt paper, but not so light as usual, seeming to be steeped in something; and here is—is it the cinder of a small charred and broken log of wood sprinkled with white ashes, or is it coal? O Horror, he is here! and this, from which we run away, striking out the light and overturning one another into the street, is all that represents him.

Help, help, help! Come into this house for Heaven's sake! (BH 479)

Since the light is in Guppy's hand as the two characters descend to Krook's level (BH 476), this passage, with its imperative "Hold up the light," seems to indicate that the narrator has temporarily quartered himself upon Jobling, Guppy's rather pitiful "inside man" at Krook's, set up in Nemo's former room to keep an eye on the old hoarder downstairs. Having taken Nemo's place, "where the two eyes in the shutters stare at him . . . as if they were full of wonder" (BH 305), Jobling now becomes a place briefly occupied by that *other* No One who narrates. Centripetal and centrifugal impulses are brought into tense proximity here, as this "localization" of our narrator within the boundaries of a character coincides with Krook's *obliteration* of boundaries, his eruption into a loathsome variety of no-one-ness and nowhereness.

There follows the abrupt and unmistakable resumption of generalizing "distance," to close out chapter, installment, and first half of the novel on what amounts to that novel's most astonishing vision of anticulture:

The Lord Chancellor of that Court, true to his title in his last act, has died the death of all Lord Chancellors in all Courts, and of all authorities in all places under all names so-ever, where false pretenses are made, and where injustice is done. Call the death by any name Your Highness will, attribute it to whom you will, or say it might have been prevented how you will, it is the same death eternally—inborn, inbred, engendered in the corrupted humours of the vicious body itself, and that only—Spontaneous Combustion, and none other of all the deaths that can be died. (BH 479)

As I have suggested, this sickening destiny of Krook's, occurring at the heart of the novel, offers up the figure who undergoes it as the defining antithesis of the model culture and self, his "inborn, inbred" death a travesty of culture's autotelic order. Literally dispersed, the essence of crookedness can now taint "everyone." At the same time, the masquerading narrator drops his Jobling act and takes to the air again, becoming once more the wide-ranging, much-traveled authority who has surveyed institutions and systems "in all places soever" and who now places his global experience before a particular auditor—"Your Highness"—who is his counterpart in authority or "highness" over one specific national community.

The many degraded or defeated interpreters among the novel's cast of characters—identified by J. Hillis Miller and including Bucket, Tulkinghorn, Jobling, Guppy, Mrs. Snagsby, and others—lend support to Audrey Jaffe's claim (cited in chapter 3) that Dickensian omniscience constructs itself "in relation to and at the expense of what it constructs as characters"; they also conform to Claude Lévi-Strauss's characterization of the ethnographic project as involving "the subject's capacity for indefinite self-objectification (without ever abolishing itself as subject), for projecting outside itself ever-diminishing fragments of itself."[61] Something like this effect occurs when Mr. Bucket, about to commence his search for Lady Dedlock, looks around her boudoir and "sees the reflection of himself in various mirrors" (BH 795).

The serious game played by Dickens's anonymous narrator may remind us as well of the pursuits of that unparalleled Victorian spokesman for mobility, Tennyson's Ulysses. Dickens discerns, I think, the paradox central to Tennyson's version of the Homeric voyager: that an open-ended commitment to abstract, worldwide "experience" in the interest of aggrandizing the self actually winds up *erasing* the self by deferring or even repudiating return to the social ground of its identity. In Tennyson's poem, Ulysses comments upon his wayfaring reputation by declaring, "I am become a name," implying that he owes it to that reputation to turn his back upon the claims of Ithaka and set out once more upon the open seas of discovery. "I am a part of all that I have met," he continues,

> Yet all experience is an arch wherethro'
> Gleams that untravell'd world, whose margin fades
> For ever and for ever when I move.[62]

But in a sly allusion to the Polyphemus episode of the *Odyssey,* Tennyson's dramatic monologue recalls the time Odysseus asserted that his name was, in fact, *Outis,* Nobody—which is precisely what the hero will become if swallowed up by the Cyclops, or even if he persists in pursuing the gleam of that untraveled world. Unable to tolerate the restriction of being simply "Ulysses of Ithaka," the Tennyson figure seeks through boundless exploration to assemble a self as big as the world it roams; but the poet who ventriloquizes him observes the logic of *anywhere's nowhere*. To trade the specific circle of duty for that ever-elusive gleam is to anonymize rather than aggrandize the self. It seems remarkably appropriate that, when Ulysses urges his men to join his last, doomed quest, his concluding and most inspiring line—"To strive, to seek, to find, and not to yield!"—is couched in the infinitive, the most abstract, most unattached, because unconjugated, verbal form.

Where there is nothing but the present for Dickens's anonymous narrator, "there's no *now*" for the suitors in Chancery, because Britain's anticulture makes them the slaves of "precedent and usage" and condemns them to await a judgment that never comes (BH 551, emphasis added; 17). Evacuation of the *now* is perhaps the chief anticultural effect and may be traced throughout the novel. Sir Leicester Dedlock, hater of all novelties as signs that "the floodgates of society are burst open," (BH 600), presides over a stagnant little kingdom of "Dandyism" aimed at "putting the hands back upon the Clock of Time" (BH 173). Allan Woodcourt's Welsh mother is tied to an outmoded clan mentality that makes her absurdly announce, upon her son's departure for India, "Wherever my son goes, he can claim

---

[61] Cf. Hillis Miller, Introduction to Penguin *Bleak House,* 17–18; Jaffe, *Vanishing Points,* 13; Lévi-Strauss, *Introduction to the Work of Marcel Mauss,* trans. Felicity Baker (London: Routledge, 1987), 32.

[62] Cf. Tennyson, "Ulysses," in *Tennyson: A Selected Edition,* ed. Christopher Ricks (Berkeley: University of California Press, 1989), 138–45, lines 11–21.

kindred with Ap-Kerrig" (BH 434). Old Turveydrop, epitome of Deportment, wages veritable war upon the coming generation, saddling his too-obedient son with the name of "Prince" in an attempt to crush the new under the pompous weight of corrupt Regency-era values. An old lady "of censorious countenance" reads him correctly when she tells Esther, "He wouldn't let his son have any name, if he could take it from him" (BH 208–9).

The performative third-person narrator I have been tracking here seems determined to display his invisibility, to court recognition for remaining unrecognizable, to signify his exemption from the British system of signification. Unlike Tulkinghorn, he is not content to lurk "watchful behind a blind" (BH 399). He distinguishes his quick forays into the domain of characters from numerous situations emphasizing the vulnerability that goes with possession of a socially recognized identity. To be lastingly visible to one's culture is to be, as Lady Dedlock says she is, "tied to the stake" (BH 609) and subject to manipulation. The agents of "fashionable intelligence" stalk Lady Dedlock like "a mighty hunter before the Lord"; and her past tracks her down, too, through the traces left by Nemo, mistakenly but tellingly identified by Mrs. Snagsby as "Nimrod"—the name of that same "mighty hunter" in Genesis 10:9 (BH 172, 156). Tulkinghorn hunts Lady Dedlock like a cool sportsman, "doggedly and steadily, with no touch of compunction, remorse, or pity"; "the two eyes of this rusty lawyer" are the negative counterpart of those "sad, gaunt eyes" that watched Nemo die in squalor (BH 423). The nobody-narrator of clear cold sunshine regards the recognition that cultures afford their members as a pitiless searchlight, like the one cast by Mr. Bucket's "bull's eye" lantern upon Jo, who "stands amazed in the disc of light, . . . trembling to think that he has offended against the law in not having moved on far enough" (BH 334).

Construed as the ability to read a system of signs, membership in a culture also means *being* a readable sign within that system, and the consequences of this reciprocal fit between cultural literacy and legibility are perceived, and shunned, by Dickens's third-person narrator. It is Lady Dedlock's recognition of her lover's handwriting that dispels her aura of inscrutability and permits Tulkinghorn to start reading *her* and to discover her secret. Once Esther is removed from her sequestered upbringing and put into social circulation, she, too, becomes subject to being read, and her likeness to her unknown mother begins to bear unwelcome fruit: when Guppy, that legal-shark-in-training, perceives it, he tries to turn his reading to advantage by attaching himself to this potentially valuable person. ("Blest with your hand," he declares in making his wholly unexpected proposal, "what means might I not find of advancing your interests, and pushing your fortunes!" [BH 138].) From the third-person narrator's point of view, to be amenable to signification on the terms laid down by one's culture is to bear a taint or a badge of shame: consider the characters darkened by their contact with writing and papers, such as the brief-writing Guppy ("[a] young gentleman who had inked himself by accident"), the enslaved amanuensis Caddy Jellyby ("I suppose nobody ever was in such a state of ink"), or the Smallweeds as they dig among Krook's documents (so "blackened with dust and dirt" that they "present a fiendish appearance") (BH 37, 47, 586).

In a striking reversal of the moral appeal arising from the idea of "consequential ground," the anonymous narrator of *Bleak House* suggests that the social domain he surveys is one in which any scribbled scrap may indict, any representation lead to ruin. Lady Dedlock's portrait at Chesney Wold leads Guppy to connect its original with Esther. Jobling unwittingly connects Nemo and his forbidden bride by adorning what used to be Nemo's room in Krook's house with "The Divinities of Albion, or Galaxy Gallery of British Beauty,"[63] which contains a "portrait of Lady Dedlock . . . in which she is represented on a terrace, with a pedestal upon the terrace, and a vase upon the pedestal, and her shawl upon the vase, and a prodigious piece of fur upon the shawl, and her arm on the prodigious piece of fur, and a bracelet on her arm" (BH 470). The setting for this picture must be the country house of Chesney Wold (with its terrace), so in placing it where he does, Jobling has in effect *answered* that question of what "connexion" might obtain between rural and urban, high and low. Hung "over the mantel-shelf" (BH 470) at Krook's, the image substitutes for the woman who ought to have been at *this* humble hearth, not at the grand one soon to be blasted by the exposure of her secret: it tells the truth "My Lady Dedlock" can never escape. Being part of a culture, in short, is understood in this half of Dickens's novel as being caught in its order of representation. Even the slippery Guppy is the subject of a portrait that "insist[s] upon him with such obstinacy" that it seems "determined not to let him off" (BH 567).

No wonder, then, that the Jarndyce case is called a "scarecrow of a suit" (BH 14), since it and the whole social system for which it stands represent everything anathema to the narrator who purports to be able to roost among characters without being lastingly classified among them. The threat of entrapment in Chancery is the same as Grandfather Smallweed's threat to George: "I'll lime you!" he mutters, referring to the substance that makes birds stick to tree branches (BH 323). To recognize oneself as a being "limed" by Chancery is to be driven to ask, just as fruitlessly as the windy Mr. Chadband does, "Can we fly, my friends? We cannot. Why can we not fly, my friends?" (BH 283).

IV

Alongside all the labor expended in *Bleak House* to characterize the male narrator as someone who has shed the limitations of cultural insideness, becoming as he does so a Nemo-in-the-positive-sense, considerable attention is also devoted to the task of making us acknowledge the other, universal method of becoming no one. When, in the "consequential ground" scene, Lady Dedlock asks Jo to point out her lover's grave, the poor boy becomes almost excessively informative:

"He was put there," says Jo, holding to the bars and looking in.
"Where? O, what a scene of horror!"

[63] This is "that truly national work" that Jobling "prizes most, of all his few possessions" (BH 305).

"There!" says Jo, pointing. "Over yinder. Among them piles of bones, and close up to that there kitchin winder! They put him wery nigh the top. They was obliged to stamp upon it to git it in. I could unkiver it with my broom, if the gate was open. . . . Look at the rat!" cries Jo, excited. "Hi! Look! There he goes! Ho! Into the ground!" . . .

She drops a piece of money in his hand, without touching it, and shuddering as their hands approach. "Now," she adds, "show me that spot again!"

Jo thrusts the handle of his broom between the bars of the gate, and with his utmost power of elaboration, points it out. (BH 240–43)

Hundreds of pages further on, when the novel returns us to this same low site to watch Esther discover her mother, this same Lady Dedlock, "cold and dead" (BH 847), the narrative has exercised *its* "utmost power of elaboration" in its determination to "show [*us*] that spot again."

The ugly vision toward which *Bleak House* repeatedly refers our gaze is that of the grave for everyone, of everyone slipping down into soil. John Ruskin complained of the novel's high body count as a symptom of the degraded taste of the age, but it might simply reflect the work's dogged commitment to the trope of memento mori.[64] The motif is there at the start, in that vision of the creatures (foot-passengers, horses, dogs) navigating the morass of the London street. Up out of the mud and the beasts arises humankind—but for what? As if anticipating the sensibility of Samuel Beckett, *Bleak House* appears to reply: to struggle over a few miserable inches of pavement, before the deluge that will engulf all combatants. It is there again at the epicenter, where Guppy and Jobling confront the blasted Krook, this truth of the body "from which we run away" (BH 479). Those two "great eyes in the shutters" of Nemo's room look in upon a coffined corpse, "that last shape which earthly lodgings take for No one—and for Every one" (BH 159).

At such moments as these (and plentiful they are), *Bleak House*'s slogan of "anywhere's nowhere" can be rendered as "everyone's Nemo." In the face of this bedrock truth, all the busy signifying and interpreting going on in *Bleak House* can come to seem quite futile. Even when Mr. Bucket succeeds in arresting Hortense, Mr. Tulkinghorn's killer, the young woman mocks his achievement by asking, "But can you restore [the victim] back to life?" (BH 773). Bucket possesses a talismanic "fat forefinger," but his pointing with it, his indication of the criminal who has ruptured the social fabric, looks just as ultimately helpless as the constant pointing of the painted Allegory on Tulkinghorn's ceiling. One day, the lawyer's corpse lies beneath it, and the narrator reminds us that

[f]or many years the persistent Roman has been pointing, with no particular meaning, from that ceiling. It is not likely that he has any new meaning in him to-night. Once pointing, always pointing. . . . There he is, no doubt, in his impossible attitude, pointing, unavailingly, all night long. Moonlight, darkness, dawn, sunrise, day. There he is still, eagerly pointing, and no one minds him. (BH 692)

---

[64] John Ruskin, "Fiction Fair and Foul," in John D. Rosenberg, ed., *The Genius of John Ruskin* (Boston, London, and Henley: Routledge & Kegan Paul, 1979), 440–41.

Dickens suggests that enabling people not to "mind" the figure that points at evidence of our common destiny is the goal of civilization. And if that labor of Sisyphus of keeping the rising mud at bay is one of the novel's governing tropes for the work of civilization—demarcating the sphere of "the human" from the always encroaching "bestial," "crooked," and "low"—*Bleak House* also implies that there can *be* no Civilization, no capital-C Culture, except in the form of ethnographic or small-c cultures, those expandable but finally closed circles of duty that Dickens sees as furnishing the largest human aggregates capable of profitably distracting us from our coming aggregation in mud.

Three *sweepers* are featured in the narrative, two of them pointedly failing at their tasks as if to highlight the path by which the third may hope to succeed. When Jo enacts his celebrated death scene, he is in effect laying down his broom for the last time, resigning his quixotic vocation of keeping *his* little space of the world clean all by himself: the maintenance of the self is the work of a whole culture. At the other extreme is the minor character named "Miss Wisk," whom Dickens permits us to classify among the self-important universalists and abstractionists whose leading figure is the telescopic philanthropist Mrs. Jellyby. Miss Wisk does not attempt practical reforms, but swipes recklessly at the entire institution of marriage in her zeal to defeat "the Tyrant, Man" (BH 445). The novel suggests that midway between Jo's futile small career and Miss Wisk's futile grandiose one lies Esther Summerson's, devoted to the taxing but limited and manageable job of sweeping out Bleak House's material and moral cobwebs (BH 110). It is her confrontation with Mrs. Jellyby and her cohorts that teaches Esther the wisdom of poor Mr. Jellyby's maxim, "Never have a mission" (BH 443). As Matthew Arnold would do in *Culture and Anarchy* (and as Burke had done before him), Esther repudiates the Jacobin chimera of an abstract and universal rights-bearing humanity in favor of the distinct, duty-bearing community: her voice might be heard in Arnold's reflection that "the deeper I go in my own consciousness, . . . the more it seems to tell me that I have no rights at all, only duties; and that men get this notion of rights from a process of abstract reasoning, inferring that the obligations they are conscious of towards others, others must be conscious of towards them."[65]

Blather about the "brotherhood of Humanity" (BH 51) and advocacy of a "mission to be everybody's brother" do not prevent a man from being "on terms of coolness with the whole of his large family" (BH 444).[66] In Esther's and John Jarndyce's ethic, to be everybody's sibling is to be nobody's. Productively being somebody and of some worthy consequence means having a place, and not laying claim to *every* place; it means standing in determinate relation to a limited group of people—and standing in *no* relation to "the world" or "Humankind." When the parasite Skimpole lavishes one of his empty encomiums on Ada Clare, calling her

---

[65] Arnold, *Culture and Anarchy*, ed. J. Dover Wilson (Cambridge: Cambridge University Press, 1932), 175.

[66] On the danger inherent in "the ideal of universal brotherhood," cf. also Marc Shell, *Children of the Earth: Literature, Politics, and Nationhood* (New York: Oxford University Press, 1993), esp. 193–94.

"the child of the universe," John Jarndyce pithily remarks, "The universe . . . makes rather an indifferent parent, I am afraid" (BH 84). In the character of Skimpole we may discern the parody in Esther Summerson's narrative of Ulyssean freefloating or expandable selfhood. It is Skimpole, of the "cosmopolitan mind" (BH 273), who expounds the pleasures of being "bound to no particular chairs and tables, but [able] to sport like a butterfly among all the furniture on hire, and to flit from rosewood to mahogany, and from mahogany to walnut, and from this shape to that, as the humour took one!" (BH 261). He toasts the theoretical "Somebody"—he doesn't care who—who will pay his bills (BH 550).

To belong to a culture, which Skimpole refuses to do, is to occupy and be identified with a "site" where, by the sort of differential processes explored by Ferdinand de Saussure in linguistics and by Claude Lévi-Strauss in anthropology, meaning and value can accrue. And what the appearance of the narrating Esther in the third chapter of *Bleak House* immediately and forcefully suggests is that the anonymous *first* narrator, purportedly beyond culture as he is, nonetheless needs to define himself through the kind of contrastive mechanisms that operate *within* and *between* cultures, by yielding a portion of the narrative space to his seeming antiself, a woman imagined as almost wholly containable in her social function. Esther assumes the narrating role with the air of having been *commissioned* to do so, not of her own volition, and her first words treat her task as if it were a burdensome assignment: "I have a great deal of difficulty in beginning to write my portion of these pages" (BH 24; but how apportioned? by whom? to what end?). Emphasizing her identity's dependence on the recognition of others in the act of telling us who she is—"they called me little Esther Summerson" (BH 25)—she reluctantly puts herself forward in a narrative of acculturation. The early stages of her discourse focus on the process by which, once a virtual nobody, she acquired a local habitation and a name—in fact, a good number of names ("Dame Durden," "Cobweb," "Mother Hubbard," and so forth [BH 111]), an oversupply of signification as if in compensation for her early lack. Raised outside the embrace of culture—"friendless, nameless, and unknown" (BH 254)—by the aptly named Miss Barbary, Esther travels from the condition of "barbarian" to that of "mistress of Bleak House." She bears the burden but also embodies the ideal of that utopian urge for the equation of self and cultural "place."

It deserves underscoring that Dickens does not make light of the burden. The acknowledgment that cultural belonging requires the acceptance of one's status as an object for others is signaled early on in the legal language of Kenge and Carboys, who have undertaken to transport Esther out of that state of internal exile to which Miss Barbary condemned her. "*We have arrangd for your being forded,*" the lawyers inform her in a telegram, "*carriage free, pr eight o'clock coach from Reading, on Monday next, to White Horse Cellar, Piccadilly, London, where one of our clerks will be in waiting to convey you to our offe as above*" (BH 35). Here Esther is treated like a consignment of goods to be carted out of Miss Barbary's warehouse and shipped on to other destinations. Like Oliver Twist, Esther is an "item of mortality" in the eyes of the social authorities charged with her disposition (OT 45). She remains just as passively parcel-like throughout many of the major, unwilled movements of her life, as Jarndyce arranges her conveyance to school at "Greenleaf"—apt name for a setting in which the potencies of the self are cultivated—then to his own hearthside at Bleak House, and finally to Allan Woodcourt's waiting arms. Within this determining framework, Dickens's heroine does, to be sure, achieve a not inconsiderable measure of tactical self-determination, but this never challenges the fundamental conditions laid down for her and even tends to endorse them. When Jarndyce offers Esther the opportunity to ask him about her background, she declines, renouncing curiosity about the given structure of her life (cf. BH 112): she will build on those given foundations, not presume to interrogate them.

The tacit argument embodied in Esther is that it takes one who has known exclusion from culture to value what culture gives: only those unacquainted with the cold outside will cavil at culture's "chancery" nature; those who have been there will consider it a stupefying pleonasm to observe that culture and its identities are arbitrary and constructed. The perspective available to such erstwhile outcasts is uniquely capable of grasping just how impoverished and vacant a self "beyond culture" might be. Early in her narrative, Esther recalls her pathetic attempts to mimic a relationship of reciprocity with a doll that, she says, was "always staring at me— or not so much at me, I think, as at nothing" (BH 24): this sad excuse for child's play suggests that the self that lacks the affirming look of others effectively *is* nothing.[67] Someone with Esther's background might well attach herself with alacrity to the identities and positions assigned her. No passing through any Teufelsdroekian "centre of indifference" is necessary for her; not for her the Victorian dark night of the soul that eventuates in the new creed of duty.[68] She absorbs Carlyle's hard-earned lesson as her second nature, without need of philosophers, recognizing her kinship with such prospective Nemos as Jo, Chadband's poster child, who is "[d]evoid of parents, devoid of relations" (BH 378) and the anonymous narrator's prime example of a being "of no order and no place; neither of the beasts, nor of humanity" (BH 669). Another such figure is Jarndyce's "little present" to Esther, Charley Neckett, whose function is to provide constant representation to the novel's heroine of her *own* salvation from placeless nonentity. When the sick Jo, who has been "tramping he [doesn't] know where" arrives in the vicinity of Bleak House, Charley sees him "as [her brother] Tom might have been, miss, if Emma and me had died after father" (BH 356, 449). And then there is Phil Squod, that luckier version of Jo, who has the habit of "tacking" across rooms with one shoulder always touching a wall, a symptom, perhaps, of the dread common to all such characters. Once a street child himself, Phil seems driven constantly to assure him-

---

[67] Cf. J. Hillis Miller, *The Form of Victorian Fiction: Thackeray, Dickens, Trollope, George Eliot, Meredith, and Hardy* (1968; Cleveland: Arete Press, 1979) on the Victorian novel's anti-Cartesian stress on intersubjectivity (e.g., 5).

[68] Carlyle, *Sartor Resartus* (London: Dent, 1973), 149. Carlyle's "[w]hatsoever thy hand findeth to do, do it with thy whole might" is matched in *Bleak House* by the late lamented Captain Swosser's maxim, "if you only have to swab a plank, you should swab it as if Davy Jones were after you." The saying is recognized by the company at Bayham Badger's as applying "[t]o all professions" (BH 247).

self that he now lives with walls around him, lives a *bounded* life of coherent self-hood, after a youth of aimless "vagabondizing" (BH 324, 388, 325).

The institutionalized structure for recognizing its members—for bestowing meaning and value upon them—a culture consists, as E. E. Evans-Pritchard said, not of "facts" or "things" available to the empirical grasp but primarily of "relations . . . and relations between these relations": like Saussure's structuralist model of language, it constitutes a "self-referential system 'without positive terms'" (quoted in Herbert 11). It is not *in themselves* that the elements of a culture are or signify anything of consequence. People can, as Ernst Cassirer put it, "construct [their] symbolic world out of the poorest and scantiest materials," so "[t]he thing of vital importance is not the individual bricks and stones but their general function as architectural form." It is this function that "vivifies the material signs and 'makes them speak.'"[69] Esther is precisely such a "material sign" endowed with the power to speak; but the landscape through which she moves is littered with reminders of the degenerative force that threatens to wreck the construction site of the self. Alone with the miserable, unvalued Caddy Jellyby, Esther sits comforting the girl until she begins "to lose the identity of the sleeper resting on [her]," and lapses into a state of semiconsciousness in which "it was no one, and I was no one" (BH 57). The criminal hollow men of this novel also exhibit this degenerative tendency: Smallweed appears "a mere clothes-bag with a black skull-cap on the top of it" (BH 309), Krook "a bundle of old clothes, with a spiritous heat smouldering in it" (BH 303). Not by accident does the slum of *Bleak House,* the place where people go to lose their names, itself go by the name of Tom-all-Alone's, in memory not only of Tom Jarndyce, driven to suicide by his dealings with Chancery, but also of the "poor Tom" of *King Lear,* the "unaccommodated man" evacuated of cultural content and reduced to the status of a "poor, bare, fork'd creature" spouting gibberish.

Esther's pragmatic refusal to be disturbed by the foundationless nature of cultural forms and values underwrites the extensive meditation on names and naming in *Bleak House,* a topic that has received considerable attention. In his seminal treatment of the theme, J. Hillis Miller responded to the gap between name and nature in a tragic key that can seem quite unsuited to that portion of the novel for which Dickens's heroine speaks. One can imagine the third-person narrator agreeing with Miller's observation that the proper name "alienate[s] the person named from his unspeakable individuality and assimilate[s] him into a system of language,"[70] but Esther, appearing to acknowledge no such "individuality," seems proof against alienation from it. Indeed, Miller's rueful reflections on how the name can never manage to identify its subject "truly or finally" would appear to be rather good news to someone whose name is, say, "Prince Turveydrop." In spite of the plot operations that tease us with the promise of "true names" being revealed, the name in Dickens is nothing more than a device of an individuating prin-

---

[69] Cassirer, *An Essay on Man: An Introduction to a Philosophy of Human Culture* (New Haven: Yale University Press, 1944), 36.

[70] Hillis Miller, Introduction to Penguin *Bleak House,* 22.

ciple that distributes across the social field the human matter that would merge into muddy senselessness if not partitioned. In crucial instances, names are surrounded by such ambiguity that the question of their being "true" names becomes nonsensical and inconsequential.

Consider "My Lady Dedlock." It is gratifying to learn, late in the novel, that this character bears the first name of Honoria (BH 762), but this is not a clue to her true character in itself. The applicability of the label is vindicated by both Esther and Sir Leicester Dedlock when *they* honor the woman who bears it even after they learn of her sin—when they forgive her, in short, proving once more that control over the meaning of one's name lies with others. And for all we may feel motivated to think that an important part of *Bleak House*'s plot is concerned to reveal who Lady Dedlock really is, we never discover her original family name. Or do we? In the chapter in which she learns Esther is her daughter, she says to herself that her sister, the woman we know as "Miss Barbary," "renounced me and my name" (BH 433): such gestures of renunciation usually involve the family name, but what was that name? There seems no reason to doubt that "Barbary" was an alias assumed by Esther's aunt when she took the illegitimate infant into hiding (see BH 254): shield and symbol at once, like the neurotic symptom, it wards off *and* points to the disgrace that necessitated it; she might just as well have called herself "Outcast." And yet Krook, of the prodigious memory, lists "Barbary" among the names involved in the Jarndyce case (BH 64). It is difficult to imagine why an alias, taken only after the birth of Honoria's unhallowed child and taken by only one member of the family as a contrivance to cut herself off from the others, should figure in a legal action that is "the only property my Lady [Dedlock] brought" into her marriage (BH 22). The question, "was her real name Barbary, or not?" is the wrong question: *everyone's* real name is Barbary, Outsider, Nemo.

A like effect obtains with Esther, who fortuitously resembles the summer sun in bringing warmth to everybody, but who bears the name "Summerson" in the consciousness that it is merely something "they called" her. Nor do the many nicknames she acquires at Bleak House—so many, she ingenuously says, "that my own name soon became quite lost among them" (BH 111)—apply to her any more or less finally than does "Esther Summerson," or for that matter, "Esther Hawdon." The snooping Mr. Guppy comes to believe that Nemo "really is" Captain Hawdon and that Hawdon is Esther's "real name" (BH 430); but the cognomen tends, when probed a bit, to devolve into the generic function of all names as *fences*. Considered as a corruption of "hawthorn," Hawdon can reverberate with meanings like "a thorny shrub or small tree, extensively used for forming hedges."[71] And, as the case of Jo demonstrates, those insufficiently girdled round by a name are quite vul-

---

[71] Among its listings under "haw," the OED gives "enclosure," "a hedge or encompassing fence (OE); hence, a piece of ground enclosed or fenced in; a messuage (OE); generally, a yard, close, or enclosure, as in *timber-haw*." Identified as "[t]he fruit of the hawthorn," a haw is "a type of a thing of no value"—meet characterization of the Dickensian heroine who endures a childhood painfully void of value, and who preserves a disinclination to *accord* herself any value throughout her happier career with Jarndyce.

nerable to the power that can make them lose definition, leak out beyond the borders of the self, and ultimately merge with brute, mute matter. With earlier Dickens characters such as Smike of *Nicholas Nickleby* in mind, readers are motivated to think that this boy started out, somewhere, sometime, with a full name, "Joseph X"; but the two letters of "Jo" are all he has left after a short life whose every experience has further erased his identity. They are the wreckage he clings to before losing hold and becoming nobody at last.

As individuating device, the personal name is a fence or container—a Bucket—for the self, which will spill out into an inconsequential everywhere if its wall is breached. This Nemo-Process happens to Lady Dedlock when she sheds her customary clothes and role. As with the "narrow track of blood" that Hortense releases from its channels in Tulkinghorn's body, it may take only a "little wound" to start selfhood leeching away (BH 744). Perhaps the most static and uninteresting character in *Bleak House*—Ada Clare—is only an extreme instance of this idea of the self as a space cordoned off to prevent contamination and spillage. Having invested Ada with all innocent goodness and identified her as the very locus of purity, Esther when dangerously ill singles out this person, who most wants to attend to her, as the one absolutely prohibited from entering her sickroom. Her frantic insistence on the matter may be taken as the amplified expression of a general anxiety to forestall leakage at the borders of self and sense. Only the watertight bucket can retain what is poured inside.

In what I have treated as the tacit authorizing narrative prior to the first chapters of *Bleak House,* we look back to a moment when some man took flight from his locatable position in culture, eradicated the recognizable contours of the self, and assumed the prerogatives of a protean overseer. The complementary movement for Esther's narrative would be to hark back to a utopian beginning when the *look* of another promised to guarantee one's identity, not arbitrarily or temporarily, but fixedly and once and for all. This look, which leaves its traces throughout Dickens's work, is the look of the mother, and it has always been lost: in a manner comparable to Scott's "translation without original," Dickens builds culture on the foundation of a necessary absence. In *Bleak House,* the funeral of Nemo draws forth a passionate evocation of the "mother at whose breast he nestled, a little child, with eyes upraised to her loving face" (BH 164). This irrecoverable exchange of gazes establishes the impossible ideal for cultural recognition, which must strive day in and day out to defend the walls of self.

Esther's years of internal exile with Miss Barbary are typified for us by the figure of the importunately *unilateral* look, with Esther's Calvinist aunt always setting her "immovable" face against the girl's appeals for reciprocity. When this aunt lies dying, Esther recalls,

> Many and many a time, in the day and in the night, with my head upon the pillow by her that my whispers might be plainer to her, I kissed her, thanked her, prayed for her, asked her for her blessing and forgiveness, entreated her to give me the least sign that she knew or heard me. No, no, no. . . . To the very last, and even afterwards, her frown remained unsoftened. (BH 28)

On its own, the unilateral gaze is powerless to create the affective social nexus that grants identity and purpose to the self. I have already referred to Esther's use of her doll, which, like the entreaties for acknowledgment in the passage above, can call to mind those psychological experiments that show infant monkeys cuddling up forlornly to forbidding mother-statues of wood and wire. Later in the novel, variations on this theme of the unreturned look associate the refusal to return it with the self-delusion of the socially exalted, who, like Sir Leicester, think it in their power to confer existence on others by deigning to "notice" or "countenance" them (see BH 176, 22). Lady Dedlock's choice of Rosa as her protégée is an ironic instance of such noticing, since in this case it is actually the *superior* woman's contact that contaminates—as "the Ironmaster" Rouncewell seems to suspect when he acts to remove Rosa from Lady Dedlock's sphere of influence (BH 169–70, 683–85). Mrs. Pardiggle's surveillance of the poor, carried on under the license of "charity visits," is another example of the self-satisfied and self-blinded look from above.

The one-way look from low to high, on the other hand, illustrates the proverb that a cat may look at a king. Consider Guppy's pursuit of Esther to the theater, where he industriously cultivates an air of lovestruck woe that she cannot help but see but refuses to reward with her "notice": "I felt, all through the performance," she says, "that he never looked at the actors, but constantly looked at me, and always with a carefully prepared expression of the deepest misery and the profoundest dejection" (BH 184). Descending from the clerkly into the laboring classes, the upward look becomes pugnacious: it emanates, for example, from the sullen brickmaker who literally lies on the floor of his hovel and "faces down" Mrs. Pardiggle while staring up at her, saying, "I wants a end of these liberties took with my place" (BH 121). Most ominous of all is the leveling menace implied in Krook's terse comment on his "brother" the Lord Chancellor, embodiment of British law and order: "He don't notice me, but I notice him" (BH 64).

In his capacity as benevolent avatar of the male narrator, John Jarndyce studiously avoids the looks of others, but he does so in order to keep the focus on his protégés, to size them up as candidates for patronage, to protect them without attracting notice, and, above all, to avoid receiving their gratitude. He rides in the carriage that bears Esther away from Miss Barbary's; he engages the girl in conversation and offers her delicacies, but he remains "wrapped up to the chin," his face "almost hidden in a fur cap" (BH 32). This is the man of whom Ada remembers that "he had once done [her mother] an act of uncommon generosity, and that on her going to his house to thank him, he happened to see her through a window coming to the door, and immediately escaped by the back gate, and was not heard of for three months" (BH 74). In the end he is still threatening to "run away and never come back" if anyone dares to acknowledge his good works (BH 891). Like the anonymous narrator in his demonstrations of a preference to remain invisible, Jarndyce creates the atmosphere in which Esther can receive the first productively requited looks of her life. He sends her to school at the nurturing Greenleaf, where Esther soon finds herself "seeing in those around me, as it might be in a looking-glass, every stage of my own growth and change there" (BH 35).[72] She "locates" herself for the first time in this circle of recognition, demarcating herself from others and so preparing herself to begin ameliorating the conditions *of* others, beginning with Caddy and her siblings, who are condemned, as she once was, to live as "nonentit[ies]" (BH 44) or barbarians (or "Wild Indians" [BH 438]). To the extent that Caddy's mother looks at her, she does so as if gazing at "a steeple in the distance" (BH 438)—an object as remote and unreadable as the top of St. Paul's is to Jo. Esther's efforts to bring such figures within the sphere of recognition and legibility earn her the reward of still further recognition: when she returns to Bleak House after bringing off Caddy's wedding, Esther finds that (as she says) "[e]verybody in the house, from the lowest to the highest, showed me such a bright face of welcome" (BH 355).

For Esther, the order of culture does not present itself as an insufficient substitute for the irreplaceable mother-child bond; on the contrary, when the mother appears, she does so as a competitor to the network of relationships in which Esther's identity has by that point been successfully constructed and sustained. Threatening to exert priority over any and all of the circles of gazes centered on her daughter, the look of the mother has to be neutralized. Endowed with the potency to give the gift of culture because she has received it herself, Dickens's heroine encounters Lady Dedlock (without knowing her relation to her) and sees in the woman's face "a broken glass" containing "scraps of my old remembrances" (BH 268). The phase of revelations culminates in Lady Dedlock's approach and confession to Esther, the one private meeting between the mother and child, during which Esther sees "a something in [Lady Dedlock's] face that I had pined for and dreamed of when I was a little child; something I had never seen in any face; something I had never seen in hers before" (BH 532).

This phase of the narrative also includes Esther's scarring by smallpox, caught through Charley Neckett from Jo. These events are almost always studied in critical accounts of *Bleak House,* but what is not often noted is the way the scarring *liberates* Esther from connection with her mother. The threat posed by the mother's return is preempted by the anticultural linkage of Jo and Esther through the trope of disease, and by the positive variety of connection that corresponds to and "heals" it. Two pages after Esther has seen her disease-transformed face in the mirror and two pages *before* her mother identifies herself, Esther describes her convalescence in the little Lincolnshire village near Boythorn's house and Chesney Wold.

---

[72] The obvious contrast for "Greenleaf" and all it conveys is "Smallweed," the name of a family identified as enemies of the nation and models of anticultural humanity, left to grow as it will (cf. BH 294, 307). Unlike Esther, Judy Smallweed "never owned a doll" (BH 309). In another setting shown to be cultureless for all its devotion to pursuits commonly designated as "cultural," we find Skimpole's daughters, who have "grown up as they could, and [have] had just as little haphazard instruction as qualified them to be their father's playthings in his idlest hours" (BH 625). Each is stunted in being defined solely by the role she plays for her father's amusement: the Beauty daughter, the Sentiment daughter, the Comedy daughter.

Charley and I had reason to call it the most friendly of villages, I am sure; for in a week's time the people were so glad to see us go by, though ever so frequently in the course of a day, that there were faces of greeting in every cottage. I had known many of the grown people before, and almost all the children; but now the very steeple began to wear a familiar and affectionate look. (BH 530)

At the nadir of her illness, Esther had hovered near death in a room without mirrors (BH 515); here, she recovers herself in the eyes like mirrors all around her. "The very steeple" seems rich with affect and meaning, as the steeple of St. Paul's is not for Jo and Mrs. Jellyby's steeple-like distant daughter cannot be for her. The disease and the recovery involve systems of connection very pointedly *not* dependent upon or dimly recalling the mother but entirely excluding her. Many readers have regarded the disfigurement that results from Esther's illness as a symbol of her mother's shame, which she takes on when she learns her parentage. But this is a form of inscription that *erases;* like the "reality effect" described by Roland Barthes, it is a sign of nonsignification, releasing its bearer from the burden of having to point to her mother. *Before* the disease has made her an "altered self" (BH 519), Esther's resemblance to Lady Dedlock renders them both liable to exploitation by opportunists like Guppy and Tulkinghorn. Once the sickness has done its work, Dickens's heroine is grateful, as she says, "that I was so changed as that . . . nobody could ever now look at me, and look at her, and remotely think of any near tie between us" (BH 535).[73]

When, toward the end of the novel, Esther finally catches up with her absconding mother—too late—she initially mistakes the dead woman for "the mother of the dead child" (BH 847), in other words, for the brickmaker's abused wife, Jenny, with whom Lady Dedlock has switched clothes. The error precisely reverses the actual situation, in which a child has now definitively survived her parent. When this child "lift[s] the heavy head, put[s] the long dank hair aside, and turn[s] the face" and sees that "it was [her] mother, cold and dead" (BH 847), there occurs a reprisal of those unilateral looks from Esther's childhood, only this time they work to the survivor's advantage. The culture-made Esther has withstood the claims of blood. In the novel's closing pages, we leave the heroine of *Bleak House* nestled with Allan Woodcourt in a Yorkshire enclosure where, she says, "I never go into a house of any degree, but I hear his praises, or see them in grateful eyes," and where "[t]he people even praise Me as the doctor's wife[,] . . . even like Me as I go about, and make so much of me that I am quite abashed" (BH 913). Secure at the center of this acknowledging circle, Esther once more recovers her value in recovering her "looks." When Allan challenges her, "don't you know that you are prettier than you ever were?" she diverts attention, as usual, away from herself to the circle of faces around her: "I know that my dearest little pets are very pretty, and that my darling [Ada] is very beautiful, and that my husband is very handsome, and that my guardian has the brightest and most benevolent face that ever was seen; and

---

[73] This is one of those instances in which, as John Kucich puts it, "[r]elease operates through [Esther], rather than involving her in the guilt of self-willed freedom": "Endings," 116.

that they can very well do without much beauty in me—even supposing—" (BH 914).

In her eagerness to accept the unforeseen gift of culture, Esther tends not to acknowledge what signs all around her are saying, and what she herself so plainly exemplifies: that the positions and identities assigned by culture are susceptible, for good or ill, to considerable refunctioning. I have in mind here, for one thing, the many discrepancies in Dickens's novel between names and the people or places to which they attach—discrepancies that do not go so far as to affirm a capacity to break free from culture's law, but suggest the latitude of that circumscribed liberty that Dickens insists is the only actual kind.[74] The relation Esther bears to the name "Hawdon" is a case in point: however much this moniker lends itself to being read as "hoyden," thus conjuring up the mother's dishonor, the daughter's behavior erases the obloquy: *honi soit qui mal y pense.*

To take another prominent instance, Bleak House, as presided over by John Jarndyce, is quite the reverse of bleak; it is both a walled-in space and "delightfully irregular" (BH 78), neither the maddening labyrinth of Chancery nor the soul-killing repetition and regularity of the tradition-bound Chesney Wold, or of the prison George lands in when he is wrongly jailed for Tulkinghorn's murder (cf. BH 733). But having made the house this way, having successfully struck this balance between enclosure and variety, John Jarndyce retains the name his predecessor gave it, demonstrating as he does so a comportment toward the past humbler than his predecessor's. Tom Jarndyce had renamed "The Peaks" "Bleak House" in reflection of his own sad consciousness, and his *act* of relabeling it illustrates a deluded or hubristic conception of how far human will should go toward the revision, uprooting, or even scrutinizing of what culture bestows—a conception manifested in the doomed effort Tom made, and Richard later makes, to penetrate the mysteries of the Jarndyce case. This attempt is bound to fail—just as Jobling discovers, when he agrees to turn himself into the infiltrating "Weevle" (the burrowing weevil?) at Krook's house, and the search for secrets leads only to the explosion of their possessor and the expulsion of the searchers. What John Jarndyce tells Esther about the Chancery case holds good for the bedrock dogma of any given culture: "it won't do to think of it!" (BH 109).

In one of its most arresting paradoxes, *Bleak House* hazards, then, that to go too deeply *inside* one's culture is to wind up outside it. Corrupt institutions and practices should indeed be exposed to the reformer's light, but the provisional nature of culture and identity forces reformers to recognize that interrogation of the origins and underlying principles of these things imperils commitment and solidarity. To probe the very basis of one's way of living and desiring is to risk reducing

---

[74] Cf. Edmund Burke on the concept of "social freedom," "that state of things in which Liberty is secured by the equality of Restraint": quoted by Conor Cruise O'Brien, Introduction to Burke, *Reflections on the Revolution in France* (1790; Harmondsworth: Penguin, 1969), 15. In Dickens, such refunctionings as I speak of may not always be beneficial: the neighborhood called "Mount Pleasant" is home to the more-than-unpleasant Smallweeds (BH 306); Miss Flite is the name of a woman who cannot bring herself to fly from Chancery.

oneself to an impotent and "inconsequential" skepticism. Up to their very elbows "in Chancery," Tom Jarndyce and Richard Carstone fall outside their culture and below human Culture as such, winding up in a condition not dissimilar from that of the more obvious outcasts, who flail and roam without object or orientation. They bear out Malinowski's contention that "[i]f you remove a man from his social milieu, you . . . deprive him of almost all his stimuli to moral steadfastness and economic efficiency and even of interest in life" (*Argonauts* 157).

Interpreting the "scientific fable" of the early nineteenth-century Wild Boy of Aveyron, Christopher Herbert extracts from it the lesson that "in order for desire to exist in any coherent, active, and potentially satisfiable form, it must embed itself in a fully social matrix, . . . [must] become directed toward objects conventionally defined and symbolically coded as desirable by human society" (Herbert 50). Jo, Dickens's Wild Boy of London, "not a genuine foreign-grown savage [but] the ordinary home-grown article" (BH 669), is constantly hounded to "move on," and all he wants to know is, "But where?" The sympathetic Mr. Snagsby seconds this desire for specific directions and positive aims when he remarks, "Really, constable, . . . that does seem a question. Where, you know?" (BH 285). "I'm a-going somewheres," the fever-stricken child mutters to Esther and Charley:

> "Where is he going?" I [Esther] asked.
> "Somewheres," repeated the boy, in a louder tone. "I have been moved on, and moved on, more nor ever I was afore, since the t'other one give me the sov'ring. Mrs. Snagsby, she's always a-watching, and a-driving of me—what have I done to her?— and they're all a-watching and a-driving of me. Every one of 'em's doing of it, from the time when I don't get up, to the time when I don't go to bed. And I'm a-going somewheres. That's where I'm a-going. She told me, down in Tom-all-Alone's, as she came from Stolbuns [St. Albans], and so I took Stolbuns Road. It's as good as another." (BH 452)

To get where Jo is doomed to go, any road will serve—for, as he knows perfectly well, "they dies everywheres" (BH 453).

In a remarkable and not much commented-on bit of business near the middle of *Bleak House,* Esther comes into her own as embodiment of the national-cultural principle so urgently argued for by the narrative logic of *anywhere's nowhere.* Convalescing in Lincolnshire, Dickens's heroine falls into her usual habit of doing small and telling acts of kindness for the people around her. Recalling the time, she writes,

> [a]mong my new friends was an old woman who . . . had a grandson who was a sailor; and I wrote a letter to him for her, and drew at the top of it the chimney-corner in which she had brought him up, and where his stool yet occupied its old place. This was considered by the whole village the most wonderful achievement in the world; but when an answer came back all the way from Plymouth, in which he mentioned that he was going to take the picture all the way to America, and from America would write again, I got all the credit that ought to have been given to the Post-office, and was invested with the merit of the whole system. (BH 530)

Identified with the unifying power of the postal service, Esther exemplifies that form of British selfhood she seeks to reproduce everywhere she goes, widening her circle of duty until at last each Briton is a self "invested with the merit of the whole system."[75] It is notable that Esther functions, here, not just as model performer of the culture-founding rites of the hearth (the role she plays at Bleak House), but as representer of the hearth, as well—both participant and observer in the national autoethnography. In a miniature ekphrasis, she writes about a picture she has drawn showing the center of the British *sailor's* circle of duty, his stool by the hearth. If we recall Walter Scott's stunning use of ekphrasis at the end of *Waverley* (discussed in chapter 4), we may wish to consider how this much less demonstrative employment of it exhibits a similar tendency: interrupting the flow of time associated with the position of cultural insideness, it grounds a claim to distanced, comprehensive ethnographic vision. Just as the anonymous narrator cannot seem to suppress his urge to return to the domain of characters, so, too, does Esther aspire to a position other than that of the mere insider: not content to be *simply* the national exemplar she so plainly is for Dickens, she insists upon practicing the qualified detachment that is insideness's necessary check and complement. Only *after* Britain as a whole has been revitalized by the inside-out labors of the autoethnographer can the sailor's promise to export Esther's picture of the British hearth to other lands be profitably entertained.

V

That ambivalent refunctioning of the cultural past that I have described above—the principle of keeping-but-changing or changing-but-keeping—works its way (as we might expect) into the very smallest details of *Bleak House*. Consider the umbrella. It is introduced in the work's first paragraph as the symbol or fetish of Victorian solipsism, the symptom of that "general infection of ill temper" (BH 11) that serves Dickens as the very type of an anticulture: each London passer-by claps one umbrella over one head, strives to keep one pair of feet out of the mud, colliding with and cursing the many others engaged in the same pursuit on the same ground at the same moment. Their common creed of "everyone for himself" makes the Londoners of *Bleak House*'s opening page epitomize the "embrace of mutual hatred" Carlyle discerned in capitalism's "cash nexus."[76] Yet the umbrella, this important emblem of malaise, undergoes a remarkable transformation in the novel's second half, where it resurfaces as the talisman of the indomitable Mrs. Bagnet, "the old girl," who has carried it with her around the world in her capacity as wife to the now-repatriated common soldier Matthew Bagnet. The umbrella, which is

[75] Cf. Steven Marcus on the conception of selfhood in which "[s]ociety and individual persons . . . are not separable or distinct phenomena, but . . . the collective and distributive aspects of the same circumstance or thing" (*Representations* 197).

[76] Cf. Graham Smith, *Dickens, Money, and Society* (Berkeley: University of California Press, 1968), 139.

still "invariably a part of the old girl's presence out of doors," has been taken from posting to posting (sites memorialized in the Bagnet children's names: Quebec, Malta, Woolwich) and has "served, through a series of years, at home as a cupboard, and on journeys as a carpet bag." As if determined to signal the symbolic rather than merely utilitarian function of this ordinary household article, the narrator indicates that Mrs. Bagnet "never puts it up" for protection from the rain, "but generally uses the instrument as a wand with which *to point out* joints of meat or bunches of greens in marketing, or *to arrest the attention* of tradesmen by a friendly poke" (BH 498; emphasis added). What it points to is not just the tradesmen's ribs but the ethic exemplified by the Bagnets: that of a resolute and resourceful lower-class patriotism that Dickens implicitly recommends to the superior orders. Like most of the Bagnets' mean objects of daily use, the umbrella testifies to extensive service on behalf of the empire. "The kit of [their] mess, if the table furniture may be so denominated, is chiefly composed of utensils of horn and tin, that have done duty in several parts of the world" (BH 408). "[A]n article long associated with the British army" (BH 498), the Bagnet umbrella is a *bayonet* of sorts, with which Mrs. Bagnet may defend herself, her family, and their British values, wherever her wide-ranging travels might lead her.

Symbolically refurbished, the umbrella has been altered from the token of a British anticulture into a sign of a positive Britishness that seems imaginable only from outside, by the traveler who goes abroad and returns—as the Bagnets and their kit have done, bringing the national self-image back with them like some trophy of an arduous crusade. Not lying within the domain of the narrated in *Bleak House,* the "beyond" of the empire exists primarily to afford an external position from which the Briton's sights may be turned *back* to Britain itself, a standpoint outside the island nation from which the collective whole of the British may be apprehended. Indeed, as if anticipating and seeking to preempt those apprehensions of "reverse colonialism" that were to inundate the late-Victorian literary imagination, *Bleak House* describes a world in which the *only* things to arrive in Britain from the colonial beyond are people and objects seemingly polished in their Britishness.[77] The Bagnets' career itinerary crosses paths here with a circuit familiar in travel writing—the kind described, for instance, by Edward Gibbon, who wrote of feeling that he had returned from his Grand Tour "a better Englishman than [he] went out."[78] Only former expatriates like the Bagnets can comprehend that highest praise that they give their son in declaring him "a Briton. That's what Woolwich is. A Briton!" (BH 406). The "old girl" herself is a quantity of Britishness brought back safely to the nation's shores: she commands her husband's awestruck admiration for the way she "[m]ade her way home once. From another quarter of the world" (BH 741). The recuperative process of carrying a perfected

[77] Cf. Stephen Arata, "The Occidental Tourist: Dracula and the Anxiety of Reverse Colonization," *Victorian Studies* 33/4 (1990); Ian Duncan, "*The Moonstone,* the Victorian Novel, and Imperialist Panic," *Modern Language Quarterly* 55/3 (Sept. 1994), 297–319.

[78] Gibbon, *The Letters of Edward Gibbon,* ed. J. E. Norton (New York: Macmillan, 1956), 1.197–98.

or recovered Britishness home from abroad mirrors the ethnographic Participant-Observer's willed submission to an alien culture and reemergence from it with new authority. Back from immersion in that destructive element of "the world" (signaled by the miscellany of their children's names), the modest Bagnets seem to have acquired the authority that arises from the autoethnographic insider's outsideness. In contrast, the more privileged Richard Carstone resigns his army commission, and so refuses the chance to subject *his* Britishness to the refining fire of the beyond, because his obsession with Jarndyce and Jarndyce requires that he remain in Britain. "I must have been ordered abroad," Richard explains to Esther, "but how could I have gone?" (BH 647).

So far I have located the constitutive ambivalence of *Bleak House* as it manifests itself through the novel's dual narration; but we need also to entertain the thought of *each* narrator's account as divided in itself. I have already suggested Esther's noncompliance with any position of simple insideness or feminine domestication: when she downplays her importance in the narrative she is writing ("as if this were the narrative of *my* life!" [BH 35]), we may read the gesture not only as an exhibition of the modesty for which Dickens wants to celebrate her, but also as indicating the wish not to be wholly confined to the story-space side of narrative's internal division, not to have her narrating function vanish entirely into her role as a *character*. During her bout of fever near the middle of the narrative, Esther's dream of herself as a bead strung on a "flaming necklace" gives powerful expression to an "inexplicable agony and misery [at being] a part of the dreadful thing" (BH 514)—to a desire, that is, to be *freed* from the ring of connection and recognition she otherwise so avidly participates in. And it is also the case that, if the anonymous narrator of half the novel's chapters is always demonstrating his freedom to revisit the culture from which he has departed, his frequent returns may also be read as compulsive, suggesting an inability to *remain* outside. As one of the most important of those partial objectifications of the third-person narrator to appear in the novel, the good doctor Allan Woodcourt not only makes an almost ghostly appearance by Nemo's deathbed, but later reenters as a "brown, sunburnt gentleman" who, compelled to leave his homeland for the vague outside, now returns bearing a new charge of authority and commitment to serve his home culture (BH 657). This improved Woodcourt is a figure tempered by the ordeal of an off-stage shipwreck in "East-Indian seas," during which he proved himself a hero. This is the man who settles down with Esther Summerson at the end of the novel. She gets "invested with the merit of the whole system" for her acts of local goodness; "[t]he whole country rings with" his fame for what he did outside it (BH 525). Woodcourt's progress describes a detachment from the space of one's culture that is not a permanent flight from it but rather a preparation for effective return: a phase in a larger process of repatriation and rededication. He returns too late to save Jo, but when we see him walk through Tom-all-Alone's full of "compassionate interest," looking "here and there" and seeming "to understand such wretchedness, and to have studied it before," we cannot easily miss the implication that he is home to stay and will find much good work to do.

And yet, in a piece of exceptionally stagy business, the novel takes its exem-

plary couple away from the metropolis and off to a bucolic Yorkshire retreat. In
order to make good on his promise to make Esther "mistress of Bleak House" without marrying her himself, John Jarndyce builds an impossibly cozy second Bleak
House in this hinterland and installs Allan and Esther in it, there to practice their
healing arts for the benefit of a suitably appreciative rural community. Prepared in
consideration of Esther's tastes but without her knowledge, the new house is

> quite a rustic cottage of doll's rooms; but such a lovely place, so tranquil and so beauti-
> ful, with such a rich and smiling country spread around it; with water sparkling away into
> the distance, here all overhung with summer-growth, there turning a humming mill; at
> its nearest point glancing through a meadow by a cheerful town, where cricket-players
> were assembling in bright groups, and a flag was flying from a white tent that rippled in
> the sweet west wind. (BH 888)

That west wind blows exactly contrary to the easterly one to which the original
Bleak House has always been exposed, the ill wind that carries the miasma of London's East End westward to more prosperous districts and insists upon their connection. All the escapist endings of earlier Dickens novels, in which a select fellowship of the saved is granted a permanent space apart from society and its
disfiguring institutions, seem alluded to and outdone here: everything is just too
perfect.[79]

As I read it, two features of this extraordinary set-piece mark it as a self-reflexive
comment on Dickens's earlier fictional practice, as an element of modesty in this
hugely ambitious novel encouraging modest good works. First is the obvious difference between this new Bleak House and its original—a glaring defiance of
mimesis involving substitution of a prettified and apparently circumscribed miniature for John Jarndyce's house, which for all its attractions was unmistakably
shown to be linked and susceptible both to the central institution of Chancery and
to its squalid urban by-product, Tom-all-Alone's. Second is the oppressively
made-to-order aspect of the new house, where Esther sees "in the papering on the
walls, in the colours of the furniture, in the arrangement of all the pretty objects"—
in "everything," in short—her own "little tastes and fancies" (BH 888–89). As a
figure for the author who created him, Jarndyce has outdone himself in his exertions to gratify an audience's tastes—he has not sought to change them. As this
novel's self-caricature, the second Bleak House would encode some of that dissatisfaction with art that makes itself felt in numerous works by this consummate
artist. It seems to involve the recognition that, sprawling and densely populated as
it is, *Bleak House* (the novel) cannot aspire to be more than a manageable miniature of *its* original, a doll's house standing in for a real and perhaps unmanageable
Britain. A place quite ludicrously out of keeping with its title, the second Bleak
House repeats as farce what the novel so much wants to insist upon, the possibility of positive refunctionings of cultural "givens."

At the same time, one might regard the decision to settle Esther and Allan in the

---

[79] Dickens's letters of the period advert to the "prettiness" of the arrangement: cf. Graham Storey,
Charles Dickens: Bleak House (Cambridge: Cambridge University Press, 1987), 84.

Yorkshire countryside as not so much at odds with the trope of a *national* "consequential ground" as it may initially seem. If we recall Mr. Gridley, "the man from Shropshire" brought into the narrative in order to give substance to the claim that Chancery wreaks its effects not just in London but "in every shire," we may be inclined to consider the ostentatiously pastoral home that the novel awards the Woodcourts at the end as complementing and at least promising to counteract the anticultural axis linking center to margin, the Lord Chancellor's court and the yeoman Mr. Gridley. Such an interpretation would accord with the impression the narrative seems determined to make on us, of Allan and Esther's marriage as inaugurating in prospect a new Britain in which every former nobody will be granted recognition and consequence. Esther is of course well suited to usher in this new dispensation. Offspring of a Barbary and a Nemo, she is doubly a nobody herself, her parents being associated with the two complementary boundaries with which communities define themselves: the boundary *around* the community, which excludes "barbarians," and the boundary *through* it, which eclipses from view the deviant "nonentities" who count for nothing. To have such parents is to confront the moral irrelevance of parentage. Holding to her belief that "I was as innocent of my birth as a queen of hers" (BH 543), Esther effectively *"becomes* a Queen"— so Bucket pronounces her (BH 834)—and this new Queen Esther evokes, of course, the Biblical heroine who saves her people from destruction. Miss Barbary raised her, of all places, in Windsor, though for most of the novel her royal court is situated in St. Albans, a town named for England's first Christian martyr (A.D. 303) and thus linked to the destinies of those latter-day English martyrs, Nemo and Jo. Esther goes on to wed a man half Welsh and half Highland Scot who has had to overcome the parochial loyalties of his ancestors and embrace the British union (BH 31, 255–56, 434).

Around their marriage crowd those restless ghosts of the national past that have been conjured up in seemingly "every" odd corner of Dickens's narrative.[80] It is as if the coherent narrative of British history has spontaneously combusted just as Mr. Krook has done, scattering its shrapnel all over the fictional field. Norman Conquest, Peasant Rebellion, Popish intrigues, Civil War, Jacobite Risings, Industrial Revolution, the domestic scandals of George IV—all are woven into the fabric of a text that appears bound to raise Great Britain's dead, even, or especially, in its "throwaway" details. We read, for instance, of the marriage of a Prince (Turveydrop) and a Caroline (Caddy Jellyby), and of the conflict between a George (Rouncewell) and his enemies (the Smallweeds), one of whom habitually calls out for "Charley over the water" (BH 310). We meet the puppet-like Mr. Smallweed, who bankrupts George and gains control of the decisive Will in the Jarndyce case: he is likened to a Guy Fawkes effigy, and looks as if he "might be expected immediately to recite the popular verses, commemorative of the time when they did contrive to blow Old England up alive" (BH 390). His entourage seems "scarcely

---

[80] On *Bleak House*'s use of gothic, cf. Arac, *Commissioned Spirits,* 114–38; Herbert, "The Occult in *Bleak House,*" 125–30; and Richard Maxwell, *Mysteries of Paris and London* (Charlottesville: University of Virginia Press, 1992), 160–90.

reconcilable with any day in the year but the fifth of November" (BH 389). We read, of course, of a doomed marriage—the Dedlocks'—a failed union to contrast with the novel's closing and crowning one: it recapitulates the strife between Cavaliers and Roundheads that sundered the Dedlock family in the seventeenth century. The ghost of that past Lady Dedlock who betrayed her Royalist husband and secretly aided Cromwell's cause stalks Chesney Wold (BH 102–5), reminding successors of this unsettled conflict that was "domestic" in both the household and the national senses. We read of a wicked Frenchwoman (Hortense) who threatens to revive vanquished Jacobinism and bring its bloodlettings to British soil. We read of an "Ironmaster" (George Rouncewell's brother) who confronts Sir Leicester Dedlock, turning his "strong Saxon face" against the "Norman house" and refusing to defer to it (BH 417, 654); industrialization thus becomes legible as a long-deferred casting-off of the Norman Yoke, with Lady Dedlock's chosen companion, Rosa, as the English Rose whose future hangs in the balance of this conflict of races and classes. The Ironmaster's own son is named "Watt," after the inventor, but the appellation has a different resonance for the Dedlock ear, attuned as it is to the slightest hints of insurgent Wat-Tylerism (BH 22, 98).

All the national work of memory that is done through the handling of these characters is organized around two centers: Allan and Esther's nation-curing marriage, on the one hand, and Nemo's and Jo's deathbeds, on the other. As loci and stimulants to national memory, Nemo and Jo are like the Unknown Soldiers commemorated by most countries today: they serve as the catalysts for an affective bond capable of both expanding to the conceptual horizon of the nation (because they are personally unknown to us, are in fact unknown to *all* of us) and *stopping there* (because they are *ours*). The fates met by Nemo and Jo are rebukes to "this boastful island" (BH 165), not to the human race at large. Their deaths point to the space where a genuine British culture ought to be, and even—who knows?—where British heroes might have been, had that culture been there to sustain them. As a former officer, Nemo was once in a position to play an important role in the national defense. Skimpole's tasteless remark that Jo, already desperately ill, might turn out "like Whittington to become Lord Mayor of London" (BH 457) serves as a reminder to British readers that, since their civic leaders might arise from "anywhere" among them, they stand to gain from a system that acculturates every Briton.

This Whittington motif (which attaches to the character of Walter Gay in *Dombey and Son*) is also applied to Richard Carstone shortly after his first appearance in *Bleak House*. When, en route from London to Jarndyce's house for the first time, Richard observes that the sound of bells along the road "has been reminding [him] of [his] namesake Whittington," and when, two pages later, he "confesse[s] . . . to feeling an irrational desire to drive back [to London] again," the text is reminding us of the legend in which, on his way out of the city, the original Dick Whittington heard the church bells call out to him, "turn again, Whittington, Lord Mayor of London" and rode back to commence a career of public service and renown (BH 73, 75). The Lord Mayor motif is there to suggest how much potential will be lost in Richard Carstone when he proves himself incapable

of resisting the disastrous call of the Chancery Court and dies in despair of his failure to penetrate that heart of darkness. But it is the death of Jo that most effectively
consolidates the national "us" in the gesture of indicting it: when the narrator caps
his announcement of the event with the phrase, "And dying thus around us every
day" (BH 677), he identifies it as a mundane occurrence, one all too easily dupli-
catable in other spots on Britain's consequential ground. Jo and Nemo exemplify
the "*general* details" by means of which a narrative conveys the "sociological solidity" of the nation: as Benedict Anderson put it, "none [is] in itself of any unique
importance, but all [are] representative (in their simultaneous, separate existence)"
of the national life. Readers' indignation and pity have nothing to do with "who
the dead vagrant individually was"; they center on "the representative body, not
the personal life."[81]

With its insistence that "everyone's Nemo," its stress on a common inheritance
of mud, *Bleak House* appears to echo Thomas Hobbes's conception of the "functional equivalence of persons" in a state, since as this novel sees it, everyone will
do equally well to fill a grave.[82] But this premise does not provide the basis for
any "leveling" sympathies. On the contrary, Dickens's point is that culture constitutes not only the moral oneness of the nation but the system of internal differences
that delineates meaningful roles and identities. As did Scott, Dickens seeks a vantage point from which different parts of the whole can appear "united by the strife
that divides them."[83] Near its end, *Bleak House* intimates this vision in its account
of the rapprochement between Sir Leicester Dedlock and his neighbor Boythorn,
whose longstanding dispute over the border between their properties has been
transformed into a sort of collaboration, rekindled by Boythorn for the purpose of
giving the bereft baronet something to live for. "Mr. Boythorn," we read, "found
himself under the necessity of committing a flagrant trespass in order to restore his
neighbour to himself" (BH 907). When we take our leave of these characters, the
contest between them is continuing "to the satisfaction of both" (BH 908). This
situation describes the very dream of intranational differences: maintained and defended in a form of serious play, division and inequity obscure but also imply a
"deeper," systemic interconnection and likeness. Elsewhere, landed and industrial
interests reconcile themselves as parts of one family, their opposition not rending
but rather defining and securing the national culture that contains them both: the
runaway George Rouncewell refuses his brother's offer of a job in his works, preferring instead to serve as steward for the ailing Dedlock. Though making peace
with his brother, George accepts the duty of sustaining the element of national difference embodied by the Dedlocks, rather than to take the side of the rising class
and assist it in eliminating that difference.

---

[81] Benedict Anderson, *Imagined Communities: Reflections on the Origin and Spread of Nationalism* (London: Verso, 1983), 36, 35, 37, respectively.

[82] See Poovey, *Making a Social Body,* 28–29.

[83] T. S. Eliot, "Little Gidding," *Four Quartets,* in *The Complete Poems and Plays, 1909–1950* (New
York: Harcourt, Brace, and Company, 1958), 143.

VI

If there was one piece of "consequential ground" in Britain in that season immediately preceding Dickens's composition of *Bleak House,* all the organs of official and mainstream opinion declared it to be the 772,824 square feet of Hyde Park enclosed within Joseph Paxton's iron and glass Crystal Palace for the Great Exhibition of 1851. As if determined to provoke comparisons with the expansive products of the nation's foremost novelist, the Exhibition's promoters treated it as a kind of text in which was written not just the British national story but the tale of all humankind. "Here in a great Open Book," the *Illustrated Exhibitor* proclaimed, "we read of the industry of our brethren of the north, the south, the east, and the west."[84] It was a book "everybody" in Britain was reading in 1851; it was, as William Howitt said, "the one great topic of conversation."[85] "Everything" made reference to it: it might seem to have cornered the market on British representation, even to have absorbed or annihilated space (in concentrating all the world upon a single spot in London) and time (in suggesting that all history had pointed to this one great trial of Civilization). Prince Albert declared that the whole spectacle would "afford a true test of the point of development at which the whole of mankind has arrived . . . and a new starting point from which all nations would be able to direct their further exertions."[86]

Central to this world-historical enterprise was the delineation of Britain itself as leader among developed nations and seat of a rational power that could overcome a world of challenges. The nation's willingness to host the amicable contest bespoke, it was said, a "conscious greatness, on the part of our country sufficient to warrant such a bold and unprecedented step."[87] In the picture of the world implied by the Great Exhibition, *Hoggs' Instructor* argued,

> Britain stood out in bold relief the principal figure . . . occupying and engrossing mainly the foreground, a rich and troubled sky above her, the principal light issuing from one cloudless spot, and of which she was the recipient, her surrounding grouped neighbours being but partially within its blaze, dimness and darkness increasing with the distance, till the horizon and sky blended, completing the picture. (quoted in Andrew Miller 75)

Here, plainly, in the promotional rhetoric of the Exhibition, and not in the novel that responded to it, was what Edward Said called the colonial power's "departmental view," with its tendentious, self-centered mapping of the world (see Andrew Miller 72). Conveying "the image of a 'non-exclusive interior'" in its walls

---

[84] Quoted in Asa Briggs, *Victorian Things* (Chicago: University of Chicago Press, 1988), 61.

[85] Quoted in Tatiana Holway, *"A Capital Idea": Dickens, Speculation, and the Victorian Economies of Representation* (Ph.D. diss., Columbia University, 2002), 209.

[86] Quoted in "History of the Great Exhibition," in *The Great Exhibition: A Facsimile of the Illustrated Catalogue of London's 1851 Crystal Palace Exposition* (New York: Grammercy Books, 1995), xi.

[87] Quoted in Andrew H. Miller, *Novels Behind Glass: Commodity Culture and Victorian Narrative* (Cambridge: Cambridge University Press, 1995), 76; henceforth Andrew Miller.

of glass, Paxton's palace could be read as suggesting that the great book of the Exhibition scarcely *needed* to be read, because its meanings appeared so self-evident: the structure might appear to imply that international capitalism and perhaps the reasons for British world dominance were transparent, plain for all to see.[88] As the least site-specific of buildings—made out of materials not bearing the signature of any particular terrain, capable of being taken down and re-erected elsewhere—the Crystal Palace might seem to say that its message was universally exportable and applicable. And the displayed items inside it, nestled snugly in their categories, bore no price tags, as if they held their value wholly in themselves, as if that value were non-negotiable and owed nothing to the variegations of demand.

The much-publicized labors of preparation for the Exhibition—of the builders, to put up Paxton's structure with amazing speed and precision; of the organizers, to arrive at a workable scheme for classifying the myriad objects to be displayed; of the institutions of transport and accommodation, to move and house the millions of visitors—all these contributed to the rhetorical labor of showing Britain meeting its unprecedented challenge of managing the world. An implicit authorizing narrative in which the enterprise was framed described the nation's willing engagement with a dizzying array of details to be handled, and its triumphant reemergence to a position of mastery over the whole. The audience for this rhetorical enterprise was assured that, "[f]ar from being abandoned in a labyrinth of cosmic alienation," it would discover "'[t]he mighty maze' has not only its plan, but a plan of the most lucid and instructive kind . . . as in a well-arranged book."[89]

The social and architectural text of the Exhibition and the seemingly self-replicating mass of words and images that promoted it bore down upon Dickens as he prepared to write his most ambitious work. "*Il n'y a rien—rien—partout excepté l'Exposition,*" he wrote to Count D'Orsay two weeks after the Exhibition opened: there was nothing anywhere but it.[90] In sympathy with many of its aims, he viewed askance its ubiquitous self-congratulation. He visited the Crystal Palace *only* twice. In a magazine piece entitled "The Last Words of the Old Year," he had the spirit of the departing year speak of having seen "a project carried into execution for a great assemblage of the peaceful glories of the world," but then ask, "Which of my children shall behold the Princes, Prelates, Nobles, Merchants, of England, equally united, for another Exhibition—for a great display of England's sins and negligences, to be, by steady contemplation of all eyes, and steady union of all hearts and minds, set right?"[91]

By the time he began writing *Bleak House* in the fall of 1851, Dickens seems to have come to regard Paxton's glorified greenhouse as yet one more symbol of

[88] Andrea Kahn, "The Invisible Mask," in Kahn, ed., *Drawing Building Text* (Princeton: Architectural Press, 1991), 85–106, see 96.

[89] "Far from . . . ": Philip Landon, "Great Exhibitions: Representations of the Crystal Palace in Mayhew, Dickens, and Dostoevsky," *Nineteenth-Century Contexts* 20/1 (1997), 30. "'The mighty maze' . . . ": Anon., *The Crystal Palace and its Contents,* quoted in Landon, 30.

[90] In Graham Storey, Kathleen Tillotson, and Nina Burgis, eds., *The Letters of Charles Dickens,* Volume VI, 1850–52 (Oxford: Clarendon Press, 1988), 392.

[91] *Household Words,* 4 January 1851, 338.

British anticulture, as a colossal "oblong cistern to hold the fog" of obscurantism, for all its purported transparency. Seeing nothing anywhere *but* the Exhibition was a step toward seeing the Exhibition as the gigantic nothing that was everywhere. Succeeding it in becoming the cultural event that "everybody talked about," the serial publication of *Bleak House* responded to the triumphant universalism of 1851 by exhibiting, not the works of industry of all nations, but the neglected human by-products of the national anticulture. Instead of a sweeping celebration of general human "Progress," *Bleak House* recounted "*A* Progress": that is the title of the novel's third chapter, in which Esther first introduces herself and begins her always local and nationally allegorical story of development and promised redemption. Like the Exhibition, the novel attempted to make its audience into observant participants in a narrative of modernity; but mobilizing its readers around the monthly ritual of the new installment, it aimed at effects quite opposed to those envisioned by the planners and trumpeters of the Great "Eggs-and-Bacon." If the Exhibition's open book lay out a putatively indisputable and universal teleology, the Dickens serial sought to actualize a single culture around a national spectacle of waste and neglect—and, "[i]n a novel where the life of England in 1851 is otherwise fully represented," it gave no space at all to the site that was everyone's destination and the subject on everyone's lips.[92]

[92] John Butt and Kathleen Tillotson, *Dickens at Work* (London: Methuen, 1957), 182. Landon and (much more thoroughly) Holway have fleshed out Norman Page's suggestion that Dickens aimed in *Bleak House* to "depict England in terms almost exactly the opposite of those implicit in the idea of the Exhibition": Page, *Bleak House: A Novel of Connections* (Boston: Twayne, 1990), 27.

PART THREE

Charlotte Brontë's English Books

Identities, Locations, and Media

As for translating the letters into French, he considered that the spontaneity of intimate letters gave them "une grace, un charme *intraduisibles.*"
   —Margaret Smith, quoting Constantin Heger[1]

I

DICKENS'S DECISION to build his metanovel *Bleak House* around the tense juxtaposition of two stances—those of the erstwhile outcast who comes to treasure cultural belonging and of the self-exiled authority who grasps the cultural totality from without—finds a match in the shape of Charlotte Brontë's brief novelistic career, and, as with Dickens, we should note in Brontë the presence of a definitive structuring opposition not only *between* leading tendencies but also incorporated *within* each. Each of Brontë's four adult fictions can be characterized as either a narrative of departure from an oppressive anticulture (*The Professor, Villette*) or one of internal exile within one (*Jane Eyre, Shirley*). In her first and fourth novels, *The Professor* and *Villette,* Brontë detaches her protagonist-narrators from the territory and the degraded culture of their homelands, exposing them to alien influence in a series of controlled, though perilous, experiments that structure a quest for the elements of a genuine Anglocentric culture. In *Jane Eyre* and *Shirley,* Jane Eyre and Caroline Helstone endure miserably alienated existence *within* their native lands, finding true homes at last through the defeat of their anticultural opponents and intimating as they do so the conditions required for Britain to become (once more?) an authentic home and culture.

The metaphorizing of cultures as places establishes cultural identity as a "hereness," a quality properly belonging to, though separable from, a specific place. Broadly speaking, narrative conflict in Brontë's novels is generated by: 1) the displacement of hereness—the identity that ought to go with a place—from the *here* to which it properly belongs; and 2) the invasion or occupation of the here by alien forces. The first plot pattern works toward (but does not necessarily arrive at) resolution under the auspices of a master trope of return or repatriation, the second toward resolution in accordance with a master trope of expulsion or purgation. The

---

[1] *The Letters of Charlotte Brontë,* Vol. 1 (1829–1847), ed. Margaret Smith (Oxford: Clarendon-Press, 1995), 34; henceforth *Letters 1.*

fundamental axes of Brontë's fiction become visible on a Greimasian semiotic rectangle we may describe in the following manner:

	HERE	ELSEWHERE
HERENESS	#1: Non-narratable resolution of narrative of displacement: Trope of Return	#2: Narrative of displacement seeking resolution in #1: *The Professor, Villette*
ELSEWHERENESS	#3: Narrative of invasion or occupation seeking resolution in #4: *Jane Eyre, Shirley*	#4: Non-narratable resolution of narrative of invasion or occupation: Trope of Purgation

A structuralist diagram like this one oversimplifies the relationships among the novels, but it can still make a convenient starting point.

In this and the subsequent chapters, I examine the interplay of geographical identity categories in Brontë's adult fiction, the repeated, interrelated, ambivalent evocations of locality, nationality, and internationality through which that fiction performs the "work of producing localities" as well as those larger units of space against which local identities come into view.[2] In every one of the novels, Brontë both constructs and investigates the ramifications of constructing an autoethnographic authority that might be capable of grasping and "restor[ing] to rectitude" what she called "the warped system of things" in her native land.[3] Her fictions attempt to gain distance on a domestic British anticulture that seems both warped in respect to Britain's proper condition and in total possession of the domestic scene. I have already cited, in chapter 3, the striking evocation of totalitarian rule under which the heroine languishes at the beginning of *Jane Eyre:* a state of affairs in which John Reed "bullie[s] and punishe[s]" Jane "not two or three times in the week, nor once or twice in the day, but continually," such that "every nerve I had," Jane says, "feared him, and every morsel of flesh on my bones shrank when he came near. . . . I had no appeal whatever against either his menaces or his inflictions" (JE 16). Resolution of this narrative would call for the elimination of forces seeking to exert total control over Jane—and in the end, something very like this has happened, through the death of John Reed, the breaking of Brocklehurst, and the permanent expatriation of St. John Rivers, three successive events enshrining the central one in which Edward Rochester is purged of those defects of character that have led him to betray what it means to be British.

But where the Greimasian diagram might encourage us to dissociate the two pairs of Brontë's novels from each other, interaction of the two leading tropes creates the warp and woof of *each* novel, giving to each its distinctive imbalance or self-interrupting tendency. Robert Moore, the reluctant, chastened hero of *Shirley,*

---

[2] Arjun Appadurai, "Sovereignty without Territoriality: Notes for a Postnational Geography," in Patricia Yaeger, ed., *The Geography of Identity* (Ann Arbor: University of Michigan Press, 1996), 42.

[3] From the preface to the second edition of *Jane Eyre:* Charlotte Brontë, *Jane Eyre* (1847; Harmondsworth: Penguin, 1996), 6; henceforth JE.

says that he "daily find[s] it proved—that we can get nothing in this world worth keeping, not so much as a principle or a conviction, except out of a purifying flame, or through strengthening peril."[4] To varying degrees, all Brontë's fiction invokes this metallurgical metaphor according to which national culture and identity must pass through the cauldron of alienation in order to become their better selves, yet this process of "tempering" cultural identity Brontë also—problematically—tropes as recuperation, restoration, return.

Brontë relentlessly questions the narrative tools in her hands: she seems never to use a plot structure or figural strategy without considering and putting on display her device's limitations, a habit which then leads to similarly qualified or interrupted investment in another device whose implications run contrary to the first. The trope of purification is disqualified to the extent that Brontë indicates a partiality for mixed conditions over undiluted ones; its counterpart, the trope of return, is in like fashion undermined whenever her narrative relies on concepts or situations that raise the question of how one can properly be said to "return" to a state of being from which it is impossible to "depart" (a racial inheritance, for example), or of how it can be felt as a "return" when one arrives somewhere one has never been before (for example, a promised "homeland" never yet seen).

Brontë never practices the self-interrupting tendency I am describing here so remorselessly as in *Villette,* with its famously frustrating reticence and its apparently principled irresolution. Thus, for example, the gothic framework of *Villette* is seriously compromised by (among other factors) the heroine's scorning of any attempt to imagine her the imperiled maiden required by the mode. The gothic's strict division of domestic and foreign realms is just as devotedly problematized: too trusting reliance on the gothic lens will obscure the fact that the left-behind homeland represents no safe haven for the threatened English maiden but rather a wholly inhospitable domain of dead loves, ruined hopes, lost possibilities. Moreover, that which defines England for the protagonist exhibits an *unheimlich* tendency to show up on the foreign landscape she comes to inhabit, to map that landscape for her as something *other* than simply or neatly Other. And the alien force through contact with which the Anglocentric principle is to refine itself—or so the metallurgical metaphor has it—is not permitted to remain *entirely* alien, but is brought nearer, is incorporated or at least seriously considered for incorporation into an expanded sense of national identity that might shed its insularity and become its better self by becoming more than just itself. Readers who infer Paul Emmanuel's loss at sea at the novel's end may find this supposed event to bring *Villette* finally under the rule of the purifying-flame master trope: they may see the abrasive intimacy that has developed between Lucy and Paul as fortifying Lucy's English Protestantism, an essential national-religious identity that even Paul comes to validate—just before his necessary demise ("Remain a Protestant," he writes. "My little English Puritan, I love Protestantism in you. I own its severe charm. There is something in its ritual I cannot receive myself, but it is the sole creed for 'Lucy'" [V 594–95]). But excessive investment in this attractively tidy

---

[4] Charlotte Brontë, *Shirley* (1849; Harmondsworth: Penguin, 1974), 505; henceforth S.

reading, according to which the narrative dispenses with its serviceable destructive element as soon as that element's catalyzing function has been fulfilled and a unilateral declaration of cultural relativism has been extracted from it, will, I think, lead us to flatten out Brontë's novel and underrate the radical thrust of a work that, written in part during the upsurge of Protestant paranoia arising from the so-called Papal Aggression of 1850, gave sustained consideration to the possibility of a Protestant Englishwoman's finding happiness and even the fulfillment of her national and religious identities by becoming the wife of a devout Belgian-Spanish Catholic. And last, because, among its many silences, *Villette* does not divulge the location from which Lucy is supposed to be writing her retrospective account, we are left with a possibility that would constitute a conclusive frustration of gothic expectations, namely that this Englishwoman, upon completing her strengthening trials, has decided to remain English *abroad*. If this is the case, only Lucy's *narrative* could be said to "return" to England, an invisible import whose message might revitalize English readers.

If we look back from *Villette* with this perspective in mind, we will be in a position to appreciate the demonstrated limitations of both of Brontë's master tropes in the earlier fiction, as well. It may strike us that not *all* the Frenchness residing in *The Professor*'s Frances Henri is supposed to be "burned off" by the refining re-education in Englishness that she receives at the hands of the novel's narrator, William Crimsworth; Brontë appears to suggest that its retention as a strong if supplementary aspect of Frances's personality will enliven that recovered Englishness to which it is fundamentally opposed. Similarly, in *Shirley,* the hybrid Robert Moore is not to *overcome* his hybridity in assuming—or resuming?—the role of a morally engaged Englishman. Brontë challenges us to think of that part of Moore proudly self-identified as "*Anversois*"—as Francophone native of Antwerp—as a possible element *in,* not a dilution of, the re-energized Englishness that his marriage to Caroline (and his brother Louis's marriage to Shirley Keeldar) appears to promise. Where Caroline herself is concerned, the prospect that Robert's purification trope might be realized in his own case, making him "purely English" in the sense of wholeheartedly devoted to the English side of his nature and to the English community he lives in, would be a disaster. For her, a viable or valuable English existence seems impossible unless it can *also* be in some vital measure a "French" one, too, and it is primarily Robert who provides her with access to those enlivening qualities she identifies as French.

In *The Professor, Shirley,* and *Villette,* Brontë drew, of course, upon the variety of "Frenchness" she had personally encountered in Brussels in the early 1840s, during those seasons of ferment that marked an epoch in her emotional and intellectual development. Belgium, a nation whose very existence testified to the reduced power of France in the wake of Waterloo and the July Revolution of 1830, could be seen as the home of a Frenchness singularly useful for generating narratives of English self-recovery: a Frenchness threatening enough (especially in its Catholic aspect) to stir up significant narrative conflict yet comparatively "safe," neither enjoying complete dominion over its own territory (since Belgian Frenchness had to coexist with Flemishness) nor striving beyond its boundaries for Continental predominance—nor, for that matter, possessing quite the reputation for indecency of its Parisian counterpart. (Indeed, the comparative respectability of Brussels over Paris did much to secure Patrick Brontë's approval of Charlotte's plan to "immerse herself" in a French-speaking culture.) In a manner comparable to that of Walter Scott's formula of *intelligible foreignness,* Brontë's Belgian Frenchness frees up aesthetic qualities and "cultural" identity from the historicopolitical forces that once put "that which is French" beyond the pale of any positively asserted English or British identity.

In her one novel making substantive use of *Parisian* Frenchness—*Jane Eyre*—Brontë imports into her narrative the prefabricated stereotype of the dangerously alluring and amoral coquette, Céline Varens, and her recourse to this standardized element of unassimilable, purely destructive foreignness is responsible for the fact that this most celebrated of her novels lacks certain of the complexities that define (and, some might say, contort) her fictions of encounter with Belgian Frenchness. More neatly than does any of Brontë's other fictions, *Jane Eyre* conforms to the metallurgical logic of nation making or nation saving: the reformation of Rochester as modern Englishman appears to require the painful purgation of those "impurities" in him that have led him to desire alien succubi like Céline or Bertha Mason. This process is replicated, one should add, in miniature form, as Adèle, who throughout the novel has been present largely for the purpose of replicating in miniature form the horrid charms of her Gallic mother, undergoes a "solid English education [that] correct[s] in a great measure her French defects" (JE 500). Furthermore, one could hardly ask for a more forceful realization of the refining-fire model of national imagining than Bertha's self-immolation at Thornfield toward the close of *Jane Eyre,* the event necessary to free Jane to marry her broken but essentially mendable Rochester. Yet even this novel, otherwise so devoted to servicing the trope of purification, opens up the possibility of thinking about exemplary Englishness as involving the recognition of oneself as a "heterogeneous thing" (JE 23). As is true, to different degrees, in the other novels as well, *Jane Eyre* invokes a heterogeneity that must be confined within limits if it is to take productive rather than destructive form.[5] The autoethnographer must get outside the hereness of her culture, but not too far outside, and not forever.

At a time when post-Napoleonic "Teutomaniacs" were encouraging English people to consider their supposed Germanic racial inheritance the fount of all civilized virtue, Brontë's insistence upon keeping Englishness open to the influence of "French" qualities—an influence she accorded much greater emotional and imaginative weight than that of the customarily approved, superficially acquired "social graces"—deserves commendation, even if it necessitated the use of the "safer" Belgian Frenchness and even if Brontë did not always steer clear of the Teutomaniacs' enthusiasms. An instance of this latter phenomenon in Brontë may be noted in the pivotal scene in which Jane Eyre first comes upon (or recovers) her

---

[5] In this tendency Brontë follows Scott, whose novels foster "the foundation of a nation and a national identity that represents *Britain's* 'natural' heterogeneity": Homer Obed Brown, *Institutions of the English Novel from Defoe to Scott* (Philadelphia: University of Pennsylvania Press, 1997), 14.

unknown English relatives, an event that begins the reconstruction of her own sense of worthy selfhood: when the destitute and friendless Jane looks in through the window of Moor House, in that part of England to which her flight from Rochester has brought her, she is granted the *tableau vivant* of Diana and Mary Rivers studying German, as if they, too, are attempting to find their way (back) to a genuine Anglo-Saxonism by (re)connecting themselves to their own long-lost "cousins," the German people whose blood they share.[6] Most of the time in Brontë it is Frenchness, not Germanism, that supplies the "outside" to which the English autoethnographer must repair; but to emphasize as Brontë does the role of a version of Frenchness in the construction of Englishness is not to reiterate the truism that national identities are formed by opposition to what they are not. Her regular practice is to usher us briskly past the reach of such clichés, demanding again and again to know *what kind* and *how much* of foreignness a positively held Anglocentric identity can accommodate before losing its definition. In her autoethnographic fiction, that national identity cannot become its true self unless it is somehow taken outside its own space and thereafter returns with, and *as,* something more than itself; but not every kind or degree of alterity will serve this supplementary function.

Not only does Brontë tend, for the most part, to shun the Teutomaniacs' invitation for Britons to step out into the warm wide bath of the Germanic bloodstream, where they might find a broader identity than their insular one to honor and exemplify. Her authorizing exit from the space of her culture is also defined in opposition to the kind made available to Britons by the possession of their empire. It would be a mistake to construe this structural contrast as "anti-imperial" in any straightforward sense; it is the sort of maneuver available only to those who *have* an empire, and in any case Brontë does not oppose colonization per se or the missionary work that operates within colonial institutions. Yet her fiction does differentiate, almost programmatically, between the positive, productive transcendence of ordinary boundaries of the self or nation and the fatal step outward into colonial space, whether that space is associated with old-style mercantilist colonialism (in the West) or with the newer, evangelically inflected imperialism of the "civilizing mission" (in the East). In the dramatis personae of Brontë's major characters who go or have been to the colonies, only Rochester comes back, and he, of course, returns bearing an awful burden, which he can shed only by "pass[ing] through the valley of the shadow of death" (JE 495).

Opposed to this excessive or unproductive displacement is the out-of-the-body experience, the *ecstatic* surpassing of the customary limitations of self, which Brontë uses to bring Rochester and Jane finally together, in the famous sequence in which each hears the other's call, though separated by hundreds of miles. Whatever one may say about this flamboyant narrative gesture, it functions in a manner not dissimilar to that of the spontaneous combustion in Dickens's *Bleak House,* in

---

[6] Cf. Frederic E. Faverty, *Matthew Arnold the Ethnologist* (Evanston, Ill.: Northwestern University Press, 1951), and Clare A. Simmons, *Reversing the Conquest: History and Myth in 19th-Century British Literature* (New Brunswick, N.J.: Rutgers University Press, 1990).

this case by creating the impression of a definitively *local* connection—two characters speaking to each other—that can overcome the usual restriction of locality but that is carefully distinguished from the vast reaches of the imperial or universal domain. In their experience of this more-than-local, less-than-global connection, Jane and Rochester enter into a union intimating what the national union could be. Hearing Rochester's desperate plea for rescue, Jane is herself rescued from the peremptory proposals of St. John Rivers, who wants to enlist her in his missionary labors in India. This effectively answers Jane's declared determination to "know for certain, whether [she] cannot be of greater use by remaining in [England] than by leaving it" (JE 461). Rochester's subsequent report that he heard Jane's voice replying "I am coming: wait for me" then contrasts precisely with the words St. John writes from India, where he has gone alone after failing to compel Jane to accompany him: Jesus, he says, has given him warning of his impending death, "[d]aily . . . announc[ing] more distinctly,—'Surely I come quickly!'" (JE 502). In the novel's closing juxtaposition of the two "calls," national belonging becomes particular and local to the degree that it is demarcated against the world-historical vocation of empire: the latter beckons in the voice of the Absolute, overriding and negating all contingent, particular forms of belonging.

In Brontë's logic, the framework of the universal and colonial must "die" so the national culture can live. Though Jane approves of St. John's work so far as to believe he merits a "sure reward" (JE 502), she leaves no doubt that acceptance of Rivers's mission as her own would have proved just as fatal for her as it has for him, and the union she enters into with the repaired Rochester carries the weight of a national allegory in suggesting what kind and degree of union a remade, repatriated English culture might constitute. This novel that has so often in recent years been read as a kind of manual for the production of liberal individualism is also, at its close, a work idealizing a condition of possible English togetherness that rivals Hegel's vision of the state as "the I that is a we and the we that is an I":[7]

> I know what it is [Jane writes] to live entirely for and with what I love best on earth. . . . I am my husband's life as fully as he is mine. No woman was ever nearer to her mate than I am: ever more absolutely bone of his bone, and flesh of his flesh. I know no weariness of my Edward's society: he knows none of mine, any more than we each do of the pulsation of the heart that beats in our separate bosoms; consequently, we are ever together. To be together is for us to be at once as free as in solitude, as gay as in company. We talk, I believe, all day long: to talk to each other is but a more animated and an audible thinking. All my confidence is bestowed on him, all his confidence is devoted to me; we are precisely suited in character—perfect concord is the result. (JE 500)

As I have suggested earlier, the discourse of culture can be placed neither at the pole of classical liberalism nor at the opposite one of irrationalist antiliberalism; it constitutes one of modernity's most influential attempts to think its way *out* of the antinomy of blood and choice, of inherited and elective affinities. We should

---

[7] G.W.F. Hegel, *The Phenomenology of Spirit*, trans. A. V. Miller (Oxford: Oxford University Press, 1977), 110.

not overlook the fact that, at the close of *Jane Eyre,* Jane's marriage is supplemented by her other intimacy, both chosen *and* discovered, with her newfound blood relations, her Rivers cousins "whose qualities [are] such that, when [Jane] knew them but as mere strangers, they had inspired [her] with genuine affection and admiration" (JE 429).

Throughout her fiction's quest for *culture,* Brontë explores versions of *elsewhere* and *elsewhereness* that can augment rather than waste English moral, spiritual, and imaginative power—autoethnographically productive versions, that is. Whenever she invokes the vast regions of colonial space, setting her narrative in that context, Brontë tends to present mixture as a problem to be overcome and tends to give precedence to the trope of purification. Thus, in *Jane Eyre,* Bertha Mason's brother, returned from Jamaica, provides the novel with an anti-Rochester, roughly the hero's age and like him in being weakened by exposure to the colonial atmosphere, but lacking any Jane to save him and the Englishness *in* him. Mason's appearance of being "not precisely foreign, but still not altogether English" is a mixture wholly negative, as is his embodiment of a condition at once "unsettled and inanimate. His eye wandered," Jane notes, "and had no meaning in its wandering": this is a man infected by the meaning-eroding anticultural virus whose chief symptom and metaphor is vagabond motion. Mason "repel[s] [Jane] exceedingly" by exhibiting to her the spectacle of a man leeched of all vitality by his immersion in the radical otherness of the colonies: Jane sees "no power in that smooth-skinned face . . . no firmness in that aquiline nose, and small, cherry mouth . . . no thought on the low, even forehead; no command in that blank, brown eye" (JE 215). In a striking instance of that *dissociation* of culture and place that makes the necessary ground of culture's figuration *as* place, Mason's physical return to England only points up the fact that he can *never* really return to Englishness: his Creole mother has bequeathed him a form of mixture finally destructive to the constitution of Englishmen, a form that represents the dialectical opposite of Brontë's desideratum: a national identity that can be understood as a condition of *bounded* heterogeneity.

The narrative of *The Professor* is also structured around a contrast between destructive and productive departures, the one for the colonial arena from which no one or nothing good ever returns, and the other for an area of Frenchness from which Englishness might be rescued and repatriated. As I will demonstrate in the next section of this chapter, this inaugural novel of Brontë's adult career pits the immature homosocial bond between the narrator, William Crimsworth, and his boyhood friend Charles against the mature heterosexual one William develops with Frances Henri over the course of the narrative. The disappearance of Charles into an undifferentiated imperial space not only leaves William to grow up and to grow past his schoolboy attachments on his own; it also changes the novel from the private letter to Charles that William intended it to be, into a public document laden with national-allegorical significance and addressing an audience at least potentially national in scope. Recognizing this additional dimension in the structural opposition at the heart of Brontë's first novel helps alert us to the fact that, while Brontë's novels dwell repeatedly on the theme of an "Outlandish Nationalism" involving complex negotiations across the boundary dividing nation from nation and the national from internationality, they also operate within an intranational frame, considering what it takes for merely local attachments to give way to a fully national identity and demanding to know what place and value can be retained for "the local" in any national culture requiring (as it must) the local's subordination or supercession.

In *The Professor* and *Villette,* the novels of extraterritorial authority, the category of locality is generally subordinated, much as it can be for travelers abroad who find themselves regarded by foreigners not as Glaswegians or Yorkshirewomen or Cornishmen or Mancunians but simply as Britons (who are somehow personally responsible for every act of the British state, even the acts of politicians they may despise). In these novels, locality or regionality gets almost wholly swallowed up in nationality, as if, displaced from our ordinary vantage points, we were looking through the eyes of foreigners. In *Jane Eyre* and *Shirley,* the novels of internal exile sandwiched between *The Professor* and *Villette,* however, the local or regional acquires greater force, refusing to be simply transubstantiated out of existence in becoming part of the higher-order unity of the nation. I think that the case for the intractability of local attachments is argued most strenuously in *Shirley,* where it informs a vision of culture and language we might call a "National Pentecostalism," counterpart of that Outlandish Nationalism put forward in *The Professor* and *Villette.* (The structural center of *Shirley* is the holiday of Whitsuntide or Pentecost, and both Shirley Keeldar's powers and those of the novel's nation-reforming narrator are implicitly modeled on the powers granted to Christ's apostles in the second chapter of Acts.)

In *Jane Eyre,* Brontë may not have felt ready to carry her thinking far in this direction. The emphasis in that novel is mainly upon the process by which Jane endures and then transcends limiting, merely local relationships—those that live through face-to-face contact and speech—becoming the authoritative woman who writes to many unseen readers, on behalf of a possible modern Englishness she aims to exemplify. The domains of the voice and of the pen or of print are almost completely opposed to each other for much of the narrative, although toward its end this novel, too, gives signs of wanting to reclaim the transcended local and oral. In her restorative season with the Riverses at Marsh End, Jane begins teaching a group of village girls who "speak with the broadest accent of the district" and records that she and they "have a difficulty in understanding each other's language" (JE 401). She does not (as Scott would) cite examples of their dialect in her text, but it stands in "silent" contrast to Jane's own ongoing narrative "voice" of educated standard English. By the time she has learned of her relation to the Rivers family and has come into her inheritance, Jane has converted half a dozen of these girls into "as decent, respectable, modest, and well-informed young women as could be found in the ranks of the British peasantry" (JE 434). In fact, the passage I quote partially here seems a miniature example of Brontë's tendency to start thinking in *international* terms just as soon as a particular locality within Britain has given way to British nationality: Jane goes on to say "[a]nd that is saying a great deal; for after all, the British peasantry are the best taught, best mannered, most self-respecting of any in Europe: since those days I have seen paysannes and Bäuerinnen; and the best of them seemed to me ignorant, coarse, and besotted, compared with my Morton girls" (JE 434). At the passage's end, we return from these remembered Continental travels of Jane's to the specific local designation "Morton girls," as if we needed reminding that in becoming British they did not cease being local, and that using the metaphor of "conversion" to describe how locality becomes national may obscure as much as it illuminates.

Of course, the most striking indication that Brontë's thought was turning back to reclaim the local or regional as she approached the close of *Jane Eyre* is to be found in the model union of Rochester and Jane, who "talk . . . all day long" and for whom "to talk to each other is but a more animated and an audible thinking." If, on the one hand, the supernatural phenomenon of lovers' voices that are capable of overcoming local limitation mimics the extensive, potentially national reach of Jane's written text, on the other hand Jane bids farewell to her widely scattered readers from a position securely defined as *within earshot* of the husband's voice. And we are certainly not expected to imagine the happy couple conversing by means of the same distance-defying magic that brought them together. Brontë is not about to invent the telephone: Jane's ten years of marriage have been spent by her husband's side. Many critics have disparaged this ending for its appearance of proposing merely private remedies for a "warped system of things," of suggesting that an England built around millions of such marriages would see all its troubles evaporate. They are partly right in this criticism, but they have not sufficiently appreciated Brontë's determination to keep the frame of locality in play *even as* she asserts the superior range and authority of the national and of her printed work of fiction over spoken communication. Jane's and Rochester's marriage offers in miniature that idealized "community of speech where all the members are within earshot" that may be found in nearly every fantasy of the "genuine culture."[8]

In a significant recent essay, Ivan Kreilkamp has helped loosen the hold of feminist criticism's habit of reading Brontë as "the model of a female author who triumphantly finds her own 'voice' in writing," maintaining that Brontë in fact "resists the equation of novel-writing with speech in order to develop a more effective means by which women writers might participate in the public print sphere." Kreilkamp's emphasis upon the phenomenon of "withheld speech" represents both a welcome advance in Brontë criticism and a salutary attempt to interfere with the workings of the seemingly unkillable "voice" metaphor for authorship. But Kreilkamp's argument "that Brontë rejects a model of authorship based on voice and embodied personality in favor of one based on the material possibilities of print" seems overstated.[9] In my view, Brontë does not so much "reject" the lure of voice or the local as subject it to the same process of displacement or defamiliarization she puts her other regularly referenced metaphors and identity categories through,

[8] "Community of speech": Jacques Derrida, *Of Grammatology,* trans. Gayatri Chakravorty Spivak (Baltimore: Johns Hopkins University Press, 1976), 136.

[9] Ivan Kreilkamp, "Unuttered: Withheld Speech and Female Authorship in *Jane Eyre* and *Villette,*" *Novel* (Summer 1999), 331–54.

a process that always involves attempts to "return to" and revalidate the revised, freshly problematized unit, in order to use it as a mechanism for defamiliarizing *another* metaphor or category. Complacent, naturalized nationalisms must be troubled by contact with the other-national or the international; but Brontë despises conventional, complacent stances of cosmopolitanism and will not permit her story lines to move far in their direction. (Witness the critique of the much-traveled Rochester or of Mr. Yorke in *Shirley*.) Local parochialisms must be lifted from their narrow sphere onto the national plane; but the local "community of speech" must retain its force in order to disrupt the hegemony of merely *abstract* or anonymous national identities, and of one standardized dialect, issuing from one centralized authority. Yet without the mediating term of the national, locality threatens to degenerate into a swamp of sanctimonious factionalisms, of premodern mentalities and social formations, while the other-national or international domain—because it is filled by Catholic, culturally French Belgium—may turn vertiginously universal, seeking to impose upon Britons either a globally ambitious ("catholic") religion or an equally aggressive "French" Enlightenment skepticism. Against these world-hungry ideologies British nationalism must stand its ground, must make the Protestant refusal. Without locality, the national can *have* no specificity and no "place" of its own; it lays itself open to the depredations of the "anywhere." Without nationality, on the other hand, the place of the local becomes its prison.

My readings in this chapter will not emphasize biographical factors, but it would be remiss not to take note of the elements in Charlotte Brontë's particular situation that surely encouraged reflection on the kinds and the competing claims of different geographical identity categories. This was a novelist, after all, whose father, perpetual curate at Haworth in the West Riding of Yorkshire, was an Irishman of initially humble station whose remarkable career had taken him to St. John's, Cambridge, and to a secure position in the English religious establishment. Along the way on this uncommon trajectory he had cut his ties to Ireland, purged his accent of Celticism, and apparently altered the spelling and pronunciation of the family name from "Brunty" to the higher-toned, less Irish-sounding "Brontë," perhaps, it has been suggested, out of a zealous convert's admiration for Lord Nelson.[10] He had married a woman from Penzance in Cornwall—a kind of long-distance connection highly unusual except through the network of associates he had acquired through the church—so neither he nor his bride were bound by inherited ties to the county of Yorkshire. Patrick Brontë's settlement there, an outcome encouraged by the rapid population growth in the region around Bradford, which brought about

---

[10] On Patrick Brontë's accent, appearance, and surname, cf. Elizabeth Gaskell, *The Life of Charlotte Brontë* (1857; London: Penguin, 1997), 33 (henceforth Gaskell); Juliet Barker, *The Brontës* (New York: St. Martin's, 1994), 1–2, 6 (henceforth Barker); Lyndall Gordon, *Charlotte Brontë: A Passionate Life* (New York: Norton, 1994), 6–7. Mary Taylor remembered Charlotte herself as speaking "with a strong Irish accent" in her schooldays (Gaskell 78). On the role of Irishness in the Brontës' fiction, cf. Terry Eagleton, *Heathcliff and the Great Hunger: Studies in Irish Culture* (London: Verso, 1995) and Kathleen Constable, *A Stranger Within the Gates: Charlotte Brontë and Victorian Irishness* (Lanham, Md.: University Press of America, 2000).

a concomitant need for more Anglican clergymen, was rendered more likely as well by the county's reputation as fertile ground for the Anglican evangelism he and so many other avid clergymen were promoting around the turn of the nineteenth century, in an attempt to combat the alarming success of Methodism and other Protestant factions.

In this new setting, Patrick Brontë's Irishness was, to the degree it needed to be acknowledged at all, a kind of open secret, not exactly to be lied about but submitting itself to quiet burial under the daily demonstration of accent, opinions, and behavior well within the pale of Englishness. The death of his wife, occurring shortly after the family's arrival in Haworth, had the effect of increasing the usual gap between the clergyman's family and the lay families of the district. Both because evangelicals saw the need for the national church's representative to stand "outside" or "above" local social hierarchies so as to avoid partisanship, *and* because this particular minister had come from so far away and never remarried into local society, the Brontë children were, as all their biographers have emphasized, thrown very much upon themselves for company, likely to grow up conscious of being perpetually on the margins of the community where their father held his perpetual but semidetached position.

It is with such considerations in mind that we should think about the legendary circle of gifted siblings gathered around the parsonage dining table, the circle that provided Charlotte Brontë with a lasting image of the "face-to-face" local community, a kind of microlocality distilling the essence of "genuine culture" in presenting talk as "animated and audible thinking" and thinking as the talk of others in one's head. Even if some of Brontë's energy always harks back to this ideal, lost condition of sibling togetherness whenever she imagines the category of "the local," it is important to recognize that such a tendency does not necessarily involve her in evocations of the kind of purity or homogeneity familiar to us from classic ethnographic accounts of "traditional village life." Living through her own personal version of modernity's tragic narrative—the passing of traditional local communities—Brontë nevertheless postulates no mythical "homogeneous local culture" to be wrecked by alien influences. Juliet Barker has usefully corrected Gaskell's presentation of the Brontës' Haworth as a kind of "remote rural village of *Brigadoon*-style fantasy," showing that "the period of Patrick Brontë's ministry there, from 1820 to 1861, saw some of the fastest growth and biggest changes that were to take place in Haworth and the surrounding area" (Barker 92). In the Brontë household itself, the children listened to the West Riding dialect of their servant, Tabitha Ackroyd, and the Cornish inflections of their aunt, Elizabeth Branwell, who had come to care for them after their mother's death. These and their father's determinedly self-anglicizing accent surrounded and interpenetrated their own discourses, as did the dialects used in the periodicals they read, most notably that of the nationally circulating *Blackwood's Edinburgh Magazine*. And this was all before Charlotte went abroad to Belgium in the early 1840s, returning to supplement the heterogeneity inside her household and the heterogeneity around it with the bold question of what role Frenchness might have in strengthening the local and national identities of Britons.

Children so situated might well come to think of attachment to the locality in which one lived as a matter not simply natural, but requiring exertion of will and self-conscious fiction making. Their family's experience had driven a wedge between ethnic and geographical senses of belonging: unlike people born, raised, and remaining in the place of their ancestors, they were so positioned as to feel the difference between identity and location, and were perhaps predisposed to think about situations in which identity and place might therefore *need* (re)connecting.

As with the other novelists studied in this work, Brontë commands attention not just for providing us with subtle and sustained handling of autoethnographic themes but also, crucially, for using the distinctive resources of narrative to give formal embodiment to the idea of an Anglocentric culture. In Brontë as in Dickens and Eliot, the textual space of the book becomes a testing-ground for imagining national-cultural space, for playing off against each other the claims of local, national, and international allegiances. Brontë's habitual practice is to establish a strong conceptual linkage among three distinctions: the distinction between speech and writing or print becomes associated with that between observable or listable traits, practices, and beliefs, on the one hand, and the holistic *culture* these comprise, on the other; and these two distinctions are also yoked to the one between local (provincial, regional, parochial) and fully national space. Imagining an English culture is likened to *writing an English book* and, just as she does with English culture, Brontë subjects her books to the challenge of elements emanating from local and international contexts, exposure to these supplying the refining fire without which the category of the national cannot come into its own. The reign of the printed text written in standard English for silent, unknown readers across the nation is both imperiled and authorized through Brontë's twin investments in local oral/aural phenomena and in French. The latter may be seen in the numerous passages of untranslated French, some of which convey information vital to the plot, as well as in the highly demonstrative manner in which Brontë's English narrators address their relationship to the French language. In *The Professor* and *Villette,* and especially in *Shirley,* Brontë seems intent on asking, in effect, how much French, and how strong a commitment to the emotional energies accessible *through* French, an English book can accommodate.[11]

At the other end of the spectrum, the productively disruptive power of the local and oral/aural manifests itself not just, as in Scott, in the plentiful use of dialect speech, but even more importantly in such striking returns to the realm of the voice as we encounter at the end of *Jane Eyre,* and in the strategic recourse to what Garrett Stewart has called the *phonotext,* the aural dimension of language usually suppressed in silent reading.[12] Like the language spoken by the ancient Hebrews as Herder described them, Brontë's English often lives in its utterance and "elude[s]

---

[11] Cf. *The Letters of Charlotte Brontë,* Vol. 2 (1848–1851), ed. Margaret Smith (Oxford: Clarendon, 2000) on the concern that the extensive use of "French in 'Shirley' might be cavilled at" for having "a pretentious air" (257n1); henceforth *Letters 2.*

[12] Garrett Stewart, *Reading Voices: Literature and the Phonotext* (Berkeley: University of California Press, 1983).

containment in letters."[13] Brontë disrupts any smooth procedure of imagining a national community of silent readers by insisting (or at least suggesting) in various ways that we route our reading experience back through the domain of the voice and ear, which until the invention of the telephone and radio remained co-extensive with the category of locality. Her vision of modernity resolutely does *not* involve the wholesale superceding of storyteller or bard or inspired orator by print author, of local by national, of aural by visual; but it *is* a vision of modernity, equally committed to the irreducibility of the local and to its containment within the frame of the national, as a variety of a more general sameness. Another way to put this is to say that Brontë refuses Whig history and other such unidirectional temporal schemes: making brilliant use of the potentialities and the limitations of its medium, her work travels back and forth along the line that connects the local to the national, retrieving both from dilution in the destructive element outside them.[14]

II

One of Mary Taylor's reminiscences of getting to know Charlotte Brontë at school, recorded in Elizabeth Gaskell's *Life* of the novelist, illuminates a moment in the history of media, identity, and the body. Taylor recalled that Brontë

> had a habit of writing in italics ([i.e.] printing characters), and said that she had learnt it by writing in their magazine. They brought out a "magazine" once a month, and wished it to look as like print as possible. She told us a tale out of it. No one wrote in it, and no one read it, but herself, her brother, and two sisters. She promised to show me some of these magazines, but retracted it afterwards, and would never be persuaded to do so. (Gaskell 79)

What must strike us about this memory, and what evidently struck Taylor, was the peculiar lack of "fit" between a certain literary form, firmly identified with the medium of print, and the Brontë children's laborious manual production and rigorously limited circulation of miniature texts designed to imitate that form. The magazine, a form that flourished in the post-Napoleonic decades in which these children grew up, lives in print and aims at breadth of circulation: it is a leading instance of the sort of text Benedict Anderson has in mind (though he focuses on the newspaper) in his account of the link between print technology and national consciousness. Critics have long recognized the importance of *Blackwood's Edinburgh Magazine* and other periodicals to the Brontë household, and it is undeni-

---

[13] Johann Gottfried Herder, in *On the Origin of Language: Jean-Jacques Rousseau, Essay on the Origin of Languages; Johann Gottfried Herder, Essay on the Origin of Language,* trans. John H. Moran and Alexander Gode (New York: Frederick Ungar, 1966), 94–95.

[14] Cf. Homi Bhabha, *The Location of Culture* (London: Routledge, 1994): "Cultures come to be represented by virtue of the processes of iteration and translation through which their meanings are very vicariously addressed to—*through*—an Other" (58).

able that they performed a function like the one Anderson emphasizes, the lifting of local perspectives up to the national plane: from such publications the children gained much of that precocious knowledge of national and world affairs—and those passionately held political opinions—that impressed numerous visitors to the parsonage (cf. Gaskell 115–19; Barker 149). As they had done for Carlyle in tiny Craigenputtock,[15] magazines bridged the family's nearby community and the wider world, providing a conduit of information, taste, and ideology that helped bind that family to a greater British public. I want briefly to consider two points arising from Taylor's remembrance that complicate this Andersonian perspective, however.

The first of these has to do with the fact that the periodical long acknowledged as holding pride of place at Haworth Parsonage was *Blackwood's* Edinburgh *Magazine*. Anderson emphasizes the standardizing, centralizing force of nationally circulating media, focusing on how the almost infinitely "varied idiolects" of French, English, Spanish, and so on, were "assembled . . . into print-languages far fewer in number" that could serve as "unified fields of exchange . . . below Latin and above the spoken vernaculars." The users of print language "gradually became aware," he says, "of the hundreds of thousands, even millions, of people in their particular language-field, and at the same time, that *only those* hundreds of thousands, or millions, so belonged. These fellow-readers . . . formed, in their secular, particular, visible invisibility, the embryo of the nationally-imagined community."[16] Yet in *Blackwood's* and in other influential Scottish periodicals of the post-Waterloo period we confront texts of the "great age of Scottish literary journalism" in which devotion to Great-British nationality could be counterbalanced by commitment to the maintenance and promotion of a distinct regional (once a separate national) identity and dialect.[17] On the pages of *Blackwood's,* an increasingly "standard" English shared space with Scots, and subjects of national interest with those peculiar to Scotland. Reading *Blackwood's* at Haworth between the 1820s and 1840s did not mean absorbing one uniform message emanating from a metropolitan center; it meant encountering mixed messages from "Auld Reekie."

Thanks very largely to the novels of Scott, readers like the Brontës could feel that history had sufficiently progressed—Jacobites long since quelled and Highlands cleared—for "the Scottish" to be reconcilable with Anglocentric British nationality *without* requiring diminution of its distinctive characteristics. A Scot could be a patriotic Briton in the same breath in which he asserted his positive Scottishness. To the children of a transplanted Irishman, the example of *Black-*

---

[15] When Goethe asked whether he did not feel isolated there, Carlyle replied "Nay, even at this time, I have a whole horse-load of French, German, American, English Reviews and Journals . . . encumbering the tables of my little Library": *The Collected Letters of Thomas and Jane Welsh Carlyle,* ed. C. R. Sanders, K. J. Fielding, et al. (Durham, N.C.: Duke University Press, 1970–), 4. 408.

[16] Benedict Anderson, *Imagined Communities: Reflections on the Origin and Spread of Nationalism* (London: Verso, 1983), 46–47.

[17] Robert Crawford, *Devolving English Literature* (Oxford: Clarendon, 1992), 145; cf. chaps. 1, 2, and also Linda Colley, *Britons: Forging the Nation, 1707–1837* (New Haven: Yale University Press, 1992), chap. 3.

wood's would likely have stimulated reflection on the asymmetrical relationships of different localisms to the state that encompassed them, and on Scotland's head start over Ireland in the process by which erstwhile nations got converted into respectable regions (or cultures) in the overarching multicultural union. Patrick Brontë had done his part to ease his native land along in this process by publishing in *Blackwood's* (anonymously, in 1818) a National Tale entitled *The Maid of Killarney, or Albion and Flora; a modern tale; in which are interwoven some cursory remarks on religion and politics.* Though the Brontës' family biographer has called this "the most Irish" of Patrick's many writings for its detailed descriptions of scenery and customs, its tendency, like that of other National Tales, is to smooth Ireland's passage to permanent subject status. In a familiar United Kingdom allegory, the novella arranges the marriage of its "appropriately named English hero," Albion, to the Hibernian Flora, insisting for good measure that this union will prosper only under the aegis of an evangelized national Protestant church (Barker 76).

The second point arising from Mary Taylor's reminiscence is that the Brontë children paid homage to their favorite periodicals in a weirdly unsuitable fashion. The young mimics worked with their hands to produce effects resembling those of mechanical printing processes, but they created something utterly unlike the models they admired: single-copy "magazines" meant for their eyes only. Mary Taylor placed inverted commas around "magazine" when she wrote about the Brontë siblings' texts because she recognized how oddly the label attached to the product. These children made *manuscript magazines,* and no hand written sonnet sequence ever had a more defensively exclusive circle of personally known readers. The young Brontës submitted the nation-evoking periodical they started with—the form that gathers around itself the anonymous siblinghood of compatriots—to an act of mimesis that actually "translated" it back into the most local context imaginable, a context in which an irreproducible text is restricted to a few individual readers intimately known to, *and indeed identical to,* the producers. The resemblance between a printed character in a periodical and that character reproduced by the Brontës' penmanship merely heightens the difference between the two.

Charlotte Brontë's unwillingness to share the family magazines, her refusal to "go public" by opening the circle to include her school friend evinces a hesitation to present herself as an *author* that never entirely left her, even as she learned to enjoy the power and prerogatives of anonymous relation to a large, unseen, and potentially nationwide readership. In recognizing the importance of the author-to-public relationship to Brontë the novelist, we ought not lose sight of the degree to which her appreciation for that professional and abstract connection remained qualified by the contrary commitment to the intensive bond of the local speech community. During a minor controversy with her publishers about whether to attach a preface to *Shirley* that would vindicate *Jane Eyre* against the *Quarterly Review*'s charges of immorality, Brontë wrote to W. S. Williams that she found it "a deplorable error in an author to assume the tragic tone in addressing the public about his own wrongs or griefs," for "what does the public care about him as an individual?" (*Letters* 2. 246; cf. 254). The next year, 1850, she wrote her "Biographical Notice of Ellis and Acton Bell," giving her sisters' Christian names and recounting their short careers and deaths. By that time, the true identity of Currer Bell had become widely known, but she still signed the piece with her pseudonym. This sort of oscillation between reticence and disclosure marks all her fiction, right from the astoundingly inauspicious start of her first novel, *The Professor.*

Writing to her friend Ellen Nussey on 4 July 1834, Charlotte Brontë offered up the sweeping recommendation, "[f]or fiction—read Scott alone all novels after his are worthless" (*Letters 1.* 130). Anyone who knew that the author of *Jane Eyre* had ever expressed a sentiment like this would have been struck, when that novel was published and became the literary sensation of 1847, by how manifestly unlike Scott's works it was. Instead of Scott's customary third-person narration—detached, genial, ruminative—a female first-person narrator, dispensing with preamble, lay urgent claim to readers' regard with "there was no possibility of taking a walk that day." In place of the historically particular terrain of the Scott novel, readers of *Jane Eyre* encountered an allegorical landscape on which was enacted a feminist *Pilgrim's Progress.* If they thought of Scott's fiction mainly as an affair of swashbuckling romance (which Brontë had indeed drawn upon in her "Glasstown" juvenilia), readers might even have seen Brontë as engaged in a deliberate debunking of her teenage idol: the chivalric afflatus they associated with Scott seemed to be violently dispersed when the "hero" of *Jane Eyre* entered the novel and promptly fell off his horse.

Yet Brontë's career needs to be looked at not as involving repudiation of a master and the discovery of the author's own "voice," but rather as a series of ongoing negotiations with aspects of Scott's influence. Divesting her fiction of many superficial Scottisms, Brontë in her first two novels strove to isolate some of the Waverley novelist's central aims. *The Professor* certainly operates less obviously in Scott's shadow than does the juvenilia, but it exhibits a relationship of similarity-and-difference to Scott's familiar narrative structure and to the narrative voice of one particular Scott novel. Even *Jane Eyre* can be read as adapting the Waverley novelist's favorite situation, transposing it into the codes and contexts of domestic fiction but placing its heroine on the seam between successive historical epochs and embroiling her personal destiny in the clash of old and emergent ideologies. It is as if Brontë needed to isolate this core Scott interest in *Jane Eyre* before she could "return" to a fictional mode more plainly indebted to Scott's in *Shirley,* a "novel of the recent past" whose manipulation of the historical distance between the Yorkshire of the 1840s and that of the turbulent 1810s might make us think it deserves some Scott-like subtitle such as *'Tis Thirty-Eight Years Since.*

In most of Scott's best-known works—*Waverley, The Heart of Midlothian, Old Mortality, Ivanhoe,* and others—a third-person voice or a series of frame narrators contains and distances the personal and national fates recounted in the tale. The engaged first-person account supplied by William Crimsworth in Brontë's *The Professor* does, however, recall the one given by Frank Osbaldistone in *Rob Roy,* the 1817 novel that was Scott's only one to use sustained first-person narration. The element that most plainly likens *The Professor* to *Rob Roy*—and sets these novels apart from a book like *Jane Eyre*—is the evident undermotivation of the two men's stories. Brontë's narrator resembles Scott's in nothing so much as his inability to convey any clear sense of why he should be bothering to write his tale, much less publishing it. "Why should I bestow all my tediousness upon you," the narrator of *Rob Roy* asks the friend to whom he writes, "[simply] because I have you in my power, and have ink, paper, and time before me?"[18] Frank recognizes a certain obligation to set down for posterity his youthful encounters with the dashing title character, but *Rob Roy* is not really about Rob Roy, and it cannot be said that the now-aged storyteller has felt any urgency about the business. It is only now that "Providence has blessed the decline of [his] life" with leisure that he resolves to bestow some of that leisure on his memoir. In doing so, he is chary of the "seductive love of narrative, when we ourselves are the heroes of the events which we tell" (RR 66), and it may be only the knowledge that, when all is said and done, he is not a very heroic hero, only (as usual in Scott) a romantic-minded youth to plot a story around, that emboldens him to write. He goes on to relate a young life's journey structurally similar to Edward Waverley's, a circular tour into Scotland, intrigue, and romance that concludes when Frank, once a powerless London clerk, is transformed into "Lord of Osbaldistone Manor" in the North of England, happily if improbably united with the fiery Catholic Jacobite Diana Vernon. So much of the book's point about the economic and moral unity of Britain seems summed up when Frank is struck by the idea his own experiences bear out, the "very singular" fact that "the mercantile transactions of London citizens" are bound up in one narrative and one destiny "with revolutions and rebellions [in Scotland]" (RR 307). The marriage of Frank to Diana makes this singular fact of common destiny into a single British family.

Both Frank Osbaldistone of *Rob Roy* and William Crimsworth of *The Professor* are figures ill suited to the commercial or industrial pursuits to which iron-willed male relatives—a father in *Rob Roy,* an older brother in *The Professor*—devote themselves. Both resist the martinets who try to bend them to the purposes of trade; both wind up exiled to alien, gothicized realms pervaded by sinister Catholic influences. Both narrators unfold plots that cleave to the romance pattern of a dangerous, strengthening immersion in otherness, a subjection to *others'* plots. Both undertake their narratives as letters to old friends; neither claims any very compelling reason for doing so.

Yet whereas Scott's entire narrative in *Rob Roy* is contained within the frame of the private letter, Brontë's introduces that frame only to depart from it in pointed fashion at the end of the first chapter. And whereas Frank Osbaldistone merely commits to paper and posterity a tale he has often recounted in person to a "dear and intimate friend" with whom he is still in contact, William Crimsworth addresses a comrade from his schooldays whom he has not seen or communicated with in years. "It is a long time since I wrote to you and a still longer time since I saw you," William writes. What has prompted him to end the long silence? "[C]hancing to take up a newspaper of your County, the other day, my eye fell upon your name—I began to think of old times; to run over the events which have tran-

---

[18] Scott, *Rob Roy,* ed. Ian Duncan (Oxford: Oxford University Press, 1998), 66; henceforth RR.

spired since we separated—and I sat down and commenced this letter; what you have been doing I know not, but you shall hear, if you choose to listen, how the world has wagged with me."[19] William proceeds to fill most of his opening chapter with recollections of his Eton education, his refusal of the patronage offered by aristocratic relations, his rash decision to go into trade with his cruel elder brother, and his cold reception at that brother's splendid home. The letter, but not the chapter, concludes as follows:

> I soon left Mr. and Mrs. Crimsworth to themselves; a servant conducted me to my bedroom; in closing my chamber-door I shut out all intruders, you, Charles, as well as the rest.
> Good bye for the present.
> William Crimsworth. (TP 11).

Two short paragraphs addressed not to Charles but to some other audience—unknown, unhailed—then bring the chapter to a close. Charles will be heard of no more.

With its introduction and then brisk disposal of the epistolary model, this opening chapter of Brontë's *The Professor* points up the work's divergence from *Rob Roy,* a divergence that comes into focus only once we have grasped the works' basic similarities. The Scottish author's narrative stance now appears, as Brontë might have seen it, an enviably comfortable one, the kind of stance available to a man at ease in his relations with institutions of government, law, and publishing in both Scotland and England. A national institution himself, such a writer seems capable of containing a narrative of public, national-allegorical dimensions within the time-honored fictional convention of the private letter to a friend *without* stumbling over any precarious frontier between private and public, local and national domains. In marked contrast, the first chapter of *The Professor* identifies its author as one for whom the linking of friend and fellow national, known addressee and unknown audience, speech and published writing, is entirely problematic. Attempting to re-establish contact with a long-lost interlocutor, that boy with whom he once "walked and talked continually" (TP 3), William Crimsworth charts his own passage from boyhood to maturity as a transition from a state of affairs in which one can continually walk and talk with one's friend to a condition in which one is reduced to chancing across one's friend's name in the newspaper. Through William, we experience the change from the intimacy of an idealized local speech situation into the faceless one of publication and print as nothing but an alienating fall.

Brontë's narrator halts uncertainly at the borderline between a defunct homosocial ideal of community and some vague alternative whose contours and purpose he cannot confidently imagine. In his letter, he underscores his estrangement by referring to his own brother as "Mr. Crimsworth" and also by admitting that he must now class even Charles among the "intruders" upon his authorial solitude. Enclosed in his chamber, he writes in a feeble, self-contradictory attempt to re-

[19] Brontë, *The Professor* (Oxford: Oxford University Press, 1991), 3–4; henceforth TP.

cover the broken habit of verbal communication: he offers his reader the option of "choos[ing] to listen" to the silent pages he will dispatch. The effort is quickly shown up as a complete failure. William concedes that his letter "never got an answer": "before my old friend received it, he had accepted a government appointment in one of the colonies, and was already on his way to the scene of his official labours. What has become of him since I know not" (TP 11).

What, then, is William to do with the rest of that autobiographical narrative he commenced in his letter to Charles? He and the author who has created him do not seem sure. *The Professor*'s first chapter concludes:

> The leisure time I have at command, and which I intended to employ for [Charles's] private benefit—I shall now dedicate to that of the public at large. My narrative is not exciting and, above all, not marvellous—but it may interest some individuals, who, having toiled in the same vocation as myself, will find in my experience, frequent reflections of their own. The above letter will serve as introduction—I now proceed. (TP 11)

Even the modest Frank Osbaldistone of *Rob Roy* never undersells his material like this. With seeming determination to minimize the novel's claims and to narrow its target audience, Brontë permits William Crimsworth no vision of the reach and power potentially available to authors working for "the public at large." Between local and global there is no correspondence, no mediating term. No sooner does this collective "public" get invoked than it recondenses into the separate "some individuals" who "may" find interest in the tale, and then only because they have had experiences very closely resembling William's. The category of "the national," that abstract body of anonymous compatriots imaginable through the medium of print, most pointedly does *not* suggest itself as making possible a form of belonging whose breadth can compensate us for the loss of those bonds that survive only through intimate contact and spoken exchange. And this seeming diffidence in addressing or even imagining the public turns out to consort very oddly with the novel's ambitious national allegory, which presents William's personal adventure as a romance of British selfhood, struggle, and survival in an alien clime. (I examine that national allegory in the next chapter.)

Reading the start of Brontë's first novel this way brings us within the orbit of Raymond Williams's famous argument, in *Culture and Society,* about the compensatory magnification of the romantic artist's aims and asserted powers in the face of the breakdown of patronage relationships.[20] The first chapter of *The Professor* provides an account of the birth of authorship—nearly the stillbirth—that can profitably be compared not only with the concerns of romantic-era novels like Scott's but with those of romantic poems and collections of songs or ballads—among them Scott's own *Minstrelsy of the Scottish Border.* With their printed, published collections "salvaging" oral forms of literature, their modern evocations of such forms (as in *Lyrical Ballads*), their "conversation poems," British authors and editors of the period worked in an atmosphere of heightened awareness of the his-

---

[20] Williams, *Culture and Society 1780–1950* (1958; New York: Columbia University Press, 1983), chap. 2.

torically fraught relationships between speech and publication, locality and nationality, the perspectives of informant and ethnographic authority.[21]

Brontë's career as a novelist begins with the unsatisfying fragment of a process that all her novels perform and seek to understand. William Crimsworth's story, which is the story of how William Crimsworth becomes an author to a nation, commences when locality presents itself to his consciousness as irrevocably lost. His narrative will be the very opposite of the romantic National Tale—of such works as *The Maid of Killarney*—in which the traveling Englishman comes calling upon the ethnic woman in her native land; *he* must travel outside his nation to seek its *own* cultural identity, which he can find nowhere in it. The anthropologist Roy Wagner has described a process very like the one I am attempting to describe here in his book *The Invention of Culture*. Immersion in the lifeways of another group, Wagner writes, enables the fieldworker to comprehend

> for the first time . . . what anthropologists speak of when they use the word "culture." Before this he had no culture, as we might say, since the culture in which one grows up is never really "visible"—it is taken for granted, and its assumptions are felt to be self-evident. It is only through "invention" of this kind that that abstract significance of culture . . . can be grasped, and only through the experienced contrast that his own culture becomes "visible."[22]

Inventing English culture by expatriating himself from its territory, by "gaining distance on it" so as to grasp it true and whole, William Crimsworth enacts the first of Brontë's mature fictional investigations of Outlandish Nationalism. To borrow Wagner's language once more: Brontë's fiction is all about "the paradox created by imagining a culture for people who do not imagine it for themselves"—the British.

---

[21] Cf. Penny Fielding, *Writing and Orality: Nationality, Culture, and Nineteenth-Century Scottish Fiction* (Oxford: Clarendon Press, 1996).

[22] Roy Wagner, *The Invention of Culture*, rev. ed. (Chicago: University of Chicago Press, 1981), 4. The subsequent quotation is from 27.

CHAPTER SEVEN

An *Échantillon* of Englishness: *The Professor*

> Monsieur, might one not learn something by analogy? An—échantillon—a—a
> sample often serves to give an idea of the whole.
>   —Frances Evans Henri in Brontë, *The Professor*[1]

THE PROFESSOR is a narrative of rescue and return that makes national avatars of its male and female leads and subjects them to a process of exilic tribulation during which whatever is English in them risks being dissolved in the surrounding swamp of Belgian "Frenchness" and Catholicism. Brontë's story tells of an English castaway who winds up in Brussels, working in a boys' school he characterizes as "merely an epitome of the Belgian nation" (TP 61); he soon begins to teach as well at the girls' school next door and is astonished to encounter there, among the clamor of alien tongues, a shy girl speaking in the "voice of Albion" (TP 115). Obedient to his principle of "always tak[ing] voices into account in judging of character" (TP 9), he determines to "learn what she has of English in her besides the name of Frances Evans" and quickly discovers that "she is no novice in the [English] language" although "she ha[s] neither been in England, nor taken lessons in English, nor lived in English families" (TP 123–24). With the very name of France in it, "Frances" signals from the start Brontë's determination to seek a view of Englishness as profitably incorporating rather than simply being opposed or threatened by "French" qualities. The heroine's full name is actually Frances Evans Henri, her father having been Swiss and her "Evans" mother possibly of Welsh extraction; nevertheless, as the novel proceeds, William begins to mythologize his pupil as a kernel of pure Englishness, doing so in about equal measure as *she* mythologizes the English homeland she has never seen.[2] Her one aim being "[t]o save enough to cross the Channel" (TP 163), Frances is engaged in the paradoxical effort to "return" to a land she never actually left (because she was never there). William notes that "she said 'England' as you might suppose an Israelite of Moses' days would have said Canaan" (TP 131).

---

[1] Brontë, *The Professor* (Oxford: Oxford University Press, 1991), 132; henceforth TP.

[2] Brontë's specification of non-English British identities as markers of "Englishness," a practice repeated across all four novels, reflects the expansive sense of the English identity gaining currency over the first half of the nineteenth-century, in which, not only for English but for Scots and Welsh (and perhaps even Irish?), "Englishman's the common name for all": cf. Linda Colley, *Britons: Forging the Nation, 1707–1837* (New Haven: Yale University Press, 1992), 162–63, and Daniel Defoe, "The True-Born Englishman," in *The True-Born Englishman and Other Writings,* ed. P. N. Furbank and W. R. Owens (Harmondsworth: Penguin, 1997), 35.

The *devoirs* that Frances produces at her English teacher's request reveal her fixation on ideas of out-of-place Englishness. One of her essays is an imaginary "emigrant's letter to his friends at home" (TP 137); another adopts the voice of the deposed King Alfred, driven into "the hills of Wales" by invading Danes (TP 122–23). Reflecting morosely upon the depredations of the pagan marauders, Frances's Christian Alfred, "whose inheritance was a kingdom," says, "My throne is usurped, my crown presses the brow of an invader; I have no friends; my troops wander broken in the hills of Wales; reckless robbers spoil my country; my subjects lie prostrate, their breasts crushed by the heel of the brutal Dane" (TP 123). The Alfred-in-exile narrative supplies Brontë's novel with its autoethnographic model of a native authority cast out into alien climes in which, though it may in time acquire foreign fathers and surnames, it may nonetheless cling to its original nature, an identity that this novel imagines as passing through the maternal line and denotes (as we shall see) with certain fetishes of the mother. Paternity, associated with the accidental accretions of history, leaves its mark upon Frances's essay on Alfred in the form of the numerous "errors of orthography," "foreign idioms," "faults of construction" that almost, but do not entirely (and, it is implied, *cannot ever*), obscure the English imagination at the core of this piece of imperfectly written English prose. William recognizes that Frances has "appreciated Alfred's courage under calamity" and grasped what seems to be his proto-Protestant reliance on "the scriptural Jehovah for aid against the mythological Destiny" (TP 123).

Frances has imaginatively apprehended all this, we are to conclude, not only because she shares Alfred's character traits of courage and faith, but more importantly because such character traits are the distinctive and undying racial inheritance of the English. Her calamitous destiny is more or less equated with her parents' intermarriage, residence, and death on the Continent, which have left Frances in an unsupported condition even more dire than Alfred's.

> "Have the goodness [William says] to put French out of your mind so long as I converse with you—keep to English."
> "C'est si difficile, Monsieur, quand on n'en a plus l'habitude."
> "You had the habitude formerly I suppose—? No, answer me in your mother-tongue."
> "Yes, Sir—I spoke the English more than the French when I was a child."
> "Why do you not speak it now?"
> "Because I have no English friends." (TP 128)

Friendlessness means here more than just a pitiable lack of companions surrounding the self; it threatens a deculturating erosion *of* the self. At the time William encounters it, Frances's self is a site under occupation by alien forces: not only is she stranded outside of England, but outside-of-England has gotten inside of her. This would-be sample of Englishness speaks English "outlandishly." Frances stutters her way through an expression of what, the novel suggests, *ought* to be her own relationship to English nationality, saying, "An—échantillon—a—a sample often serves to give an idea of the whole" (TP 132).

In the first of her trenchant portrayals of friendless women, Brontë makes "friends" stand for the intersubjective network of custom and value that constitutes and situates the self as a member of a particular community. To put the matter just a little too simply, Frances in Belgium represents English race deprived of any ongoing English culture, and the critical question underlying Crimsworth's entire narrative about her is the nineteenth-century anthropologist's question par excellence (even though nineteenth-century anthropologists did not use *culture* as we now conveniently may): does race *imply* culture? Do language, custom, belief, moral character *express* racial type, and will that force of expression override environmental influences—no matter where and among whom one lives, and for how long? It is certainly possible to find in Brontë the expression of racialist certitudes, yet her work also productively exploits the theoretical "confusion" still surrounding questions of racial determinism circa 1850.[3] Brontë explores again and again the unsettled boundary between race and culture by focusing on the friendless English self who is subject to the seemingly genuine threat of national decomposition or un-Englishing. She anticipates by fifty years Joseph Conrad's plotting of this same border, and it seems a happy irony that Brussels, the imperial capital in Conrad's most famous tale, was her heart of darkness.

Frances Evans Henri embodies the question of an English cultural identity that might rest secure in the blood, enabling English people to withstand perhaps even permanent dislocation from their native milieu. If race breaks down under the pressure of the surrounding social environment—if, in other words, culture overcomes race (as it does in most accounts of the transition from nineteenth- to twentieth-century anthropology)—then what will become of that Scott-like narrative pattern of *return* that *The Professor* and all of Brontë's other novels evoke? If the Englishness *can* be crushed out of someone by long immersion in a foreign culture, then *even if* such a person whose original identity was English but has never been to England is *brought* to England at the end of the story, that bringing will not be felt as a *return*. Only adherence to the fixity of race makes possible that paradox of "coming back to somewhere one has never been" that supports notions of motherland and mother-tongue. When Frances tries to explain why she wants to go to England, William notes "the difficulty she experienced in improvising the translation of her thoughts from French to English" (TP 132). Many people who have lived all their lives in a French-speaking culture and who themselves speak French almost exclusively would have similar difficulties, but only an appeal to English as the culture and language *proper* to Frances but from which she has become estranged can endow this observation with pathos and make it function as part of a plot of recuperation and return.[4] Yet if cultural identity is fixed in the blood, how are we to generate a narrative about its loss and recovery?

In so effectively ventriloquizing Alfred, the exiled English king, Frances has also unwittingly arranged for her own myth of identity to dovetail with William's, for the novel's narrator presents *his* life as a story of a legitimate English authority banished by an illegitimate one but ultimately to return in triumph. As the book

---

[3] Cf. Stocking, *Victorian Anthropology* (New York: Free Press, 1987), 63.

[4] Here I follow Walter Benn Michaels, *Our America: Nativism, Modernism, and Pluralism* (Durham, N.C.: Duke University Press, 1995).

of Genesis frequently does, *The Professor* confounds prevailing understandings of legitimacy and succession, preferring a younger son to an older. The second son of an aristocratic mother and a father "in trade," William has been educated at Eton with the evident intention of binding him entirely to his mother's social class. But when William's maternal uncles Lord Tynedale and the Hon. John Seacombe present him with their plan for his future as a clergyman (which includes a comfortable living and a socially acceptable wife), he perversely declines it. He turns for help to his industrialist older brother, a man who has already and quite ruthlessly purged himself of his mother's class identity—especially of that identity's more benign aspects. Edward Crimsworth illustrates for William a model of identity based on the trope of *conversion*, according to which one can drastically change one's social position and identity, as he has done, but one can occupy only a single position and have only a single identity at a time. Demanding to be assured that William has definitively broken with their aristocratic maternal relatives, the zealous convert Edward reminds his younger brother that "no man can serve two masters" (TP 8). The one master Edward now serves, he virtually declares, is Mammon. This older son of the house of Crimsworth has crushed out of himself not only every emotion linked to his mother's class but every extracommercial consideration, devoting every atom of his being to the cause of making himself the perfect representative of the new industrial class. Any thought that his brother might have claims upon him greater than or even different from those of other employees, Edward dismisses as "humbug" (TP 15). To use Frances's French term, Edward is determined to become an *échantillon*, or sample, not of Englishness but of one single class, since to him, nothing exists *but* classes—that is to say, single positions and their corresponding sets of interests. For Edward Crimsworth, there is no such *thing* as "Englishness" or "England," no such thing (to quote Mrs. Thatcher) as "society."

Not surprisingly, Brontë quickly negates any possibility that her narrator and leading man could ever have emulated Edward and adopted his conversion model of identity. Without such a negation there would have been no journey abroad and no hearing of the voice of Albion in foreign fields. Moreover, whatever there is of interest in the character of William Crimsworth derives from his incapacity to occupy any single position or sense of identity—he must remain true, in a way, to the principle of heterogeneity inscribed in him by his mixed-class parentage. Raised among competing forms of singleness—maternal uncles enforcing the codes of the upper class and elder brother enforcing those of the middle—William develops a disaffection for singularity. Disenchanted with the only class position he has ever known but incapable of trading it in for another, he represents a type of the class "alien" later described by Matthew Arnold in *Culture and Anarchy*.[5] These are the figures who fail to adapt themselves to living comfortably within the confines of the "ordinary self" that everyone acquires through the process of socialization in a particular social location. Arnold's ordinary self accepts the values inculcated in him as natural and true: ordinary selves live by "a routine which they

---

[5] *Culture and Anarchy* (Cambridge: Cambridge University Press, 1932), 108; henceforth Arnold.

[have] christened reason and the will of God, in which they [are] inextricably bound, and beyond which they [have] no power of looking" (Arnold 46). Arnold describes here precisely the kind of ethnocentrism that twentieth-century anthropology came to ascribe to its "natives," except that in the former instance Arnold's concept of culture offers the way out of such a condition, while in the latter (and later) one, it is precisely culture in which the native is trapped. Arnold's aliens exhibit some peculiar "bent" of curiosity that "always tends to take them out of their class" (Arnold 108). Only after this dislocation has occurred does the class misfit acquire the potential to develop through Arnold's culture a second, "best self" that can transcend the different but equally limited perspectives and interests of all classes.[6] Like Malinowski, Arnold believes that no mere participant in a way of life possesses a view of the interconnected whole precisely because such participants are "inside" it. The desocialization that the class alien has to undergo en route to attaining the vision of culture is presented by Arnold as a break-out from a confining location, an escape that might lead to an authoritative stance "outside" or "above" the space containing that original location and all other "positions" within the social whole. Until that happens, one has only the narrow sightlines of the insider and can imagine only a plurality of such standpoints, not an organized totality.

In *The Professor,* the elder brother Edward Crimsworth has forfeited his birthright by effectively denying that England is anything more than an assortment of positions or competing outlooks. He believes that one can defend the interests of the aristocracy today and those of the industrialists tomorrow, but one must defend either of these to the death, for there is nowhere to "stand" in England but inside one or another antagonistic camp. With no English whole greater than the sum of its parts, there can also be no self beyond the ordinary, no vision of social life as anything but the endless conflict of equally self-righteous ideologues. As long as William remains in an anticultural England dominated by such ignorant armies as his brother's class, on the one hand, and his maternal uncles', on the other, he will be judged an admonitory specimen, an *échantillon* of the man who is an *échantillon* of nothing because he has been so foolish as to turn his back on one battling class without securing himself a position in another. An acquaintance of William's, Yorke Hundsen, thinks that William *could* have played the aristocratic heir's role, the role repudiated by Edward, to perfection, had it been his to play. "What a nobleman you would have made, William Crimsworth!" he exclaims,

> You are cut out for one; pity Fortune has balked Nature!—Look at the features, figure, even to the hands—distinction all over—ugly distinction! Now if you'd only an estate and a park and a title, how you could play the exclusive, maintain the rights of your class, train your tenantry in habits of respect to the peerage, oppose at every step the advanc-

---

[6] Arnold does come close to adumbrating an ethnographic conception of culture when he aligns his version of it with the power of a *"national* right reason" to embrace and reconcile conflicting factions (cf. Arnold 69, 94, 97; emphasis added). Cf. George W. Stocking Jr.'s "Matthew Arnold, E. B. Tylor, and the Uses of Invention," in *Race, Culture, and Evolution: Essays on the History of Anthropology* (New York: Free Press, 1968), 69–90.

ing power of the people, support your rotten order and be ready for its sake to wade knee-deep in churls' blood. As it is you've no power; you can do nothing; you're wrecked and stranded on the shores of Commerce; forced into collision with practical Men, with whom you cannot cope, for *you'll never be a tradesman.* (TP 32)

For William, the only alternative to an incapacitating positionlessness is to travel the treacherous path of romance leading him outside of actually existing England's collection of hostile standpoints. Encountering Frances abroad and finally bringing her "back" to an England that has forsaken the values stored in her, William turns displacement from England into the precondition of authority over it. His story makes the state of exiled "friendlessness" an essential step in the recovery of Englishness.

The romance field on which Brontë's hero and heroine must endure their strengthening trials is organized around two adjoining schools presided over by the cunning Mlle. Zoraïde Reuter and the blithely amoral M. Pelet. At these acculturating institutions, veritable factories for the mechanical reproduction of anticulture, a new generation absorbs its fatal lessons in Popish superstition, hypocrisy, and cynicism. William and Frances must strive in this most unpropitious setting to sustain their little flames of English Protestantism. Their destinies are bound together in a question of language: if the English teacher cannot help Frances oust the usurping alien culture within her and restore Englishness to the throne of her self, then her spoken English will remain the broken and hesitant hodgepodge that it is when William first meets her, and the narrative William writes about her, in which he needs must quote her a great deal, will be disfigured through and through by the monstrosity of an English woman's spoken English that is actually badly translated French. For the first time in her career, Brontë is exploring what it means to write "an English book." Only if William succeeds in educating Frances in the language that is the "outward expression of the inner essence of [her] nation" can the story William writes about the process become the English book he wants it to be, one in which he locates and retrieves his English "treasure" from those who have "snatched [her] from [his] hands and put [her] away out of [his] reach" (TP 148).[7] If he fails to return both Frances to Englishness and the reanglicized Frances to England, his book may even suffer the indignity of turning into what he disdainfully labels a "modern French novel" (TP 174).

This would be its fate if William were to get waylaid, on his campaign to rescue Frances, by Mademoiselle Reuter, whose character and establishment furnish the handiest of *échantillons* of "French" femininity and Catholicism. Hers is a "Romish school" where Frances must submit to Jesuitical surveillance, a school at which duplicity is the most thoroughly mastered subject: it is "a building with porous walls, a hollow floor, a false ceiling," where "every room . . . has eye-holes and ear-holes, and what the house is, the inhabitants are, very treacherous" (TP 133–34). The manageress tries, of course, to get William in her clutches, and she

---

[7] Linda Dowling, *Language and Decadence in the Victorian Fin de Siècle* (Princeton: Princeton University Press, 1986), 15.

temporarily succeeds so far as to make him set about deluding himself that, were they to wed, he might be the means of anglicizing and protestantizing *her.* He starts to believe, in other words, that he can export Englishness to Zoraïde instead of ful- filling his vocation to reimport it to England in the figure of Frances. "Even if [Zo- raïde] be truly deficient in sound principle," he thinks,

> is it not rather her misfortune than her fault? She has been brought up a Catholic—had she been born an Englishwoman and reared a Protestant—might she not have added straight integrity to all her other excellencies? Supposing she were to marry an English and protestant husband, would she not, rational, sensible as she is, quickly acknowledge the superiority of right over expediency, honesty over policy? (TP 99)

Within a few pages, William has blundered onto the truth of Zoraïde's character, and he forswears the theory of cultural conversion he has briefly been led to en- dorse: "our souls were not in harmony," he now affirms, "and . . . discord must have resulted from the union of her mind with mine." The recognition switches William's narrative from a campaign of English culture-for-export—a campaign licensed, like colonialism, by thoughts of the other's misfortune in not being En- glish—to a project of autoethnography aimed at the insider's outsideness toward English culture.

But even when Mlle. Reuter decides to marry Pelet, this does not entirely lib- erate William from the danger of being embroiled in her plot. He has to quit his positions at both schools and remove himself from Pelet's house, of which Zoraïde will shortly be mistress, for (he says)

> it would not do for me to remain a dependent dweller in the house which was soon to be hers. Her present demeanour towards me was deficient neither in dignity nor propriety— but I knew her former feeling was unchanged. Decorum now repressed, and Policy masked it, but Opportunity would be too strong for either of these—Temptation would shiver their restraints.
>
> I was no pope—I could not boast infallibility—in short—if I stayed, the probability was that in three months' time, a practical Modern French novel would be in full process of concoction under the roof of the unsuspecting Pelet. Now modern French novels are not to my taste either practically or theoretically. (TP 173–74)

Unless he decisively places himself beyond the traditional temptation of the field- worker in foreign parts—the temptation to "go native"—the autocthnographer of Englishness risks letting his English book become a French novel in which he must give over his author's mantle and act his scripted and degrading part.

The national pedagogy William begins practicing upon Frances makes promi- nent use, naturally enough, of English books.[8] At tea in Frances's small apartment, the teacher commands her, "Get one of your English books, Mademoiselle," whereupon "up she rose, got her book and accepted at once the chair I placed for her at my side. She had selected 'Paradise Lost' from her shelf of classics . . . I told

---

[8] Cf. Homi Bhabha, "DissemiNation: Time, Narrative, and the Margins of the Modern Nation," in Bhabha, ed., *Nation and Narration* (London: Routledge, 1990), 291–322.

her to begin at the beginning" (TP 162). What other text could she have chosen, this woman who thinks of England as her Canaan? At this same tea, William is struck by the "sort of illusion [that consists] in seeing the fair-complexioned, English-looking girl presiding at the English meal and speaking the English language" in a house on the Rue *Notre Dame aux Neiges* (TP 161). The entire important scene is appropriately enough shot through with evocations of Freud's *Unheimlichkeit,* since the siting of Frances as the English treasure in exile coincides with the recovery, through fetish objects, of lost maternal powers—powers, that is to say, of an *English* "our lady" to be contrasted with the Catholic one.[9] The paradoxical idea that we might call it *returning* when a woman goes to a country she has never been to before gets secured *as* paradox (rather than remaining nonsense) by a talismanic tea set, which once belonged to Frances's English great-grandmother and was passed down through the maternal line until, Frances says, "my mother brought them with her from England to Switzerland and left them to me; and ever since I was a little girl, I have thought I should like to carry them back to England, whence they came" (TP 160–61). In a woman's version of what Dickens in *Great Expectations* will fixate on as "portable property" and Virgil long ago represented in the household gods Aeneas carries with him out of Troy, Frances's tea set is Brontë's objective correlative for the continuous racial memory that Crimsworth's English book requires if it is to turn what might otherwise be an affectless succession of events (Frances lives in Europe, then in England) into a pathos-laden *plot* of exile and return.

Not much later, William acquires his own maternal fetish, through a sequence of events commencing when Yorke Hundsen visits Brussels, bearing the news that Edward Crimsworth's business has failed and that "Crimsworth-Hall is sold" (TP 192). This collapse of the turncoat older brother clears the way for the younger. In an act of somewhat cynical benevolence, Hundsen sends William the portrait of William's mother that has been "saved . . . out of the wreck of Crimsworth-Hall and now committ[ed] to the care of its natural keeper" (TP 194). We could hardly request a fitter emblem of the well-known salvage motif of ethnography, the "saving" of vanishing traditional cultures that requires their transformation into effects of the ethnographer's text. Out of this picture there gazes

> a pale, pensive looking female face . . . [with] large, solemn eyes [that] looked reflectively into mine. . . . A listener (had there been one) might have heard me after ten minutes' silent gazing, utter the word 'Mother!' I might have said more—but with me, the first word uttered aloud in soliloquy, rouses consciousness; it reminds me that only crazy people talk to themselves, and then I think out my monologue, instead of speaking it. (TP 194)

As we have also seen in Dickens, the tableau of the face-to-face look between mother and child supplies a powerful myth of origin for both identity and narrative; it is the "ground zero" of the idea of locality. In the beginning, this myth sug-

---

[9] The street name may encourage us to think of Brontë's last novel, which is presided over by an English Protestant "translation" of *Notre Dame aux Neiges:* Lucy Snowe.

gests, the recognizing gaze of the mother stamped identity and value upon the child, but that moment is present to the child's consciousness only as something lost. In this plot about the (re)discovery of Englishness abroad, what also gets recovered is, not the mother herself, but her substitute and image: a culture, an identity-sustaining network of "friends" that represents and stands in for that always-lost moment of supposedly natural identification, just as Frances, to the extent that she will come to occupy the wifely domestic role, will do vis-à-vis the Mrs. Crimsworth who preceded her. Receiving the picture seems to embolden William to free himself once and for all from the Pelet-Reuter sphere of influence by obtaining a new job, and, like Brontë's hero Wellington before him, he now strives iron-willed toward triumph in Belgium. "Feverish and roused, no disappointment arrested me; defeat following fast on defeat served as stimulants to will; I forgot fastidiousness, conquered reserve, thrust pride from me: I asked, I persevered, I remonstrated, I dunned. It is so that openings are forced into the guarded circle where Fortune sits dealing favours round" (TP 196). He is rewarded with "the appointment of English professor to all the classes of _____ College, Brussels" (TP 197).

Culture's re-presentation of the mother and her meaning-conferring look inspires Brontë's hero to achieve his Englishness by extricating himself from foreign entanglements and extirpating foreign influences over his life. But it also introduces hazards of its own, as William's peculiar comments on the habit of talking to oneself might indicate. A very few pages after telling us that the recovery of his mother's portrait had brought him to the verge of this habit indulged in "only [by] crazy people," William writes of accidentally overhearing Frances as she engages at length in this same activity that he denies himself. (Always opposed to Jesuitical surveillance, Brontë nonetheless permits much of her plot to turn on instances of overhearing, but she is scrupulous to distinguish what she regards as honest Protestant overhearing from Catholic eavesdropping.) There are, it seems, good forms of talking to oneself as well as bad. Overhearing Frances exposes William to the possibility of a redeemed or a *translated* talking-to-oneself that will become one of Brontë's favorite figures for the true relationship or culture. The redemption can occur only if William and Frances pass through a phase of trial wherein the racial foundation of cultural identity threatens to crumble, exposing the expatriated heroine to the danger of a total and final de-anglicization.

Approaching her door, William is caught up short by the sound of a voice "so low, so self-addressed, I never fancied the speaker otherwise than alone; Solitude might speak thus in a desert, or in the hall of a forsaken house" (TP 199). The beloved is reciting poetry. First comes a fragment of an "old Scotch ballad"—not really so old, since it is Scott's "The Covenanter's Fate"—which parallels Frances's and William's own stories inasmuch as it dwells upon a refugee driven into hiding from a battlefield on which, as in the anticultural homeland, Britons contend with Britons. As with the possibly Welsh surname of Evans, the invocation of a poem by Scott on an episode in Scottish history to serve as a pathway to recovered *Englishness* is entirely characteristic of Brontë and reflects that expanding, inclusive sense of the identity "English" on the rise since 1801. In the quoted excerpt from Scott, a "wanderer" "[i]n persecution's iron days, / When the land was left by God," flees "[f]rom Bewley's bog, with slaughter red" and eludes the pursuing victors in a dismal cavern. Like that wanderer in a time of civil war, William and Frances both have hidden themselves away from Britain's domestic conflict.

Breaking off her recital of Scott just when she has brought the fugitive panting to his cave, Frances then embarks upon a second poem, her own, in French. This one seems to revoke the refugee model for Brontë's heroine that Scott's verses had made available. Rather than dive shivering and silent into the cave of the friendless self, Frances in this second poem speaks out, using what William perceives is "the language of her own heart"—whereas "Sir Walter Scott's voice" is "to her a foreign, far-off sound" (TP 200). Here again is the dilemma of the displaced Englishwoman, who may have passed too far into the embrace of the importunate Francophone culture surrounding and trying to "befriend" her to be amenable to reanglicization. The poem tells of the growing love of a pupil for her master, but the way to their true union seems blocked so long as French remains the language of Frances's heart.

What Brontë does next recalls, in inverted form, Scott's elaborate business with the bard's battle song in *Waverley* (discussed in chapter 4). The communication changes its medium from overheard speech to silently read text: William enters the room after the first lines of these verses have been recited, picks up the sheet of paper on which the poem is written, and, exercising his teacher's prerogative, waves aside all Frances's demurrals and reads. This shift recalls the one William himself made at the start of the novel, from the conversation of boyhood companions to the production of a text that translates that talk into something silently read by those out of earshot. In his book, William supplies a lengthy portion of Frances's poem, which develops its tale of burgeoning love between teacher and pupil, including the near loss of the beloved student to illness, her impending departure, and his culminating cry—like Rochester's in *Jane Eyre*—"Come home to me again!" After the fashion of *Waverley,* Brontë's narrator here evokes an alien original but gives only an English translation that he describes as "nearly literal" (TP 202): the purported French original will not appear in William's English book. In a manner developed by the ballad-collectors and novelists of the United Kingdom's secondary nations at the beginning of the century, Brontë confronts us, here, with the abiding strangeness of a medium in which dark markings on a white page conjure up people speaking in a shared physical space. Brontë's novel appears to be arguing that it is just as impossible for French to be the language of an Englishwoman's heart as it is for the spoken voice to be heard in print. William does more than simply translate Frances's verses and the sentiments they express into English; informing us of the existence of an absent original permits us to register his *suppression* of it—and this in an English novel containing plenty of untranslated French—as if, in "silencing" it, he could make his translation *itself* an original. Just as in Scott, though, Brontë leaves wide open the question: how nearly literal is a nearly literal translation?

Translators in every age have had to be satisfied with the "good enough," but since the philological revolution commencing in the later eighteenth century made

each separate people's language the index of its cultural identity, translation became an inescapably ethnographic and perhaps even an impossible endeavor: the
trope of an ultimate untranslatability vouched for the integrity of cultural identities, heightening awareness of "the lack of an 'equals' sign, the reality of what's
missed and distorted" in the attempt to understand the Other.[10] Similarly, commitment to the spatial metaphor of cultures as discrete, nonoverlapping domains
can underwrite a corresponding set of metaphors for describing processes of acquiring or unlearning or relearning a culture: the idea of cultures as mutually exclusive encourages reliance on the tropes of conversion or purgation, tropes that
are themselves hard to purge from narratives of national pedagogy such as the one
William Crimsworth is engaged in with Frances Henri. The proposal scene that
follows William's translation, centering upon roughly a page of dialogue that al-
ternates between the two languages vying for Frances's soul, comes close to driving us into the arms of such tropes, close to making us think of English cultural recovery as a process that must entail radical de-gallicization. We can imagine the
teacher's frustration as his every English question meets a French response:

> "Frances, how much regard have you for me?"
> "Mon maître, j'en ai beaucoup," was the truthful rejoinder.
> "Frances, have you enough to give yourself to me as my wife? To accept me as your
> husband?" . . .
> "Monsieur," said the soft voice at last, "Monsieur désire savoir si je consens—si—enfin,
> si je veux me marier avec lui?" (TP 206)

And so forth. Brontë's heroine eventually has to be ordered to stop relying on the
language that has so adventitiously managed to become the language of her heart
and to accept translation into her "mother tongue." Nowhere in the novel does the
temptation to conceive of national pedagogy as the authoritative extirpation of foreignness make itself more plainly felt than in the curt command that ensues the
proposal: "Will my pupil consent to pass her life with me? Speak English now,
Frances" (TP 207).

And yet, as we might have suspected from William's own divergence from the
conversion model of class identity provided by his brother, it would be a mistake
to stop there. Just as soon as Frances has consented, in English, to marry William,
all those factors contained in the novel that run *contrary* to the de-Frenchifying or
one-making national pedagogy begin to reassert themselves. The making of
Frances English, as well as the recovery of Englishness in Frances, is not an end,
but a new beginning: the affirmation of this primary identity supplies the foundation on which a new plurality of roles and identities can emerge, and even substantial forms of difference, once shunned, can be reintroduced to a certain degree.
In other words, it is only after the fundamental identity of a national culture is
placed beyond dispute that differences may be permitted and recognized in rela-

---

[10] James Clifford, "Traveling Cultures," in *Routes: Travel and Translation in the Late Twentieth
Century* (Cambridge, Mass.: Harvard University Press, 1997), 42.

tion to and even within it.[11] This readmitted difference comes in several forms. Less than a page after accepting her teacher's proposal, Frances is arguing for the right to go on teaching after marriage; she prevails, with the result that, when the narrating William looks back to survey their years together, he finds it cause for satisfaction rather than disturbance that he has "seemed to possess two wives"— both Mrs. Crimsworth and "Madame the Directress" of the school they have founded—"[s]o different was she under different circumstances" (TP 230).

In addition, it turns out that while Frances can be instructed to adopt certain English ways, she remains impervious to others. William enables her to do justice to her mother's tea set by teaching her "how to make a cup of tea in a rational English style" so that she becomes capable of "administer[ing] a proper British repast," but his wife persists in many of her gallicisms, preferring to call her husband "Monsieur" in part because, as she says, "I cannot pronounce your W" (TP 227, 228). She persists in disavowing the sound that starts her husband's name and that helps distinguish English from many Continental languages. Their marriage establishes itself according to a pattern by which, William says, "she teased me in French [and] entreated me in English" (TP 234). He does continue to employ English books in a campaign originally designed to de-Frenchify his wife, but he gradually comes to realize the pleasurable tension that her supplementary foreignness brings to their marriage, so that the campaign turns into something of a running joke shared between them. When Frances teases him about some "bizarreries anglaises," some "caprices insulaires" in his character, he makes her "get a book, and read English to [him] by the hour by way of penance." "I frequently dosed her with Wordsworth in this way," he tells us—another William, and one whose name positively brims with those "W's" Frances cannot pronounce. For an Englishman of the 1840s to make his French-speaking wife read Wordsworth aloud (and even to say the name "Wordsworth") is to compel her to use her body as a vehicle for definitively English sounds and meanings, to train her in habits of pronunciation and association that had come to be exalted *as* definitively English, in large measure for their repudiation of the Francophile enthusiasms of the poet's youth.[12] Yet although William claims that the tonic Wordsworth always damped down his wife's Gallic passions, always "steadied her soon," these sessions seem to have acquired the second, contrary function of providing opportunities for the demonstration, not of Frances's amenability to wholesale angliciza-

---

[11] Cf. Marshall Sahlins, *Waiting for Foucault* (Cambridge: Prickly Pear Pamphlet no. 2, 1993): "In order for the categories to be contested at all, there must be a common system of intelligibility" (13–14).

[12] Cf. James K. Chandler, *Wordsworth's Second Nature: A Study of the Poetry and Politics* (Chicago: University of Chicago Press, 1984). Frances's responses to British poets—"Byron excited her; Scott she loved; Wordsworth, only, she puzzled at, wondered over, and hesitated to pronounce upon" (TP 233–34)—run opposite to John Stuart Mill's. In the chapter of his autobiography entitled "A Crisis in My Mental History," Mill famously writes of being left cold by Byron but of finding in Wordsworth "the very culture of the feelings, which [he] was in search of": *Autobiography,* ed. Jack Stillinger (Boston: Houghton Mifflin, 1969), 89.

tion, but rather of her *persistence* in finding Wordsworth foreign to her. "[S]he had a difficulty in comprehending his deep, serene and sober mind," William notes: "his language too was not facile to her; she had to ask questions; to sue for explanations; to be like a child and a novice and to acknowledge me as her senior and director" (TP 233). Their interaction over Wordsworth preserves *both* the pedagogic relationship and the intransigent Frenchness commonly thought excluded from definitions of Englishness and indeed regarded as the very ground of opposition upon which those latter definitions could take shape.

Further indication that *The Professor* does not conclude in any simple vision of achieved national purity comes when, soon after their engagement, William and Frances play host to the visiting skeptic Hundsen. This man with the "broad Saxon forehead," who has come to Belgium "just fresh from his island-country," confronts Frances's idealized conception of the motherland with a cynical nominalism on the question of Englishness (TP 217). Happy to be out of "that dirty little country," Hundsen demands of Frances, "is it possible that anybody with a grain of rationality should feel enthusiasm about a mere name, and that name England?" This challenge spurs the following exchange:

> "England is your country?" ask[s] Frances.
> "Yes."
> "And you don't like it?"
> "I'd be sorry to like it! A little corrupt, venal, lord-and-king cursed nation, full of mucky
>   pride . . . and helpless pauperism; rotten with abuses, worm-eaten with prejudices!"
> "You might say so of every state; there are abuses and prejudices everywhere, and I
>   thought fewer in England than in other countries."
> "Come to England and see. Come to Birmingham and Manchester; come to St. Giles in
>   London." (TP 218)

Hundsen reveals more here than his tendency to accentuate the negative in accounts of his native land; he exhibits the materialist habit of thought also shown by Edward Crimsworth, according to which the nation is nothing more than an itemizable assortment of people, places, and things. Where Frances extols the affective bonds between individuals and their nations, Hundsen calls it "mad as a March hare to indulge in a passion for millions of ship-loads of soil, timber, snow and ice" (TP 221). In Malinovskian parlance, Hundsen's is the perspective of one who is *in* and *of* his national anticulture but possesses no vision of the whole. Even when he gets physically outside of England and converses with the living spirit of Englishness, he cannot see it.

In her debate with him, Frances speaks up not simply for Englishness: for the first time in the novel, she explicitly defends her identity as Swiss, abjuring Hundsen's slanders against this people she now claims as her own: "Do you call my countrymen servile? . . . Do you abuse Switzerland to me, Mr. Hundsen? Do you think I have no associations?" (TP 220). The heroine and her foil articulate Brontë's vision of national-cultural authority and its defining opposite:

> "Were you born in Switzerland?" [Hundsen asks.]
> "I should think so, or else why should I call it my country?"

"And where did you get your English features and figure?"

"I am English too—half the blood in my veins is English; thus I have a right to a double power of patriotism, possessing an interest in two noble, free and fortunate countries."

"You had an English mother?"

"Yes, yes; and you, I suppose, had a mother from the Moon or from Utopia, since not a nation in Europe has a claim on your interest."

"On the contrary, I'm a universal patriot; if you could understand me rightly; my country is the world."

"Sympathies so widely diffused must be very shallow." (TP 222)

Like another character named Yorke in Brontë's later novel *Shirley,* Hundsen is a man at once too local and too universal: he lacks all grasp of the mediating term of nationality. His professed but meaningless universal patriotism leads him, as it led the *Philosophes* and Jacobins, to indulge in many pointless "polyglott [sic] discussions" with "driveling theorists" (TP 238–39). It is not just the strong feeling of belonging to a distinct community that Brontë opposes to Hundsen's Enlightenment cosmopolitanism here and elsewhere in the book, but a *double* power of patriotism, as if it takes the person animated by the sense of belonging to *two* different nations to understand, and properly value, what it means to belong to *one*.

During that quest to recover the identity that flows from the motherland, the quest that structures William and Frances's marriage plot, the claims of Frances's Swiss fatherland lay dormant. Once that quest has concluded with the engagement of Frances and William, it becomes possible in some measure to revalidate the paternal by admitting feelings of patriotism toward the country where one was born and raised. Race and the mother hold sway, but now birthplace and childhood associations can receive their due. This readmission of patrimony into the logic of Brontë's novel brings home the novel's implicit and paradoxical argument about the necessity of double or plural identifications to the maintenance of single ones: as in *Shirley,* much of Brontë's narrative labor is devoted to confounding the urge (which she also exhibits) "not to be other than one thing."[13]

Around the middle of Brontë's first novel, at a point when, Frances having left Mlle. Reuter's school, William has lost contact with her, the hero resolves to "seek her through Brussels" (TP 151). The plot of her restoration to England provides an image of what threatens to derail that plot when William finally spots her in "the protestant Cemetery, outside the gates of Louvain."

[F]or those who love to peruse the annals of grave-yards [he writes], here was variety of inscription enough to occupy the attention for [hours]. . . . Hither people of many kindreds, tongues, and nations had brought their dead for interment, and here, on pages of stone, of marble and of brass, were written names, dates, last tributes of pomp or love in English, in French, in German and Latin. . . . Every nation, tribe and kindred mourned after its own fashion and how soundless was the mourning of all! (TP 153–54)

This polyglot necropolis stands in defining contrast to the dream of a positive Protestant nationalism toward which Brontë's plot moves. "[H]ere was my lost

---

[13] Cf. chap. 9 below, on *Shirley.*

jewel," William writes, "dropped on the tear-fed herbage, nestling in the mossy and mouldy roots of yew-trees!" (TP 155). Finding her means rescuing the possibility of a relocatable national identity from the infectious nation-dissolving tendencies of "the catholic." The cemetery's "pages of stone" inscribed with the languages of many nations stand opposed to the pages of the English book we hold in our hands, which aims to revive the principle of Englishness and return it to its proper place. In that book, William hopes, we will not read the "soundless" voices of all nations but will somehow magically *hear* the voice of Albion he has heard in Frances.

Remembering this central tableau can also help us account for one of the most peculiar moments in this weird novel, which occurs immediately after Frances has accepted William's proposal of marriage. The union of the pilgrim and his national icon cannot be achieved without one final crisis: the successful suitor must pass a dark night of the soul during which "Hypochondria" assails his new-found joy. William personifies this affliction as an incubus angered by his infidelity to her.

> She had been my acquaintance, nay my guest, once before in boyhood; I had entertained her at bed and board for a year; for that space of time I had her to myself in secret; she lay with me, she eat with me, she walked out with me, showing me nooks in woods, hollows in hills, where we could sit together, and where she could drop her drear veil over me, and so hide sky and sun, grass and green tree; taking me entirely to her death-cold bosom, and holding me with arms of bone. What tales she would tell me, at such hours! What songs she would recite in my ears! How she would discourse to me of her own Country—The Grave!—and again and again promise to conduct me there ere long; and drawing me to the very brink of a black, sullen river, shew me on the other side, shores unequal with mound, monument, and tablet, standing up in a glimmer more hoary than moonlight. "Necropolis!" she would whisper, pointing to the pale piles, and add, "It contains a mansion, prepared for you." (TP 211)

To the *ordinary* patriot, *all* other lands are Hypochondria's own country: all particular manifestations of the Not-Us merge into undifferentiated otherness; all the world's other capitals are Necropolis. Hypochondria is that force of ordinary patriotism that William must overcome in himself, the model of identity he must repudiate, en route to Brontë's emerging ideal of an extraordinary, expatriated patriotism.

In token of their quest's success, William and Frances name their child Victor; but the name does not signal any triumphalist conclusion. What seems most striking about the novel's handling of this boy, who combines the traits of his parents, is the fact that all the hospitality toward supplementary foreignness that William found himself able to extend to his wife once he had won her gets revoked when attention shifts to their son and heir—as if the pedagogic quest for Englishness has to be started over from scratch with each generation, each time requiring the setting aside of secondary identities and submission to the purgative lesson. With regard to his son's education, William becomes the mouthpiece for stern necessity: the foreignness in his son represents for him some "leaven of the offending Adam," which must be driven out at all costs, chiefly by driving Victor physically away from the look of his mother. Victor "must soon go to Eton," William tells us, "where, I suspect, his first year or two will be utter wretchedness" (TP 244). But after all, he asks,

> will reason or love be the weapons with which in future the world will meet his violence? Oh no! for that flash in his black eye—for that cloud on his bony brow—for that compressure of his statuesque lips, that lad will some day get blows instead of blandishments—kicks instead of kisses—then for the fit of mute fury which will sicken his body and madden his soul—then for the ordeal of merited and salutary suffering—out of which he will come (I trust) a wiser and a better man. (TP 245)

Brontë's next novel would devote considerable attention to the "mute fury" of a sick and maddened man, who must pass through the refining fire of much "merited and salutary suffering" in order to become a wiser and better Englishman. And at the end of *Jane Eyre,* along with his still wiser and better wife, the chastened Edward Rochester will set about building a model of English concord to counterbalance the domain of furious antagonism to which William Crimsworth commits his son. Until all England became home to that concord, no Englishman could truly be called victor.

CHAPTER EIGHT

The Wild English Girl: *Jane Eyre*

Thus from a Mixture of all kinds began,
That Het'rogeneous Thing, *an Englishman* . . .
  —Daniel Defoe, "The True-Born Englishman"[1]

I was a discord in Gateshead Hall; I was like nobody there; I had nothing in
harmony with Mrs Reed or her children, or her chosen vassalage. If they did not
love me, in fact, as little did I love them. They were not bound to regard with
affection a thing that could not sympathize with one amongst them; a
heterogeneous thing, opposed to them in temperament, in capacity, in
propensities; a useless thing, incapable of serving their interest, or adding to their
pleasure; a noxious thing, cherishing the germs of indignation at their treatment,
of contempt of their judgment.
  —Jane Eyre[2]

I

READINGS OF *Jane Eyre* and of Charlotte Brontë's work as a whole have derived
much energy from the idea that Brontë had to drop the pretense of *The Professor*'s
masculine narrator in order to "find her voice," and that she found and used that
voice triumphantly in her impassioned second novel. This chapter will consider
the phenomenon of voice in *Jane Eyre* as a much more paradoxical and ambiva-
lence-generating issue than critics have been inclined to regard it. It seems to me
that *Jane Eyre* cultivates considerable suspicion about the powers and tendencies
of the voice, holding apart Jane the speaker and Jane the retrospective narrator and
deeming the latter to possess advantages of perspective that the former was too
young, too degraded, too enraged, too narrow-sighted to have access to. In this,
the novel exploits a possibility inherent in all first-person narration, heightening
the effect of the split between narrating and narrated selves. Its tense play with
writing and speech also harks back to Scott and the authors of the National Tale,

---

[1] Defoe, *The True-Born Englishman and Other Writings,* ed. P. N. Furbank and W. R. Owens (Harmondsworth: Penguin, 1997), 35; Benedict Anderson uses this passage as an epigraph to *Imagined
Communities.*
  [2] Brontë, *Jane Eyre* (1847; Harmondsworth: Penguin, 1996), 23; henceforth JE.

for whom Celtic-speaking voices could be "heard" only if translated into the silent markings in an English or self-anglicized text: *Jane Eyre* is an *English* National Tale that subjects the speech of its narrator's former self to just such translation.[3]

Yet the crucial business of the telephonic communication between Jane and Rochester at the close of the novel routes us *back* to the domain of the voice and disrupts any simple progress from voice to print, from local to abstracted national consciousness. Moreover, throughout the narrative, we may detect intimations of a persistent aural dimension whenever we find Jane Eyre being placed in situations that emphasize her status as a figure of *ire,* as someone who longs to fly off into *air,* as a dispossessed *heir*(ess), and, most tenuously yet most intriguingly of all, as having something to do with *Eire* or *Erin.* Circulating amidst these possible associations is the suggestion that it just might matter how one *pronounces* the heroine's name, as if the recommended method for dealing with *Jane Eyre* were to read it aloud to hearers within the reader's immediate vicinity, not to peruse it in solitary silence. The national consciousness Brontë seeks to cultivate cannot be permitted to remain simply abstract; it has to reincorporate the elements of locality (the body, the voice) rather than simply trade these in for an anonymous comradeship whose image is "the reading public." As in *The Professor,* though now working from the inside out (that is, from local to national) instead of from the outside in (from expatriation to repatriation), *Jane Eyre* describes a quest for a positive national identity that will supplement and transcend other identities but not obliterate them, that will sustain the condition of being other than one thing. This means, as in all Brontë's work, confronting and resisting the allure of those one-making tropes of purgation or conversion to which a significant segment of Brontë's own imaginative energy is undeniably attracted. It means actualizing, through the resources distinctive to narrative—chiefly the relationships between discourse- and story-spaces, silent print and evoked voices—the powers distinctive to Englishness as a "heterogeneous thing." The shift to a female narrator enables *Jane Eyre* to succeed *The Professor* as a revisionary romance in which the protagonist develops into the kind of heroine capable of saving the novel's hero and of complementing Defoe's one-sided account of the hybrid English*man* with an Englishwoman no less mixed in her nature than he. But, as I indicated above, Brontë's aim is a strictly regulated heterogeneity that has to turn aside from engagement with forms of otherness deemed unmanageable or threatening to the integrity of the system of differences constituting the national culture.[4]

---

[3] Whereas most of the internal evidence suggests that the events Jane narrates took place in the 1820s, one anomalous reference to Scott's *Marmion* (1808) as a "new publication" (JE 414) would make Jane's story contemporaneous with the non-English National Tales of Owensen, Maturin, and others.

[4] Brontë is thus well ahead of the trend Robert J. C. Young locates in the later nineteenth century "for the English to invoke Defoe's account of 'that Het'rogeneous Thing, An Englishman', and to define themselves as a hybrid or 'Mongrel half-bred Race'": Robert J. C. Young, *Colonial Desire: Hybridity in Theory, Culture, and Race* (London: Routledge, 1995), 17. In her interesting *Imperialism at Home: Race and Victorian Women's Fiction* (Ithaca: Cornell University Press, 1996), Susan Meyer attributes to Brontë too uncomplicated an investment in the trope of purification and thus constructs a

The general tendency in *Jane Eyre* to move from the domain of voice to authorship and print and then, jarringly, back through voice again, fits the pattern of return on which—as many have noted—much of the novel is organized. Here again Brontë mobilizes, and provides repeated thematic echoes of, an intrinsic potentiality of her form. Not only does retrospective first-person narration lend itself to figuration as a return to the past; the plot of *Jane Eyre,* too, is filled with returns. On the novel's very first page, Jane refers to her childhood dislike of returning from cold walks outside to the morally cold interior of Gateshead. Later on, when in Rochester's employment, she leaves Thornfield to go back to Gateshead to visit the dying Mrs. Reed and learn of her uncle John's earlier attempts to locate her; this departure from Thornfield allows both for a space of reflection on what has been happening there and for a first-ever return to Thornfield itself, where Jane is now courted in earnest by Rochester. Later, fleeing Thornfield after the revelation of Rochester's existing marriage, Jane makes a paradoxical "homecoming" to a set of relatives she has never known she had, the Riverses at Moor House. We can call this a return or recovery, or call the Riverses Jane's "long-lost" relatives, to the extent that we invest in the idea that blood relation makes abiding claims having nothing to do with an individual's actual experience: it is the *cri du sang* that draws Jane at her time of utter "friendlessness" toward this home she never knew she had.[5] A little later, though, pressed to leave England on St. John Rivers's missionary campaign, Jane hears the far-off pleadings of Rochester and returns once more to Thornfield to find it a ruin.

Only after undergoing all these trying and recuperative returns can Jane the character move *beyond* this pattern of return, to Ferndean, where she enters into her definitively new state as savior of Rochester, as wife and mother, and, of course, as an author capable of enacting the very different *kind* of return constituted by the first-person narrative. Rochester himself has all the while been moving through a pattern of return, as well: his first appearance in the novel and first encounter with Jane—we learn much later—coincides with his return to England after ten long years of hopeless wandering. He contrasts the "quiet little figure" of Jane he sees on that day to a catalogue of female foreignness—not only the Creole Bertha but, in efficient succession, the Parisian Céline, the Italian Giacinta, and the German Clara—with whom he has spent his years as a "Will-o'-the-wisp," just as he will later contrast her to the anticultural Englishwoman Blanche Ingram (JE 348). If he were to marry Blanche, their marriage would offer a precise opposite to the possibility Rochester and Jane's marriage holds out: instead of a model of English culture balancing the claims of individual and collectivity (see my dis-

---

neater opposition between "plague-cursed colonial environments" and a bourgeois ideal of "England, cleanliness, and home" than I would draw (87; cf. chap. 2). Cf. Firdous Azim, *The Colonial Rise of the Novel* (London: Routledge, 1993), for the argument that Jane's ties to the colonial domain "Creolise" her into a figure "whose inscription within English society remains heterogeneous" (177): Azim misses the national allegory through which *Jane Eyre* recommends a *restricted* heterogeneity as a formula for modern Englishness.

[5] Cf. Ruth Perry, "De-Familiarizing the Family; or, Writing Family History from Literary Sources," *Modern Language Quarterly* 55/4 (Dec. 1994), 415–27.

cussion in chapter 6), a jail or "Bridewell," as the charade enacted in the Thorn-field drawing room suggests (JE 208–9).

Had all these returns in the plot not occurred, the authoritative Jane who revis-its her past by narrating it would never have come into being. Jane's authority to author her own life is secured every time she can demonstrate the vital difference between her former and her present selves, and between successive stages of her former character. Revisiting Gateshead, for example, Jane finds "the inanimate ob-jects . . . not changed[,] but the living things . . . altered past recognition":

> On a dark, misty, raw morning in January, I had left a hostile roof with a desperate and
> embittered heart—a sense of outlawry and almost of reprobation. . . . The same hostile
> roof now again rose before me: my prospects were doubtful yet; and I had yet an aching
> heart. I still felt as a wanderer on the face of the earth; but I experienced firmer trust in
> myself and my own powers, and less withering dread of oppression. The gaping wound
> of my wrongs, too, was now quite healed; and the flame of resentment extinguished. (JE
> 256)

Over the next few pages, Jane the narrator is at pains to assert how fully her character-self had *already* liberated herself from the psychological barriers im-posed on her at the aptly named Gateshead, that factory for making "mind-forg'd manacles." Her cousins' contempt "had no longer that power over me it once pos-sessed"; "their airs gave me no concern either for good or bad"; "Eliza did not mor-tify, nor Georgiana ruffle me" (JE 257). That narrator remembers being "surprised to find how easy [she] felt" when subjected once again to her cousins' barbs. Look-ing back, she shows her achieved detachment by generalizing philosophically on her earlier experiences of both the original oppression and the later recognition of how much she had overcome its effects:

> It is a happy thing that time quells the longings of vengeance, and hushes the promptings
> of rage and aversion: I had left this woman in bitterness and hate, and I came back to her
> now with no other emotion than a sort of ruth for her great sufferings, and a strong yearn-
> ing to forget and forgive all injuries—to be reconciled and clasp hands in amity. (JE 259)

This outlook that subordinates personal experience to the function of illustrating maxims ("It is a happy thing that time . . . ") is plainly opposed to the perspective conjured up at the novel's beginning, in the famously terse remark "There was no possibility of taking a walk that day" (JE 13). There Jane the narrator returns mo-mentarily to the mentality of her child-self, so deeply inside the deadening night-mare of Gateshead life that she has no thought of any viewpoint *outside* it that might contextualize her circumstances. To the child Jane, those circumstances are the extent of the real and the possible, until the moment ("that day") when she be-gins to question her fate.

Not only does the narrative of *Jane Eyre* enact a return and describe several, it also includes reflection on the idea of return. Around the middle of the novel, telling of her journey back to Thornfield after the return to Gateshead, Jane the nar-rator writes:

> How people feel when they are returning home from an absence, long or short, I did not
> know: I had never experienced the sensation. I had known what it was to come back to
> Gateshead when a child, after a long walk . . . and later, what it was to come back from
> church to Lowood. . . . Neither of these returnings were very pleasant or desirable: no
> magnet drew me to a given point, increasing in its strength of attraction the nearer I came.
> The return to Thornfield was yet to be tried. (JE 272)

Shortly after this, Jane will blurt out to Rochester, "wherever you are is my only
home" (JE 276).

It scarcely needs to be said that this novel's much-exampled commitment to the
idea of return derives in great part from the model of *Pilgrim's Progress* and the
Christian tradition narrating life as a journey of the soul toward its spiritual home.
This and other novels' secularization of such time-honored topoi is well known.
But Brontë's adaptation of the model in *Jane Eyre* leads its journeying protagonist
along a path that stretches not simply from homelessness to home, but from a series of *antihomes* to the idealized home these define by opposition. The right kind
of home turns out to be the kind of place to which one can make the right kind of
return, which of course implies that one needs to be displaced from it first.

The novel opens by evoking a return that doesn't happen: Jane and the Reeds
don't take a walk "that day," so they don't come back to Gateshead. On the same
page we find those unpleasant memories of past returns from such walks, which
Jane "never liked" because "dreadful to [her] was the coming home in the raw twilight" (JE 13). These maneuvers set up twin negative versions of the pattern governing the entire narrative: one state of affairs to which there is no possibility of a
return because one doesn't get out of it, and another in which the getting out of it
is rendered valueless because there must always be a return to exactly the same
(miserable) situation one has left. In contrast, all *productive* returns in *Jane Eyre,*
including the return involved in retrospective first-person narration, make themselves felt as returns-with-a-difference, the identity that establishes the event as a
return being qualified by a difference that insists upon recognition. We have seen
(in chapter 4) Scott making powerful use of such qualified returns in *Waverley,*
where the re-presentation of Tully-Veolan to the Baron of Bradwardine and Waverley's own gaze at the dual portrait of himself and Fergus MacIvor seem designed to problematize Scott's own effort to represent "Scotland" as its self-
designated autoethnographer. In *Jane Eyre,* the identity over time that is vouched
for by the *name* the character and narrator share, the identity that makes the novel
the "autobiography" its subtitle claims it to be, is complicated by the oppositional
logic in which Brontë conceives of the novel's several determinative social environments. The allegorical-sounding Gateshead, Lowood, Thornfield, and Whitcross are differentiated from each other in several ways, but each supplies a variety of anticulture against which the final ideal of a genuine culture (figured in
Jane's account of her married state) can be imagined: a utopian vision somehow
magically capable of sustaining *both* a Protestant, protofeminist individualism and
a condition of intersubjective integration that I likened (in chapter 6) to Hegel's
"the I that is a we and the we that is an I."

The differences between the Gateshead Jane and the narrating Jane suggest that Brontë is traveling in the conceptual territory mapped out by the later, post-Boasian anthropologists of the so-called Culture-and-Personality School, for whom human character came to seem almost wholly malleable.[6] The deformative cultures that successively shape the young Jane are made visible in the older Jane's backward-looking narrative by the productive tension between ethnography's Observer and Participant functions, a tension that endows first-person narration with the specific force of a "cultured" self's return to lived-through versions of anticulture and to the antiselves they manufactured or were designed to create. With the exception of Whitcross, where Jane briefly inhabits a condition that is anticultural in the sense of being wholly *outside* the domain of civilization, the stages of Jane's life-travels represent protoethnographic perversions of the utopian culture at which she will finally arrive. Systematically pressuring their inmates to conform to and internalize normative models of character, Gateshead, Lowood, and Thornfield are all *cultures:* both the forms of selfhood they seek to produce in Jane and the forms they actually produce bear the inscription of their acculturating power. At Gateshead in particular, her "native environment," Jane in childhood exhibits pathologies of character and mentality that take their shape very precisely, *even in rebellion,* from the totalitarian regime in which she has been raised. To borrow a phrase of Christine Froula's, one could say that *Jane Eyre* practices autoethnography in the form of a portrait of the artist *as* her culture.[7]

That claim requires two immediate qualifications, however. First, the claims of the blood never entirely disappear from Brontë's exploratory fiction of cultural determinism: they are there all the time, unforgettably embodied in the figure of Bertha Mason, and where Jane is concerned they return in force at her severest moment of exile from all forms of culture whatever, at Whitcross. Second, reading *Jane Eyre* as an autoethnographic "portrait of the artist as her culture" does not entail the claim that, chameleon-like, Jane the character assumes a completely different hue every time she is placed in a new environment. On the contrary, the novel emphasizes the accretive, sedimentary nature of the acculturation process, showing how habits of response instilled at Gateshead persist and crop up under later, different conditions, alongside traits of more recent vintage. Chief among these habits is the tendency to regard human relations through the lens of a fundamental antinomy wherein all social existence presents itself as unmitigated servitude and the only possible freedom as utter isolation. Like the antinomy "race versus culture," that of "society versus freedom," Brontë suggests, is a symptom of social pathology, not a "problem" for which one should seek a "solution" by proving the final predominance of one side.

---

[6] Cf. George W. Stocking Jr., ed., *Malinowski, Rivers, Benedict and Others: Essays on Culture and Personality* (Madison: University of Wisconsin Press, 1986), and David Simpson's recent revisiting of the issue in *Situatedness, or, Why We Keep Saying Where We're Coming From* (Durham, N.C.: Duke University Press, 2002), chap. 3.

[7] Cf. Froula, *Modernism's Body: Sex, Culture, and Joyce* (New York: Columbia University Press, 1996).

Brontë's emphasis in *Jane Eyre* upon the power of culture is counterbalanced by all those vital elements in the text that come from domains *outside* the merely cultural: God, whose law Jane resolves to keep, in the face of Rochester's anti-nomian urgings; the monitory spirits who visit Jane when she is in extremis at Gateshead and later at Thornfield; the mad savagery of Bertha Mason; the cri du sang that brings her to the Riverses; St. John Rivers' divine vocation; the "natural sympathies" that ultimately reunite Jane with Rochester; above all, the funda-mental "restlessness" Jane comes to discover inside herself, a literally "hyper-bolic" drive to "overpass [the] limit" of any condition (JE 125). The visitations of these forces from beyond the social world break into and disrupt the otherwise dominant naturalizing ideologies of culture. Jane says of the strange visionary light that sometimes comes over her that it strikes her "into syncope" (JE 358), a word suggesting not just loss of consciousness but a violent truncation or interruption of consciousness's normal flow: the word derives from the Greek *sunkoptein,* to chop up or cut off. So steadily peremptory is the authority of culture (whether that authority is wielded by John Reed, Mr. Brocklehurst, Edward Rochester, or St. John Rivers) that it appears to require nothing less than repeated recourse to the heavy machinery of supernaturalism to put a check upon it. At the same time, the built social environment of a national culture appears to afford us our only means of curbing the dangerously alluring powers of the "beyond." Interrupting and in-terrupted in turn, the forces of culture and their opposites weave the fabric of Brontë's autoethnography. In the process, Jane the character's spoken voice is *shown* to us as possessing a power that cannot be permitted free rein, even when Jane speaks out in justified indignation against her oppressors. To appreciate the way Brontë makes Jane's writing an instrument for containing and even breaking off the flow of Jane the character's speech, it will be useful to contrast this novel with Anne Brontë's earlier novel of a downtrodden but ultimately triumphant gov-erness, *Agnes Grey.*

Both of these works participate in a particular brand of autobiographical narra-tive we might call "me-narrative," the driving impulse of which is to assert and ex-ercise the *right* to tell one's own tale. Not all first-person accounts of a life exhibit this distinctively modern tendency (whose current avatars choke the airwaves and dull the mode's critical potency). Me-narrative beseeches readers to examine things from the narrator's point of view, aiming not simply to convey information about, or lessons derived *from,* a life, but above all else to authenticate and justify that life. Like Coleridge's ancient mariner, me-narrators are under a powerful com-pulsion to narrate, to command attention and sympathy: they exhibit none of that seeming undermotivation we observed in Scott's *Roy Roy* and Brontë's *The Pro-fessor.* Their hunger for justification leads them to court and apostrophize their reader, appealing to the absent, faceless public as if it were a single listener phys-ically before the writer, capable of responding to imploring voice and looks rather than merely reading a text. And yet they may align the relationship between writ-ing and speech with that between past powerlessness and present authority. A me-narrator like Anne Brontë's Agnes Grey sets about her task with a certain eager-ness because being able to write her life story compensates for the muteness once imposed upon her as a dependent subordinate. Her previous life one long affair of *l'esprit de l'escalier,* Agnes "burned to contradict" the false monologues of the powerful: "I was used to wearing a placid smiling countenance when my heart was bitter within me," Agnes tells us.[8] The definitive effect of her text occurs whenever she points, as she repeatedly does, to the gap between the character in the past and the narrator in the present. Recalling one of the many snubs she received at her employers' hands, for instance, Agnes writes, "I wished to say something in my own justification, but in attempting to speak, I felt my voice falter, and rather than testify any emotion, or suffer the tears to overflow, that were already gathering in my eyes, I chose to keep silence, and bear all, like a self-convicted culprit" (AG 47–48). Protected now by the screens of time and text, the narrator's "voice" does not falter, but "speaks out"—in print. In order to utter all that she could not say in the face-to-face exchanges that the book recounts, the me-narrator has to turn her thwarted voice into silent words on a page, which now affirm, for anyone who might happen to be reading—and will her past oppressors be among them?— that she was in the right, though sorely misused. The me-narrator protests those past situations of silencing but requires them as the basis of her authority as a writer.

Apart from the authority to narrate, the me-narrator insists upon her right to desire. To write is to "give voice" to longings once condemned to remain unspoken. Drawn to the good curate Mr. Weston yet blocked from seeing him by Rosalie, the coquette in her charge, Agnes Grey consoles herself with the reflection that, "though he knew it not, I was more worthy of his love than Rosalie Murray, charming and engaging as she was" (AG 145). "Nobody knew him as I did," she boldly, inwardly resolves; "nobody could appreciate him as I did; nobody could love him as I . . . could, if I might" (AG 147). Jane Eyre has her comparable moment when she is compelled to sit in the drawing room of Thornfield and watch Rochester pay court to Blanche Ingram. "He is not to them [Blanche and the others] what he is to me," she writes that she then thought: "he is not of their kind. . . . I understand the language of his countenance and movements: though rank and wealth sever us widely, I have something in my brain and heart, in my blood and nerves, that assimilates me mentally to him." But all the while that this volcano of self-justification smolders silently in their midst, the denizens of the drawing room go on with their deadening rites: in the text, Jane's inner monologue is broken off with the devastating "Coffee is handed" (JE 199).

Me-narratives about once-silenced characters may be placed on a continuum whose opposite poles would involve either complete acceptance of the trade-off of voice for print (of then for now) or lasting dissatisfaction with that exchange. In the former case, the deferred gratification offered to the narrator in surrogate form would not generate any turbulence but would insert itself smoothly and frictionlessly into the psychic slot once occupied by the silenced character's resentment, describing an airtight economy whose chief products are forgiveness and the psychological liberation of the forgiving self. In the latter, no amount of emphasis

---

[8] Anne Brontë, *Agnes Grey* (1847; Oxford: Oxford University Press, 1998), 145; henceforth AG.

on the advantages of "distance" from past sufferings would quell the desire to go back, not just through the medium of reflection and writing but *actually,* to relive and revise painful scenes by speaking up. Neither *Agnes Grey* nor *Jane Eyre* belongs at either end of this continuum, but it is obvious that Anne Brontë's novel deserves a spot far closer to the "accepting" side than is warranted for her older and more famous sister's masterpiece. Even in *Agnes Grey* it is occasionally possible to detect that turbulence I refer to, whenever Agnes the character's stifled desire and rage finds a substitute agent in some creature lower in the hierarchies of society or nature than is Agnes herself. A nursemaid named Betty, for instance, provides the much put-upon governess with some vicarious satisfaction when she confesses herself untroubled by the former's scruples about corporal punishment: "I don't vex myself o'er 'em as you do," Betty says: whenever the monstrous children of the household deserve it, "I hit 'em a slap sometimes; and them little uns— I gives 'em a good whipping now and then—there's nothing else ull do for 'em" (AG 41). In another passage, Agnes recalls her mistress's cruel, vulgar brother and admits that "poor as [she] was, [she] would have given a sovereign any day" to see one of the dogs he regularly brutalized bite him (AG 43). But for the most part, Agnes Grey is content with her bargain, grateful for that state of affairs in which "shielded by [her] own obscurity, and by the lapse of years, and a few fictitious names," she need "not fear to venture, and [may] candidly lay before the public what [she] would not disclose to the most intimate friend" (AG 1). Her narrative remains a tale of quiet virtue rewarded: potentially messy feelings are efficiently borne away by proxies, purifying the heroine in preparation for her inevitable marriage to Mr. Weston, which comes about without Agnes's having to say a word.

Where *Jane Eyre* is concerned, the critical template established by Gilbert and Gubar's *The Madwoman in the Attic* has accustomed us to regarding Bertha Mason as the vehicle for Jane's own inexpressible fury over the false liberation Rochester promises her in "wedlock." But here the use of a substitute as vehicle and sacrificial victim, a device whose troubling implications postcolonial readings have alerted us to,[9] seems but one manifestation among many of Brontë's self-consciousness with regard to the tropes and modes basic to her own fictional practice. For *Jane Eyre* is a me-narrative featuring a character whom many attempt to silence but who seems determined to anticipate the advent of her authorship by speaking out a good deal. "*Speak* I must," writes Jane the narrator, referring not to her writing as a kind of long-deferred speech but to what she could not stop herself from doing many a time in the past (JE 45). Among the simplest gratifications on offer in this complex book is the vicarious pleasure we get when the young Jane fires off salvoes of righteous retaliation, as for example when she explodes with "How dare I, Mrs Reed? How dare I? Because it is the *truth.* . . . I will tell anybody who asks me questions, this exact tale. People think you are a good woman, but you are bad; hard-hearted"—and so forth (JE 45–46). Jane's self-quotation at moments like this appears to take us straight to that burning core of resentful au-

---

[9] Cf. Gayatri Chakravorty Spivak, "Three Women's Texts and a Critique of Imperialism," *Critical Inquiry* 12 (1985), 243–61.

thenticity, that sense of "Eyre" as *ire,* which scorns the charge of lying and turns it back upon the authorities of the warped system that imprisons her. Here is that titanic anger whose rupturing of the surface of Brontë's fiction has given critics of opposite tendencies cause for distress or celebration but which in any event has occupied much critical attention ever since *Jane Eyre* was published. Another often-cited instance occurs later on, when, thinking Mr. Rochester intends to see his feigned courtship of Blanche Ingram through to its culmination, Jane bursts forth:

> "I tell you I must go!" I retorted, roused to something like passion.
> "Do you think I can stay to become nothing to you? Do you think I am an automaton?—
> a machine without feelings? and can bear to have my morsel of bread snatched from
> my lips, and my drop of living water dashed from my cup? Do you think, because I
> am poor, obscure, plain, and little, I am soulless and heartless?—You think wrong!—
> I have as much soul as you,—and full as much heart!" (JE 284)

In such passages, "Eyre" means both *ire* and *air,* the breath of the vehement speaker-on-her-own-behalf.

Without disputing Jane the character's right to be as angry as she frequently was, however, we may observe that it is Jane the narrator's regular practice to subject her earlier and now self-quoted outbursts to the countervailing effort to frame and control them, to keep the indignant voice, however just its cause, from having uncontested sway.[10] In the early stages of the novel, the me-narrator's drive to speak out on her own behalf is both staged and examined, in acts of oral autobiography first delivered "without reserve" (JE 69) and then with a greater attempt to guard "against the indulgence of resentment" (JE 83). At Lowood, seizing upon Helen Burns's request for information about her circumstances, Jane gives voice to that "exact tale" she had threatened to relate about the Reeds' abuse of her: "I proceeded forthwith," the narrator recalls, "to pour out, in my own way, the tale of my sufferings and resentments. Bitter and truculent when excited, I spoke as I felt, without reserve or softening" (JE 69). Two chapters later, under the beneficent influence of Helen and the teacher Miss Temple, Jane offers a different kind of narrative in defending herself against Mr. Brocklehurst's charge of mendacity.

> I resolved in the depth of my heart that I would be most moderate: most correct; and,
> having reflected a few minutes in order to arrange coherently what I had to say, I told her
> all the story of my sad childhood. Exhausted by emotion, my language was more sub-
> dued than it generally was when it developed that sad theme; and mindful of Helen's
> warnings against the indulgence of resentment, I infused into the narrative far less of gall
> and wormwood than ordinary. Thus restrained and simplified, it sounded more credible:
> I felt as I went on that Miss Temple believed me. (JE 83)

In such passages, Jane the character begins the journey toward her later narrative authority, trying out in speech the narrator's role that can be accomplished only

---

[10] Compare those passages toward the end of *Shirley,* when the title character's expressions of scorn for her narrow-minded uncle Sympson are so little checked that one starts to feel rather sorry for the man.

upon accession to the abstracting and "distancing" medium of print (though not with perfect security even then).

Later in the novel, when Jane has left Lowood, she begins to learn a new reason to contain her own speaking voice. After a childhood crushed by authorities who do not want to hear what she has to say (the Reeds, Mr. Brocklehurst), she enters into womanhood to find herself subject to masculine authorities who may pressure her to speak of herself for purposes not in her own interest. Rochester, who makes a show of divulging his sordid past to Jane but who actually conceals the most important fact about himself, tries to use this false candor as a lure to make Jane reveal herself to him—and, when that fails, resorts to the disguise of a Gypsy fortune-teller to enable himself to plumb Jane's secret soul unimpeded. This is the man who announces "I am disposed to be gregarious and communicative" but who really wants to know his new governess without fully being known by her, the master who says, "It would please me now to draw you out: to learn more of you—therefore speak" (JE 151). Her experiences with Rochester doubtless prepare Jane for St. John Rivers's later protest, "if I know nothing about you or your history, I cannot help you," so that she furnishes him with only the sketchiest of accounts, saying, "I will tell you as much of the history of the wanderer you have harboured, as I can tell without compromising my own peace of mind—my own security, moral and physical, and that of others" (JE 388). Sure enough, when he has learned her true identity and parentage, Rivers turns out to be yet another incarnation of those powers that have sought from the beginning to cast Jane in scripts of their own construction, asking for her voice only insofar as it can be made to endorse those scripts.

And there is still a further reason, virtually absent from *Agnes Grey,* why *Jane Eyre* cultivates skepticism about this voice to which part of the imagination informing the text also longs to return. When young Jane talks so stirringly back to her aunt, she also feels that her utterances are "scarcely voluntary . . . as if my tongue pronounced words without my will consenting to their utterance: something spoke out of me over which I had no control" (JE 36). Her tirade is followed—or broken off—by the narrator's recollection, "Ere I had finished this reply, my soul began to expand, to exult, with the strangest sense of freedom, of triumph, I ever felt. It seemed as if an invisible bond had burst, and that I had struggled out into unhoped-for liberty" (JE 46). An invisible bond *has* burst, but the thing struggling out into unhoped-for liberty is actually larger and other than the "I." In *Jane Eyre,* me-narrative is complicated by the vision of desire as an impersonal force that disdains to be thought the servant of this or that self, and that uses the self as *its* agent and vehicle. Let loose upon Jane's tongue, this desire would rupture not only the invisible bonds of social constraint but the integrity of self as well (as it seems to have done to Bertha Mason): only the cultured self's inscription in a "system of desire" may constrain it.[11] What Jane has achieved by

---

[11] Christopher Herbert, *Culture and Anomie: Ethnographic Imagination in the Nineteenth Century* (Chicago: University of Chicago Press, 1991), 51.; cf. Patricia Ticineto Clough, *Autoaffection: Unconscious Thought in the Age of Teletechnology* (Minneapolis: University of Minnesota Press, 2000),

the end of the story is not just the freedom to speak-in-print, but also the recognition that this power that welled up within her and that often impelled her to speak was not in any final or complete way *her own.*

When this alien "something" in Jane forces its way into her words and out of her mouth, the result is a displacing or uncanny effect that parodies the signature effect the text regularly aims at, namely that of an *autoethnographic uncanny* arising every time Jane the narrator makes her presence strongly felt alongside her younger speaking self. Those raging moments in her youth placed Jane (she later writes) "beside myself; or rather out of myself" (*JE* 19): within the story-space of the novel is reproduced in distorted form the fundamental narrative dichotomy of discourse- and story-spaces. Imprisoned for her insolence in the unused "red-room" at Gateshead, Jane remembers, "My heart beat thick, my head grew hot; a sound filled my ears, which I deemed the rushing of wings: something seemed near me; I was oppressed, suffocated: endurance broke down—I uttered a wild, involuntary cry—I rushed to the door and shook the lock in desperate effort" (*JE* 24). At this moment of greatest vulnerability to the "something" newly felt within herself, the child Jane tries to burst out of the room, just as that power has burst out of *her* in the form of that involuntary, inarticulate cry.[12] "I never forgot the, to me, frightful episode of the red-room," she writes, "in detailing which, my excitement was sure, in some degree to break bounds" (*JE* 83). If revisiting such episodes by narrating them can arouse the same bound-breaking energy then let loose, the medium of writing or print must assume the function of distancing and containing desire even while "recalling" it.

One can see it playing this role in the famous scene at Thornfield in which Jane begins to frequent the rooftop to soothe that "restlessness" within her that being a governess has failed to quell. Summarizing her earlier self's burning dissatisfaction, her desire to "overpass [the] limit" of her horizons of possibility, the narrator fully sympathizes with those feelings and embarks upon her famous plea for understanding of the fact that women require "exercise for their faculties, and a field for their efforts as much as their brothers do" (*JE* 125). Without negating or qualifying the justice of her earlier discontentment, Jane the narrator nevertheless gives us her retrospective account of her feelings on such occasions, rather than exposing us to them in the form of self-quoted involuntary cries or anguished soliloquies. She knows that more expresses itself in the utterance of discontentment than is subject to control by the discontented one who utters: she substitutes her narrative for the "tale" her frustrated self then heard with her "inward ear . . . a tale that was never ended—a tale [her] imagination created, and narrated continuously; quickened with all of incident, life, fire, feeling, that [she] desired and had not in

---

on autoethnographic sociology's programmatic "forgetting . . . of the unconscious and desire altogether, so that what began as a criticism of the authority produced in ethnographic writing comes back at times as a naïve production of autobiographical authority" (16–17).

[12] This was one instance in which Brontë may have felt she could not trust the partitioning force of print: the words "I uttered a wild, involuntary cry" appear in manuscript but were deleted from the published text; they have been "restored" in the Penguin and some other editions of the novel.

[her] actual existence" (JE 125). It is this inward, endless tale of a bottomless desire to which Bertha's "distinct, formal, mirthless" laugh (JE 122) offers pitiless punctuation and the novel's ending dream of a genuine culture offers utopian resolution.

We also see the form of self-splitting that parodies the autoethnographic uncanny in those much-noted instances of mirroring—simultaneously self-recognizing and self-alienating—when Jane the character looks at some vision of herself and we look *at* that looking through the retrospective narrator's lens. In the red-room, the child Jane "had to cross before the looking-glass" and saw a "strange little figure there gazing at me, with a white face and arms specking the gloom and glittering eyes of fear moving where all else was still" (JE 21). To her own self she "had the effect of a real spirit: [she] thought [the figure in the mirror] like one of the tiny phantoms, half fairy, half imp" she had heard of in tales told by a Gateshead servant (JE 21–22). Later the effect acquires additional layers of mediation, in the scene in which Jane tells Rochester about her "dream" of seeing "a woman, tall and large" (Bertha) trying on Jane's wedding veil the night before Jane's nuptials and then turning to look at herself in a mirror that is so positioned as to afford Jane a view of the woman's reflected face, as if standing before that mirror herself (JE 317). If the first instance records an experience that set a seal upon Jane's recently commenced break from complete absorption in her native social environment, the second not only displays the existence of another "Mrs. Rochester" but also suggests that Jane's mistake in thinking she has found a properly nurturing new environment at Thornfield threatens to put her in essentially the same position as her predecessor and dark double.

A third moment transmutes these earlier two, in preparation for Jane's recovery of both identity and culture on a higher plane. This occurs in the passage in which St. John Rivers presents Jane, heretofore known to him as "Jane Elliott," with a piece of paper bearing her true name in her own hand. "He got up," Jane recalls, "held it close to my eyes: and I read, traced in Indian ink, in my own handwriting, the words 'Jane Eyre'—the work doubtless of some moment of abstraction" (JE 426). Instead of seeing her ghost-like, Gateshead-crushed antiself or her monstrous, Thornfield-imprisoned doppelgänger, Jane sees in her written name the prospect of the self she might become. We discern here the progressive move, typical of me-narrative, from voice to print, from local bonds to the author's power of "abstraction,"[13] but we should not overlook the fact that this moment of self-representation in and as *text* coincides precisely with the countervailing and (in this novel) the powerfully *localizing* force of the blood ties Jane discovers to exist between her and the Riverses.[14]

---

[13] Cf. Sharon Marcus, "The Profession of the Author: Abstraction, Advertising, and *Jane Eyre*," *PMLA* 110/2 (1995), 206–19.

[14] For Brontë, blood makes a double-edged claim: her siblings afforded her the very quintessence of *locality* (voices and faces intensely present), but where her parents were concerned blood ties could be powerfully *dislocating,* a constant reminder of far-off places (Cornwall, Ireland) involved in the formation of her identity.

The book Jane Eyre writes about her life functions as a cage or box—perhaps as a jail—for the voice imperfectly controlled by her former self. In the context of 1840s Britain, that voice does not simply express the insatiable yearnings of the Id or the Dionysian element in human nature, but more specifically those increasingly identified with the *Celt*. We have seen how, in *Waverley,* Scott self-consciously aligns his practice as an autoethnographer with the dispensing of English justice after the Jacobite Rebellion and presents his translating book as the modern British container (perhaps the coffin) for the Celtic voice. Approaching the middle of the century, the increasingly prestigious, pseudo-scientific distinction between supposed Germanic and Celtic traits was making ever more widely available the explanation of Ossianic melancholy as a symptom of a whole race's susceptibility to unfulfillable desire. The Celt, the limit of whose powers had been shown time and again in the history of the British Isles, who had been driven to the fringes of Britain and beyond the Pale in Ireland, was the pawn of a longing *without* limit, both symptom and cause of his historical failures. The "Celtic sadness" stemmed from the "Celtic longing for infinite things."[15] In the context in which such stereotypes were coming to acquire the authority of science, Brontë appears to be placing within her model English heroine the boundless and self-defeating hunger suited to this racialist stereotype.

To make this connection is not to suggest that Brontë does anything so positive as try to identify Jane as covertly Irish; but Irishness remains the limit-case in her exploration of a possibly heterogeneous Englishness. It seems no accident that the final ploy of Rochester in his effort to get Jane to declare her feelings for him is the lie that upon his marriage to Blanche Ingram Jane will be sent off "to undertake the education of the five daughters of Mrs Dionysius O'Gall of Bitternut Lodge, Connaught, Ireland." Rubbing salt in the wound, Rochester says, "You'll like Ireland, I think: they're such warm-hearted people there, they say," adding, "and when you get to Bitternut Lodge, Connaught, Ireland, I shall never see you again, Jane: that's morally certain. I never go over to Ireland, not having myself much of a fancy for the country" (JE 282). Having before her the example of a father who had made the one-way journey out of Ireland to England and Englishness, Brontë can think of no prospect more cruel than that her English heroine be condemned to make a one-way journey in the opposite direction.[16] In her autoethnographies of English culture as a heterogeneous thing, it remained an open question whether an expansive Englishness could really come to include Irishness—in other words, whether the latter could ever provide the position of an *insider's outsideness* for the English, rather than remaining simply, ineluctably beyond the pale (as racialist explanations would have it).

---

[15] Cf. Fredric Faverty, *Matthew Arnold the Ethnologist* (Evanston: Northwestern University Press, 1951), 154.

[16] Cf. *The Letters of Charlotte Brontë,* Vol. 1 (1829–47), ed. Margaret Smith (Oxford: Clarendon Press, 1995), 269, for Brontë's sole (and oblique) reference to her father's Irishness, and *The Letters of Charlotte Brontë,* Vol. 2 (1848–51), ed. Smith (Oxford: Clarendon, 2000), 497 ff., for her interesting correspondence with an Irish fan, "K. T."

II

Foucauldian perspectives on *Jane Eyre* have highlighted those elements in the narrative that are devoted to the production of a model modern subject. It is certainly, forcefully true that the initial chapters, larded as they are in terminology drawn from the lexicon of political theory and starkly contrasting two social environments in a manner comparable to Foucault's at the start of *Discipline and Punish,* seem to indicate that the private history of Jane Eyre will encode an allegory about the birth of modern subjectivity out of the ruins of the ancien régime. Foucault's opposition of a premodern social order focused on the body of the king and a carceral modernity aimed at the production of self-regulating subjects is almost too neatly anticipated in the opposition of Gateshead to Lowood, the former run according to the fiat of its rulers and devoted to the commemoration of a dead father-king, the latter a highly regimented "Institution" in which natural differences are suppressed and every movement of the day strictly scheduled. Yet while Jane does acquire at Lowood lessons in the cultivation of interiority that stand her in good stead for the rest of the narrative, it would be a mistake, in view of the rapturous vision of intersubjectivity that ends the novel, simply to conclude (whether one approves of liberal individualism or mistrusts it) that such individualism is *in itself* the novel's aim: to read *Jane Eyre* in this way is to miss its devotion to producing reciprocally defined ideals of selfhood and culture as heterogeneous things. It is also to operate at a level of generality on which different modernities, including the specific United Kingdom variety I am investigating here, remain analytically invisible. Brontë draws upon the national allegories of the Waverley Novels and the National Tales of her father's generation, but where Scott produces narratives about a male character's accession to a modernity and a maturity that balance nostalgic antiquarianism with the virtues of a commercial, voluntarist social order, Brontë's revisionary romance seeks the freedom to realize the powers of the female self within the constraints of an intersubjective order, a genuine culture, far more positive and forceful than the pale contractual models of society permitted under classical commercial liberalism.

To be sure, the early chapters offer considerable support for a reading of Jane as the rights-bearing liberal subject just beginning to emerge. On the momentous "that day" of the novel's abrupt opening, Jane shatters her bonds of servitude, casting off the mental blinders imposed on her by Gateshead the moment she questions the legitimacy of its rule and demands to know, "Why is he [John Reed] my master?" (JE 19). Here we see Jane as the subject of a society recognizing no rights, only revocable "privileges," and as having "no appeal" against capricious authority. John Reed appears to Jane as a "tyrant" and "slave-driver," akin to the more bloodthirsty of the "Roman emperors" (JE 17). A "rebel slave," she "resist[s] all the way" against his "violent tyrannies"; she cries "Unjust!—unjust!" against the "insupportable oppression" she endures, longing to mount an "insurrection" (JE 22, 19).[17] Thrown like some sacrificial virgin into the mausoleum of the dead

---

[17] It was this language, concentrated in the early scenes, that led the reviewer for the *Christian Remembrancer* to the hyperbole of saying that "[e]very page burns with moral Jacobinism" and that "'Un-

patriarch—the red-room where Mr. Reed had lain "in state"—she perceives a chair looking "like a pale throne" and the massive bed standing "like a tabernacle" in the center of the room. The images recall how absolutism legitimated itself (and the heirs fathered on such beds) through appeals to divine right. When Jane sees them, both the furniture and the chamber that contains it are things of "vacant majesty": absolutism's era has passed, and we are on the cusp of something new, but Mrs. Reed carries on oblivious of the fact that the girl she harbors and mal-treats belongs to a future in which she and her kind will have no place. At the novel's start, she sits like a queen in her court, "her darlings" "clustered round her" like fawning courtiers (JE 13). Peremptory and arbitrary, she will not submit her rule to the scrutiny of "cavillers or questioners" and will not even answer Jane's plea to know what she has done to deserve punishment (JE 13). Gateshead life amounts to a weird cultural "survival," a holdover from a bygone epoch in human development.[18] We learn enough about the kindness of the deceased Mr. Reed (e.g., JE 24) to infer that absolutism could in former days be benevolently prac-ticed, but we also note the close coincidence of his death and Jane's birth, which seems to suggest that Jane embodies a principle whose entry into the world is in-imical to absolutism per se, whether benevolent or not. Reproved by John Reed as a "bad animal," little Jane is the rough beast of a new era whose hour has come round at last.

Writing of her incarceration in the red-room, Jane sums up her new-found awareness of her position at Gateshead in that famous passage I have used as one of the epigraphs to this section, a passage that rings the changes upon some of the best established metaphors for describing fixed, hierarchical social orders. Jane's identification of herself as "a discord" derives from traditional appeals to natural and social hierarchies (or chains of being, in the related trope), appeals stretching back at least to Plato's *Republic* and descending by way of such famous instances as the "untune that string" speech in Shakespeare's *Troilus and Cressida:* accord-ing to these, justice in the soul and in society is the harmony of lower, middle, and higher elements. Calling herself "a noxious thing," Jane invokes the time-honored figure of the "body politic," which, like the trope of social harmony, defines indi-vidual members of societies entirely in terms of their function as parts within and servants of the total structure. The statements that she was "like nobody" and "a useless thing" at Gateshead proceed from this, for in beginning to assert needs not congruent with her allotted role, Jane is laying claim to a dimension of selfhood not even visible (or so the tendentious modern argument runs) in traditional soci-eties. A self whose worth and identity are drawn from inner reservoirs of thought

---

just, unjust,' is the burden of every reflection upon the things and powers that be": cf. Miriam Allott, ed., *The Brontës: The Critical Heritage* (London and Boston: Routledge and Kegan Paul, 1974), 90.

[18] Cf. JE 38, for an image of the passing social order dabbling in the ways of the new one: "[Eliza Reed] had a turn for traffic, and a marked propensity for saving; shown not only in the vending of eggs and chickens, but also in driving hard bargains with the gardener about flower-roots, seeds, and slips of plants; that functionary having orders from Mrs Reed to buy of this young lady all the products of her parterre she wished to sell." Brontë, who had considered Peel a traitor when he capitulated to the anti-Corn-Law faction, objects here to a system of trade rigged in favor of the landed classes.

and feeling strictly partitioned from given role or level does not even figure in absolutism's calculus, has no weight on its evaluative scales; modern selfhood is *definitively* "useless" by the ancient standard. When she labels herself "a heterogeneous thing," Jane is not signaling that she, homogeneous within herself, does not belong in the otherwise homogeneous social universe of Gateshead but, rather, that modern selfhood is *intrinsically* heterogeneous, founded as it is upon the distinction between role and core. More specifically than this, she alludes to the distinctive heterogeneity of the English that Defoe (in this chapter's other epigraph) expressed solely in racial terms but which Brontë explores in more registers than merely that one.

In the twilight of its epoch, with its hold beginning to weaken, absolutism becomes both more violent and more erratic in its attempt to retain power. One sign of its decadence is the latitude Mrs. Reed grants to her torturer or chief of secret police—her son John—to keep order by any means. On his watch, the unconditional authority of the monarch extends itself in efforts to exercise surveillance and control over absolutely every aspect of its subject's existence, and, in striving toward totalitarianism, Gateshead life becomes the anticulture that sets in motion Jane's quest for its structural opposite. But first Jane has to surmount the other antithesis inscribed in her by the very oppression she longs to escape, the opposing idea of a freedom as unconditioned and solitary as Gateshead society is intrusive and "airless." Jane the narrator's account of the crisis that precipitated her expulsion from the negative Eden of her childhood both analyzes her Gateshead-nurtured pathology of thinking in terms of extremes without middles (as in *society vs. freedom*) and suggests the terms in which such dichotomous structures have *themselves* been opposed and overcome in the mature authorial Jane.

When, in chapter 1, Jane manages to steal a few minutes' solitude behind the "folds of scarlet drapery" in the drawing-room window seat, she daydreams herself away to the barren climes reachable only by the subjects of the book in her hand, "Bewick's *History of British Birds*." Her imagination dilates upon "the haunts of the sea-fowl . . . 'the solitary rocks and promontories' by them only inhabited," upon "the vast sweep of the Arctic zone, and [its] forlorn regions of dreary space": the oppression of Gateshead stimulates in reaction the imagination of freedom as flight from all human habitation, a one-way flight into the "death-white realms" of the north (JE 14). Before John Reed has a chance to reassert his punitive power by literally throwing the book at her, Jane flies off in reverie from human society in its entirety, as yet incapable of envisioning any form of society other than Gateshead's crushing despotism. She escapes in imagination to a state of uncompromised animal purity achievable, if anywhere, only on a landscape as barren to human purposes as those ice floes. As Jane describes the several "vignettes" in Bewick on which her imagination alighted, we note the way her former self inclined toward those images showing unpopulated land- or seascapes, scenes or events remote from or inimical to human good: "the broken boat stranded on a desolate coast"; the "wreck just sinking"; "the quite solitary churchyard" (JE 15). The only individual human figure she pauses over ("the fiend pinning down the thief's pack") is bent on nefarious purposes, and him Jane "passe[s] over quickly," fleeing his company. She seems to perceive as the essential character of all human society what the final vignette shows her in depicting a "black, horned thing" sitting "aloof on a rock, surveying a distant crowd surrounding a gallows" (JE 15). Young Jane herself—rough beast—might *be* that strange creature, the deformed or deviant subject who looks on with jaundiced eye at this rite whereby communities achieve cohesion by the elimination of the deviant. Here is a vision of anticulture to rival Joseph de Maistre's chilling celebration of the executioner as the figure on whom "all greatness, all power, all subordination rest," the "terror and the bond of human association."[19] We recall how, at the start of the novel, Jane was banished from the Reed family circle, "exclude[d] from privileges intended only for contented, happy, little children" (JE 13), and how she refers to herself as "the scape-goat of the nursery" (JE 23).

If *Jane Eyre* were simply an instruction manual in docile liberal subjectivity, we would expect to see in the ensuing sections of the novel an unambiguous endorsement of all those forces encouraging Jane to develop the inner landscape of her soul and recommending the taking of refuge therein. It is true that in the opening chapter, Jane describes herself as "shrined in double retirement" (JE 14) when she sequesters herself with Bewick in the window seat, drapery on one hand and window panes on the other, and that this self-enshrining both contrasts with the deference paid to absolutist authority in the "tabernacle" of the red-room and points forward to the Lowood portion of the novel, where, encouraged by Helen Burns and instructed by Miss Temple, Jane begins to learn the self-discipline necessary for the construction of her own private temple of interiority. Thus far, the details line up in support of a reading of the novel as more or less enacting, in a Foucauldian key, the process described in Keats's "Ode to Psyche." But the admiration Jane the narrator expresses for Helen and for Miss Temple is anything but unqualified: both figures offer too extreme a swing of the pendulum away from Gateshead-Jane's wild rebelliousness, a self-composure that relinquishes all claim whatever upon the order of society or even (in Helen's case) upon mortal existence.

Helen receives the novel's implicit approval when she argues that the forgetting of grievances is necessary to psychological liberation, but not when she turns forbearance into utter passivity: her capacity to "live in calm, looking to the end" of life (JE 70) differs completely from Jane's later, hard-won independence, which is sustained on the principle that "God did not give me my life to throw away" (JE 461). Helen Burns's life *is* thrown away, and the girl acquiesces to the act. Where Miss Temple is concerned, all the respect and gratitude Jane feels for her do not dispel the memory of the "petrified severity" she imposes upon herself when she withdraws in silence from the noisy tyranny of Mr. Brocklehurst: Jane recalls how, under the hail of his abuse, Miss Temple "gazed straight before her, and her face, naturally pale as marble, appeared to be assuming also the coldness and fixity of that material; especially her mouth closed as if it would have required a sculptor's

---

[19] Quoted in Isaiah Berlin, "Joseph de Maistre and the Origins of Fascism," *The Crooked Timber of Humanity: Chapters in the History of Ideas,* ed. Henry Hardy (Princeton: Princeton University Press, 1990), 117.

chisel to open it" (JE 75). This is making oneself into a temple of interiority in a wholly negative sense, a self-petrification and self-silencing that represents but the extreme reversal of the Gateshead Jane's bound-breaking fits and cries. Together, Gateshead and Lowood offer complementary situations of extremes without middles, the hallmark of anticultural situations. When disease brings the icy hand of death to Lowood, it comes in a "bright May" teeming with flowers (JE 90); the relaxation of Brocklehurst's disciplinary system that occurs during this crisis sends Jane careening back into a state of total license in which a new companion (an anti-Helen) gives "ample indulgence" to Jane's faults, "never imposing curb or rein on anything" she says or does (JE 90–91). When Miss Temple marries and leaves the school, Jane backslides to a position from which she "gasp[s]" for an impossibly abstract "liberty," then scorns her own desire and calls out cynically for "a new servitude" (JE 99). Genuine culture, when it is finally attained, will offer itself as mediating these hypostatized alternatives: Burke's ideal of a "*social* freedom . . . in which Liberty is secured by the equality of Restraint."[20]

At Thornfield, Jane is so worked upon by Rochester's deceit as to believe that she has found the means of obtaining all the freedom and self-realization she is entitled to there by marrying the master, in the style of Richardson's *Pamela.* Yet, along with many other disturbing signs, the recurrence of situations of stark antithesis or extremes without middles identifies the place, in keeping with its name, as another variety of anticultural wasteland. Shortly after arriving at Thornfield, Jane gazes from the rooftop and then hears the "curious laugh" of the incarcerated wife she knows nothing about: she looks out upon a broad horizon and "a propitious sky, azure, marbled with pearly white"—a sky that seems to promise her greater reach and range than she has yet known—then immediately down through the trapdoor back to the attic: "I could scarcely see my way down the ladder," she writes, "the attic seemed black as a vault compared with that arch of blue to which I had been looking up" (JE 122). Jane's later discovery of what was always the truth about Thornfield brings on one more passage of heightened oppositions, similar to the kind we saw in the Lowood portion of the novel. Jane writes that her "cherished wishes, yesterday so blooming and glowing . . . lay stark, chill, livid corpses that could never revive": "A Christmas frost had come at midsummer; a white-December storm had whirled over June; ice glazed the ripe apples, drifts crushed the blowing roses; on hay-field and corn-field lay a frozen shroud: lanes which last night blushed full of flowers, to-day were pathless with untrodden snow; and the woods, which twelve hours since waved leafy and fragrant as groves between the tropics, now spread, waste, wild, and white as pine-forests in wintry Norway" (JE 330).

Brontë's fiction implicitly suggests that oppositions like the one between discourse- and story-space in narrative become autoethnographically productive to the extent that they generate tension at their boundary and begin to suggest that significant kinds of trespassing are going on across it. One striking method for en-

---

[20] Quoted by Conor Cruise O'Brien in the introduction to Burke, *Reflections on the Revolution in France* (Harmondsworth: Penguin, 1969), 15.

abling this tension or trespass is Jane the narrator's occasional lapse into the present tense when representing past moments of particular emotional intensity. Recalling her first, silent admission of love for Rochester while watching him amidst the ladies and gentlemen in the drawing room, the narrator elides the inner monologue she engaged in then and her retrospective account of the scene: the character thinks, "He is not to them what he is to me" and "while I breathe and think I must love him," and then the narrator writes, "Coffee is handed. The ladies . . . have become lively as larks" (JE 199). For a little less than a page, the temporal frontier between the two Janes vanishes. Later, describing her return to Thornfield from Gateshead, where she was impressed by her lack of vengefulness toward the Reeds, Jane assumes the present tense once more, in a passage that points forward to the winter-in-summer one quoted just above. Once more thinking of her feelings for Rochester, the writer gives us this:

> They are making hay, too, in Thornfield meadows: or rather, the labourers are just quitting their work, and returning home with their rakes on their shoulders: now, at the hour I arrive. I have but a field or two to traverse, and then I shall cross the road and reach the gates. How full the hedges are of roses! But I have no time to gather any; I want to be at the house. I pass a tall briar, shooting leafy and flowery branches across the path; I see the narrow stile with stone steps; and I see—Mr Rochester sitting there, a book and pencil in his hand: he is writing. (JE 274)

At such moments we confront the double uncanniness of a narrator whose usual effect is to stress her difference from her narrated self, now dropping into the perspective of that former self. The compulsion to relinquish authorial control and fully to inhabit that earlier viewpoint, felt in the insistent "now, at the hour I arrive," is felt even more strongly and strangely when we notice that all of a sudden it is Rochester who is writing, not Jane. The remembered pleasure of seeing him again is accompanied by the disturbing thought that he was even then writing Jane as a character into his plot, subordinating her to his duplicitous narrative. This is the false summer of Jane's hopes.

A third such passage, the most arresting and sustained, occurs immediately after Jane has fled the fraudulent promise of Thornfield and finds herself "absolutely destitute" "at a place called Whitcross" (JE 362). If we recall Jane's Gateshead-inspired longings to be free of all human society, we will be prepared to read the ensuing episode as a terrible vision of those very longings realized. "Not a tie holds me to human society at this moment," she writes, "not a charm or hope calls me where my fellow-creatures are—none that saw me would have a kind thought or a good wish for me" (JE 362). The narrator's adoption of the present tense in this instance strongly suggests that she is rehearsing a central problem of romanticism, the desire for a spontaneity and fullness of being thought to exist among the unreflective animals. The relationless liberty imagined to be found outside of human culture would be a condition without past and future, an atemporal unconsciousness such as Wordsworth ascribed to the hares "running races in their mirth" while he brooded upon mutability, in "Resolution and Independence." At Whitcross, experience loses its layered temporality as the narrating Jane disappears behind her narrated self. "I have no relative but the universal mother, nature," she declares, "I will seek her breast and ask repose" (JE 363). But in the words of John Jarndyce in Dickens's *Bleak House,* "the universe makes an indifferent parent." "[N]o town, nor even a hamlet," but a mere "stone pillar set up where four roads meet," Whitcross is Jane's crossroad. Like Wordsworth, like Coleridge in such poems as "The Eolian Harp," she will turn back from the path of self-annihilating boundless desire, affirming that *human* freedom is constituted in and through time and the claims of others, that the apparent freedom of the beasts is subjection *to* time. With this affirmation comes the resumption of past-tense narration and the capacity to analyze the desire rather than simply to submit to it. Jane writes that, alone upon the moor, she "wished [she] could live in it and on it": "I saw a lizard run over the crag," she remembers; "I saw a bee busy among the sweet bilberries. I would fain at the moment have become bee or lizard, that I might have found fitting nutriment, permanent shelter here. But I was a human being" (JE 364). Saved by the providential light that guides her to her unsuspected relatives, Jane recovers her self and name not upon the moor but at "Moor House," and she recovers these, as we have seen, in writing.

With Diana and Mary Rivers she finds "perfect congeniality of tastes, sentiments, and principles," and through them learns to "comprehend the feeling" of their "perfect enthusiasm of attachment" to the particular landscape they inhabit, and also to "share both its strength and truth." They teach Jane "the fascination of the locality" and in doing so the value of locality as such (JE 391). St. John, in contrast, "considers himself an alien from his native country" (JE 395), and turns from local attachment to its extreme opposite, abstract, universalizing philanthropy. Like Jane in being prone to "insatiate yearnings and disquieting aspirations," he manifests the same cruel self-conquering discipline shown earlier by Miss Temple (JE 394). Jane watches him "sitting as still as one of the dusky pictures on the walls; keeping his eyes fixed on the page he perused, and his lips mutely sealed. . . . Had he been a statue instead of a man, he could not have been easier [to examine]." With "Greek face" and forehead "colourless as ivory," he marbleizes himself in acts of "despotic constriction" against the sensuous appeal of Rosamund Oliver, the "Rose of the World" (JE 386, 407, 419). Had he married Rosamund and acquired control of her father's sizeable fortune, he might have exercised his formidable gifts in England. It is against the backdrop of St. John's boundless and self-consuming vocation that Rochester's call to Jane comes into focus as effecting a bond *both* translocal and demarcatable, a voluntary union animated by the energy of a quasi-religious *calling:* a national culture.[21]

The appellation "Moor House" encodes the refusal of singleness required of deliberately heterogeneous things: it beckons toward the natural expanse and the domestic enclosure alike. We saw such a gesture at the beginning of the novel, in that suggestive tableau of Jane in the Gateshead window seat, "shrined in double retirement." She sat there dreaming in the most conventional of metaphors for a state

---

[21] As Rochester's servant says of his wounded, regenerate master after the destruction of Thornfield, "he's in England; he can't get out of England, I fancy—he's a fixture now" (JE 476).

of perfect liberty, but the book she used to imagine herself flying away from social toils was a book of *British* birds.[22] Can there exist a creature both British and as free as a bird? An ideal culture would give its members the feeling that their natural longings and their social needs were being satisfied in equal measure. In the Gateshead window seat, only glass divides Jane from the domain of "the natural"—but she can see it; only a curtain divides her from that of "the social"—she can temporarily block it out but never escape it while living, and so must begin the search for a home she might fly in. But she can find it, evidently, only at the cost of proving true what she suspected and dreaded about cultures when she fixed her eye upon that final vignette from Bewick. Both narrative closure and national closed unity *do* turn out to require the elimination of some element—Bertha, of course, but also Irishness, perhaps?—*too* deviant to be admitted within the culture of heterogeneous things without blasting it apart.

[22] Or, as actually titled, *A History of English Birds* (1804).

CHAPTER NINE

National Pentecostalism: *Shirley*

For about a quarter of an hour he dug on uninterrupted; at length, however,
a window opened, and a female voice called to him:—

"Eh, bien! Tu ne déjeunes pas ce matin?"

The answer and the rest of the conversation was in French, but as this is
an English book, I shall translate it into English.

— Brontë, *Shirley*[1]

To make a Frenchman English, that's the devil.

— Defoe, "The True-Born Englishman"[2]

I

SHIRLEY, a blend of industrial novel and "novel of the recent past" in the manner
of Scott, is the work of Brontë's that people will think of first as being ethnographic
in tendency. Like early twentieth-century anthropological monographs and like the
early nineteenth-century fiction of Scott and the authors of the National Tale, it
provides a wealth of detail about the customs of a specific "culture area," Brontë's
own West Riding in the years 1811–12, the time of the Luddite uprisings Patrick
Brontë had witnessed. Like Scott's *Waverley,* it is a work of third-person narration
that looks back to a period in the not too distant past that is felt to lie on the other
side of a dividing line in history. Again like Scott's novels, it gives the impression
not of a quaintly uniform rural community but rather of a strikingly diverse one.
Right from the start Brontë seems determined to show the region her novel deals
with as anything but the homogeneous backwater that visitors from the south or
from cities—visitors like Elizabeth Gaskell—might take it to be. The community
described in *Shirley* is one in which the Anglican Church must compete for souls
in a market-like setting it shares with several other robust Protestantisms; in which
we find Irishmen, Welshmen, Scots, Germans, and Anglo-Belgians settled amidst
an indigenous population; and in which an international crisis is dividing the
landed, industrial, and working classes into separate, hostile camps.[3] This is not

---

[1] *Shirley* (1849; Harmondsworth: Penguin, 1974), 91; henceforth S.

[2] "The True-Born Englishman," in *The True-Born Englishman and Other Writings,* ed. P. N. Furbank and W. R. Owens (Harmondsworth: Penguin, 1997), 32.

[3] Juliet Barker's family biography of the Brontës and Margaret Smith's ongoing edition of Char-

diversity on the scale of the metropolis, of course, but it *counts* as diversity in the specific local context in which Brontë works. The portrait of an industrializing rural community given in *Shirley* illustrates the cultural relativity of difference and makes it clear that outsiders should not approach this community with a preconceived notion of its uniformity.

Also from the very beginning, the novel signals its apparent determination to pluralize the society it represents by indicating that it, too, as a text, is going to be more than one type of thing. The first paragraphs make a point of confounding expectations, of keeping the reader off balance. The book begins with the phrase "Of late years," but then announces that it is not, in fact, concerned with the present but with the early years of the century. Having said this, it denies whatever expectations may be forming in its reader's mind that it is going to deliver a period romance, promising instead to deal in cold hard facts, "[s]omething real, cool, and solid," as "unromantic as Monday morning" (S 39). Yet "[i]t is not positively affirmed" that readers "shall not have a taste of the exciting" later on, even though "it is resolved that the first dish set upon the table shall be one that a Catholic— ay, even an Anglo-Catholic—might eat on Good Friday in Passion Week: it shall be unleavened bread with bitter herbs, and no roast lamb:" a collation wholly lacking in flavorful appeal. Statements are made only to be qualified or have their direction reversed by subsequent statements: the effect is not to negate the prior statements but to maintain that both they and their qualifying or reversing ones are true.

And this book that starts out by indicating that the story it has to tell needs to be described in more than one way also begins by situating readers in two places at once, foregrounding narrative fiction's irreducible doubleness. Brontë's culinary metaphor for the story she is starting to serve up to her readers leads, rather uncannily, into a scene of three Church-of-England curates eating a meal, a scene initially represented in the present tense. Discourse- and story-spaces are treated as separate, yet wholly continuous with one another, the line between them capable of being leisurely traversed. "Step into this neat garden house," the narrator invites; "walk forward into the little parlour—there they are at dinner. . . . You and I will join the party, see what is to be seen, and hear what is to be heard. At present, however, they are only eating; and while they eat we will talk aside" (S 40). It turns out that the small grouping of curates embodies in itself something of the heterogeneity Brontë is at pains to exhibit throughout her depiction of West Yorkshire country life: one, Mr. Sweeting, is unplaceable, but apparently an outsider to the district, while the others, Mr. Malone and Mr. Donne, hail from Ireland and from the south of England, respectively.

Another strange echo of the narrator's domain arises within the domain of the characters when this "lamb" that Brontë mentions in denying that it will appear in the first course of her narrative meal seems to appear anyway, spoken of by a

---

lotte Brontë's letters help correct the image of Haworth as isolated and remote set down in Gaskell's *Life*. Cf. *The Letters of Charlotte Brontë,* ed. Margaret Smith, Vol. 1 (1829–1847) (Oxford: Clarendon, 1995), 213–15 (henceforth *Letters 1*).

character. Sweeting says that a local troublemaker, "an Antinomian, . . . a violent Jacobin and leveller," has been threatening the mill-owner Robert Moore, "affirm[ing that] Moore should be chosen as a sacrifice, an oblation of a sweet savour" to warn the other industrialists not to invite the workers' wrath (S 48). Catholics (and Anglo-Catholics) abstain from eating lamb on Good Friday because that is the day the Agnus Dei was given in sacrifice for the sins of humankind. Violence against Moore—which eventually happens—would constitute a travesty of the divine sacrifice all Christians claim to believe in; it would be a human offering to the god of an anti-Christian culture, the god of class and sectarian enmity. As in Dickens, a metaphor for describing what the narrator is doing crosses over to figure importantly in the narrated world.

Indeed, later on in *Shirley* we encounter numerous other sacrifices, enacted or merely contemplated. The novel describes a society in which women are routinely laid upon the altar of pitiless gentility, given to esteemed men who cannot know their worth and consumed in the furnace of an antimarriage. In this, of course, it follows *Jane Eyre*'s much-noted motif of suttee, the barbarous rite rhetorically serviceable to the English in justifying their rule over India but oddly enough emulated by them in their marital customs.[4] In *Shirley,* consumption by a marriage that offers her nothing and cuts her off from all other possibilities of realization has been the fate of Mary Cave, the memory of whom floats through the novel like a monitory specter: loved by the scion of the family "first and oldest in the district," she was consigned instead to the Reverend Helstone "for his office's sake" and shriveled away under the scorching beam of his neglect (S 79, 81). (Like *Jane Eyre*'s Miss Temple, Mary Cave is a "girl of living marble; stillness personified" [S 81], and her surname links up with other images developed throughout *Shirley* of women's secret inner spaces and unrealized powers.) During the course of the narrative, Mr. Helstone contemplates taking a second bride, the much younger Miss Sykes, whose parents, we read with a chill, "would have delivered Hannah over to his loving-kindness and his tender mercies without one scruple" (S 139). Caroline Helstone's long-lost mother, who enters the novel incognito as Mrs. Pryor, has also suffered immolation in wedlock, and at the hands of a husband even less worthy than Mr. Helstone: his abusive brother James. Further acts of virgin sacrifice are attempted on the novel's title character, whose uncle tries to bind her on the altar of respectability though she declares herself "[a]n infidel to [his] religion; an atheist to [his] god" (S 518):

> Sir, your god, your great Bel, your fish-tailed Dagon, rises before me as a demon. You, and such as you, have raised him to a throne, put on him a crown, given him a sceptre. Behold how hideously he governs! See him busied at the work he likes best—making marriages. He binds the young to the old, the strong to the imbecile[,] . . . the dead to the living. In his realm there is hatred—secret hatred: there is disgust—unspoken disgust:

---

[4] Cf. *Jane Eyre* (1847; Harmondsworth: Penguin, 1996), 306, 450 (henceforth JE): on the latter page, Jane reflects that marrying St. John Rivers would require her to "throw all on the altar—heart, vitals, the entire victim."

there is treachery—family treachery: there is vice—deep, deadly, domestic vice. In his dominions, children grow unloving between parents who have never loved: infants are nursed on deception from their very birth; they are reared in an atmosphere corrupt with lies. Your god rules at the bridal of kings—look at your royal dynasties! your deity is the deity of foreign aristocracies—analyze the blue blood of Spain! Your god is the Hymen of France—what is French domestic life? All that surrounds him hastens to decay: all declines and degenerates under his sceptre. (S 519)

With a fervor rivaling that of any of Jane Eyre's outbursts, Shirley repudiates the anticultural dominion of an England whose ruling classes have unanglicized themselves in emulation of heartless Continentals.

While arranged and coerced marriages are the central means of perpetuating English anticulture, they represent but the leading variety of a pervasive sacrificial theme that accompanies Brontë's interest in the social grounds of Bildung or self-realization (the older sense of *culture*) as its dialectical opposite. In their own ways, Caroline Helstone and Robert and Louis Moore all suffer the wasting of their powers in the service of a tyrannical social order that obliges them to offer themselves up to the labor of continuing it. Robert, the indebted industrialist, has accommodated himself more completely than have the other two: declaring that "[t]he poor ought to have no large sympathies; it is their duty to be narrow" (S 99), he shuts down whatever better feelings exist within himself, curbing himself with a violence reminiscent of St. John Rivers's whenever that character looks upon Rosamund Oliver. In doing so, he condemns Caroline to the Hobson's choice of a life of "brain-lethargy" spent doling out tea to curates amid the "unmeaning hum" of parlor prattle (S 141) or one of petrification through entire self-abnegation in charitable work (cf. S 190–99): the fact that no other option is offered her serves as the basis for one of the novel's most famous passages, in which she challenges in silent thought the men of both Yorkshire and England to "give [women] a field in which their faculties may be exercised and grow" (S 378). Louis Moore, under the thumb of Mr. Sympson as tutor to his son, himself enjoys no such field, enduring a state in which "[h]is faculties seemed walled up in him, and were unmurmuring in their captivity" (S 430). It begins to look as if the lesson inferable from Jane Eyre's vision of the horned thing and the scaffold—that social cohesion requires the identification and elimination of some deviant as sacrificial victim—has to be revised, for the maintenance of the "warped system of things" presented in this novel seems to demand not just that *somebody* be sacrificed, but that *everybody* be "martyrized" (S 128).

The theme of sacrifice we can discern throughout the novel emanates from the first chapter's indications that both the society depicted and the novel depicting it are "heterogeneous things" that cannot be reduced to a single outlook or tendency. But is this mixed condition the problem or the potential for a solution? On the one hand, the recognition of heterogeneity in a manifestly divided and enervating social system will tend to encourage a narrative of purgation that identifies some aspect of that heterogeneity as the problem to be overcome, the alien element to be expelled, so that the society can "become one again." On the other, the recognition that more and more characters are susceptible to having the theme of sacrifice applied to them suggests the presence of a massively uniformitarian tendency already at work flattening out specific differences, the juggernaut of an inescapable social law crushing all in its path. This would be the law of culture, the tacit consensus anthropologists ascribed to traditional cultures, appearing here in its nightmarish, anticipatory avatar. The method for escaping anticulture and finding one's way to a genuine culture would then involve the *cultivation* of differences, the multiplication of vantage points and vocabularies for looking at and describing social life. Brontë, characteristically, is drawn in both directions, giving a mixed answer to the question about the value of mixture in both societies and the books that represent them. The one figure around whom Brontë's ambivalence on these questions circulates most electrically is Robert Moore.

Brontë introduces Moore to us as a man whose mixed ancestry is the key to his failure to acknowledge his moral connection to Yorkshire and to England:

> Mr Moore, indeed, was but half a Briton, and scarcely that. He came of a foreign ancestry by the mother's side, and was himself born, and partly reared, on a foreign soil. A hybrid in nature, it is probable he had a hybrid's feeling on many points—patriotism for one; it is likely that he was unapt to attach himself to parties, to sects, even to climes and customs; it is not impossible that he had a tendency to isolate his individual person from any community amidst which his lot might temporarily happen to be thrown, and that he felt it to be his best wisdom to push the interests of Robert Gérard Moore, to the exclusion of philanthropic consideration for general interests: with which he regarded that said Gérard Moore as in a great measure disconnected. (S 60).

From such a passage it is easy to envision an ensuing narrative focused on the purgative re-education or conversion of this troublesomely divided character, a process in which Moore would unlearn the distracting and diluting foreign side of his nature, that side making him argue for England's capitulation to Napoleon so that normal trading can resume. This reading would reason that one cannot be both English and foreign—especially *Francophone*-foreign: one must choose, and the urgency of making that choice is intensified in times of international crisis like the one dealt with in *Shirley,* the period of showdown between Napoleon's Continental System and Britain's "Orders in Council."

In Moore's dealings with Caroline Helstone, however, it quickly becomes apparent that the Frenchness in Moore, the non-national Frenchness of the "Anversois" is to be prized for its capacity to inject an acculturating potency back into a Yorkshire and an England wholly evacuated of it. And through another diagnostic lens, it is not Moore's hybrid ethnicity but his willed one-dimensionality, his reduction of himself to an agent obeying the directives of only one motive, that constitutes the imperfection in his character. This one motive is not, as is usually suggested, simply that of the *homo economicus* of political economy; in fact its derivation is to be looked for not in modern liberal social arrangements but in much older ones. Moore is driven by filial loyalty to a deceased father he considers to have been the victim of both bad fortune and betrayal. He takes up trade not out of rational self-interest but as a "hereditary calling" (S 60): his furious impatience in pursuit of it—"he foam[s] at the mouth" when circumstances narrow his opportunities (S 61)—is the symptom of how desperately he longs to redeem his fallen patrimony. He strives not so much to expand his trade and income as to keep it from bankruptcy, fearing that "a second failure" in the family business "would blight the name of Moore completely" (S 180).

Another kind of determined singleness is to be found in Robert's sister Hortense, who radiates "blissful self-complacency" in her unswerving adherence to all "her old Belgian modes" and to the conviction that they are identical with civilization itself, no matter where she might happen to reside (S 113, 92). The eternal outsider, "she [does] not choose to adopt English fashions because she was obliged to live in England" (S 92). Brontë lards Hortense's speech with untranslated words like *bouilli* and *choucroute* and has the character expatiate at length on the merits of *sabots noirs* ("très propres, très convenables") and the foolishness of Yorkshirewomen for not apprehending them. She delivers herself of a kind of motto when she censures Caroline's (to her) senseless improprieties by saying, "I ever disapprove what is not intelligible" (S 95). In a scene I will examine later, Caroline diagnoses this same singular propensity in Robert when she likens him to Shakespeare's Coriolanus, that rigid hero-tyrant animated by the drive "not to be other than one thing."[5] And Robert's opponents the Luddites exhibit their own variety of the same flawed singularity in being unable, or so Brontë depicts them, of thinking themselves outside of their class positions or provinciality. So while it is true that some part of Brontë—the Wellington-worshipping part, perhaps—does remain bound to the habit of thinking of identities as describable in terms of purity versus impurity, singleness versus corrupting mixture, in *Shirley* she counterbalances that habit with an effort to conceive of a redeemed Englishness as something definitively plural, going so far, in fact, as to raise the question of whether one can be in some sense both English and "French"—the most radical of questions, when posed in 1811–12—and the further question of how much of French or Frenchness an "English book" might safely contain. As in Dickens, the condition of Brontë's book offers to stand for the condition of England, and both novelists subject the coherence of their novels to considerable strain in using them to ask where the boundary should be drawn.

Shirley's seemingly ambivalent, self-correcting first chapter has been a problem for readers of Brontë ever since the manuscript was in the hands of her publishers. Writing to W. S. Williams on 1 March 1849, she responded to his charge that the "opening scene [seemed] irrelevant to the rest of the book" by promising "there are other touches in store which will harmonize with it," and in subsequent letters she continued to insist on the chapter's close connection to the rest of the narrative.[6] I have already suggested how this recurrently problematic chapter introduces

---

[5] Cf. Margaret J. Arnold, "Coriolanus Transformed: Charlotte Brontë's Use of Shakespeare in *Shirley*," in Marianne Novy, ed., *Women's Re-Visions of Shakespeare: On the Responses of Dickinson, Woolf, Rich, H. D., George Eliot, and Others* (Urbana and Chicago: University of Illinois Press, 1990), 76–88.

[6] *The Letters of Charlotte Brontë*, ed. Margaret Smith, Vol. 2 (1848–1851) (Oxford: Clarendon

the idea of sacrifice and testifies to the narrator's determination to cross over the fundamental line in narrative, to make her presence felt among the characters she moves across her fictional landscape. This determination, which gives rise to many subtle narrative effects throughout, strikes us full in the face at the novel's end, where Brontë's narrator suddenly becomes a character and has a conversation with someone who knew the main personages of the now-concluding story (cf. S 599, discussed below). This crossing over from discourse- into story-space is the narrator's act of return to the culture that formed her, the one she shares with her readers and subjects but had to remove herself from in order to "see" it: it is the act that defines what the narrator has been doing as an autoethnographic labor. I now want to examine the initial scene in a little more detail, for in it Brontë begins to outline a leading antithesis of the autoethnographic authority she claims for her narrator.

It appears that the meal the three curates are sharing together is scarcely an infrequent occurrence: these three men, drawn to West Yorkshire from their various points of origin, seek each other out for dinner, drink, and disputation, and make extra work for their landladies by doing so, on an almost obsessively regular basis. Mrs. Gale, Mr. Donne's landlady, "considers that the privilege of inviting a friend to a meal . . . has been quite sufficiently exercised of late" (S 41). Brontë's narrator ponders the "unintelligible zeal" with which these men pursue their "rushing backwards and forwards, amongst themselves"—for "[w]hat attracts them, it would be difficult to say. It is not friendship; for whenever they meet they quarrel. It is not religion; the thing is never named amongst them: theology they discuss occasionally, but piety—never." Nor can "the love of eating and drinking" explain it, since "each might have as good a joint and pudding, tea as potent, and toast as succulent, at his own lodgings, as is served to him at his brother's." Their gatherings represent not hospitality, but a "system of mutual invasion" (S 40–41).

Much of the intercourse among the three consists of the two Englishmen joining forces to taunt the Irishman into a rage, and such is the state of affairs when Mr. Helstone, vicar of one of the nearby communities, stops by. He rebukes them for broadcasting their discord, asking,

> "What! has the miracle of Pentecost been renewed? Have the cloven tongues come down again? Where are they? The sound filled the house just now. I heard the seventeen languages in full action:—Parthians, and Medes, and Elamites, the dwellers in Mesopotamia, and in Judea, and Cappadocia, in Pontus and Asia, Phrygia and Pamphylia, in Egypt and in the parts of Libya about Cyrene, strangers of Rome, Jews and proselytes, Cretes and Arabians;—every one of these must have had its representative in this room two minutes since." . . .
>
> "What do I talk about the gift of tongues? Gift, indeed! I mistook the chapter, and book, and testament:—Gospel for law, Acts for Genesis, the city of Jerusalem for the plain of Shinar. It was no gift, but the confusion of tongues which has gabbled me deaf

---

Press, 2000), 185 (henceforth *Letters 2*). Cf. Brontë's letter to G. H. Lewes of 1 November 1849 declaring, "All mouths will be against that first chapter—and that first chapter is true as the Bible—nor is it exceptional" (275).

as a post. You, apostles? What!—you three? Certainly not:—three presumptuous Babylonish masons,—neither more nor less!" (S 45–46)

Helstone's scathing oratory raises two issues that will preoccupy the entire narrative of *Shirley*. One is the reference to a post-Babel "confusion of tongues," which introduces those many elements throughout the novel that invite reflection on the existence and value of linguistic and cultural difference. As Helstone presents it, the national church's representatives are turning the Pentecostal power to spread the gospel across all cultural and linguistic divides *into* the disunity that that power was meant to overcome. But in a novel as energetically devoted to activating our auditory imagination as Scott's ever were, a novel that highlights time and again the different sounds coming out of its characters' mouths, that sets different accents and languages before us, offers commentary on them by characters and narrator alike, and demonstratively, self-consciously, self-critically translates them into the narrator's standard English, it is difficult to come to any easy judgment on whether this disunity is not after all a productive phenomenon, the means rather than the obstacle to national redemption. I will return in a moment to Brontë's insistence on making us come as close to *hearing* her characters as a book can do.

The second preoccupying concern to emerge in Helstone's diatribe arises over the nature of this bond that joins the curates together (even in enmity) and isolates them from their flocks, a form of identification (among themselves, as clergymen) that involves a concomitant disidentification (from the Yorkshire folk among whom they live). (Mrs. Gale mutters the opinion that "these young parsons is so high and so scornful, they set everybody beneath their 'fit' . . . they are always speaking against Yorkshire ways and Yorkshire folk" [S 41].) I will call this *horizontal identification,* for it involves loyalty to affiliations stretching across space, without regard to particular places. Horizontal identification is the force that makes members of the same translocal group, even when personally unknown to each other and even if not personally fond of each other, nevertheless seek each other out whenever they wind up together in the same area. (Think of college alumni associations, for instance.) This type of affiliation commonly harks back to some formative location (in the case of the clergymen, Oxford or Cambridge), but it is definitively unrestricted to that location. For Brontë and, one could venture to say, for all nineteenth-century Britons, the paramount example of a group surviving on horizontal identification *alone* is the diasporic Jews. It seems to me, and I must wait to give substance to the claim, that Brontë associates horizontal affiliation with the metonymic axis of narrative, with the powers of the father, and with writing or print publication.

Vertical identification, in contrast, mobilizes those forces binding people to a particular place *and* to the entire social structure established in that place. The thrust of Mr. Helstone's critique of his subordinates—though he is liable to it, too—is that, in exalting their horizontal comradeship at the expense of any vertical one, in never attaching themselves to the local populations they have been sent to serve, these emissaries of the Church of England have in effect turned "Jews." This is why Helstone finds it necessary to turn back from New to Old Testament, from spirit to letter, in seeking a comparison for them, rather than forward from Old to New, as Christians are supposed to do. They represent the devolution of Christianity and, under their leadership, English people may wind up living "like Jews" in their own country. The curates are "Babylonish masons" rather than builders of true community—they are incapable of building true community even among themselves—because their solely horizontal identification lacks weight, remains abstract and "ungrounded." Like the masons of the tower of Babel, they create the conditions for their own sundering; they turn their own homeland into a place of exile, a Babylon. Happening to find themselves in the same district, they band together, but in the weakest and least productive of unions, a togetherness that is little more than chance contiguity in space, when it is not positively antagonistic.

The champion of vertical identification in *Shirley* is Caroline, who thinks of herself as "a Yorkshire girl" and thus shares the reaction of Mrs. Gale, "hat[ing] to hear Yorkshire abused" by pretentious "southrons" (S 137). Authorized by metaphors of rootedness or grounding, vertical identification is associated with metaphoricity as such and with the powers of the mother, and it is daily secured in face-to-face exchanges of speech. Within the confines of the particular place, it enables solidarity across class and other boundaries because the members of different classes or sects are known individuals to each other, capable of becoming interlocutors in specific speech situations. That is what it *means* to live in the "same place." But the nation is not a "place" in this sense: nation-feeling is definitively anonymous, like the bond an author may have with readers never seen or spoken with. What Brontë tries to do in *Shirley* is argue that the grounding function of vertical identification acquires positive efficacy for the maintenance of a national culture only when it is yoked to an equally strong force of horizontal identification, while, on the other hand, horizontal connections—such as common nationality— require the gravity supplied by vertical ones if they are not to dissolve into empty abstractions. In my discussion below, vertical identification must be distinguished from a provincialism that does not involve cross-class affiliation. Caroline Helstone can arise out of her feeble state of *mere* locality only when she gains access to insights of the more widely traveled figure of Shirley, who, for her part, has never yet known the value of locality until she returns home to Fieldhead and is tutored by Caroline. The overlapping bonds that develop in the course of the narrative between Caroline and Shirley, Caroline and Robert, and Shirley and Louis, all exemplify the ideal of a self-regulating system combining elements whose reciprocal enabling is the flipside of their reciprocal checking.

A clergyman arriving in a community from outside should not, and probably cannot, become a complete insider: his vocation can be fulfilled only if he remains enough on the outside of insiders' perspectives to judge and correct them. But neither should he remain wholly detached: successful performance of his mission depends upon the achievement of an outsider's insideness. This, of course, Brontë's curates do not even aim at: they do not so much live *in* the community where they are quartered as live *on* it, as parasites. They all have "good appetites" and the food they criticize nevertheless disappears before them "like leaves before locusts" (S 42). But not only do the curates hold themselves aloof from even partial assimilation in their surrounding community; their own miniature community of the aloof is constantly fracturing in rancor. Their "system of mutual invasion" exemplifies the anticulture brought about by exclusive devotion to horizontality, a way of being together and sharing an identity that, unsupported by vertical ties, devolves *into* disidentification. The Lord of Misrule is Malone, a man whose face and voice instantly proclaim him "a native of the land of shamrocks and potatoes," and who drunkenly taunts Sweeting and Donne on their particular susceptibilities, eliciting their Celtophobic barbs in return (S 41). This lout with the "genuinely national" countenance seems to become more Irish as he grows more agitated, "revil[ing his companions] as Saxons and snobs at the very top pitch of his high Celtic voice" and "menac[ing] rebellion in the name of his 'counthry'" (S 42, 44). A monstrous negative of the abstemious, self-anglicized Patrick Brontë, Malone forces the question of how far horizontal identification can go in forging an effective community—a question behind which lies the further, abiding one of whether, or how successfully, an Irishman can act as the agent and bear the moral authority of the Church of England.

II

The importance of the curates in *Shirley* has partly to do with the fact that they define by opposition the stance of autoethnographic authority that the novel attempts to establish for its narrator, partly with their status as potential husbands for Caroline (altars on which she might immolate herself), and partly with their prominent role in that hell of hollow gentility to which Caroline is condemned so long as Robert closes himself off to her. The chapter in which Caroline discovers that, after a moment of intimacy, he has hardened himself against her is called "The Curates at Tea," and in it, she looks into the abyss of her probable future:

> Caroline at intervals dropped her knitting on her lap, and gave herself up to a sort of brain-lethargy—closing her eyes and depressing her head—caused by what seemed to her the unmeaning hum round her: the inharmonious, tasteless rattle of the piano keys, the squeaking and gasping notes of the flute, the laughter and mirth of her uncle and Hannah and Mary [Sykes], she could not tell whence originating, for she heard nothing comic or gleeful in their discourse; and, more than all, by the interminable gossip of Mrs Sykes murmured close at her ear; gossip which rang the changes on four subjects: her own health and that of various members of her family; the Missionary and Jew baskets and their contents; the late meeting at Nunnely, and one which was expected to come off next week at Whinbury. (S 141).

Though obsessed with local goings-on, Mrs. Sykes and the others manifest not vertical attachment to locality but devotion to the horizontal bond of class. The minutest details of the well-being and daily doings of the genteel caste are thought worthy of review, while the welfare and activities of nongenteel locals are a nonissue except insofar as they impinge upon the former.

At the same time, *charity* is implicitly defined as the act of self-importantly busying oneself about abstract, remote, meddlesome, sanctimonious causes—telescopic philanthropy, in short. The "Missionary and Jew baskets" function as ritual objects that bind this segment of the population together and give it purpose, creating an anticultural cohesion that extends horizontally anywhere but isolates the defined group from others on the local hierarchy. The narrator breaks into the story to describe the use of the Jew basket, much as Malinowski interrupts his narrative in *Argonauts of the Western Pacific* to characterize and situate sociologically a particular item or custom:

> It ought perhaps to be explained in passing, for the benefit of those who are not "au fait" to the mysteries of the "Jew basket" and "Missionary-basket," that these "meubles" are willow repositories, of the capacity of a good-sized family clothes-basket, dedicated to the purpose of conveying from house to house a monster collection of pin-cushions, needle-books, card-racks, work-bags, articles of infant-wear, &c. &c. &c., made by the willing or reluctant hands of the Christian ladies of a parish, and sold per force to the heathenish gentlemen thereof, at prices unblushingly exorbitant. The proceeds of such compulsory sales are applied to the conversion of the Jews, the seeking up of the ten missing tribes, or to the regeneration of the interesting coloured population of the globe. Each lady-contributor takes it in her turn to keep the basket a month, to sew for it, and to foist its contents on a shrinking male public. (S 134)

Though the item may appear the very quintessence of the *local,* needing to be explained to readers elsewhere, we can be sure of finding likenesses of it in Cornwall and in Kent, making the rounds of *those* counties' self-isolating gentlefolk. Its use demonstrates which people are suited to use it and implies which people are not.

Some recognition of this ritual purpose seems to lie behind Robert Moore's otherwise puzzling remark that it would be difficult to conceive of anything more *Jewish* than the Jew basket. When Caroline informs him that she has to knit some children's socks for it, Robert replies, "Jew's basket be—sold! Never was utensil better named. Anything more Jewish than it—its contents, and their prices—cannot be conceived" (S 101). Moore makes use, here, of the anti-Semitic stereotype of the diasporic Jew as economic parasite, the one whose usury and exorbitant prices sap the strength of Christian nations. But apart from the clever paradox of saying that something used in the proselytizing of Christianity is the most Jewish object one could think of, Moore's words hark back to Helstone's and the opening chapter's critique of the curates as cultivating only horizontal affiliation. *They* were parasites, Christians degenerating into Jews by withholding themselves from the local community they lived in.

The genteel classes' combination of surface *locality* and exclusive horizontality is manifested by the eponymous Mr. Yorke, the head of that family that is "first and oldest in the district" (S 79). In Brontë's ideal of English identity-in-difference, signs of positive regional identity would be reconcilable with those of the nation as a whole, regionality becoming an indispensable supplement to nationality rather than a challenge to it. The achievement of this ideal would be all the more remarkable in the case of those northern areas, like Yorkshire, traditionally marked as the provincial domains of "dialect" speakers, areas whose inhabitants just as traditionally feel resentment and scorn toward putatively more civilized southern ways.[7] What Mr. Yorke, the landlord of Briarmains, exemplifies is the phenomenon of the prickly provincial who is also a committed European or cosmopolitan *without* being fully national—a state of affairs at odds with what ought to be, since he *appears* both "a Yorkshire gentleman . . . par excellence, in every point," and "thoroughly English, not a Norman line anywhere" (S 76). The joint regional-national exemplarity written on his countenance lies undeveloped in his character, so that, lacking that mediating term Brontë always looks for, Yorke oscillates between pugnacious regionalism and ostentatious cosmopolitanism: he is *capable* of being more than one thing, but not all at once, or not in the proper way (his manner is definitively "inconsistent" [S 77]). He can speak "very pure English," but generally chooses to employ "broad Yorkshire," "preferring his native Doric to a more refined vocabulary" (S 79). Veering to the opposite extreme, he speaks at length in French "with nearly as pure a[n] . . . accent" as that of Moore (S 74).

In one of the novel's most remarkable exchanges, a passage beginning with a line from Helstone but then consisting solely of dialogue between Yorke and Moore, we might be likely to forget it is an *English* book we are holding in our hands:

> "Moore, are you ready to go?" inquired the Rector.
> "Nay; Robert's not ready [says Yorke]; or rather, I'm not ready to part wi' him: he's an ill lad, and wants correcting."
> "Why sir? [asks Moore.] What have I done?"
> "Made thyself enemies on every hand."
> "What do I care for that? What difference does it make to me whether your Yorkshire louts hate me or like me?"
> "Ay, there it is. The lad is a mak' of an alien amang us: his father would never have talked i' that way. Go back to Antwerp, where you were born and bred, mauvaise tête!"
> "Mauvaise tête vous-même; je ne fais que mon devoir: quant à vos lourdauds de paysans, je m'en moque!"
> "En revanche, mon garçon, nos lourdauds de paysans se moqueront de toi; sois en certain," replied Yorke, speaking with nearly as pure a French accent as Gérard Moore.
> "C'est bon! c'est bon! Et puisque cela m'est egal, que mes amis ne s'en inquiètent pas."
> "Tes amis! Où sont ils, tes amis?"
> "Je fais ècho, où sont ils? et je suis fort aise que l'ècho seul y rèpond. Au diable les amis. Je me souviens encore du moment où mon père et mes oncles Gèrard appellèrent autour d'eux leurs amis, et Dieu sait si les amis sont empressés d'accourir à leur secours! Tenez, M. Yorke, ce mot, ami, m'irrite trop; ne m'en parlez plus."
> "Comme tu voudras."
> And here Mr Yorke held his peace. (S 74–75)

I will return to consider Moore's role in this dialogue later on; for now I want to complete the portrait of Yorke as a figure of wasted potential to build the kind of national culture Brontë is trying to envision. His command of French (matched by

---

[7] Cf. S 88, for the northerner's disdainful parody of southern English speech.

an equal facility in Italian) is like the "many good paintings and tasteful rarities, with which his residence [is] . . . adorned," collected on a protracted Grand Tour in the years before the French Revolution (S 79): it links him with the Continental elite, a horizontal affiliation whose importance to his sense of self is evident in his imperious manner. Yorke speaks French as if always aware he is speaking the traditional language of European courts, the language of diplomacy and refinement. At the same time, he noisily espouses Jacobin and anticlerical views—more souvenirs from abroad—that even Moore would hesitate to claim. These Shirley Keeldar repudiates when she tells him, "all arraying of ranks against ranks, all party hatreds, all tyrannies disguised as liberties, I reject and wash my hands of. *You* think you are a philanthropist; *you* think you are an advocate of liberty; but I will tell you this—Mr Hall, the parson of Nunnely, is a better friend both of man and freedom, than Hiram Yorke, the Reformer of Briarfield" (S 356–57).

Plainly, it will not be until Mr. Yorke, "one of the most influential men" in the vicinity (S 79), unlearns his habit of "crying up" a single class, whether high or low, not until he turns his devotion from abstract causes to the pragmatic concerns of the nation's and the region's limited system of differences, that Brontë's national culture can be born. Two linked diagnoses of Yorke's malformed condition are implied. On the one hand, recognition of Yorke's ethnic makeup—"thoroughly English, not a Norman line anywhere" (S 76)—suggests Matthew Arnold's later argument that vital Englishness *needs* the French or "Celtic" element of flexibility and sympathy and that too strict an adherence to its Germanic origins will deaden the sensibility of the race.[8] In the framework of nineteenth-century ethnological generalization, Yorke's signal failing is that of the unqualified Saxon, an incapacity to "place himself in the position of those he vituperated" (S 77). This reckoning of the fault in his character accords with the second diagnosis, focused on the fact that Yorke is that unrequited lover of Mary Cave who never got over her marriage to another and her early death. Had she married him and lived, the novel suggests, her hidden powers might have nurtured his and turned him from barren horizontality to the fruitful tension of a national-regional culture. The unmistakable implication of Brontë's aligning of these two readings—one based on ethnicity, the other on gender—is that the wasted female powers of Mary Cave are in some sense akin to "French" ones. Not "French" in any sense *independent* of Englishness, but as that ingredient *of* Englishness that saves it from becoming wholly German. A hypothesis of great significance for the two female leads of this novel arises out of the analysis of Mr. Yorke: that English women must learn to be "French" (must be permitted to be French, must recognize the French in themselves) if they are to restore the nation of heterogeneous things.

Down below in those orders of society to which the genteel assiduously blind themselves we find another version of the paradox of a local identity combined with an unchecked horizontality. This is to be found among the Luddites who smash Moore's machinery and later lay siege to his mill. In the novel's second

---

[8] For discussion, cf. Vincent P. Pecora, "Arnoldian Ethnology," *Victorian Studies* 41/3 (Spring 1998), 355–79.

chapter, the Luddites are introduced in a manner that sets them and Moore up as opposite extremes—they are provincials, below the level of nationality, while Moore acts like a foreigner, outside the sphere of the national. These positions are mediated by Brontë's narrator, whose standard English is differentiated from both of the antagonists' languages. Nervously awaiting delivery of his new machines, Moore drops into his native, alien tongue, as he tends to do at moments of excitement: "Chut!" he says "in his French fashion" (S 63). The frame-breakers, for their part, call out in dialect, "Ay, ay, divil, all's raight! We've smashed 'em" (S 63), and they leave Moore a warning note whose place- and class-bound character is so strongly marked as to require translation if it is to be understood by English people from different parts of the country. Informing us that the note bears a superscription reading "To the divil of Hollow's-miln," the narrator then drops transcription in favor of rendition into the common national tongue: "We will not copy the rest of the orthography, which was very peculiar," she writes, "but translate it into legible English" (S 64). Both Yorkshire dialect and French call out for such translation because after all, as the narrator announces—and apparently we need to be told it—"this is an English book" (S 91). But neither does Brontë always translate the French some of her characters use, nor does she treat the conflict between workers and employer in a way that encourages simple equation of working-class identity and the localizing force of vertical identification. In neither its territorial nor its sociological senses can *unredeemed* locality—the mere occupation of a particular spot of ground or figurative "site" within a social order—provide the basis for the autoethnographic authority Brontë is in quest of: only a locality reclaimed after productive displacement can do that.

Chapter 8 bears an ironic title—"Noah and Moses"—linking it to the opening one, "Levitical," that established the character of the de-Christianizing clergymen: both chapters set up figures of false leadership or antiauthority against whom the novel's narrator and favored characters are meant to be measured. Brontë's Noah and Moses are the hypocritical, narcissistic rabble-rousers of the Luddite mob, and they appeal to a class identity *not* specific to place or nation, that of the proletariat. Writing in the immediate aftermath of 1848's season of revolutions, when bourgeois Europeans were recoiling from Marx's call for a horizontal comradeship of labor stretching across the artificial barriers of nationhood—"Workers of the world, unite!"—Brontë makes it difficult to form any automatic connection between dialect speech and the advocacy of local community interests: the use of class-indexed, place-specific speech habits, deriving from a lack of opportunities for exposure to a larger world via education and travel, may now signal a dangerous susceptibility to the appeals emanating from the vastest and most dangerous of larger worlds, that of international communism. In the paranoid bourgeois imagination, dialect speakers are now likely to have already transferred their loyalties from the local to this abstract, universal, and horizontal fellowship of class. This is the vision activated, anachronistically, by the rhetoric Brontë's proletarian patriarchs employ. One of them says to the defiant Moore, "I would beg to allude that as a furriner, coming from a distant coast, another quarter and hemisphere of this globe, thrown, as I may say, a perfect outcast on these shores—the cliffs of Albion—you have not that understanding of huz and wer ways which might conduce to the benefit of the working-classes" (S 154). Evocations of the distinctively local ("huz and wer ways") and the national ("the cliffs of Albion") do not disguise the primacy awarded here to the location- and nation-obliterating category of a working class universally extended. Later on the antilocal nature of the Luddite cause is underscored when assorted "strangers . . . emissaries from the large towns" arrive to whip up the mob (S 370).

To counteract the leeching power of horizontality, a true English Moses capable of conducting his people out of their internal exile, their homelessness within their own borders, must move among the fixed positions, the outlooks narrowed by caste and sect, must ceaselessly cross those inner boundaries and actualize the social whole in the shape of his itinerary, and this Brontë's narrator is continually, demonstratively doing, in ways repeatedly mimicked by movements or features in the story-space. Caroline longs for "Prince Ali Baba's tube" to transport her across the "chasm" separating her from Robert Moore; like a narrator, she spies unseen on Moore and Shirley, leading him, when he discovers what she has been doing, to teasingly ask her if she wears the ring of Gyges (S 235, 257). Shirley challenges the men who assert their superior wisdom, "Acute and astute, why are you not also omniscient? How is it that events transpire, under your very noses, of which you have no suspicion?" (S 351–52). Only the mobile third-person narrator can escape this charge. In Chapter 8, having started the account of the standoff of employer and workers by showing us Moore inside the mill and then bringing him out to meet his challengers, the narrator then departs from Moore and his circle, following the honorable workman William Farren home to afford bourgeois readers a privileged look at the family life of this worthy but frustrated and unemployed man. The narrator's movement across class frontiers is then doubled in the story-space when the Reverend Mr. Hall promptly arrives at Farren's, bringing with him the genuine concern, the strengthening counsel, and the material assistance that Farren and all such sober hands can put to good effect to see them through the worst of times (cf. S 158–60). Like Caroline Helstone, though enjoying opportunities for the exercise of his faculties denied to her as a woman, Mr. Hall embodies the force of vertical identification. The narrator mentions that he "not only spoke with a strong northern accent, but, on occasion, used freely north-country expressions" (S 159): a Yorkshireman himself, he will not permit Yorkshire people of whatever rank to slip outside the sphere of his notice and care. In this he differs not only from the outsider curates (his charitable incursion into Farren's home standing opposed to their "mutual invasion") but also from Caroline's clergyman uncle, the militaristic vicar who sides exclusively with those segments of the local population admissible into his parlor. Yet Mr. Hall's efficacy in this cause depends on the fact that, though a native to the region, he approaches its people from the extraregional perspective, and with the extraregional authority, of a Church of England representative.

Robert Moore's potential to become the kind of leader Brontë is looking for is then suggested by the staging of chapter 9, where we see Moore, made thoughtful by his confrontation with the respectful Farren, take steps to assist him, as Mr. Hall has already started to do. Taking these steps involves crossing another divide in the social landscape, the one between the industrial and landed classes—Moore goes to Hiram Yorke to ask him to find Farren a job—and the one kind of partition that we are urged to cross (that of class versus class) is set against another kind that, the novel suggests, remains uncrossable: that between orthodoxy and an unassimilable "horizontalist" nonconformism (S 163).[9] The way to Briarmains passes before the village's "large, new, raw, Wesleyan place of worship," where a raucous service is in progress. The evening walker hears "a hymn of a most extraordinary description" (S 163) dwelling with bloodthirsty glee upon the conflicts to precede the Last Days. This is religion as *ressentiment,* the indulgence of the downtrodden in compensatory fantasies of vengeance: the faithful sing of the warrior Jesus who will come to put his "foes"—everybody outside the chapel—to the sword. As she had done with the Jane Eyre of Gateshead, Brontë shows here how people whose condition prevents them from imagining any possible form of *social* freedom grasp for *absolute* freedom instead, as out of the "clamorous prayer" that follows the cruel song there arises a single voice shouting "I've found liberty!" (S 163). Such assertions of individual salvation, not merely unchecked by any episcopal authority but positively encouraged by the riotous congregation, fascinate and repel the Anglican witness.

The chorus that responds to this self-proclaimed deliverance mixes self-congratulatory exclusivity, the transfer of all value out of earthly existence, and the fatal devolutionary tendency of all unqualified horizontalists: the hymn dissolves into a cacophony of "shouts, yells, ejaculations, frantic cries, agonized groans" (S 164), and, although the final stanza of the hymn asserts that the faithful are prepared to "[s]hout in the refiner's fire" and "clasp [their] hands amidst the flame" (S 165), the community it describes remains the placeless one of the solely horizontal bond. The great paradox of Brontë's establishmentarianism consists of the fact that she identifies the *Nonconformists* as the ones who refuse "to be other than one thing," seeing them as cleaving to the single viewpoint of the laboring classes and developing no consciousness of the plurality of standpoints involved in vertical affiliation.[10] While the industrialist Moore attempts to enlist the aid of the rentier Yorke for the operative Farren, the Methodists are busily validating the viewpoint of a single class and fueling the resentment and self-righteousness of that class. The resulting militant factionalism drives a body of desperate men to mount an attack on Moore's mill. To counteract them, Brontë proposes a militancy without factional-

[9] Unorthodox in relation to the existing Anglican Church, Brontë's doctrine of Universal Salvation (cf. *Letters 2:* 343 and 345n4) *would* be at home in the new orthodoxy envisioned in *Shirley.* An Anglicanism of Universal Salvation stands in sharp contrast to the exclusivist Nonconformism expressed in the hymn discussed immediately below. Cf. *Letters 2.* 160–61.

[10] Cf. *Letters 1.* 581, for Brontë's pleasure in receiving a favorable review of *Jane Eyre* in the *Church of England Journal* "chiefly because it *was* the *Church* of *England* Journal . . . to the Establishment, with all her faults—the profane Athanasian Creed excluded—I am sincerely attached." The anticultural authority Mr. Helstone commands Shirley to recite not only the Apostles' Creed but the Athanasian Creed as well, holding the latter to be "the test" of orthodox Anglicanism (cf. S 211 and 609n2).

ism—an elusive ideal, but one very much in the spirit of the holiday of Whitsuntide or Pentecost, which takes place in the middle of *Shirley*.

The Whitsun sequences unfold over four chapters (16–19) whose central position is not at all accidental, for it is here that the novel suggests most forcefully that its aim is a *National* Pentecostalism. In this section, the forces of Anglican militancy-without-factionalism put to rout an army of Nonconformists, and Shirley Keeldar preaches a new gospel of a female spiritual energy that claims recognition as the savior and supplement of masculine powers—a gospel the English will have to heed if they are to make themselves a culture and find themselves a home in their native land. National Pentecostalism is the power of the Anglican Church as Brontë imagines it might be—a church including Shirley—to hail a definitively *pluralized* English people, a people whose differences of class, region, gender, and even (to a degree) ethnicity, might be sustained and acknowledged as ways of being English. It is in the pursuit of such an ideal that the speech of *southern* English people gets "dialecticized" in *Shirley*, as part of an effort to denaturalize England's normalization of southern voices as standard or national ones. Mr. Donne, for instance, is represented as delivering one of his many disparagements of Yorkshire in the following terms:

> I could never have formed an idea*r* of the country had I not seen it; and the people—rich and poor—what a set! How *corse* and uncultivated! . . . [Y]ou scarsley—(you must excuse Mr Donne's pronunciation, reader; it was very choice; he considered it genteel, and prided himself on his southern accent; northern ears received with singular sensations his utterance of certain words); you scarsley ever see a fam'ly where a propa carriage or a reg'la butla is kep; and as to the poor . . . [t]hey pos'tively deserve that one should turn a mad cow in amongst them to rout their rabble-ranks. (S 286–87)

Similarly, Mr. Sympson, Shirley Keeldar's outraged uncle, delivers himself of the southron's outburst, "Good *Ged*!"—prompting the narrator to remark that "*Ged* . . . must be the cognomen of Mr Sympson's Lares," since, "when hard-pressed, he always invokes this idol" (S 582).

On Whitsuntide, the soldier manqué Mr. Helstone gets to assemble three "regiments," arrayed in their finery, to march in procession around the district, in observance of longstanding West Yorkshire custom. At the exact midpoint of the novel, Brontë's narrator savors the spectacle's redemptive promise. "It was," she writes, "a joyous scene, and a scene to do good: it was a day of happiness for rich and poor: the work, first of God, and then of the clergy. Let England's priests have their due: they are a faulty set in some respects, . . . but the land would be badly off without them: Britain would miss her church, if that church fell. God save it! God also reform it!" (S 298). A Church of England reformed as Brontë envisions, realizing the power of National Pentecostalism, would not have to contend with encroaching sects—as its unreformed antitype has literally to do in chapter 17, when the Anglicans' procession encounters another one consisting of an "unholy alliance" from "[t]he Dissenting and Methodist schools, the Baptists, Independents, and Wesleyans," seemingly intent, says Helstone, on "obstructing our march and driving us back" (S 300). In one of the absurdest episodes in her fiction, the Anglican body led by Helstone and "Captain" Shirley Keeldar literally runs the challenging Nonconformists off the road, singing "Rule Britannia" as they go (S 301).

But if Shirley is capable of acting in her male and militaristic guise in league with the flinty, unforgiving Helstone, she soon gives voice to a feminist protest against England's merely existing orthodoxy of Protestantism. In chapter 18, Shirley and Caroline skip the evening service to join with "Nature . . . at her evening prayers" (S 314), and Shirley takes inspiration from the scene to personify Nature as the non-Miltonic Eve, the aboriginal "woman-Titan" whose powers patriarchal tradition has studiously suppressed (S 315). The two women stand before the door of the church, like Luther with his list of grievances; Shirley's open-air sermon coincides with the one Mr. Donne is giving inside. I will not dwell further on Shirley's Pentecostal homily, which feminist readings of the novel have duly considered, except to note its emphasis on the *recovery* of powers long lost or forgotten under patriarchal rule, like those powers associated with the memory of Mary Cave. When Shirley entered the novel some hundred pages earlier, she brought with her Caroline's own long-lost mother, the "Mrs Pryor" who served as Shirley's governess: at the time of the Whitsuntide sequence this woman's true identity has still not been revealed, but the bond that continues to develop between Shirley and Caroline does for both women, in complementary ways, what Caroline's eventual recovery of her mother does: it equips them to exercise an efficacious national womanhood. What each partner in this comradeship needs is suggested by the contrast between their reveries after Shirley leaves off sermonizing about Nature and Eve in chapter 18: whereas Shirley's expansive imagination fixates on the universal "mother Eve, in these days called Nature," Caroline's constricted one centers "not [on] the mighty and mystical parent of Shirley's visions, but [on] a gentle human form—the form she ascribed to her own mother; unknown, unloved, but not unlonged-for" (S 316). By the end of the novel these two will have found their way by opposite paths to the mediating ideal not of universal or of particular but of national femaleness.

The Whitsun sequence has a third act, in chapter 19, that joins with the battling processions of chapter 17 to sandwich the feminist ideals that Shirley gives voice to and that are seeking a home in Brontë's redeemed England. Here we watch as Caroline and Shirley watch the Luddites' assault on Moore's mill, and they and we witness another antithesis of the goal Brontë strives for:

> A simultaneously-hurled volley of stones had saluted the broad front of the mill, with all its windows; and now every pane of every lattice lay in shattered and pounded fragments. A yell followed this demonstration—a rioters' yell—a North-of-England—a Yorkshire—a West-Riding—a West-Riding-clothing-district-of-Yorkshire rioters' yell. You never heard that sound, perhaps, reader? So much the better for your ears—perhaps for your heart; since, if it rends the air in hate to yourself, or to the men or principles you approve, the interests to which you wish well, Wrath wakens to the cry of Hate: the Lion shakes his mane, and rises to the howl of the Hyena: Caste stands up, ireful, against Caste; and the indignant, wronged spirit of the Middle Rank bears down in zeal and scorn on the famished and furious mass of the Operative Class. (S 335).

Brontë's description of the rioters' yell exhibits a funnel effect, a rapid narrowing of the constituency giving voice to it and hailed by it. This evocation of a regressive, exaggerated regionalism offers the very antipodes of that class-transcending national culture and vertical identification Brontë is at pains to advance. When the narrator turns to her readers, however, the untranslatably local cry turns into an *example* of a widespread phenomenon: it becomes merely the local variety of proletarian anger extending horizontally everywhere, the West Yorkshire inflection of the "howl of the Hyena." Also noteworthy is the shattered windowpane: as in *Jane Eyre,* Brontë chooses the window as a partition that does not blind one to what lies on the other side of it—a figure for that interplay of distinction and connection she seeks in her model of culture.[11] The window is the kind of partition to have *inside* a culture, keeping the different regions, stations, genders, and individuals apart but keeping all of them conscious of the others.

III

Brontë's interest throughout *Shirley* and in the particular moment of the rioters' yell centers on the perception—it was Scott's—of how public crisis narrows and rigidifies identities, fuels the determination "not to be other than one thing." The relentless logic of crisis, which makes everyone start acting according to the dictates of only a single identity—whether Lion or Hyena—had to be resisted, just as militant factionalism had to be counteracted by the paradox of a militant antifactionalism. While the historical conditions that triggered adherence to exclusive identities lay outside the scope of individual agency, and while Brontë herself was not immune to the appeal of such identities, she tried in *Shirley* to disrupt the logic of crisis by showing critical moments succeeded or interpenetrated by others in which multiple identities might coexist and reciprocally reinforce one another. This effort is most plainly visible in the symbolic transactions around which the novel's three central relationships are built: those between Shirley and Caroline, Caroline and Robert, and, finally, Shirley and Robert's brother Louis.

Shirley Keeldar's entrance into the novel coincides with the very nadir of Caroline Helstone's descent into despair: Robert's resumption of indifference toward her has brought her to confront the vacancy of the landscape of her prospects. Her efforts to submerge herself in philanthropic labors bring her "neither health of body nor continued peace of mind" and she grows "more joyless and more wan . . . the heaviness of a broken spirit, and of pining and palsifying faculties, settl[ing] slow on her buoyant youth" (S 199). As readers have always noted, Shirley bursts upon the scene with all the vigor and determination that have been crushed out of Caroline, and she provides the latter with her first truly gratifying relationship. The famous scene at "Nunnwood" where the bond between the two women is conse-

---

[11] The figure later returns in the description of the illness that represents the "valley of the shadow of death" through which Caroline must pass: a "yellow taint of pestilence . . . dim[s] the lattices of English homes with the breath of Indian plague" (S 399).

crated goes beyond this, however, representing them as bringing complementary strengths of vertical and horizontal identification into concord, and thus foreshadowing the conjunction of forces necessary for the invention, or the recovery, of a genuine national-regional culture. The passage must be quoted at length.

> They both halted on the green brow of the Common: they looked down on the deep valley robed in May raiment. . . . On Nunnwood—the sole remnant of antique British forest in a region whose lowlands were once all sylvan chase . . . slept the shadow of a cloud; the distant hills were dappled, the horizon was shaded and tinted like mother-of-pearl; silvery blues, soft purples, evanescent greens and rose-shades, all melting into fleeces of white cloud, pure as azury snow, allured the eye as with a remote glimpse of heaven's foundations. The air blowing on the brow was fresh, and sweet, and bracing.
>
> "Our England is a bonnie island," said Shirley, "and Yorkshire is one of her bonniest nooks."
>
> "You are a Yorkshire girl too?"
>
> "I am—Yorkshire in blood and birth. Five generations of my race sleep under the aisles of Briarfield Church: I drew my first breath in the old black hall behind us."
>
> Hereupon Caroline presented her hand, which was accordingly taken and shaken. "We are compatriots," said she.
>
> "Yes," agreed Shirley, with a grave nod.
>
> "And that," asked Miss Keeldar, pointing to the forest,—"that is Nunnwood? . . . What is it like?"
>
> "It is like an encampment of forest sons of Anak. The trees are huge and old. When you stand at their roots, the summits seem in another region: the trunks remain still and firm as pillars, while the boughs sway to every breeze. In the deepest calm their leaves are never quite hushed, and in a high wind a flood rushes—a sea thunders above you."
>
> "Was it not one of Robin Hood's haunts?"
>
> "Yes, and there are mementos of him still existing. To penetrate into Nunnwood, Miss Keeldar, is to go far back into the dim days of eld. Can you see a break in the forest, about the centre?"
>
> "Yes, distinctly."
>
> "That break is a dell; a deep, hollow cup, lined with turf as green and short as the sod of this Common: the very oldest of the trees, gnarled mighty oaks, crowd about the brink of this dell: in the bottom lie the ruins of a nunnery."
>
> "We will go—you and I alone, Caroline—to that wood, early some fine summer morning, and spend a long day there. . . . It would not tire you too much to walk so far?"
>
> "Oh, no . . . and I know all the pleasantest spots: I know where we could get nuts in nutting time; I know where wild strawberries abound; I know certain lonely, quite untrodden glades, carpeted with strange mosses. . . . I know groups of trees that ravish the eye with their perfect, picture-like effects. . . . Miss Keeldar, I could guide you."
> (S 220–21)

This striking and much commented-upon set-piece takes us to a scene of aboriginal female power, a power still lingering around the ruined site of a women's spiritual community, though it lies deep, deep down in that "hollow cup." The reverberations of Mary Cave and Mrs. Pryor are set to work here: the cup is like a cave, full of secret magic; the place radiates with the energy of a prior, far-off era when English soil could still nurture and be nurtured by the might of women.[12] Here, through Shirley, Caroline emerges as *genius loci,* exercising that genius of place that others stifle in her: one has to note the new sound of authority in her voice ("I know . . . I know . . . I could guide you"), as she introduces Shirley to this primal scene of vertical identification. Her intimate familiarity with the landscape, down to its smallest details and down in its nethermost depths, gives her vision the grounding force required by true communities both local and larger. Shirley, on the other hand, brings to this encounter the breadth of experience of a more-traveled woman: she has just returned to the region after ten years away, much of the time in the south of England; she is the one who can generalize about the condition of "Our England" and then file Yorkshire under its heading as one of England's "bonniest nooks."[13] Through Caroline she is able to affirm for the first time that she is, indeed, a *local,* "Yorkshire in blood and birth"; through her, Caroline comes to recognize her native locality, centered on this special site—verticality's ground zero—as an *English* nook. The idea that Shirley is Caroline's route of access to a national plane gets reinforced later, when upon learning Mrs. Pryor is her mother, Caroline tells her, "I like your southern accent: it is so pure, so soft. It has no rugged burr, no nasal twang, such as almost everyone's voice here in the north has" (S 424). Between mother and daughter lies the mixture of identity and difference in which the nation's north can appreciate southern difference (and vice versa) even while claiming the different as kindred. Nunnwood lies at the crossroads where locality and nationality meet, the place where vertical and horizontal energies can declare "we are compatriots" and begin to bring England's internal exile to an end.

As I suggested earlier, these two Englishwomen—the one who comes from outside to claim the local home she has never known, the other who has been stifled in the prison of *mere* locality and now reaches outward from there to acknowledge her nationality—can fully and efficaciously *become* English only the extent that they can also be "French," and this they do by marrying Anglo-Belgian husbands. The resolution of *Shirley* has often been disparaged as excessively tidy and as a backsliding into gender conventionalities after the daring intimations of Sapphism surrounding Caroline and Shirley's interactions. Just as in *Jane Eyre,* however, the marriage plot Brontë resorts to in this novel cannot simply be dismissed, for the heterogeneity Brontë seeks to cultivate must include the category of gender. Even if it must be admitted that Louis Moore is brought into the action two-thirds of the way through the book by an act of unparalleled shoehorning, the comple-

---

[12] A further line may be drawn between this section and the ballad of "Puir Mary Lee" that Caroline thinks of when she is spurned by Robert: the ballad expresses the rejected woman's desire to be buried in snow, to become invisible to the world of faithless men. Cf. *Villette* (1853; Harmondsworth: Penguin, 1979), for Lucy Snowe's comparison of her soul under the influence of John Graham Bretton's attention to a "sad, cold dell [that] becomes a deep cup of luster" when a woodman's axe lets the sunshine in (334).

[13] One notes the expansive use of "England" to name the entire island-nation.

mentarity of Shirley and Caroline's alliance has suggested all along that the two "different-same" women would require two different-same men with whom to establish two further, complementary forms of different-sameness. In the case of Robert Moore, the novel has indicated from its earliest stages that we must pass through French to find the Englishness in the man. In that passage cited above where Yorke warns Moore about the antagonism he is generating in the district, the latter says, among other things, "*Au diable les amis. Je me souviens encore du moment où mon père et mes oncles Gérard appellèrent autour d'eux leurs amis, et Dieu sait si les amis sont empressés d'accourir à leur secours!*" Brontë's publishers worried that the lengthy passages of untranslated French in *Shirley* would seem pretentious, but here as in some other instances the novelist appears to be using it to enact in linguistic terms the pattern of departure-and-return she so often favors in her plots and figurative strategies. Readers who can temporarily *leave* English for French will discover here the source of Moore's pitiless drive: loyalty to an English father betrayed by the so-called friends he called upon for help in time of need. Such readers will note at once that this fidelity to English patrimony does not preclude loyalty to his "French," maternal ancestry: like Yorke, Robert is a man of potentially flexible and multiple identities (as his name, "Robert Gérard Moore" suggests), warped by fate into a form that negates his potential. The lesson Robert has erroneously derived from his father's and uncles' collapse is that he needs to adopt the exclusivist, anti-English style of Frenchness put forward by the logic of crisis and embodied, for the English, by Napoleon. It is this definition of Frenchness Caroline refers to when, in a well-known scene of instruction, she seeks Robert's guarantee that he is "*not* going to be French, and skeptical, and sneering" (S 115; emphasis added) and tries to head off the juggernaut of his Enlightenment incredulity toward the bonds of community by making him read Shakespeare's *Coriolanus*. "To-night you shall be entirely English," she tells him: "you shall read an English book" (S 114).

To activate a Frenchness in himself that can coexist with, and even strengthen, Englishness, Moore has to pass through the English book, identify with its protagonist, and bend in mercy as that protagonist famously does. More specifically, he has to read that book aloud with Caroline, to experience what it feels like to say the English words Shakespeare wrote for that character. Caroline says, " you must hear [Shakespeare's] voice with your mind's ear" (S 115).

"And have you felt anything in Coriolanus like you?" [she asks.]

"Perhaps I have."

"Was he not faulty as well as great?"

Moore nodded.

"And what was his fault? What made him hated by the citizens? What caused him to be banished by his countrymen?"

"What do you think it was?"

"I ask again—

> 'Whether was it pride,
> Which out of daily fortune ever taints
> The happy man? whether defect of judgment,

> To fail in the disposing of those chances
> Which he was lord of? or whether nature,
> Not to be other than one thing, not moving
> From the casque to the cushion, but commanding peace
> Even with the same austerity and garb
> As he controlled the war?'" (S 117)

Instead of the fatal consistency that led Coriolanus to carry a single demeanor into all contexts, from the casque of the soldier to the cushion of the senator, Brontë recommends an identity capable of being differently embodied or enunciated in different settings, though stopping short of protean. The national pedagogy she puts Moore through cannot be represented under the sign of a once-and-for-all "conversion," for that would entail simply the exchange of one exclusivity for another; the identity she instructs him in is tactical and occasional—for "tonight."

In return for Caroline's tutelage, Robert makes *her* recite André Chenier's "La Jeune Captive," *Frenching* her just as she has *Englished* him. Here Brontë's text again includes a block of untranslated French whose relevance to the narrative makes it something of a rebuke to monolingual English readers. The poem expresses, in the compass of its twelve lines, all the longing for self-realization Caroline has felt, longing it would take a full-fledged woman's Bildungsroman to bring to fruition. "Je ne suis qu'au printemps," the verse says; "Je veux achever ma journée!" By requiring Caroline to make her body a vehicle of these French sounds and sentiments, Robert affords her access to territories of feeling and prospects of fulfillment closed off to her in her current English life, and the importance of maintaining such access strikes Brontë as so great that she makes her case using nationalities that, at the time of her story, could hardly be more committed to mutual exclusivity. At the moment when Napoleon's Continental System is choking Britain off, when English and French people are under intense pressure to "declare themselves" the adherents of one identity only, Brontë's lovers declare themselves in each other's native tongue, each recovering in that other language some lost, indispensable component of the self.

Working with three main characters in *Shirley* afforded Brontë the opportunity to emphasize the mediatedness of culture and desire, the way a single character's thoughts and feelings are channeled through others and single relationships overlap with other ones. Such mediatedness is the curse of every anticulture but would be the crowning glory of a genuine culture: in either case, culture could be imagined as a bounded structure of interlocking triangles—like a geodesic dome. The symbolic transactions I have already surveyed begin to suggest the operation of a cultural principle of transitivity, as a bond between Robert and Caroline leads to one between Caroline and Shirley, so that we might expect to see the cultural circle closed with a third bond between Shirley and Robert. To satisfy readers wishing to see all three of the protagonists happily married in the end Brontë would obviously have to introduce a fourth figure to break the triangle into two pairs, and she went about this business with an ironic self-consciousness that matches anything to be found at the end of an Austen or a Scott or a Dickens novel. (The title of her final chapter—"The Winding Up"—suggests an author visibly dusting off her hands upon completion of a job well done.)

But her particular choice for that necessary fourth cannot be explained solely by reference to readers' conventional expectations and the novelist's acquiescence to them. For as I have argued, that unstable model of culture as an object in space, that attempted "spatialization of difference" we associate with twentieth-century cultural anthropology and (this book contends) can find adumbrated in nineteenth-century novels, generates a position outside itself from which its integrated structure may be seen. In the hands of nineteenth-century novelists, the narrator came to occupy just such a position, an outside vantage point that was presented as having been attained by some erstwhile insider and as such could then become the point of departure for numerous *revisitings* of the story-space and cultural interior. In Greek mythology, a disguised god's presence in the world of humans could be detected by the turbulence that figure created in entering or leaving the human domain; something similar could be said about the authorizing trope of many nineteenth-century novels, according to which the narrator makes return visits to the world of characters. Louis Moore, in short, "is" the narrator—in reverse. An outsider to England who has learned how to be English (and a man who has learned to develop "female" strengths), he turns inside out the position of an English indigene who has learned to look at England from without, a woman who has become more mobile and knowing than any of her male characters.

With Louis's appearance upon the scene in chapter 23 comes an instance of that uncanniness so often signaling Brontë's autoethnographic aim: Hortense calls out excitedly to Caroline, "venez voir mon frère," and Caroline wonders, "What does this unwonted excitement about such an everyday occurrence . . . portend?" (S 395). When she enters the parlor, Hortense "seize[s] her hand" and leads her

> to Robert, who stood in bodily presence, tall and dark against the one window, present[ing] her with a mixture of agitation and formality, as though they had been utter strangers, and this was their first mutual introduction.
>
> Increasing puzzle! He bowed rather awkwardly, and turning from her with a stranger's embarrassment, he met the doubtful light from the window: it fell on his face, and the enigma of the dream (a dream it seemed) was at its height: she saw a visage like and unlike, Robert, and no Robert. (S 395–96)

Only when the actual Robert appears, too, does Louis's identity separate itself out from his brother's: he has a look, Caroline resolves, "less decisive, accurate, and clear than [that] of the young mill-owner," but also a more "deliberate and reflective" air (S 397). Louis embodies what Caroline has tried to accomplish, namely the *translation of Robert into English*. This calmer Moore, self-controlled rather than self-curbing, not prey to Gallic impetuosity and so not requiring the punishing restriction of it, has absorbed the influence of an English education Robert never had, and he wins the hand of Shirley not by bold or headstrong action but by patiently keeping faith as she rejects a series of conventionally preferable suitors. While waiting, he keeps a secret diary of his observations and desires, cultivating those powers of interiority so much recommended to Victorian women denied the opportunity to act in a male-controlled public sphere.[14] His writing and the narrator's overlap; the boundary between them sometimes blurs. Louis even takes up the role of the "me-narrator," writing, "It is pleasant to write about what is near and dear as the core of my heart: none can deprive me of this little book, and through this pencil, I can say to it what I will—say what I dare utter to nothing living—say what I dare not *think* aloud" (S 487).

The autoethnographic uncanny occurs when we get the feeling that the narrator has brought a productively alienated perspective to stand alongside the viewpoint of another figure contained in the story-space and in the culture from which that narrator has distanced herself. Squeezed awkwardly into the novel, Louis Moore possesses a few distinctive characteristics and performs a few functions suggesting that he might be such an avatar for the disembodied "voice" that tells the story. After many chapters showing characters watching one another and partially or incompletely coming to understand each other's motives, Louis enters the narrative and does virtually nothing else but wait for and watch the title character. He is the only man in the novel who can come close to meeting that challenge that Shirley flung at the feet of the community's male authorities: "Acute and astute, why are you not also omniscient? How is it that events transpire, under your very noses, of which you have no suspicion?" (S 351–52). Where Shirley is a dreamer, Louis is a *writer:* the narrator even invites us, in a strange self-reflexive moment, "Come near, by all means, reader: do not be shy: stoop over his shoulder fearlessly, and read as he scribbles" (S 487). In the past, he has tried to discipline Shirley to become a writer, too. We are informed that

> if Shirley were not such an indolent, a reckless, an ignorant being, she would take a pen at [her] moments [of inspiration]; or at least while the recollection of such moments was yet fresh on her spirit: she would seize, she would fix the apparition, tell the vision revealed. Had she a little more of the organ of Acquisitiveness in her head—a little more of the love of property in her nature, she would take a good-sized sheet of paper and write plainly out, in her own queer but legible hand, the story that has been narrated, the song that has been sung to her, and thus possess what she was enabled to create. (S 374)

A Shirley who possessed her own visions and narrative might be a first-person narrator like Jane Eyre, but instead she has become an inspired orator who needs another to do the writing.

In the novel's final scene of instruction and symbolic transaction, Shirley's former French master makes himself the pupil, by reciting from memory one of the French compositions she wrote at his request, "La Première Femme Savante," another reverie of the primordial, anti-Miltonic Eve: envisioning the marriage of this figure to the "glorious Bridegroom" "Genius," it represents one more variation (one straining under its own mythological weight) on the kind of tense combination of forces Brontë has been seeking throughout the novel. Brontë makes "La Première Femme Savante" echo the Nunnwood scene in several respects, setting

---

[14] Cf. S, chaps. 29, 36. I borrow the thesis of Nancy Armstrong's *Desire and Domestic Fiction: A Political History of the Novel* (New York: Oxford University Press, 1987).

it in the same kind of "forest valley" we saw there, a space of "island oak-woods" not in some far-off cradle of civilization, some Mesopotamia or Africa, but "in our own seas of Europe" (S 456). Our attention is drawn down into that valley "with rocky sides and brown profundity of shade, formed by tree crowding on tree, descend[ing] deep"—there, we might think, to find that same ground zero of vertical identification to which Caroline guided Shirley at Nunnwood (S 456). But what we actually encounter is a series of displacements right at the heart of the culture-rooting myth: the "original" that expressed this vision was a *text,* not a piece of charismatic oratory; it was in French, not English (though when Louis speaks it the narrator says she "must translate [into English], on pain of being unintelligible to some readers" [S 455]). It centers not upon a bygone integrated female community but upon a lone female figure, an orphan "[n]one cares for" (S 456). It is rendered into impassioned speech not by a woman-prophet but by the male authority who now acts as her disciple.

Local and abstract communities, voice and text, man and woman, insider and alien: Brontë's archaeology of culture, her search for old foundations on which to build a new England, takes us deep, deep down to the bedrock of a fundamental ambivalence, where once lay a document that contained the key to the reformation of England and was written in French. When Louis then goes on to demand from Shirley a recital of "Le Cheval Dompté"—the tamed horse—he is ironically acknowledging the impossibility of ever fully domesticating the woman who will become his wife. She, in terms that make many modern readers cringe, refuses to marry any man "who cannot hold [her] in check" as Louis can (S 513). But in Brontë's lexicon, being *checked* is not the same as being crushed, incarcerated, neglected, negated, consumed; it describes the condition of a social freedom, a limitation that is the ground of any valuable liberation. Exactly where one draws the line between acceptable and excessive forms of limitation remains the subject of further negotiation.

IV

For much of the novel, Brontë's focus rests on Robert Moore, a man between two women and a figure embodying the "confusion of tongues" that Brontë explores as either cultural entropy and chaos or the principle of multiplicity that enlivens culture. For what, after all, are we to call him? His middle and last names seem easily divisible into the Francophone and Anglophone sides of his character: Gérard Moore. But what of his Christian name? To speak it is to be forced to choose: the English (or North-of-England) "ROH-but" or the French "Ro-BAIR"? The presence of Hortense in the narrative, and Brontë's calling of attention to the fact that sister and brother speak in French to each other, is a reminder that we should not feel too comfortable saying his name the English way. If we read the novel aloud, we will constantly be confronting that discomfort. The oral performances Brontë's central characters put each other through, acquiring their significance in relation to the international crises of both 1811–12 and 1848, the seasons of the novel's story and of its composition, involve the recognition that people will always, sometime or other, be called upon to "declare themselves," but that they can also be trained to speak as something *other* than what they are compelled to be. Always drawn back to the ideal of a face-to-face community of speakers, Brontë nevertheless learned to appreciate the privileges of authorship and the corresponding privileges of silent readers, faceless to her, who could enjoy the pleasure of *not* having to choose between Robert and Robert. On the other hand, anyone taking the silent, anonymous community of readers for an image of a wholly abstract national community might be checked by considering that this and other of Brontë's devices seem designed to reroute the reading experience back through the domain of the oral or aural, back through the frame of the local, which progressivist narratives of nationality suggested could simply be left behind. In Brontë's modernity, we cannot turn our backs for long upon the rural and the regional, with their older forms of sociality that refuse to conform to the new normative model of the bourgeois private citizen (reading the novel alone at home) who recognizes only voluntary and horizontal affiliations.

Shirley ends with a reminder that the *fairies,* thought to have been driven away from the district by the one-making forces of industrialization and enclosures, have still been *heard,* though not seen, in recent times. On the last pages of the novel, the narrator enters the community she has been overseeing, becoming a character herself, capable of talking with other characters in the book and of writing such things as "[t]he other day, I passed up the hollow, which tradition says was once green and lone, and wild; and there I saw the manufacturer's day-dreams embodied in substantial stone and brick and ashes." (S 599). The last character to speak in the novel is this narrator's servant, Martha, who, even in commenting on the obvious changes modernization has brought to the region, refuses simply to bury the local and invites us silent readers to "listen" for it.

> "What was the Hollow like then, Martha?"
>
> "Different to what it is now; but I can tell of it clean different again: when there was neither mill, nor cot, nor hall, except Fieldhead, within two miles of it. I can tell, one summer-evening, fifty years syne, my mother coming running in just at the edge of dark, almost fleyed out of her wits, saying, she had seen a fairish (fairy) in Fieldhead Hollow; and that was the last fairish that ever was seen on this country side (though they've been heard within these forty years)." (S 599)

CHAPTER TEN

Outlandish Nationalism: *Villette*

For whosoever entreth into anothers dominion, is Subject to all the Laws thereof; unlesse he have a privilege by the amity of the Soveraigns, or by speciall license.
—Thomas Hobbes[1]

That England may be spared the spasms, cramps, and frenzy-fits now contorting the Continent, I earnestly pray. With the French and the Irish I have no sympathy. With the Germans and the Italians I think the case is different; as different as the love of freedom from the lust for license.
—Charlotte Brontë, in a letter of 1848[2]

I

IN AN ARGUMENT about the Victorian novel's anticipation of ethnographic concepts, *Villette,* like *The Professor,* might readily appear a promising selection, for its narrative could be read as one about Lucy Snowe's fieldwork "immersion" in the alien culture of a fictional Catholic European country based on Belgium. No twentieth-century anthropological monograph arising out of fieldwork in a far-flung tribal society can outdo *Villette*'s representation of the disorientation and helplessness likely to beset the visitor newly arrived upon the scene of research. Mary Louise Pratt has written persuasively about the rhetorical function of arrival scenes in ethnographic writing, contending that, by magnifying the strangeness of the visited culture at the outset, such scenes assist in the accreditation of the figure writing the book, who purports to have overcome all that strangeness and organized it into knowable form.[3] If the other place is depicted from the start as positively teeming with otherness, we will be more inclined to give credit to the author who has won her way through that baffling plenitude and found a way to bring it to order. And Lucy Snowe's initial encounter with Labassecour would appear ideally suited to this ethnographic topos.

[1] Hobbes, *Leviathan,* ed. Richard Tuck (Cambridge: Cambridge University Press, 1996), 154.

[2] *The Letters of Charlotte Brontë,* ed. Margaret Smith, Vol. 2 (1848–1851) (Oxford: Clarendon, 2000). 48; henceforth *Letters 2.*

[3] Pratt, "Fieldwork in Common Places," in James Clifford and George E. Marcus, eds., *Writing Culture: The Poetics and Politics of Ethnography* (Berkeley: University of California Press, 1986), 27–50.

Lucy had left England full of hope about the prospects she might realize abroad: while crossing the Channel, she had indulged in a "reverie" in which, she recalls, "I saw the continent of Europe, like a wide dream-land, far away. Sunshine lay on it, making the long coast one line of gold. . . . For background, spread a sky, solemn and dark-blue, and—grand with imperial promise, soft with tints of enchantment—strode from north to south a God-bent bow, an arch of hope."[4] Her experiences upon arrival put paid to such optimism and make Lucy the narrator savagely undercut the memory of it: "Cancel the whole of that, if you please, reader," she remarks, "or rather let it stand, and draw thence a moral—an alternative, text-hand copy—Day-dreams are the delusions of the demon. Becoming excessively sick, I faltered down into the cabin" (V 117–18). Thoroughly irritated by the "teazing peevishness" of a fellow-traveler, she disembarks to face "the cold air and black scowl of the night," which "seemed to rebuke me for my presumption in being where I was: the lights of the foreign sea-port town, glimmering round the foreign harbour, met me like unnumbered threatening eyes" (V 118). Unlike the other passengers, she has no one to meet her as she disembarks; she has trouble communicating with her porter, absentmindedly trying to tip him with a sixpence, then a shilling, and earning another kind of rebuke when he "speak[s] rather sharply, in a language to me unknown." Her money, she is made to recognize, is now "foreign money, not current here" (V 119).

It is forcefully impressed upon her that, just as she is now outside the domain where English currency is the coin of the realm, she has also passed beyond the limit of that sphere in which English customs and language and, in fact, the whole system of interpretation and valuation that comprises existing English culture, hold sway. She does not know how to interpret and assess what takes place around her. When a "rough man" arrives at her hotel room the next morning and brusquely demands the keys to her trunk, she cannot immediately classify his actions as relating to the custom-house rather than to the customs of foreign thieves (V 120). Arriving at the inland city of Villette—again in darkness—she fears her trunk has indeed gone astray and lacks the ability to inquire about it, for she has come there "not possessing a phrase of *speaking* French: and it was French, and French only the whole world seemed now gabbling round me" (V 123). She is reduced to a counterproductive pantomime: "Approaching the conductor, I just laid my hand on his arm, pointed to a trunk, then to the diligence-roof, and tried to express a question with my eyes. He misunderstood me, seized the trunk indicated, and was about to hoist it onto the vehicle" (V 123). Only the providential appearance of that trunk's true owner, an "English gentleman," can clear up the confusion and set Lucy on her way to a respectable inn (V 124). Even then, the murk of night and the unfamiliar streets, populated only with insolent "moustachioed men," cause Lucy to lose her way (V 125). Providence again intervenes and brings her to the doorstep of the "Pensionnat de Demoiselles" where she will eventually find work and increased confidence as a teacher of English.

---

[4] Brontë, *Villette* (1853; Harmondsworth: Penguin, 1979), 117; henceforth V.

Devoting this much attention to heightening our impression of the incapacitating otherness of Labassecour, Lucy the narrator might seem, then, to be preparing us for a narrative about how she triumphed over the frailties of her former self and gained mastery over the once oppressively foreign culture by grasping it *as* a culture rather than remaining overwhelmed by it as an agglomeration of alien stimuli. And one would have to say that, in part, this is a fair description of what *Villette* is about. But modern ethnographic narratives that move from disorientation to mastery regularly present that passage as one validating a cultural-relativist outlook. The anthropologist who can change her relationship to a culture from that of befuddled visitor to that of sympathetic authority offers powerful testimony to the relativity of cultures: that change occurs as the visitor comes to recognize that the cacophonous array of bizarre practices that assaulted her when newly arrived actually have an order and make perfect sense on their own terms. As she learns "the native's point of view," the ethnographer becomes convinced that these people she once thought senseless savages in fact possess "a culture of their own."

One problem with any attempt to read *Villette* ethnographically is that Lucy Snowe never does decisively unlearn her proclivity for regarding the Francophone Catholics among whom she lives in Villette as uncivilized savages. On the contrary, growing understanding of them tends to confirm and activate British Protestant values that were perhaps underdeveloped or dormant in her when she lived in Britain: Lucy's narrative presents a strong variety of that truism about foreign travel that holds that "the more we become acquainted with the institutions of other countries, the more highly must we value our own."[5] In only one relationship to what ethnographically minded later readers would call the "culture" of Labassecour does she even approach the attitude that acknowledges there might *be* such a thing as a culture of Labassecour: in her doomed love for Paul Emmanuel, a devout half-Spanish Catholic she both admires and explicitly tells us she does *not* wish to convert to her Protestantism.

Most of the time what goes on in Labassecour strikes her as evidence, not of another culture than her own, but of a condition of anticulture that helps mark out the conceptual space for a possible British culture by opposing it in two distinct ways. On the one hand, the power-hungry Catholics, aggressively seeking to universalize their (to Lucy) absurd and deleterious creed and customs, call forth the self-universalizing response of British ethnocentrism, from the perspective of which the Catholics appear the antithesis of a globally applicable Civilization that is deemed equivalent to British custom. When Lucy's narrative oscillates in this direction, the Catholics seem to have no culture at all, only a set of hypocritical and harmful practices that will, Lucy hopes, be swept into oblivion on that glorious day when Protestants stop warring among themselves and join in a new kind of "Holy Alliance" based on "the Bible itself, rather than any sect, of whatever name or nation" (V 514). I will suggest below that this pole on the spectrum described by Lucy's narrative corresponds with the subplot focused on the charismatic Brit-

---

[5] Samuel Rogers, *Italy: A Poem* (London: Cadell & Moxon, 1830), 173.

ish hero, John Graham Bretton, whose trajectory from "faithless" youth to reformed young professional is aligned with Britain's imperial destiny to export capital-C Culture to the world at large (V 73). Remembering his "chivalric" behavior in guiding her through the gloomy streets of the foreign city that first night, Lucy reflects, "I believe I would have followed that frank tread, through continual night, to the world's end" (V 125).

To the extent that Lucy remains willing to be led by this fearless bearer of light through all the world's darkness, she will endorse a concept of Britishness *as* Civilization that underpins the nation's imperial project and, accordingly, represents even *Continental* differences from Britishness as evidence of an uncivilized or simply mistaken way of life.[6] When she operates in this mode, she reports on the foreigners' way of doing things almost solely for the purpose of denigrating or even mocking it, as, for example, when she writes that "[t]he Labassecouriens must have a large organ of philoprogenitiveness: at least the indulgence of offspring is carried by them to excessive lengths; the law of most households being the children's will" (V 166). Her consideration of Catholic beliefs and rites (such as the central rite of confession) is steadily, almost jingoistically ethnocentric: "Romanists" remain "strange beings" throughout her account (V 486); "the more I saw of Popery," she tells us late in the book, "the closer I clung to my Protestantism" (V 516); and she concludes, without the slightest qualification, that "God is not with Rome" (V 515). It is not as a fully ethnographic culture or "system of desire" different from her own that the way of life in Labassecour makes Lucy recoil and go on recoiling; that way of life signifies to her the pre-ethnographic anticulture of limitless or "catholic" desire, of desire and the hunger for power run amuck.[7] In that realm, everyone schemes and spies ceaselessly on everyone else, hoping to gain some decisive advantage; everyone has to be enmeshed in a plot and pressured to convert; the "Catholic," by definition, knows no bounds. In the final analysis the desires animating the proprietess of the Pensionnat, Mme. Beck, whose system of surveillance may be juxtaposed with Lucy's perspective as knowing retrospective narrator, do not differ materially from those driving the authorities of the Catholic Church in the Jesuitical machinations in which Paul Emmanuel, and Lucy through him, are embroiled.

Yet her immersion in the alien realm *also* stimulates Lucy to begin forming an ethnographic rather than ethnocentric conception of the identity, mentality, and place appropriate to *Britons*. "Lucy" contains the possibility of becoming a different *kind* of light than the civilizing beacon of the imperial project. The counterhegemonic possibility of a Victorian Briton's coming to regard Britishness as a *culture* rather than "how everyone ought to live" arises from the recognition that the Catholics bent on converting and manipulating Lucy evince, not a devilishly

---

[6] The picture-book Graham gives to Polly Home in the Bretton segment of the novel portends this imperial orientation and prominently features a "good, good Englishman" preaching to natives under a palm tree (V 88).

[7] Christopher Herbert, *Culture and Anomie: Ethnographic Imagination in the Nineteenth Century* (Chicago: University of Chicago Press, 1991), 51; henceforth Herbert.

effectual "license," but a self-defeating addiction to incompetent troublemaking. None of the Catholic threats to which Lucy is subjected even comes close to appearing as if it might come to fruition: Lucy really does seem to possess a special *license*—in Hobbes's sense of the term—to move among the aliens untouched.

As Christopher Herbert has demonstrated, one vital sign of the culture concept's advent in modern consciousness appears in the shift in representations of the Natural Man extolled by romantic political theorists and reviled by Calvinist theologians: whereas these imagined "unaccommodated man" as either potently pure or potently wicked, writers in the early decades of the nineteenth century began to show him the way he appeared in the notorious Wild Boy of Aveyron case (first reported on in 1801), as a figure whose subjection to constant, conflicting, undirected bouts of desire leaves him virtually incapable of meaningful or efficacious expressions of desire. The lesson of the Wild Boy case, Herbert says, "is that in order for desire to exist in any coherent, active, and potentially satisfiable form, it must embed itself in a fully social matrix, which is to say, become directed toward objects conventionally defined and symbolically coded by human society" (Herbert 50). As the counterproductive activities of Mme. Beck and the other Jesuitical authorities in *Villette* repeatedly attest, desire *not* so contained, desire that seeks to lay its hands upon just everything it can—"catholic" desire, in a word—negates itself. Mme. Beck does not succeed in discovering incriminating secrets about Lucy, in luring Lucy's friend John Bretton into her trap, in preventing a deep attachment from forming between Lucy and Paul; just so does a priest's plan to win Lucy for Rome resoundingly come a cropper. As in Dickens—think of the self-canceling violence of the demonic Quilp, in *The Old Curiosity Shop*—the evil that can be represented as altogether unfettered by culture tends to foil its own plots.

Indeed, in *Villette,* every attempt to control Lucy Snowe and Paul Emmanuel moves them closer to freedom from control: every attempt to make inroads on Lucy's Protestant self-government both proves and *improves* the inviolability of that defining core. As Brontë wrote to her publisher George Smith in the midst of the "Papal Aggression" uproar that immediately preceded the composition of *Villette:* "We are in no danger" (*Letters* 2. 522). But in its exhibition of what I have called pre-ethnographic anticulture, Labassecourian life appears to enlighten Lucy to the possibility of a Britishness that British people ought to adopt and live up to, not because it is what people everywhere should adopt and live up to, but because it is what defines and separates, limits and directs the energies of, Britons. In *Villette*'s enactment of the principle of *anywhere's nowhere*—a principle to which this supremely strange novel commits itself both inconsistently and strikingly— Britons have to *decatholicize* their view of themselves in order to reap the benefits of having "a culture of their own."[8]

---

[8] The decisive moment of decatholicization takes place when the spectral nun haunting Lucy throughout the middle of the novel as a distorted mirror of her cloistered self is revealed not to have been supernatural at all but, rather ridiculously, a disguise worn by Colonel de Hamal on his nocturnal visits to Ginevra Fanshawe. Overcoming one's temptation to believe the European Catholic Other in possession of supernatural powers is vital to the Briton's recovery of a nonimperialist British culture not *itself* buttressed by claims of supernatural authority to conquer and convert the world.

Much of the narrative tension in *Villette* can be described as a conflict between the two senses of "license" referred to in my epigraphs above: on the one hand, the negative license of unrestraint that Brontë associated in 1848 with the French and the Irish, with Catholicism's global aggression, and, in *Villette,* with characters like Mme. Beck and Ginevra Fanshawe; on the other, the license of diplomatic immunity Hobbes refers to in *Leviathan,* which shields the emissary from the laws of the foreign country in which he resides. Diplomatic immunity or extraterritoriality involves the legal fiction that certain sites within a foreign land—an embassy's grounds, an ambassador's vehicle—are not actually "in" that land at all, but are part of, and under the governance of, the land from which the ambassador has come. *Villette* explores the *cultural* fiction that the person of its narrator and protagonist might be read as such a site. In order to obtain the Hobbesian license, it suggests, Britons would have to restrict or at least to counteract their own tendencies toward license of the other variety, tendencies that manifested themselves not simply in Chartism or other protorevolutionary causes, but also in the self-universalizing mentality of the successful and expanding empire.

But *Villette* also suggests that Britons could so restrict themselves only to the extent that Catholics restricted *their* longing for self-universalization. A staunch Anglican writing in the wake of the Oxford Movement's implosion and of Cardinal Wiseman's arrival in Britain could hardly be expected to think most Catholics ready to do this. Brontë does, however, create in Paul Emmanuel one honorable Catholic who, by the end of the novel, appears prepared to redefine his faith as the phenomenon of a certain distinct and limited culture, rather than seeking always to impose it everywhere. Before going off to his ambiguous end (shipwrecked, we assume), he unambiguously relinquishes the desire to bring Lucy within the ever-spreading Popish plot, writing affectionately to her, "Remain a Protestant. My little English Puritan, I love Protestantism in you" (V 594–95). Nineteenth-century British fiction can offer few more remarkable passages.

Brontë is able to position her unlikely hero this way because in the midst of that pre-ethnographic variety of anticulture that Labassecourian life never really ceases to embody for Lucy, there begins to emerge as well a *protoethnographic* variety, a negative and deleterious version of the organizational ideal attributed to so-called genuine cultures, whose "every leaf and twig is fed by the sap at the core." As she begins to discern the possibility that seemingly random bits of behavior among the Catholics may in fact form parts of a coherent scheme, Lucy comes to entertain the vision of a sinister total system in which nothing can be left unexamined for its anticultural import. "These Romanists are strange beings," Lucy comes to perceive:

> Such a one among them—whom you know no more than the last Inca of Peru, or the first Emperor of China—knows you and all your concerns; and has his reasons for saying to you so and so, when you simply thought the communication sprang impromptu from the instant's impulse: his plan in bringing it about that you shall come on such a day, to such a place, under such and such circumstances, when the whole arrangement seems to your crude apprehension the ordinance of chance, or the sequel of exigency. Madame Beck's

suddenly recollected message and present, by artless embassy to the Place of the Magi, the old priest, accidentally descending the steps and crossing the square, his interposition on my behalf with the bonne who would have sent me away, his reappearance on the staircase, my introduction to this room, the portrait, the narrative so affably volunteered—all these little incidents, taken as they fell out, seemed each independent of its successor; a handful of loose beads; but threaded through by that quick-shot and crafty glance of a Jesuit-eye, they dropped pendant in a long string, like that rosary on the prie-dieu. (V 486)

With the dawning of *this* variety of anticulture comes the recognition of Paul Emmanuel as a figure just as much crushed and stunted by the system he is doomed to serve as the figures in later ethnographic texts are (or so the texts say) nurtured and directed by the genuine cultures whose members they are fortunate enough to be. Remarkably, the transformation of the forbidding professor into the sympathetic fellow-sufferer capable of telling Lucy to remain a Protestant is underscored by an apparent alteration of his race: "the very complexion seemed clearer and fresher; that swart, sallow, southern darkness which spoke his Spanish blood, became displaced by a lighter hue" (V 407). The lightening of the Spanish in Paul corresponds with his growth away from *inquisitorial* Catholicism toward a utopian proto-"relativist" variety. To the extent that Brontë succeeds in working this de-hispanicizing magic upon Paul, in characterizing him as the victim of Catholic plotting rather than its agent, in making his Catholicism appear a godly, Christian resistance to the forces of either priestly hypocrisy or freethinking atheism,[9] and in getting him to issue his unilateral declaration of cultural relativism, to just that extent (and no farther) is it even possible to think of Catholicism and Anglicanism as cultures in the modern ethnographic sense and as accepting confinement to their own proper spheres.[10]

Another productive difficulty for any straightforward ethnographic reading of *Villette* arises from the fact that, in its opening chapters, the text seems no less determined to highlight the disorienting and estranging effects of *British* settings than it is in highlighting these same features in its later representations of Labassecour and Villette. Here Brontë significantly alters the pattern found in Scott, in the Irish National Tale and, indeed, in much gothic fiction. As in these works, an alien territory and the narrative's story-space, while not exactly coextensive, are closely aligned with each other, so that, for the bulk of the novel, the foreign land simply *is* the domain where the characters interact. Beginning with a few chapters set in

[9] Cf. Paul's contrast to the educated but unbelieving and amoral Boissec and Rochemorte (drywood and deadrock) who stalked Lucy in the streets of Villette on the night of her arrival and later turn up as colleagues of Paul's to witness Lucy's examination.

[10] In the hallucinatory "Cloud" chapter (chap. 38), Lucy appears to attain a comprehensive vision of the Labassecourian anticulture when she slips through a gap in the fence at the city park and sees virtually every important character from the Labassecourian portion of the narrative arrayed in significant groupings. The vision culminates with a tableau of the chief Catholic schemers who have tried to entrap her: "There, then, were Madame Walravens, Madame Beck, Père Silas—the whole conjuration, the secret junta. The sight of them thus assembled," she writes, "did me good" (V 558).

England—as Scott does in *Waverley,* for instance—enables Brontë to narrate the experience of crossing the epistemological border between familiar and alien realms, to register the impact of arrival among strangers. But where Scott heightens the effect of difference, Brontë blurs it, situating the unfamiliar in the spaces of the local and national home and then transporting significant features of home to the alien realm. Lucy's first view of the *British* capital, where she stops on her way to the Continent, discloses, as she says, "a Babylon and a wilderness of which the vastness and strangeness tried to the utmost my powers of clear thought and steady self-possession" (V 106). The "strange speech of the cabmen and others waiting round" seems to her as "odd as a foreign tongue"; she has "never before heard the English language chopped up in that way" (V 106). As in Villette, later, she finds herself "unfurnished with either experience or advice to tell me how to act, and yet—to act obliged" (V 106). And the purpose of all this emphasis on the alienating feel of London is not to set the metropolis in opposition to more hospitable country scenes; on the contrary, it comes at the end of a process in which the possibility of Lucy's finding *any* home within British territory is systematically eliminated. I will discuss that process in some detail a little later. For now, the point not to be missed is that Lucy is driven to the nation's capital and then beyond the boundaries of the nation because nowhere in the Britain that actually exists for her is there a place for the Britishness whose unconventional, unvalued, and virtually *invisible* embodiment she is. In the narrative that follows, the social invisibility of the "extraneous" woman is figuratively linked to: 1) the invisible authority of the fictional narrator, secure in her discourse-space from the entanglements of characters; 2) the invisibility of *culture* itself, as the "placeless" (abstract, nonempirical) totality among seemingly disparate objects; and 3) the vital worth of the invisible export, which, like Brontë's novel, does not actually *leave* the country but nevertheless brings it riches from "outside."

Tensely unstable on the question of whether British Protestantism can be thought a culture among many, *Villette* pushes the *outsideness* phase of the autoethnographic process as far as it can, not by its handling of the possibility that Lucy might convert to Catholicism (it rapidly closes off that possibility) but by refusing the easy resolution of marrying Lucy to a charismatic British hero (John Graham Bretton) and instead pointing its narrative logic directly toward the unrealizable vision of uniting Lucy with Paul Emmanuel. The marriages in *Jane Eyre* (involving the reclamation of an Englishman) and *Shirley* (involving Englishwomen's fulfillment through union with half-foreigners living in England) give way here to the far more radical image of a marriage that does not occur but that we are compelled to confront as the British heroine's one chance at happiness, even though it would have yoked Lucy to a Labassecourian Papist with no thought of becoming Protestant or living in Britain.[11] To complain about the suddenness and ambiguity of the ending, in which we *think* we are justified in believing Paul lost at sea, would be churlish, when the novel has exhibited such resolve in pursuing to its very limit or

---

[11] I do not mean to suggest that Lucy's *only* source of fulfillment is lost with Paul's apparent drowning; she has broken free of Mme. Beck and set up on her own as the director of a successful *pensionnat.*

even beyond it the idea that Britons must come to know themselves as displaced persons.

While the proposition that modern Britishness or Englishness was to an important degree forged outside of Britain, that it constitutes an "offshore" phenomenon rather than an autochthonous one, has gained wide assent among readers influenced by postcolonialist perspectives, it has tended to remain confined—if at times uncomfortably confined—within the oppositional scheme in which the *only relevant elsewhere* for the making of modern European identities *must* be "the colonized space [that] was instrumental in the invention of Europe."[12] Linda Colley, in *Britons* (1992), perhaps overemphasized British self-definition by opposition to France, leaving "the Empire . . . strangely peripheral" to the argument;[13] postcolonialists have done precisely the reverse, replacing the catalyzing *European* Other with the far-flung spaces of an actually or prospectively imperial domain. But it is not as though, come 1815, Britons simply stopped having to think about the Continent of Europe and started fabricating their sense of their collective self solely in relation to the colonial domain, nor is it the case that every bit of land outside Europe was easily categorizable by them as "colonial" or "awaiting colonization."[14] In this context, Brontë's *Villette* valuably differs from Austen's *Mansfield Park* as Edward Said influentially read it a decade ago in *Culture and Imperialism*. It is not simply that in Brontë's novel a fictionalized version of Belgium functions as the offshore site for making or remaking British identities, but that the procedures of British national identity-formation get embroiled in an imperial project that is *not* Britain's.

Toward the end of the novel, the decisive step in the development of Lucy's admiration for Paul Emmanuel comes when she discovers how self-sacrificingly he has committed himself to support the family of his dead fiancée, a family that rejected his suit and placed its daughter, Justine Marie, in a convent to wither and die when Paul's own family lost its fortune. The rejecting family went on to lose *its* fortune, too, but Paul stepped in nobly to ensure its maintenance at the cost of

---

[12] Simon Gikandi, *Maps of Englishness: Writing Identity in the Culture of Colonialism* (New York: Columbia University Press, 1996), 6. In Edward Said's well-known reading of *Mansfield Park,* in 1993's *Culture and Imperialism,* the proverbial narrowness of the Austen world rested upon foundations half a world away, though invisible both to those within it and to those readers who looked no farther than the boundaries of the text. (But cf. Franco Moretti, *Atlas of the European Novel* [London: Verso, 1998], 24–29 for questioning of Said's assumptions.) For many critics working after Said, Salman Rushdie's quip from *The Satanic Verses,* placed in the mouth of a stuttering character, that "[t]he trouble with the Engenglish is that their hiss hiss history happened overseas, so they dodo don't know what it means" has acquired status of a truism: cf. Ian Baucom, *Out of Place: Englishness, Empire, and the Locations of Identity* (Princeton: Princeton University Press, 1999), 4.

[13] Theodore Koditschek, "The Making of British Nationality," *Victorian Studies* 44/3 (Spring 2002), 394.

[14] Recent and ongoing work re-examining either intra-European relations or European involvement in extra-European but noncolonial spaces promises to help break down the persistent and disabling binarism of "the West and the Rest." As an example of the first, cf. Margaret Cohen and Carolyn Dever, eds., *The Literary Channel: The Inter-National Invention of the Novel* (Princeton: Princeton University Press, 2002).

impoverishing himself. That fortune, devoured in "some financial transactions which entailed exposure and ruinous fines" (V 485), can be redeemed, apparently, only by Paul's going off to "Basseterre, in Guadaloupe [sic]" to oversee the reorganization of the Walravens' estate there and render it profitable once more (V 559). Attempting to return to Lucy after three years' toil, Paul is, or so we infer from the novel's unforthcoming ending, drowned in the violent storms that wrack the Atlantic. Brontë's novel *triangulates* the single European nation's relationship to empire, making us see the British heroine's prospects for self-realization as mediated by the Labassecourian hero's entanglement in *his* nation's colonies. Instead of a situation in which one nation and its empire, or one "West" and all "colonial space," are oriented solely toward each other, *Villette* emphasizes each imperial nation's implication in what other imperial nations are up to. The British woman's "fall" into the low country—*là bas*—of Labassecour, that fortunate fall that is the route to recovered Britishness, turns out to involve still *another* fall, into a state of entanglement in the condition of the low country's *lower* country, Basse-terre. This situation of separate European identities dependent not only upon each other for definition-by-opposition (as in Colley), and not only upon each one's exclusive relationship with its "dependencies" (as in postcolonialism), but also upon *each other's* dependencies, represents something like the pre-emptive transfer to the international plane of the web or network metaphor later used by the developers of the ethnographic culture idea to characterize the organization of elements *within* an individual culture. In the vision of global ecology vouchsafed by *Villette,* the single nation's identity and way of life may appear elements in a worldwide system in which each element must endure the condition of "waiting upon" (deferring to) the others, as Lucy waits for Paul's return at the novel's end. In this vision, even the world's most powerful nation can come to know itself and fulfill its destiny only through acceptance of the "intersubjective" nature of international relations, in which it functions the way each element of a *single* culture has been supposed to function, namely as "in some sense a corollary of, consubstantial with, implied by, immanent in, all the others" (Herbert 5).

I believe that, for some leading English writers of the 1840s and 1850s, merely to glimpse this vision was to trigger the reaction against it that is implied in the slogan *anywhere's nowhere.* Ian Baucom has argued that, from the high imperial era to the era of decolonization, "Englishness has [both] been identified *with* Britishness, which in its turn has been identified as coterminous with and proceeding from the sovereign territory of the empire, and . . . defined itself *against* the British Empire," and that the primary nineteenth-century method for accomplishing the latter involved "retaining a spatial theory of collective identity but privileging the *English* soil of the "sceptered isle" or, more regularly, certain quintessentially English locales, as its authentic identity-determining locations."[15] For the half-Irish and nonmetropolitan Brontë however, even as Englishness moves to demarcate itself and its territory from the vertiginous expanses of British and other empires, it still needs to demonstrate the elasticity shown by *Britishness* in

---

[15] Baucom, *Out of Place,* 12.

that category's (supposed) inclusion of the Celtic. *Villette*'s two narratives—focused on Lucy and on John Graham Bretton, respectively—permit Brontë to work through and work *past* the allegories of nation making laid down in the early nineteenth-century National Tale and in Scott's historical fictions. The Bretton narrative rehearses the familiar pattern of inventing modern Britishness out of the raw material of a "faithless" Celt and faces "outward," toward empire and the corresponding notion of Britishness as exportable, universalizable Culture with a capital C. It is also outward-looking in the sense of being focused on two tranquilly nonintrospective characters, the Adam and Eve of a new world order, whose innocent lack of interiority could not be more unlike the character of Lucy Snowe.

Lucy's story, in contrast, attempts the more difficult and possibly impossible task of honoring these two and their vocation while seeking at the same time to construct a sense of Britishness that belongs at home, one that learns in another nation how to begin thinking of itself as a territorially limited, small-c culture among others. If the Bretton story held sway, or if Brontë had permitted Lucy to marry her Bretton hero, this latter, bounded identity could not even have begun to develop. By displacing and interrupting it, by reversing the customary gender positions employed in Scott's national-allegorical romances and in the National Tale,[16] and by pushing her story's search for emotional fulfillment beyond the stereotypically passionate Celt to a figure of seemingly unaccommodatable difference, Lucy strives toward an alternative British identity at once more definite and restrictive than the abstract imperial model and, paradoxically, more flexible and open to (some kinds of) difference.[17] The attempt ultimately fails, but not at demonstrating a mid-Victorian drive to imagine Britain as a relocatable culture.

II

Even when her imagination burrows deep in the soil for images of a rooted cultural identity, as it does in the Nunnwood section of *Shirley,* Brontë is liable to complicate her own quest by introducing discordant elements that point to nomadic or mobile forms of social life rather than grounded ones. As a ground zero of vertical identification, Nunnwood may be the resting-place of age-old (though nearly forgotten) female energies capable of reforming English culture, but it is also, Caroline Helstone says, "like an encampment of forest sons of Anak" and "one of Robin Hood's haunts."[18] These references to Old Testament and to English legend run contrary to the more commonly noted aspects of the Nunnwood scene, evoking varieties of men's migratory groups, for whom the site provides a

---

[16] Marriage between Protestant and Catholic was felt admissible when Protestantism appeared in the male role, as in Owensen's *The Wild Irish Girl* or Scott's *Rob Roy.*

[17] I differ here from Cannon Schmitt, who argues in *Alien Nation: Nineteenth-Century Gothic Fictions and English Nationality* (Philadelphia: University of Pennsylvania Press, 1997), that the strand of Bildungsroman in *Villette* "detach[es] an individual woman's fate from the fate of the nation" (17).

[18] *Shirley* (1849; Harmondsworth: Penguin, 1974), 220; henceforth S.

temporary encampment or occasional haunt, to complement that spiritual sorority that rests on lasting foundations deep down in the hollow cup of the dell.[19] No *single* history lies awaiting recovery and reactivation in the forest of Nunnwood.

If this scene consecrates the "planting" of the newly returned Shirley Keeldar in her local community, it also reminds us of the value of *not* being fixed in one spot, a form of relationship to the location of culture that Brontë does not always restrict to men, though in *Shirley* she ultimately does. It is Robert Moore's *departure* from the region and his travels throughout England in the latter part of the novel that illustrate to him the necessity of attending to concerns "beyond a man's personal interest; beyond the advancement of well-laid schemes; beyond even the discharge of dishonouring debts" (S 506). "While I was at Birmingham," he tells Yorke,

> I looked a little into reality, considered closely, and at their source, the causes of the present troubles of this country; I did the same in London. Unknown, I could go where I pleased, mix with whom I would. I went where there was want of food, of fuel, of clothing; where there was no occupation and no hope. I saw some, with naturally elevated tendencies and good feelings, kept down amongst sordid privations and harassing griefs. I saw many originally low, and to whom lack of education left scarcely anything but animal wants, disappointed in those wants. . . . I saw what taught my brain a new lesson, and filled my breast with fresh feelings. (S 506)

Here is the breadth of experience, the empirical evidence gathered from a wider than local field ("I saw . . . I saw"), to pair with Caroline's matchless mastery of the local *lieu de memoire* ("I know . . . I know") in remaking the national-local culture. Importantly, Robert's itinerary comprehends the nation's capital as well as other areas that possess the status (as Yorkshire does) of localities or regions in relation *to* that capital. Between them, the reformed Robert and Caroline approximate the double strength laid claim to by Brontë's autoethnographic narrator.

Not in its attachment to historically resonant sites alone, then, but also in its distinctive forms of motion or movability, is national culture to be looked for. This is the suggestion that arises from the presentation, in *Shirley,* of the Jew basket as the identifying feature of an English anticulture too much devoted to horizontal affiliations: the Jew basket and its contents are "meubles," transportable commodities rather than real estate, whose handling both defines a limited, horizontal stratum within England and diagnoses what is wrong with the English culture in which such a limited stratum might succeed in isolating and flattering itself as this one has done. Not by its memory-sites alone but also by what Dickens would famously

---

[19] It adds another layer of complexity to *Shirley*'s critique of a "judaicized" English people to note that the Anakim (cf. Num 13:33 and Deut. 9:2) were those primordial giants of Canaan whom the chosen people had to wipe out in order to take possession of their land. In creating an image of rooted, indigenous culture, Brontë simultaneously recalls an image that *discounts* the claims of indigenousness and represents prior inhabitants as merely "encamped" on the land until their appointed successors arrive.

call in *Great Expectations* its "portable property" can one know the national culture and seek to reform it.[20]

In *Villette,* the power of *meubles* to evoke a national culture becomes all the more important because, after two narratives of internal exile, Brontë returns in her last novel to *departure,* to the necessity of, and the powers of, displacement from Britain in the effort to relocate a vital national identity. As in *The Professor,* British *meubles* become the "household gods" of a people uprooted from Britain and obliged, like Aeneas's Trojan refugees, to carry the fetishes of their collective identity on their wanderings (V 240). When the trappings of a British household appear, transplanted to the Continent, at the beginning of *Villette*'s second volume, their uncanny effect (described below) signals their participation in the auto-ethnographic process by which erstwhile mere insiders might obtain the extraterritorial authority of insider's outsideness. John Graham Bretton is the anglicized Celt of British national fantasy, bearer of that self-universalizing sense of imperial identity from which a relocatable British culture must diverge, as Lucy's history does from Bretton's in *Villette.* Bretton's ultimate marriage to Polly Home carries with it all the allegorical suggestiveness of the unions that culminate romantic-era National Tales and historical novels: settlement of internal United Kingdom conflict ushers in an era in which "Home" for the consummated Briton might now be anywhere at all, since modern Britishness means nothing less than (and nothing more than) universally applicable Civilization itself. As in Virgil's *Aeneid,* the lares and penates containing the essence of a lost locality are transformed into symbols of the definitively portable authority befitting an expansive empire putatively unlimited in space or time. It is against the massive authority of the British epic of John Graham Bretton—or John Great Britain—that Lucy Snowe struggles to get her story told in Brontë's outlandish last novel. Herself a definitively British meuble, Lucy seeks an autoethnographically productive style of detachment, one that, in turn, might lead to a new and autoethnographically conscious Britishness.[21]

Villette's opening recalls *Jane Eyre* in its allegory of epochal change: we begin in the waning days of an era in which it was still possible (though even then delusory) to imagine Britain as a place of rooted identities, a homogeneous homeland, notwithstanding the long history of mixture Defoe had satirically celebrated in "The True-Born Englishman." We first encounter Lucy Snowe in "the clean and ancient town of Bretton," where she is staying with her godmother, whose "husband's family had been residents there for generations, and bore, indeed, the name

---

[20] Dickens, *Great Expectations* (1860; Harmondsworth: Penguin, 1996), 201. John Plotz's ongoing work has stimulated my thinking here.

[21] Cf. Amanda Anderson on *Villette* in *The Powers of Distance: Cosmopolitanism and the Cultivation of Detachment* (Princeton: Princeton University Press, 2001), 34–62. My argument below about the rhetorical function of "depthless cosmopolitanism" in Ginevra Fanshawe should not be taken as saying Brontë repudiates cosmopolitanism as such, only that she seeks a variety that preserves and perfects Britishness rather than evaporating it.

of their birthplace—Bretton of Bretton" (V 61). This tidy formulation suggests an autochthonous identity and a series of almost comically circular questions-and-answers reinforcing a certain people's claim on a certain piece of land ("Who lives in Bretton? The Brettons." "Where are the Brettons from? Bretton."). As Lucy the narrator is quick to indicate, it is not positively known whether this authorizing redundancy of place name and family name came about "by coincidence, or because some remote ancestor had been a personage of sufficient importance to leave his name to his neighbourhood" (V 61), and the same undecidability surrounds the allegorical inferences we seem invited to derive from the name. Once again it seems to become important how we "hear" a name in a Brontë text, a possibility that challenges the hegemony of silent reading and the wholly abstract national community instantiated by that practice. Does "Bretton" refer to "Britain," the multicultural island-nation, or perhaps to "Breton," a cultural formation at once prenational and transnational? Might "Bretton" signal a coming narrative of nation making, or one of nation losing? Thought to have descended from Britons pushed out of Britain by Teutonic invaders in the middle of the fifth century, does the Continental Celtic culture of Breton, ultimately reduced to the status of a "region" of sovereign France, furnish a cautionary example for the British expatriates we will read about in *Villette,* suggesting that they, too, risk losing their way home again and being swallowed up in a Francophone nation of Europe? Would invoking Breton in this context amount to the paradox that a modern searcher of the aboriginal Britons (those unmixed with Germanic stock) would have to look in France? Or might Breton be thought of as a kind of bridge between the "British" and the "French," a mediating position open to selected influences from both? These and other questions, which seem to circulate around "Bretton," and which seem to *begin* circulating from the very first page of the novel, drive the entire narrative of *Villette.*

Readings of this novel that emphasize its adaptation of gothic conventions have provided very valuable insights, but they are apt to impose upon it the genre's tendency to imply that the heroines whose British virtue is threatened while traveling among scheming Catholics abroad have, all the while, a safe and proper home in Britain. Lucy Snowe and the Brettons, however, are the legatees of that alarming shrinking-island effect Jane Austen produced in *Northanger Abbey,* in which Catherine Morland consigns the Continent and even "the northern and western extremities" of Britain to the powers of the gothic but fervently wishes to believe "the central part of England" demarcatable and defensible against those powers.[22] As Claudia Johnson has demonstrated, Catherine's territorial concessions do not go far enough. Even where the heart of enlightened England is concerned—even in that sphere of which Henry Tilney so pompously says, "Remember that we are English, that we are Christians"—Austen "does not refute, but rather clarifies and reclaims, gothic conventions:"[23] what Lucy Snowe refers to in *Villette* as the "flat,

[22] Austen, *Northanger Abbey* (1817; Oxford: Oxford University Press, 1990), 161.

[23] Claudia L. Johnson, *Jane Austen: Women, Politics, and the Novel* (Chicago: University of Chicago Press, 1988), 34. The next quotation is also from this page.

rich middle of England" (V 104) turns out to be no less hospitable to the disorienting effects of gothic than are the Alps, the Pyrenees, and the British Celtic fringe of Catherine Morland's imagination. And if the gothic, or more generally speaking, the romance turns out to be just as much at home in modern, civilized England as on the Catholic Continent—if it starts to appear the uncanny truth, "the inside out of the ordinary" English reality—then the nation-defining oppositions subscribed to by gothic writers break down.

Villette's beginning presents the unraveling of the calm and stable British modernity that Henry Tilney would like us to believe in and that Walter Scott tried to narrate into existence at the conclusion of *Waverley*. The novel raises the possibility of a tranquil, indisputable cultural authority only to lay waste to it swiftly and remorselessly, as part of a narrative-initiating campaign that transforms the flat, rich middle of England into something like the Waste Land of quest romance and turns the capital of the national homeland into a foreign city. Before all this commences, the Brettons of Bretton, whether they actually descend from an eponymous founder or not, have long been accorded the status of those who do, and life among these principal inhabitants of the town goes on in "large peaceful rooms" with "well-arranged furniture," looking out of "clear wide windows" upon a "fine antique street, where Sundays and holidays seemed always to abide" (V 61). To live one's life as a Bretton of Bretton, and even to be under the protection of such, is to know the epistemological ease that comes with being sure who one is and where one belongs. During her regular visits, Lucy recalls, "[t]ime always flowed smoothly . . . ; not with tumultuous swiftness, but blandly, like the gliding of a full river through a plain," and she goes on to compare her sojourns at Bretton with that "of [Bunyan's] Christian and Hopeful beside a certain pleasant stream, with 'green trees on each bank, and meadows beautified with lilies all the year round'" (V 62). Scott's smoothly flowing British river of mingled ethnic streams, from the end of *Waverley,* seems to reappear here at the outset of a novel very quickly to reintroduce into the tale of British nation making all the turbulence Scott wished to leave safely behind. To read *Villette* means not only to exchange the non-narratable stasis of a Bretton that appears *both* prelapsarian and posthistorical for a narrative that (as Tony Tanner puts it) "moves by fits and starts," a pattern of exaggerated self-interruption consisting very largely of "outbursts of emotion followed by the willful negation of feeling" (see V 32); it also means confronting the re-emergence of troublesome ethnic rivulets in Scott's placid national stream.

The trouble starts with the appearance in Bretton of the daughter of a man oddly enough named Home who turns out to be "of mixed French and Scottish origin" (V 63) and who, finding England "wholly distasteful to him" decamps to the Continent, leaving his child a homeless dependent among the Brettons. Into the supremely settled domicile of the Brettons, in other words, comes this figure suffering and representing the break-up of the family Home. To make matters worse, Lucy recalls the son and heir of the Bretton family, who at that point in his life was called by his middle name, the Scottish "Graham," as "a handsome, faithless-looking youth of sixteen," *faithless-looking* "because the epithet strikes [her] as proper to describe the fair, Celtic (not Saxon) character of his good looks" (V 73). As in *Jane Eyre,* the novel opens in a domestic setting lacking its paterfamilias; we are invited to wonder whether the survival of Mr. Bretton might have kept Graham from becoming quite so faithless or, for that matter, quite so unchecked in his Celticism. Too unqualified a Celt, not acculturated to be *other than one thing,* the young Graham will later prove susceptible to turning "French" and "Catholic" in the conduct of his Continental love affairs: he has to be rescued from his own willingness to immerse himself in the Jesuitical anticulture of scheming and spying and secrecy that defines and permeates the foreign domain. Transplanted abroad after the evaporation of the Bretton fortune, he learns to play the game of Labassecourian intrigue so adeptly that he risks losing himself in it.

If it is the scene of his temptation, the domain of French-speaking Catholics will also be the scene of his redemption, his capacity for which is signaled by his acting at critical moments in the novel as a "true young English gentleman" (V 125) and a "cool young Briton" (V 341), and by his exhibiting a "genuine English blush" even while speaking in a discernibly "Highland tongue" (V 529–30). His trajectory suggests that Britons or Brettons must learn how to embody *both* local and national identities, though as usual in Brontë the plurality they *must* demonstrate is set against varieties of mixture or multiplicity they must *not:* varieties that threaten the national integrity or evacuate the national center. Rather like Mr. Yorke in *Shirley,* who seemed both local and cosmopolitan without "passing through" the mediating position of nationality, the Homes in *Villette* are professedly "Caledonian and Gallic" (V 364).[24] Their regionality needs to be routed through English nationality rather than being permitted to bypass the center and enter into unilateral relations with the foreign. Caledonians abroad, in other words, have to conduct themselves as ambassadors of "England"—which does not imply that they have to suppress their signs of Scottishness, only that they have to cultivate a Britishness capable of keeping the former in check.

Polly Home, who has gone to live abroad with her father and whose name has rather incredibly changed to Paulina de Bassompierre by the time we meet her again, can come home to the Britishness she has never really acknowledged as hers only when she marries the reformed, and also renamed, John Graham Bretton. But this can be realized only if *he* turns his affections Home-ward from the faithless turncoat Ginevra Fanshawe, Polly's "Saxon cousin" (V 398), who manifests not the least compunction in divesting herself of all of the putative Saxon strengths, becoming in behavior more French than the "French," and finally running away with the Frenchest of them all, the *roué* Colonel de Hamal. *Villette*'s subplot about the evolution of the faithless Graham is an interrupted epic bildungsroman that proceeds through stages of estrangement during which the figure becomes unrecognizable to us under other names, finally enacting a return-with-a-difference to yield a man actively both Celtic and English: again, John Great Britain. He finds the Polly who long ago adored him at home under the cumbersome mantle of the

---

[24] Ginevra says Mr. Home "is English enough, goodness knows" (V 351); but what is English enough for Ginevra is plainly not English enough to satisfy Brontë.

Villette society heiress, and the two of these "Nature's elect" depart the narrative trailing clouds of glory (V 532). Lucy never specifies whether they remained in Labassecour, returned to Britain, or set off for "the world's end" (V 125); but when she pays tribute to their union with the words "God saw that it was good" (V 533), she suggests—and appropriately enough, where the world's leading empire is concerned—that nothing less than the recreation of the globe is at stake in the redemption of Celt as Briton.

For the Celtic Bretton, displacement from Britain carries with it the risk of irrevocable conversion to Frenchness, but it also affords the opportunity to become "English," even while retaining every Celtic feature. To the end, John remains a man of whom it may be said, as M. de Bassompierre says of him, "there is a trace of the Celt in all you look, speak, and think" (V 529–30). Polly's father says this in petulance, for he is reluctant to part with his daughter, but the novel ultimately patches up the difficulties between them, which it handles as a decidedly provincial matter pitting Scot against Scot—a conflict familiar enough from the prehistory of modern Britain. The resolution of this conflict proves easy, for both of these men have learned how to act and identify themselves as *English* during their time on the Continent. When they meet by chance after helping evacuate a burning theater (keeping their calm among the panicking foreigners, of course), they hail each other thus:

> "You are an Englishman!" said [Home-de-Bassompierre], turning shortly on Dr Bretton, when we got into the street.
> "An Englishman. And I speak to a countryman?" was the reply.
> "Right." (V 344)[25]

It turns out that Mr. Home has taken the name of his maternal relations, de Bassompierre, as a stipulation of inheriting a vast French fortune; but though the walls of his lavish Villette apartment "gleam[] with foreign mirrors," his "hearth glow[s] with an English fire" (V 345), and he thanks Bretton for his assistance "with as much earnestness as was befitting an Englishman addressing one who has served him" (V 347). Only on foreign soil, it seems, has his heart come to glow with English fire as well as his hearth. He is more than happy to join in Bretton's invitation to "toast Old England" with a "Christmas wassail-cup," and he seconds the sentiment by quoting Burns's "Auld Lang Syne" to Mrs. Bretton (V 363). These and other signs that he is now willing to put his Scottishness in the service of Englishness are part of what make his resistance to John and Polly's marriage feel so perfunctory. Just as soon as this conventional narrative obstacle of parental disapprobation has been cleared, we see Polly "plaiting together the gray lock" of her father's hair "and the golden wave" of her future husband's, using "a tress of her own" to bind them (V 531).

What interrupts and subordinates the epic Bildungsroman or British *Aeneid* of

---

[25] In the rush to exit the theater, Polly Home's shoulder is injured, bodying forth the theme of necessary displacement as both dangerous and promising to the renewal of British identity. "'Dislocation, perhaps!' mutter[s] the Doctor: 'let us hope there is no worse injury done'" (V 344).

John Graham Bretton is, of course, the main plot focused on *Villette*'s narrator, Lucy Snowe. His story of overcoming the unqualified Celt's temptation to go native among the "French" (perhaps evoking the expatriated Stuarts) is disrupted and displaced by hers, a story of struggle with the rather opposite temptation to *withhold* the self from compromising emotional investment—that hankering to retreat into the stony temple of interiority, to make oneself invisible, to crush one's desire and emulate the detachment of a fictional narrator, to withdraw from the story-space of one's own life story. These related tendencies in Lucy, all different ways of describing that seemingly perverse cold reticence that has fascinated and frustrated generations of readers,[26] become legible by the contrasting light of the John Graham Bretton subplot as symptoms of a Saxonism that, if not in sole possession of the field, is too despotic in its rule of passions that are coded Celtic-French and therefore lastingly suspect to post-Napoleonic Britons. Lucy, like the United Kingdom, seeks an equilibrium between these elements in herself, carrying the combination outside of Britain and the existing version of Britishness in order to find a modus vivendi and hospitable habitation in which the Celtic might not be crushed under the Saxon yoke—a challenge precisely reversing the terms of that "Norman Yoke" myth which Scott's *Ivanhoe* did so much to promulgate among British readers.[27] Along the way, some old battles from the history of British state-formation must be refought, and not only "the old quarrel of France and England" that Paul Emmanuel refers to in his first tussle of wills with Lucy (V 209). At one moment of heightened opposition between their characters, Lucy gives Ginevra Fanshawe a dressing-down that "might challenge comparison with the compliments of a John Knox to a Mary Stuart" (V 408)—and we are instantly in Scott country, invited to read this women's conflict as recapitulating some of the strife from the prehistory of modern multicultural Britain.[28] Ginevra embodies the license that comes of entirely casting off the restraining Saxonism of the British character, Lucy the punitive self-denial that comes of too strict a devotion to it. It would be a mistake to insist that *Villette* pursues an entirely consistent allegory of ethnicity and nationality, but it would be no more correct to neglect the self-interrupting, often paradoxical allegory that it does pursue.

---

[26] Pertinent here is Kamala Visweswaran's caution, in *Fictions of Feminist Ethnography* (Minneapolis: University of Minnesota Press, 1994), that "[a] feminist ethnography cannot assume the willingness of women to talk. . . . [It needs] to theorize a kind of agency in which resistance can be framed by silence, a refusal to talk" (51). Cf. D. A. Miller, *The Novel and the Police* (Berkeley: University of California Press, 1988), on dramatized reticence as "a mode whose ultimate meaning lies in the subject's formal insistence that he is radically inaccessible to the culture that would otherwise entirely determine him" (195).

[27] Cf. Clare A. Simmons, *Reversing the Conquest: History and Myth in 19th-Century British Literature* (New Brunswick, N.J.: Rutgers University Press, 1990).

[28] The Lucy/Ginevra opposition has parallels in the Mr. Home/Graham Bretton one. Home, evidently a Lowland or "Saxon" Scot, resembles Lucy in striking ways and may even function as her avatar in the subplot, expressing some of the disdain that mixes with her approval of the John-and-Paulina pairing. Home is Knox-like, "a stern-featured . . . man. . . . The character of his face was quite Scotch; but there was feeling in his eye, and emotion in his now agitated countenance. His northern accent in speaking harmonized with his physiognomy" (V 71).

In this context, Lucy Snowe's much-interpreted name certainly seems pertinent to the cool reserve ascribed to the Saxon temperament: the way she writes casts a cold light upon her former desires and entanglements, discouraging readers from involving themselves emotionally in her tale, much as, when a character in that tale, she serially suppressed her own longings for involvement and stimulation. In a justly famous passage, Lucy revels in the violence of a thunderstorm that makes all the Catholics in Mme. Beck's school "[rise] in panic and pray[] to their saints": she writes of her yearning, Jane-Eyre-like, "for something to fetch me out of my present existence, and lead me upwards and onwards," but then likens that yearning to the enemy Sisera in the book of Judges, whose bloody murder the preservation of the chosen people required. "This longing, and all of a similar kind," she writes, "it was necessary to knock on the head; which I did, figuratively, after the manner of Jael to Sisera, driving a nail through their temples. Unlike Sisera, they did not die: they were but transiently stunned, and at intervals would turn on the nail with a rebellious wrench; then did the temples bleed, and the brain thrill to its core" (V 176).

With this "at intervals" emerges the self-interrupting aspect of this narrative testifying to the recurrence of a desire that, given free rein, would conquer and destroy the self, and, in British fiction after the National Tale and Scott, such a desire remains associated with the powers of the subjugated, but perhaps never *finally* subjugated, Celt, the "enemy within" the modern United Kingdom, the "giant slave under the sway of [Saxon] good sense" (V 71). A later passage occurring near the middle of the novel describes how the "vindictive" force of "Reason" within Lucy—supposedly the distinguishing Germanic strength—sternly curtails every attempt to give felt emotions an outlet. The sentiment that has to be silenced in this instance is Lucy's nascent, unrequitable love for Graham, whom she has encountered in Villette many years after the fall of the Brettons of Bretton. "[I]f I feel," Lucy the character demands of her inner censor, "may I *never* express?"; Reason replies, "*Never!*" (V 307). The latter enjoins upon Lucy the joyless pragmatism of an unmitigatedly Germanic approach to life, according to which, Lucy writes, "I was born only to work for a piece of bread [and] to await the pains of death" (V 307–8). Yet, she adds, "[w]e shall and must break bounds at intervals, despite the terrible revenge that awaits our return" (V 308).

As I have suggested above, a tidier narrative, like that of *The Professor,* would have arranged for the faithless Graham to turn his affection toward Lucy, his journey toward Saxon self-control crossing and complementing her perilous forays in search of a permissible Celticism. But the national allegory in *Villette* is a good deal more outlandish than that, centering on Lucy's attraction and potential marriage to the tempestuous Continental Catholic Paul Carlos David Emmanuel, whose "deep Spanish lashes" import into the narrative of British self-making influences even more distant and alien than those of Francophone Labassecour (V 583).[29] Lucy will relinquish any claim upon John Graham Bretton and pay final

---

[29] Including the possibility that Paul Carlos David Emmanuel is the descendant of *conversos,* Spanish Jews converted under duress during the Inquisition.

tribute to her feelings for him in an exotic metaphor. Convinced that he keeps some small room for her "in that goodly mansion, his heart," she writes,

> I kept a place for him, too—a place of which I never took the measure, either by rule or compass: I think it was like the tent of Peri-Banou. All my life long I carried it folded in the hollow of my hand—yet, released from that hold and constriction, I know not but its innate capacity for expanse might have magnified it into a tabernacle for a host. (V 555)

The *Arabian Nights* tale Brontë has in mind tells of a magical tent "whose peculiar property it was to shrink or swell at need," one capable of being folded down to a tiny size, making it easy to transport, but also capable of expanding to house an entire army, or "host."[30] Brontë makes it into a something like an ark, a portable sacred space for a British household god. If unfolded, however, the tent housing these feelings would enlarge to fill every inch of Lucy's emotional world, crowding out all other possibilities: if Lucy were actually to settle down with her household god, she would lose herself in the wholly subordinated role of priestess-housewife—the role that Lucy watches Polly Home rehearse for in the early stages of the novel.[31] Completely absorbed in the husband's identity, Lucy would relinquish any hope of narrating into existence the female variety of Brontë's British ideal of being *other than one thing.*

Villette's swerve away from this partly desired conclusion constitutes the novel's comment upon an instability Brontë perceives to lie at the heart of those inaugural narratives of the United Kingdom, the National Tale and Scott's historical romances. In these works, promotion of the moral union of Celt and Saxon involved the defense on cultural-relativist grounds of distinctive non-English traditions, but it also relied heavily on figures of union (the marriage, the river) that might be read as portending the virtual *elimination* of non-English (or Saxon) elements, their total submersion within the civilized British stream. When, at the end of Owenson's *The Wild Irish Girl,* for example, the English Lord M. gives his approval for his son to marry the enchanting Irish Glorvina, he advises the younger Englishman to accept the stewardship of Ireland's especial "national virtues" on one page, but urges the couple to let "the distinctions of English and Irish, of protestant and catholic, be forever buried" on another.[32] The prospect that this latter counsel is the one Britain will follow haunts *Villette* as the ghostly nun haunts Lucy, threatening to become her fate. One of *Villette*'s most daring suggestions is that such a fate might be worse than coerced conversion to Catholicism. Reversing the expected narrative turn from exotic to acceptable British Other—the turn of Edward Waverley's desire in Scott's first novel, from Flora Mac-Ivor to Rose

---

[30] *The Book of the Thousand Nights and One Night,* trans. Powys Mathers (n.p.: Dorset Press, 1987), 3. 568.

[31] Cf. Jane Eyre, anticipating marriage to Rochester: "My future husband was becoming to me my whole world; and more than the world: almost the hope of heaven": *Jane Eyre* (1847; Harmondsworth: Penguin, 1996), 307.

[32] Sydney Owenson (Lady Morgan), *The Wild Irish Girl* (1806; Oxford: Oxford University Press), 251, 250.

Bradwardine—Lucy makes *suppressing* rather than actualizing her feelings for her Celtic fellow Briton the necessary prerequisite for recovering a multiple Britishness. Scott had revised the National-Tale formula by doubling the Scottish heroines in *Waverley*—a device that emphasized Scotland's internal plurality, its border between Highlands and Lowlands, and made it possible to cast the *burden* of English-Scottish union onto the exiled Highlanders. In *Villette,* Brontë doubles her heroes so as to transfer onto Polly Home the burden of the British marriage plot. This frees Brontë up to use the stormy courtship of Lucy and Paul Emmanuel to explore the ethnographic paradox (stated here by Laura Bohannon) that "[t]he greater the extent to which one has lived and participated in a genuinely foreign culture and understood it, the greater the extent to which one realizes that one could not, without violence to one's personal integrity, be of it."[33]

III

The interlacing of the John-and-Polly subplot and the main plot focused on Lucy herself makes visible the fact that the latter is not simply a narrative of displacement but, more precisely, one of displacement from available or conventional styles *of* displacement, and from the stories built around them. The opening chapter initially gives the impression that Lucy herself will be the consistent object of our attention, much as Jane Eyre is in the novel bearing her name. After a paragraph setting the scene at Bretton, we zero in on Lucy, the "[o]ne child in a household of grown people" who is "made very much of" by Mrs. Bretton and the others: she seems the center of the other characters' attention just as she is the central figure in the narrative. Within a few pages, however, she gets shouldered aside by the newly arrived Polly Home, and the rest of the Bretton chapters (1–3) place her on the margin of the action, the observer in the scene who records Polly's reaction to *her* displacement from her father's home and company. The precocious girl presents us with a sort of time-lapse enactment of the young woman's expected transfer of affection from father to suitor, moving with exaggerated efficiency between emotional states in which the first and then the second is all in all to her. With her father, Lucy witnesses, Polly seems to have "all she want[s]—*all* she want[s], and to be in a trance of content" (V 71); the departure of her alpha and omega, her household God-the-Father, draws forth from her "a sort of 'Why hast thou forsaken me?'" (V 79); but she installs Graham upon the vacated altar with what Lucy notes as a "curious readiness" (V 83). This approved (though accelerated) British variety of detachment and reattachment Lucy studies in the manner of a recently arrived visiting anthropologist confronting the strangest of alien customs: "One would have thought the child had no mind or life of her own," she records, "but must necessarily live, move, and have her being in another: now that her father was taken from her, she nestled to Graham, and seemed to feel by his feelings: to

---

[33] Laura Bohannon (as Elenore Smith Bowen), *Return to Laughter: An Anthropological Novel* (1954; New York: Doubleday, 1964), 291–92.

exist in his existence" (V 83). What Lucy observes here, of course, is the hothouse cultivation, the "forcing" of a flower of British womanhood perfectly conforming to the feminine norm of dependency on and deference to men, a norm Lucy herself will attempt to defy.

More generally, however, what fascinates and repels Lucy in Polly's behavior is a definitive feature of cultural belonging as such: the intersubjective character of identity that defines who we are by the roles we recognize others calling on us to play. Much of Lucy's subsequent narrative can be described as a denaturalizing quest for the boundary no culture wants its members to locate: the boundary lying between, on the one hand, specific, refusable or reformable roles, and, on the other, the general truth of culture that identity can be maintained *only* through the playing of *some* sorts of roles at another's behest. Another way of putting this would be to say that the Lucy plot recalls but reworks *Jane Eyre* in its confrontation with the ultimately self-negating desire to repudiate life in culture and the performing of roles altogether—the desire to be wholly uninscribed by culture, invisible to its circle of gazes, a blank page, "pure as the driven snow." To the extent that this longing, now coded *Saxon* and opposed to a "Celtic" urge to throw oneself into the performance of roles, gains the upper hand in Lucy, she will approximate the position she finally occupies as the narrator of her tale, when she takes up the position of no position, the state of being the light by which we see but not an object to be seen.[34]

If Polly Home's behavior upon being stranded in Bretton offers one conventional style and story of displacement, others commence when the Brettons themselves are forced to leave their British Eden. As many readers have noted, Graham's exilic career describes a bourgeois version of the Fortunate Fall narrative, in which the cosseted layabout "adopt[s] a profession" and makes good (V 95)—a culmination made possible only if Graham is ejected from the cozy nest in which he might never grow up. The idea that British mettle should be tested and British ore refined elsewhere than in Britain has been much explored by critics focusing on the role of the colonies in Victorian fiction, and the reformed John Graham Bretton whom Lucy encounters in Labassecour is not dissimilar from the self-reliant young men who return from the colonial beyond in novels like *Dombey and Son* or *Bleak House*. His temptations along the way, however, derive from different narrative paradigms, such as the one focused on the country lad lured to destruction in the wicked city (as in Wordsworth's "Michael") or the one about the British Grand Tourist who gives himself over to foreign ways. When he turns from Ginevra to Paulina, he re-enacts that change of direction from dangerous first to acceptable second object of desire that Scott had Edward Waverley perform and that Lucy Snowe will reverse in moving from Graham to Paul. The opposition of

---

[34] In one of the few tantalizing passages giving information about her current condition, Lucy the narrator writes "my hair which till a late period withstood the frosts of time, lies now, at last white, under a white cap, like snow beneath snow" (V 105). "Snow beneath snow" represents something like a culminating concentration of the coldly observant, self-erasing tendency that during the period narrated in *Villette* was still contending for supremacy in Lucy's character.

the cousins Ginevra and Paulina, as well as that between Ginevra and Lucy, is it-self configured by the dictates of another established narrative of displacement, the "family-abroad plot" in which two young women, usually sisters, exhibit con-trasting responses to the attractions and milieu of Europe, the one foolishly aping every Continental fashion and the other remaining true to the conduct and outlook befitting a Briton.[35] Ginevra's ultimate destiny of being yoked to a profligate for-eigner might have been taken straight from the pages of numerous Victorian mag-azine tales or even tourist guidebooks cautioning English maidens against the blan-dishments of Continental fortune-hunters: as John Murray III reminded readers in one of his guides to Italy, "Englishwomen by marriage with a foreigner forfeit their nationality, and are precluded from seeking redress from British consuls or tri-bunals."[36] Such women lose the Hobbesian license Lucy Snowe requires.

Accepted patterns of displacement are a culture's way of managing change and of conveying the message that no important change *cannot* be managed by its methods. Lucy Snowe is looking for a narrative of displacement more radical than these, and she is uniquely situated to undertake this quest because from the start she characterizes herself for us as someone already homeless. Bretton, where she visits twice a year, made a satisfying enough substitute until Paulina usurped her position at the center; but as for her regular abode, she speaks only, and in the most stilted manner, of "the kinsfolk with whom was at that time fixed my permanent residence" (V 62). This language gives an impression that could not be more op-posed to that of "Bretton of Bretton": rather than conveying the idea of a massively settled way of life and an indisputable authority over a particular spot of ground, it conjures up a vision in which place of residence is forever open to negotiation and alteration, something requiring to be "fixed" by somebody, as if it were bro-ken. Nothing can be called "permanent," no place a "permanent residence" under these circumstances, except ironically. A few chapters later, Lucy writes of her last departure from Bretton, "It will be conjectured that I was of course glad to return [from there] to the bosom of my kindred. Well! the amiable conjecture does no harm, and may therefore be safely left uncontradicted" (V 94). Having long ago anticipated the Brettons in undergoing irreversible dislocation from anything rep-resentable as a home naturally and unproblematically *hers,* and disdaining the amiable conjectures of her readers that would insist on locating and *fixing* her in some such place, Lucy studies the conventions of displacement through which her fellow expatriates now begin to move.

Her own movements beyond the Bretton of her childhood take her to two coun-terposed locations that function together to sum up the anticultural condition of her country and hence the need for a displacement farther-reaching than the vari-eties that existing England understands. These locations are, as I have indicated, the country's "flat, rich middle," where she cares for the dying Miss Marchmont,

---

[35] Cf. my *The Beaten Track: European Tourism, Literature, and the Ways to "Culture," 1800–1918* (Oxford: Oxford University Press, 1993), 130–54.

[36] Quoted in John Pemble, *The Mediterranean Passion: Victorians and Edwardians in the South* (Oxford: Oxford University Press, 1987), 271.

and its capital, which she visits before turning her sights abroad. If the first—rural England—reveals itself to be both physically and spiritually barren, the second, the metropolis, teems with a life that seems almost completely foreign, and contains only one reassuring symbol, though a massive one, of a national faith abiding in potential, one to which Lucy's experiences outside Britain might bring her back.

Miss Marchmont, "a rheumatic cripple, impotent, foot and hand" for the past twenty years (V 95), is an exacting and irritable mistress in whose exclusive company Lucy gains a startling image of her probable future self. The mythic Bretton now gone for good, "there remain[s] no possibility of dependence on others" (V 95). "Two hot, close rooms became my world," Lucy remembers: "[a]ll within me became narrowed to my lot" (V 97). She lives entirely alone with a woman whose life-narrative bears a relationship of uncanny similarity-with-difference to both the content and the method of the narrative about Lucy that we are still just beginning. As this "maiden lady" approaches death, she relates the tale, as she says, of "the love of my life—its only love—almost its only affection; for I am not a particularly good woman: I am not amiable." She tells of a time thirty years past when she was loved by "my noble Frank—my faithful Frank—my *good* Frank—so much better than myself." Her worship of this lover named for the Englishman's stereotypical forthrightness or frankness acquires its full dimension when Miss Marchmont recalls that it was on Christmas Eve that she "dressed and decorated" herself to await his arrival for the last time: hurrying through the snowy night to lessen his lateness, poor Frank fell from his horse and died by morning. Since then, the life of his unreturned-to beloved has been one long questioning of "why it was taken from me." "For what crime was I condemned," she still demands, "after twelve months of bliss, to undergo thirty years of sorrow?" (V 99).

It is more than plain that her story prefigures key elements in the one focused on Lucy that lies ahead, and that her admitted unamiability links her temperamentally to Lucy as well.[37] In both women's stories, the prospect of the lover's return is associated with the dawn of a new era of spiritual fulfillment, the turning of a page in human history. But Lucy's narrative submits its model to an outlandish redaction, not content simply to replace Frank with the Celtic Graham but pressing farther outward to the egregiously alien Paul. While Miss Marchmont's narrative operates within the narrow Austen world of the genteel rural English south, it can be read as repudiating Austen's customary resolution, in keeping with that destruction of the tidy Bretton world that inaugurates *Villette*'s entire narrative. English and British self-fashioning will henceforth require more capacious narratives, charged with the accommodation of levels of heterogeneity unthinkable in the Austen calculus. As I have suggested, the John Graham Bretton and Polly Home subplot of *Villette* takes up and reworks the challenge of British imperial

---

[37] Though Lucy is famously tight-lipped about what became of her after the period narrated in the book, there is evidence that the time elapsed between the (inferred) loss of Paul Emmanuel and the commencement of the task of narrating is comparable to if not longer than Miss Marchmont's thirty years (cf. V 105).

identity-formation, while the Lucy-and-Paul plot attempts to envision a complementary Britishness not wholly absorbed in the imperial project.

But the way Miss Marchmont tells her story is every bit as significant as the matter in it. The narrative is distinguished by its commitment to leap back across the span of time dividing teller from tale: all the teller's effort goes toward replicating her impressions as they arose on the fateful Christmas Eve. The invalid begins by saying that Memory (so personified) is giving her "a deep delight; she is bringing back to my heart, in warm and beautiful life, realities—not mere empty ideas— but what were once realities, and that I long have thought decayed, dissolved, mixed in with grave-mould" (V 98–99). The following will serve as an example of her method of recounting the suspense of her wait:

> Would he for once fail me? No—not even for once; and now he was coming—and coming fast—to atone for lost time. "Frank! you furious rider," I said inwardly, listening gladly, yet anxiously to his approaching gallop, "you shall be rebuked for this: I will tell you that it is *my* neck you are putting in peril; for whatever is yours is, in a dearer and tenderer sense, mine." There he was: I saw him; but I think tears were in my eyes my sight was so confused. I saw the horse; I heard it stamp—I saw at least a mass; I heard a clamour. *Was* it a horse? or what heavy, dragging thing was it, crossing, strangely dark, the lawn? How could I name that thing in the moonlight before me? or how could I utter the feeling which rose in my soul? (V 100)

It is Frank, of course, dragged to her feet to perish uttering her name.

In a recent reassessment of literary defamiliarization, Carlo Ginzburg has identified a variety of this common device he associates with writers such as Madame de Sévigné, Dostoevsky, and Proust but which seems also at particularly strenuous work in Brontë's *Villette*. Unlike the strain Ginzburg traces from Marcus Aurelius down through Voltaire and Tolstoy, which offers us "the means by which we [may] overcome appearances and arrive at a deeper understanding of reality," this alternative version of defamiliarization works in precisely the opposite direction, attempting "to preserve the freshness of appearances against the intrusion of ideas, by presenting things 'in the order of perception' and still uncontaminated by causal explanations." It aims at "an impressionistic immediacy."[38] This seems exactly the goal of Miss Marchmont's account: no summary statement of the events, no prefabricated narrative frame for them, is adequate to the experience that has shaped her life, so she must practice upon her audience that interpretation-interrupting technique that Ian Watt labeled "delayed decoding."[39] Commitment to this technique seems to animate Miss Marchmont's story at all levels, being visible even at the level of prose style—as in the stilted phrase "crossing, strangely dark, the lawn." And it is this model that Lucy's narrative will appropriate and massively

---

[38] Carlo Ginzburg, "Making It Strange: The Prehistory of a Literary Device," in *Wooden Eyes: Nine Reflections on Distance,* trans. Martin Ryle and Kate Soper (New York: Columbia University Press, 2001), 18–19.

[39] Cf. Watt, *Conrad in the Nineteenth Century* (Berkeley: University of California Press, 1979), 175–80.

extend in its campaign to displace conventional modes of displacement. Only by holding the latter at bay can she put her readers into the position in which she actually underwent her formative trials in Labassecour. I will return to consider the novel's most notorious instance of this technique below.

Soothed by the catharsis of narrating this central episode in her past, Miss Marchmont resolves to reward her caretaker and listener with a bequest in her will, but she dies before being able to realize this benevolent aim. Had the plan been enacted, Lucy might simply have settled into her dead mistress's place as a keeper of her money and memory; its foiling makes possible the expansion of Lucy's constricted world, the dislocation that lifts local mentalities up to the level of national ones. Through the intervention of the inspiring Aurora Borealis—a cold light, like Lucy herself—she gains "some new power": as her biblical diction intimates, she was on her road to Damascus.

> A bold thought was sent to my mind; my mind was made strong to receive it.
> "Leave this wilderness," it was said to me, "and go out hence."
> "Where?" was the query.
> I had not far to look: gazing from this country parish in the flat, rich middle of England—
> > I mentally saw within reach what I had never yet beheld with my bodily eyes; I saw London. (V 104)

I have already shown what a "Babylon and a wilderness" the metropolis appears to Lucy when she first sees it (V 106). As in *Jane Eyre,* the directing voice does not lastingly sustain the courage of the woman who heeds it, and, once in the great city, *Villette*'s heroine is soon overwhelmed by her aimless and friendless condition—the vision of which, she says, in terms pointing forward to the apparition of the nun that will beset her abroad, "rose on me like a ghost. Anomalous; desolate, almost blank of hope, it stood. What was I doing here alone in great London? What should I do on the morrow? What prospects had I in life? What friends had I on earth? Whence did I come? Whither should I go? What should I do?" (V 107). Comfort comes to her in the darkness of her solitary chamber when she hears the "deep, low, mighty tone" of church bells striking midnight and thinks, "I lie in the shadow of St. Paul's" (V 107). Sunrise the next morning shows her "THE DOME" (V 108). Dome, shadow, and bell-toll encode the promise of the national culture's extraterritorial license, and the driving question of Lucy's subsequent narrative of Continental adventures can be formulated by ringing the changes upon these linked figures, for the tale of Lucy abroad is concerned to determine how great is the circumference of the dome, how far that shadow can effectually extend, and at what point one passes out of earshot of those British bells. En route to the foreign land, Lucy carries the memory of that Anglican dome with her on her travels, like a protective umbrella.

As if to indicate her commitment to the narrative model bequeathed her in lieu of a pecuniary reward by Miss Marchmont—that model devoted to the revivifying liberation of impressions from established interpretive frameworks—Lucy boards a ship called "The Vivid" for her passage to the Continent. On board she encounters the figure who, among all the important "shadow selves" or partial objectifications of herself and her prospects that she has to deal with in her narrative, seems most plainly an anti-Lucy in every tendency: the much-traveled, cynically cosmopolitan Ginevra Fanshawe.[40] During the ensuing stages of their time together in Villette, Ginevra will keep Lucy close at hand as a foil for heightening her own attractions, at one point even compelling the latter to stand beside her before a mirror so that the contrast might come unmistakably into focus (V 214–16). Lucy's narrative of their interactions spins the contrast the other way, however. As the starlet of the salon, the creature positively made to be looked at and to generate plots of courtship and intrigue, Ginevra embodies the essence of fictional characters in general, those figures whose movement across the story-space of narrative we watch as we read; Lucy, even though assigned the role of a character, cannot help withdrawing into the powerful invisibility of a narrator who *watches* characters and enables our watching of them. Consequently, Ginevra is at a complete loss to comprehend or assess the phenomenon of Lucy Snowe, a woman whose value is "viewless" in the Keatsian sense of "not available to view." When she says to Lucy, "It seems so odd . . . that you and I should now be so much on a level, visiting in the same sphere; having the same connections" (V 392), she expresses the puzzlement any fictional character might feel upon registering the presence of the *narrator* in the story-space where that invisible personage does not belong. "Who *are* you, Miss Snowe?" she petulantly asks: "If you really are the nobody I once thought you, you must be a cool hand" (V 392–93). The point is that Lucy is a different *kind* of nobody from the kind Ginevra thought her, the social nobody unprepossessing in both person and status; she is incipiently the narrator who may haunt her own story but whose proper domain is that of narrative's discourse-space, the textual analogue to cultural *outsideness*.

In their meeting aboard the *Vivid,* Ginevra demonstrates her oppositional function in two striking and specific ways. First, as she blithely announces,

> I have quite forgotten my religion; they call me a Protestant, you know, but really I am not sure whether I am one or not: I don't well know the difference between Romanism and Protestantism. However, I don't in the least care for that. I was a Lutheran once at Bonn—dear Bonn!—charming Bonn!—where there were so many handsome students. Every nice girl in our school had an admirer; they knew our hours for walking out, and almost always passed us on the promenade: "Schönes Mädchen," we used to hear them say. I was excessively happy at Bonn! (V 115)

It is safe to say that this young woman knows every European language's translation for "Schönes Mädchen," and that she will just as amenably adopt the creed of

---

[40] Cf. Amanda Anderson, *The Powers of Distance,* 48ff. for a reading focused on Mme. Beck as a foil for the protagonist. One anti-Lucy less often noted is the woman whose position Lucy assumes at Mme. Beck's school, the "Mrs. Svini" who has passed herself off among the Francophones as speaking "the English tongue with the purest metropolitan accent," when in fact she speaks "a smothered brogue, curiously overlaid with mincing cockney inflections." A "native, indeed, of Middlesex," Mrs Svini—"Anglicé or Hibernice, Sweeny"—cannot shed the Irishness in her nature even if she was born and raised near London and adopts the speech patterns of the southern elite. Once again, Irishness represents Brontë's limit case for United Kingdom "Englishness."

whatever denomination offers her the most and handsomest admirers. She leeches all affect out of the question of religious conversion, treating that question—the source of so much bloodshed, generator of so much of history's narrative—as a matter of masquerade. She is the absolute obverse of *another* persona Lucy Snowe must avoid assuming, that of the Englishwoman who, having never been anywhere else, believes no other creed than her own deserves a moment's consideration. Lucy's challenge is to steer between the Scylla of depthless cosmopolitan creed-changing and the Charybdis of a blinkered chauvinism even her author could not always avoid.[41]

Every sincere Protestant and Catholic has always longed to do what Ginevra has accomplished so easily: erase the distinction between the two Christianities. But the wicked beauty in *Villette* has done this without "in the least car[ing]" for the question most pressing to Catholics and Protestants: which *side* will be erased so that conflict might cease? The tortuous narrative of Lucy and Paul's rapprochement, if permitted to culminate, would point either to Catholicism's eventual withering away (as Paul, safely back from Guadeloupe, learns at his wife's side to overcome his aversion to Protestantism's "severe charm" [V 595]) or to the even more utopian vision Paul articulates when he declares, "Whatever say priests or controversialists . . . God is good and loves all the sincere. Believe, then, what you can" (V 517). The main narrative of *Villette* cannot make it to either of these shores, but even to *glimpse* the latter one remains a praiseworthy achievement. Where it will *not* go, however, is toward that other vision for which Ginevra stands as a mocking testament: the one in which the difference between Catholic and Protestant is to be "buried" forever, as Lord M. recommends at the close of Owenson's *The Wild Irish Girl*. Ginevra embodies Brontë's repudiation of that reading of the National Tale that renders religious distinctions a matter of no consequence to the modern British nation.

The other telling trait Ginevra exhibits in her first scene with Lucy involves a quasi-Dickensian identifying tick, a cosmopolitan speech habit of enormous significance in defining the anti-Lucy. It arises when the protagonist asks her where she is currently studying, now that she is no longer in wonderful Bonn.

> "And where are you now?" I inquired.
> "Oh! at—*chose*," said she.
> Now Miss Ginevra Fanshawe [Lucy then tells us] . . . only substituted this word "*chose*" in temporary oblivion of the real name. It was a habit she had: "*chose*" came in at

---

[41] Cf. Brontë to Ellen Nussey in July 1842, on the absurdity of worrying about "the danger protestants expose themselves to in going to reside in Catholic countries": *The Letters of Charlotte Brontë*, ed. Margaret Smith, Vol. 1 (1829–1847) (Oxford: Clarendon Press, 1995), 289–90. But cf. 329–30 for Brontë on the "fancy" that made her participate in the Catholic sacrament of confession in Brussels in 1843. The episode forcefully raises the question of whether one's culture is so completely defined by what one does that the doing of Catholic things (such as going to confession) *makes* one a Catholic, or whether cultural identity resides so intransigently in one's race that even the lonely expatriate Anglican might go so far as to make "a real confession" to a Catholic priest without falling under suspicion of actually "turn[ing]" Catholic. For a pertinent argument, cf. Walter Benn Michaels, *Our America: Nativism, Modernism, and Pluralism* (Durham N.C.: Duke University Press, 1995).

every turn in her conversation—the convenient substitute for any missing word in any language she might chance at the time to be speaking. French girls often do the like; from them she had caught the custom. "*Chose,*" however, I found, in this instance, stood for Villette—the great capital of the great kingdom of Labassecour. (V 115–16)

As capital of a great kingdom of anticulture in Brontë's novel, Villette is, in fact, quite properly called by the name of "thing," and Ginevra properly understood as a convert to the mentality of thinghood. The progress of Lucy's fieldwork in the Catholic anticulture of surveillance creates the condition for making the visitor's *own* culture "visible by culture-shock": as ethnographers do, Lucy subjects herself "to situations beyond [her] normal interpersonal competence and objectif[ies] the discrepancy as an entity."[42] As I argued in chapter 2, the entity of "a culture" arises from a perspective that sees *itself* as the precise opposite of that of capitalist "reification" or "commodity fetishism." Ethnography involves the translation of discrete phenomena encountered in fieldwork from object- or event-status into the status of nodes or points of intersection in a web: a "thing" looked at through the ethnographic lens dissolves into the social networks that explain it. But in order to achieve this perspective on a social arrangement in which, purportedly, "[e]verything is somehow related to everything else"—in order to de-reify the "contents" of a culture, in other words—one must reify the culture *itself,* restricting its sphere of applicability in order to grasp the contingent differential network that endows the contents with meaning and value.[43] A way of life determinedly "catholic," always aggressively reaching out to pull more and more elements into it, can never achieve this enabling self-interruption. In the *everywhere* it longs to go, everything remains a thing.

In his stimulating introduction to *Villette,* Tony Tanner noted how "the presence of ordinary domestic articles or appliances looms very large" in the novel "and a great deal of 'affect' or excited emotion can attach itself to objects and sounds which in another fictional world might simply be incidental items in a larger circumambience" (V 13). He was putting his finger upon the novel's drive to read even the most seemingly trivial details of a social situation as charged with the significance, and radiating throughout the putative wholeness, of a culture; and, in a manner more familiar in the criticism of Joyce than in that of Brontë, he proceeded to enumerate a host of phenomena that on first glance might appear the very quintessence of obdurate phenomenality, of what Roland Barthes called the *reality effect,* but that turn out to be inscribed with that pervasive-but-elusive, hidden-in-plain-sight cultural code that the ethnographer longs to crack (cf. V 13–14).[44] To

---

[42] Roy Wagner, *The Invention of Culture,* rev. ed. (Chicago: University of Chicago Press, 1981), 9.

[43] Clyde Kluckhohn, "Cultural Anthropology: New Uses for 'Barbarians,'" in Lynn White, ed., *Frontiers of Knowledge in the Study of Man* (New York: Harper, 1956), 37.

[44] Cf. Susan Hegeman, "Imagining Totality: Rhetorics of and Versus 'Culture,'" *Common Knowledge* 6/3 (1997), 51–72, on the "trope of enumeration" used to signal the "ineffable complexity of culture" (53); also Alan Liu, "Local Transcendence: Cultural Criticism, Postmodernism, and the Romanticism of Detail," *Representations* 32 (Fall 1990), 75–113; esp. 84–87, on the role of the list and "etc." in postmodern cultural criticism.

the degree that Lucy Snowe's narrative enables its readers to *begin* envisioning Labassecourian Catholicism as a culture, to the degree that it accords the Labassecourians' life-ways even the coherence and intelligibility of an organized *anticulture,* to just that degree can the narrative enable its readers to objectify their *own* customary domain as a limited, locatable "entity."

IV

As I have contended throughout these pages on *Villette,* Brontë appears to recognize that progress toward this goal of "culturing" Britain can be made only if narratives of imperial Britishness can be held at bay—or, to put it another way, if Britons' urge to regard themselves as possessing an identity whose home is potentially everywhere can be interrupted for a time. And this is how I think we should regard one of the most peculiar features of this highly peculiar novel: the strange reappearance of the Brettons (and their things) in Villette at the start of Volume 2, and the bizarre revelation that follows from it, namely that the character we have watched moving about Villette in Volume 1 as "M. Isidore" and "Dr. John" was in fact John Graham Bretton all along, and *known to be so* by Lucy, who has deliberately withheld the information from her readers. Here is how she puts it:

> For, reader, this tall young man—this darling son—this host of mine—this Graham Bretton, *was* Dr John: he, and no other; and, what is more, I ascertained this identity scarcely with surprise. . . . The discovery was not of to-day, its dawn had penetrated my perceptions long since. Of course I remembered young Bretton well; and though ten years (from sixteen to twenty-six) may greatly change the boy as they mature him to the man, yet they could bring no such utter difference as would suffice wholly to blind my eyes, or to baffle my memory. (V 247–48)

Lucy explains that, seeing he did not recognize her, she resolved not to reveal herself, cultivating instead the satisfaction of "entering his presence covered with a cloud he had not seen through, while he stood before me under a ray of special illumination, which shone all partial over his head, trembled about his feet, and cast light no farther" (V 248). But this is scarcely an explanation for why, when narrating her tale, she felt it necessary to leave readers as much in the dark as the "illuminated" Bretton was. Registering this belated information and reassessing Lucy's entire situation in light of it, we may come to realize that the narrative of dislocation and trial we have been reading to this point was always already accompanied by that other and customarily dominant narrative of exemplary British character making centered on the scion of the Brettons.

    On the one hand, knowing he was there during the initial, punishing phase of Lucy's expatriate adventures encourages us to link Graham Bretton to the dome, shadow, and bell of St. Paul's, to consider him a guarantee of Lucy's ultimate safety as a Briton, even as she undergoes the most dangerous of her encounters with the alien. Such a silent guarantee might counterbalance the almost complete erosion of Lucy's sense of self that takes place over the course of Volume 1, culminating in the desperately lonely young woman's quasi-confession to Père Silas and her loss of consciousness on the cathedral steps. When she comes to, at the beginning of the subsequent volume, in a room filled with the strangely familiar household items of the Brettons, what we are seeing is the "return" of things and characters that were never "gone" from Lucy's life-world at all, an enactment of that paradoxical pattern Brontë had earlier associated with the racial identity that the English cannot leave behind no matter where their fortunes take them. Just as she appeared ready to lose herself and turn Catholic, the Brettons and their *meubles* reappear and turn out to have been on the scene throughout. These furnishings, objects of which Lucy "could have told the peculiarities, numbered the flaws or cracks, like any *clairvoyante,*" are the British household gods performing their identity-sustaining or identity-restoring magic (V 239, 240): *sustaining,* insofar as the identity in question (we now see) was never really in danger; *restoring,* insofar as it is possible to generate a narrative convincing us it *might* be. They complement the massive fixity of St. Paul's, its centrality and centeredness, making it possible to remake the "hearth of Old England" in other lands (V 240). "'[A]uld lang syne'" Lucy writes, "smiled out of every nook"—Burns's Scottish phrase summing up the impact of that expansive, United Kingdom "Englishness."[45]

On the other hand, it is more than possible to read the "return" of the Brettons as a matter for mixed feelings. Lucy Snowe's awareness that her space of alterity has always been less alien than her own narrative needs it to be testifies to the extreme difficulty of fostering an alternative Britishness to the one centered—like that "ray of special illumination" that prevents the illuminated from seeing beyond it—upon the "darling son." And *our* awareness, at the start of Volume 2, that Lucy has up to now hidden hers from us testifies to the determination that drives this outlandish novel, to delineate a plot of possible Britishness not wholly absorbed in the fortunes of John Great Britain—a determination leading Lucy Snowe to adopt and intensify almost to the point of absurdity Miss Marchmont's defamiliarizing or distancing narrative practice. In order to construct her own fiction of a revivified alternative Britishness, she has to *filter out* or interrupt the transmission of those of her past impressions in which her spotlighted rival appeared in his true character rather than in the persona of a Continental or Continentalized young man of wavering loyalties. Once the opening of Volume 2 permits us to know him again as he always was, it can then go on to separate Lucy's narrative from his once more, this time showing *us* the delineating operations it had to practice covertly in order to set Lucy in narrative motion.

Writing a few years after Brontë in *Villette,* and facing the prospect of a future in which expanding knowledge put "the number of doctrines which are no longer

---

[45] In a reworking of Jane Eyre in the Red Room of Gateshead, Lucy sees herself in the "gilded mirror" of the Brettons and notes that she "looked spectral, my eyes larger and more hollow" (V 238). Throughout Brontë's work, such moments of self-haunting not only convey that power of seeing while unseen that the character-turned-narrator will come to possess; they also figure culture as the *abstraction* supposedly pervading a particular territory but not empirically discernible in it. Cf. Herbert chap. 1, on the culture idea as the object of "superstition."

disputed or doubted . . . constantly on the increase," John Stuart Mill in *On Liberty* began reckoning the possible cost of a world in which everything might finally be known and every question—to use the colonialist metaphor—"settled." "The cessation, on one question after another, of serious controversy is one of the necessary incidents of the consolidation of opinion," he wrote, "a consolidation as salutary in the case of true opinions as it is dangerous and noxious when the opinions are erroneous." But he judged that

> though this gradual narrowing of the bounds of diversity of opinion is necessary in both senses of the term, being at once inevitable and indispensable, we are not therefore obliged to conclude that all its consequences must be beneficial. The loss of so important an aid to the intelligent and living apprehension of a truth as is afforded by the necessity of explaining it to, or defending it against, opponents, though not sufficient to outweigh, is no trifling drawback from the benefit of its universal recognition. Where this advantage can no longer be had, I confess I should like to see the teachers of mankind endeavoring to provide a substitute for it—some contrivance for making the difficulties of the question as present to the learner's consciousness as if they were pressed upon him by a dissentient champion, eager for his conversion.[46]

Villette's narrative of defamiliarized Britishness affords a highly demonstrative variety of Mill's wished-for "contrivance," one designed not only to overcome the great obstacle in Lucy's path but also to instruct readers about that obstacle's magnitude. Only so long as she can get out of the shadow Bretton's "special ray" places her in can Lucy become visible to us as a character whose story explores the boundaries of a British identity that might be capable of permitting extranational differences to assume the form of "another culture"; and only insofar as she can achieve *this* can she bring back to Britons the culture that is theirs. The famously reticent Lucy does not tell us whether she returned to England to stay after the period narrated in the novel; she *does* indicate that, between the time she awaited Paul Emmanuel's homecoming from Guadeloupe and the time she writes, she has "seen the West-end, the parks, the fine squares" of London (V 109), but we lack additional evidence to suggest any definitive repatriation took place. And that, of course, seems perfectly appropriate, for a writer whose career-long effort it was to stretch the categories of Britishness and Englishness to lengths from which it might *not* be possible to come back, in order to locate the kinds of distance from which it might.

---

[46] Mill, *On Liberty,* ed. Currin V. Shields (New York: Macmillan, 1956), 53–54.

PART FOUR

Around and After 1860

CHAPTER ELEVEN

Eliot, Interrupted

"As you like" is a bad finger-post.
—Eliot, *Daniel Deronda*[1]

GEORGE ELIOT, to whom I referred in chapter 1 as "the premier English [Victorian] novelist whose career unfolds entirely after the formalization of the British Empire in India," is the transitional figure between this work and its intended sequel.[2] In this chapter I provide an overview of the autoethnographic labor her novels perform even as they alter the shape of British fictional autoethnography in the changing conditions of the 1860s and 1870s; more extended analyses of *Middlemarch* and *Daniel Deronda* will begin the sequel. Chapter 12 then returns to the late nineteenth-century text introduced at the outset of this study, William Morris's *News from Nowhere*, combining with this chapter to frame the period to be covered in the next book. The overlap between the two books that will result from this way of concluding the first one is intentional, for, without diminishing differences that arise during this long stretch, I mean to emphasize continuities running from the turn of the nineteenth century to the turn of the twentieth, from the era of the National Tale and historical novel to the era of modernism. This book's stress on self-interrupting narrative—a modernist-sounding concept—as the formal signature of a developing ethnographic and autoethnographic outlook would perhaps suggest as much.

In George Eliot's incomparable *Middlemarch,* the self-interrupting nature of Victorian narratives takes on a form not often discernible in the works of Dickens or Brontë. Even their seemingly deliberate efforts to activate a British autoethnographic consciousness through regular and resourceful manipulation of the boundary between narrative's "outside" and "inside," its discourse- and story-spaces, never bring them to write anything quite like the following, from the beginning of *Middlemarch*'s twenty-ninth chapter:

> One morning, some weeks after her arrival at Lowick, Dorothea—but why always Dorothea? Was her point of view the only possible one with regard to this marriage? I protest against all our interest, all our effort at understanding being given to the young skins that look blooming in spite of trouble; for these too will get faded, and will know the older and more eating griefs which we are helping to neglect. In spite of the blinking

---

[1] *Daniel Deronda* (1876; Harmondsworth: Penguin, 1995), 278; henceforth DD.
[2] On this relationship, cf. Nancy Henry, *George Eliot and the British Empire* (Cambridge: Cambridge University Press, 2002).

eyes and white moles objectionable to Celia, and the want of muscular curve which was
morally painful to Sir James, Mr Casaubon had an intense consciousness within him, and
was spiritually a-hungered like the rest of us.[3]

In the abruptest, most demonstrative fashion imaginable, Eliot's narrator here
pulls herself back from a liability in fiction to which she elsewhere gives in and of
which she is always warily cognizant. Having created a young, intelligent, attractive but self-deluded heroine, she finds it necessary to put a check upon the compassion so easily mobilized on behalf of that character, and to disrupt the temptation to construct her fictional world the way she thinks most people construct their
view of the world around them—as wholly and steadily centered upon the privileged self. The power of that egocentric tendency, and of the urge to mirror it in
fiction, is attested to by the suddenness and seeming clumsiness of the interruption, as if the narrator exercised only the most minimal and improvised form of
control over the direction of her own gaze. The breakdown of that control would
reduce *Middlemarch*'s fictive world to the kind of simplistic, fairy-tale domain
Dorothea is prone to imagine it; the narrator *must* displace Dorothea from the center of that world, however crudely, if she is to realize her aim of a multiperspecti-
val, sympathy-spreading realism. In the specific instance of chapter 29, pushing
Dorothea brusquely aside appears to be necessary in order to get the point of view
from which the narrator can help us understand and pity Casaubon: "For my part
I am very sorry for him," she writes (M 280).

Even more striking is what happens when the narrator turns her attention, at a
later stage in the novel, to Joshua Rigg, old Featherstone's illegitimate son, the
"frog-faced legatee" who enters into the world of the novel to inherit Stone Court
and thereby to dash all Fred Vincy's cherished hopes of inheriting it himself. Dashing such hopes as Fred's and those of other expectant relatives turns out to have
been the spiteful Featherstone's purpose all along: he had "often, in imagination,
looked up through the sods above [his grave] and, unobstructed by perspective,
seen [Joshua Rigg] enjoying the fine old place to the perpetual surprise and disappointment of other survivors" (M 519). But his natural offspring has other plans.
As is so often the case with Eliot, one must quote at length to apprehend the full
significance of the old miser's failure to understand the true character of his designated heir.

> But how little we know what would make paradise for our neighbours! We judge from
> our own desires, and our neighbours themselves are not always open enough even to
> throw out a hint of theirs. The cool and judicious Joshua Rigg had not allowed his par-
> ent to perceive that Stone Court was anything less than the chief good in his estimation,
> and he had certainly wished to call it his own. But as Warren Hastings looked at gold and
> thought of buying Daylesford, so Joshua Rigg looked at Stone Court and thought of buy-
> ing gold. He had a very distinct and intense vision of his chief good, the vigorous greed
> which he had inherited having taken a special form by dint of circumstance: and his chief
> good was to be a money-changer. From his earliest employment as an errand-boy in a

---

[3] *Middlemarch* (1871–72; Harmondsworth: Penguin, 1994), 278; henceforth M.

seaport, he had looked through the windows of the money-changers as other boys look through the windows of the pastry-cooks; the fascination had wrought itself gradually into a deep special passion; he meant, when he had property, to do many things, one of them being to marry a genteel young person; but these were all accidents and joys that imagination could dispense with. The one joy after which his soul thirsted was to have a money-changer's shop on a much-frequented quay, to have locks all round him of which he held the keys, and to look sublimely cool as he handled the breeding coins of all nations, while helpless Cupidity looked at him enviously from the other side of an iron lattice. The strength of that passion had been a power enabling him to master all the knowledge necessary to gratify it. And when others were thinking that he had settled at Stone Court for life, Joshua himself was thinking that the moment now was not far off when he should settle on the North Quay with the best appointments in safes and locks.

Enough. We are concerned with looking at Joshua Rigg's sale of his land from Mr Bulstrode's point of view, and he interpreted it as a cheering dispensation conveying perhaps a sanction to a purpose which he had for some time entertained without external encouragement; he interpreted it thus, but not too confidently, offering up his thanksgiving in guarded phraseology. His doubts did not arise from the possible relations of the event to Joshua Rigg's destiny, which belonged to the unmapped regions not taken under the providential government, except perhaps in an imperfect colonial way; but they arose from reflecting that this dispensation too might be a chastisement for himself, as Mr Farebrother's induction to the living clearly was.

This was not what Mr Bulstrode said to any man for the sake of deceiving him: it was what he said to himself—it was as genuinely his mode of explaining events as any theory of yours may be, if you happen to disagree with him. For the egoism which enters into our theories does not affect their sincerity; rather, the more our egoism is satisfied, the more robust is our belief. (M 519–21)

Both Featherstone's miscalculation of Rigg's intentions and Bulstrode's self-interested interpretation of the turn of events that puts Stone Court in his possession furnish us with Eliotic object-lessons on the fallacy of "judg[ing] by our own desires": in the one case, Featherstone's aim of determining the future with his "dead hand" is thwarted, his influence cast aside as if it had the weight of a feather, not a stone; in the other, Bulstrode's self-congratulatory reading of the operations of providence is mercilessly undercut, for no sooner does he come into ownership of the estate than a hand long thought dead reaches out from *his* past, the hand of the blackmailing Raffles, whose mere existence turns the whole Bulstrodian universe to stone. Both commit the error Eliot's entire career was devoted to exposing and overcoming, the fatal error, simply put, of forgetting the existence of other people.

But I want to take the full measure of that "[e]nough" that truncates our introduction to the inner world of Joshua Rigg, returning us to the perspective of Mr. Bulstrode and more generally to the circumscribed group of characters and corresponding outlooks Eliot's narrator studies in *Middlemarch*. As in the previous example, narrative self-interruption here becomes almost embarrassingly overt, as if driven to extremes by the countervailing pressure of Eliot's commitment to penetrate beneath the surface of even the most unprepossessing of characters, to look at things through their eyes and thereby to make possible a tolerant and forgiving assessment of their behavior. By the time Eliot writes *Middlemarch,* her narrator appears to recognize herself, and, in passages like this one, to *acknowledge* herself, as endowed with the Midas-like power to turn virtually any character, however unlikable or merely useful to the plot, into the gold of a sympathy-stimulating three-dimensionality.[4] The more deeply she takes us inside of Joshua Rigg, the more even he may appear to deepen *for* us, making it difficult to dissociate ourselves from his standpoint or to hold him in place as a minor figure whose actions merely advance a plot focused on others. Even though the attitude she expresses toward Rigg's aims in life is thoroughly contemptuous, we still get the impression that Eliot's narrator needs to stop herself before going "too far," needs quite energetically to impede the further progress of the process she regularly sets in motion and defines as central to her art: that widening of our sympathies to take in not only the easy-to-sympathize-with, but also those characters who are "superlatively middling, the quintessential extract of mediocrity"—phrases used of the Rev. Amos Barton in one of Eliot's earliest works but quite suited to Joshua Rigg as well.[5] Eliot's fiction always gravitates toward those for whom "the essential *ti megethos,*" or magnitude, which Aristotle thought a necessary ingredient of tragedy, is "wanting [both] to the action" and to the situation of characters who are definitively *situated* in time and place, as classical tragic heroes never were: it aims to produce pity and terror on behalf of characters not elevated above the webs of custom but borne along—to switch to another of Eliot's favorite metaphors—upon the pitiless current of a determining social medium (MF 164). "It is the habit of my imagination," the novelist wrote to a critic of *Romola,* her detail-packed fiction of Re-

---

[4] The one glaring exception among Eliot's works in this regard is the 1860 "Brother Jacob," which Gordon Haight called "unique among [her] works in its complete lack of sympathy for any of the characters": cf. Haight, *George Eliot: A Biography* (Harmondsworth: Penguin, 1986), 340. My argument here is not that Eliot's novels actually demonstrate sympathy toward all types of characters or all segments of society (her failures with regard to the working class have been much complained of) but rather that Eliot's narrator starts to exhibit the consciousness that she *could* "enter into" any character she brings into her fiction and that she *might* do so, with disastrous consequences, if she did not check herself. When, in her later work, Eliot begins to create characters who are unrelievedly loathsome (Grandcourt, Lapidoth) or mainly unsympathetic (Rosamund Vincy), rather than just weak or corrupted fellow mortals, it may be in reaction against the omnisympathizing, or at least casuisitical tendency, she perceives in her earlier fiction. James Chandler's comments on Henri Lefebvre's comments on Pascal and casuistry are especially germane to the "case" of Eliot, the most potentially casuistical of English novelists in her talent for delving into the situational specificity of ethical life. Cf. Chandler, *England in 1819: The Politics of Literary Culture and the Case of Romantic Historicism* (Chicago: University of Chicago Press, 1998), 39n78 and elsewhere. By the time of *Middlemarch,* Eliot had long recognized her liability to the anticasuistical charge of taking a position from which "to understand is to excuse." "The casuists have become a by-word of reproach," she writes in *The Mill on the Floss,* "but their perverted spirit of minute discrimination was the shadow of a truth to which eyes and hearts are too often fatally sealed: the truth, that moral judgments must remain false and hollow, unless they are checked and enlightened by a perpetual reference to the special circumstances that mark the individual lot" (*The Mill on the Floss* [1860; Harmondsworth: Penguin, 1979], 628; henceforth MF).

[5] In *Scenes of Clerical Life* (1858; Harmondsworth: Penguin, 1973), 85.

naissance Florence, "to strive after as full a vision of the medium in which a character moves as of the character itself."[6]

But to give free rein to her powers of circumstantial analysis and sympathetic
understanding might obliterate the distinction between minor characters belonging to that medium and major characters foregrounded against it—a prospect nothing less than calamitous for the future of the novel, for a universalized fellow-
feeling would petrify narrative fiction, an open-ended pluralizing of perspectives
bring it to a grinding halt.[7] Eliot's matchless skills of thick description and devotion to expanding the circle of those deserving our commiseration bring her to the
brink of a terrible success, and, rather like Mr. Brooke of *Middlemarch*—a character mainly satirized—the novelist must "pull[] up in time" (M 17) before going
off the edge. In Dickens's *Bleak House,* as I have shown, we confront a great novelist flirting with the idea of an omnisignificant novel; Eliot later flirts with the idea
of a novel in which *every* character might become "major." (And, as W. S. Gilbert
was to observe, "When every one is somebodee, / Then no one's anybody."[8]) In
Brontë, the energizing lure of the visionary moment and the inspired oratory has
to be contained in the frame of a text, the urge simply to identify with a single,
slighted character resisted, if novels are not to degenerate into outbursts of lyric
self-justification and to shrink back from the community of readers to the merely
local sphere of embodied listeners.

George Eliot is the most ambitious and most brilliant developer of English prose
fiction in the third quarter of the nineteenth century, a period defined both by a
newly self-conscious imperial role for Britain and, not coincidentally, by the be-
ginnings of what Harold Perkin has called in a seminal book *The Rise of Professional Society.* In these years and in her works, the narrative logic of *anywhere's
nowhere* is pushed to new extremes. Across her career, Eliot repeatedly, consistently, and self-consciously defines the role of the novelist or the artist as that of a
professional sympathy-extender, a service occupation that turns out to exemplify
the increasingly common lot of the professional in its tendency to incur the burdens of its own efficiency. The better Eliot's art performs its function, the more
routine the process of generating sympathy threatens to become. A reader working her way from the early stories up to *Middlemarch* and *Daniel Deronda* might
be excused for wondering just how many times, and in how many variations, she
had encountered one of Eliot's narrators (or characters, for that matter) employing
the formulaic phrase *"poor X,"* where "X" is some character's name or more gen-

---

[6] Cited in Haight, *George Eliot,* 367–68.

[7] Concerned that the extensively researched *Romola* would degenerate from narrative into catalogue, G. H. Lewes urged Eliot's publisher to "discountenance the idea of a Romance being the product of an Encyclopedia" (cf. Haight, *George Eliot,* 353). Eliot herself thought that the book contained
"scarcely a phrase, an incident, an allusion, that did not gather its value to me from its supposed sub-
servience to my main artistic objects" (Haight 367). During the composition of *Middlemarch,* she told
Blackwood, "I don't see how I can leave anything out, because I hope there is nothing that will be seen
to be irrelevant to my design" (Haight 435).

[8] From *The Gondoliers,* in *The Complete Annotated Gilbert & Sullivan,* ed. Ian Bradley (New York:
Oxford University Press, 1996), 937.

eral designation. The gesture of compassionating a character runs the risk of turning predictable and stale, rather like the so-called poster-child syndrome faced by charity fundraisers. It is possible, then, to regard Eliotic self-interruption as an attempt to counteract the routinization endemic to professional activity as such: it might testify to the way in which the very success of a professional paradigm can bring about a crisis of its legitimacy.[9]

At the same time, Eliot's fictional practice, so manifestly different from that of Dickens or Brontë, shares with their work the tendency to raise visions of a boundless commercial or imperial domain in order to stimulate a return of the gaze to local and national contexts. In the remarkable case of Joshua Rigg, the crisis in novelistic form that might result from more prolonged occupation of his viewpoint arises as part of the autoethnographic project of grasping an English culture in its densely integrated and self-regarding totality: when we withdraw so abruptly from Rigg's point of view, we are also averting our eyes from an outward-looking orientation that seems the very opposite of the cultivated insularity Eliot's fiction aims at. The imagined reader who is reformed by that fiction and the Eliot characters whose egotism is similarly displaced and overcome in the working out of its plots receive instruction in humankind's common lot, which is, precisely, to be enmeshed in local, densely circumstantial systems of meaning-making and evaluation: readers and characters alike are enjoined to devote themselves to the study and aid of their own communities and asked to exchange global fantasies (Keys to All Mythologies, for instance) for "incalculably diffusive" acts of specific good (M 838). The fictive domain called "Middlemarch" is a place where one confronts Dante's paradox of emphasizing the commonality of "our life's journey"—a decisive, celebrated moment late in Eliot's novel involves Dorothea's feeling of identification with some strangers on a road (M 788)—while also regarding protagonists as inextricably situated in particular historical societies. The learner of Eliot's lessons would emulate the narrator's own principled refusal to disperse her attention (as Fielding had done) across the whole of "that tempting range of relevancies called the universe," instead concentrating it upon the task of "unravelling *certain* human lots, and seeing how they were woven and interwoven" in "this particular web" (M 141; emphasis added). Yet Joshua Rigg is someone who turns his back on all this: he dreams of perching on the very edge of England, his eyes upon the coming and going of ships, his hands upon "the breeding coins of all nations" (M 520). His endless conversion of money into money is made to appear an unproductive exchange—a kind of "breeding" that cultivates nothing new—in contrast to the novelist's alchemy that transforms self-isolating English individuals into elements of a common web of culture and plot. Where Mr. Bulstrode regards Rigg's destiny as pertaining to "the unmapped regions not taken under providential government," Eliot's narrator pointedly indicates that it belongs to an unmappable world not under *her* government.

---

[9] Cf. my "'Culture' and the Critics of *Dubliners*," *James Joyce Quarterly* 37/1–2 (Fall 1999-Winter 2000), 43–62, on the professional phenomenon of "reaping what one sows."

So too, at another stage in *Middlemarch,* is Mr. Brooke's insincere politicking as a supporter of "Reform" presented as the diversion of ethical attention away from pressing nearby problems onto vague "unmapped regions" (M 520). Dorothea echoes the "circle-of-duty" creed of Esther Summerson in *Bleak House* in telling her candidate uncle, "I think we have no right to come forward and urge wider changes for good, until we have tried to alter the evils which lie under our own hands" (M 389). Instead of heeding her, however, Brooke ignores the squalor in which his tenants live and takes up the banner of a cause that remains wholly abstract to him. Joshua Rigg's literal future of gazing out to sea rather than back upon inland English communities—heart-of-England communities, like "Middlemarch"—is matched in figurative terms by Brooke's disastrous speech making from the hustings. The impending speech appears to Brooke as a perilous sea-journey on which "[e]mbarking would be easy, but the vision of the open sea that might come after was alarming" (M 503). Once underway, the rhetorical voyager quickly loses his compass and begins casting wildly about the whole world of thought for a theme.

> "We must look all over the globe:—'Observation with extensive view', must look every-where 'from China to Peru', as somebody says—Johnson, I think, *The Rambler,* you know. That is what I have done up to a certain point—not as far as Peru; but I've not al-ways stayed at home—I saw it wouldn't do. I've been in the Levant, where some of your Middlemarch goods go—and then, again, in the Baltic. The Baltic, now."
>
> Plying among his recollections in this way, Mr Brooke might have got along, easily to himself, and would have come back from the remotest seas without trouble; but a di-abolical procedure had been set up by the enemy. At one and the same moment there had risen above the shoulders of the crowd, nearly opposite Mr Brooke, and within ten yards of him, the effigy of himself; buff-coloured waistcoat, eye-glass, and neutral physiog-nomy, painted on rag; and there had arisen apparently in the air, like the note of the cuckoo, a parrot-like, Punch-voiced echo of his words. (M 504)

In this diabolical parody of the autoethnographic process in which Eliot herself is engaged, departure from mere locality ("I've not always stayed at home") does not lead to a productively alienated grasp of the community's whole shape and to a re-demptive return, but only to aimless ramblings across the expanse of an exhausted Enlightenment universalism, invoked through the half-remembered citation of Johnson's "The Vanity of Human Wishes." What really strands Brooke and pre-vents the "lost exordium" of his speech from "coming back [into his memory] to fetch him from the Baltic" (M 505) is the crowd's reaction to the representation of him being held aloft as he stumbles for his words. That effigy and the response it provokes are the defining opposites or sinister doubles of Eliot's community-consolidating art.

Eliot's work as a novelist is framed by the powerful 1856 essay "The Natural History of German Life," which claims for art the high vocation of "amplifying experience and extending our contact with our fellow-men beyond the bounds of our personal lot," and by "The Modern Hep! Hep! Hep!" of 1879, which places the fixed limit of nationality—at least for the foreseeable future—on that spread of fellow-feeling that Eliot so consistently and so expertly stimulates.[10] "A common humanity," she writes in the later piece,

> is not yet enough to feed the rich blood of various activity which makes a complete man. The time is not come for cosmopolitanism to be highly virtuous, any more than for communism to suffice for social energy. I am not bound to feel for a Chinaman as I feel for my fellow-countryman. . . . Affection, intelligence, duty, radiate from a centre, and nature has decided that for us English folk that centre can be neither China nor Peru.[11]

For Eliot, the global domain across which Doctor Johnson's enlightened gaze had traveled could not be expected to confer meaningful identities or obligations upon "law-thirsty" human souls (M 73). "Every limit," she writes at the end of *Middlemarch,* "is a beginning as well as an ending" (M 832): like the rules of a game, nationality imposes the limit that makes it possible for meaningful "play" to commence. As her last novel, *Daniel Deronda,* attempts colossally to prove, a "many-sided sympathy" that encourages identification with all and sundry only "hinder[s] any persistent course of action" and ultimately cancels itself out, falling "into one current with that reflective analysis which tends to neutralise sympathy." Before Daniel discovers his unsuspected Jewishness, his "too reflective and diffusive sympathy [is] in danger of paralysing in him that indignation against wrong and that selectness of fellowship which are the conditions of moral force"; he longs for some stimulus that would "urge him into a definite line of action, and compress his wandering energy," a force "that would justify partiality" and make him part of "a binding history" (DD 364, 365, 368). When he learns the truth about his ancestry, it is "as if he ha[s] found an added soul . . . his judgment no longer wandering in the mazes of impartial sympathy, but choosing, with that noble partiality which is man's best strength, the closer fellowship that makes sympathy practical—exchanging that bird's-eye reasonableness which soars to avoid preference and loses all sense of quality, for the generous reasonableness of drawing shoulder to shoulder with men of like inheritance" (DD 745). As Mrs. Meyrick puts it, "Saint Anybody is a bad saint to pray to" (DD 370)—a phrase reminiscent of John Jarndyce's quip, in Dickens's *Bleak House,* that "the universe makes rather an indifferent parent."

Though more pronounced in her later writings, an emphasis on the *anywhere's nowhere* logic that identifies the nation as setting the outer limit of any workable sympathy, and on the national import of plots focused quite narrowly on local actions and communities, is never absent from the novelist's work. Her first novel, set in 1799, featured an idealized hero whose "tall stalwartness" identified him as "a Saxon, and justified his name"—that of the historian Bede, keeper of Saxon memory—while "the jet-black hair . . . and the keen glance of the dark eyes that

---

[10] In Eliot, *Selected Critical Writings,* ed. Rosemary Ashton (Oxford: Oxford University Press, 1992), 260–95; see 263–64.

[11] Eliot, *The Impressions of Theophrastus Such* (1879; London: Dent, 1995), 138–39; henceforth ITS.

shone from under strongly marked, prominent, and mobile eyebrows, indicated a mixture of Celtic blood."[12] It was pointedly observed of this hero by a passing stranger that "[w]e want such fellows as he to lick the French" (AB 19), though his real contributions are domestic, like those of many humble men across the country who act quietly and locally for good, "their lives hav[ing] no discernible echo beyond the neighbourhood where they dwel[l]" but setting patterns for English virtue that are applicable, mutatis mutandis, in all the nation's neighborhoods (AB 213).

In *The Mill on the Floss,* the busy, self-important doings of a community almost wholly lacking in broader historical, political, and economic perspectives are set against the deep-historical national landscape of "incarnate history" shaped by "the Roman legions," "the Saxon-hero-king," "the dreadful heathen Dane," the Normans, and others (MF 181), while the kind of intense attachment to one's native place that Wordsworth exalted as the stabilizing English excellence is preferred to the "instructed vagrancy" of modern cosmopolitans, "nourished on books of travel and stretch[ing] the theatre of its imagination to the Zambesi," "which has hardly time to linger by the hedgerows, but runs away early to the tropics and is at home with palms and banyans" (MF 352).[13] The fable of Silas Marner unfolds in a village "in the rich central plain of what we are pleased to call Merry England" and implies that all England should emulate the redeeming love consecrated in the tale set there.[14] *Romola* centers on a heroine whose "nature, . . . recoil[s] from [a] hopelessly shallow readiness which professed to appropriate the widest sympathies and had no pulse for the nearest"; "her feelings," she discovers, cannot "go wandering after the possible and the vague: their living fibre [is] fed with the memory of familiar things"; she strives to find a "consistent duty" amid the cynical power struggles of Savonarola's Florence, and her story was conceived during the final movements of the Italian Risorgimento.[15]

Felix Holt, The Radical examines the transformation of "a respectable market-town [at] the heart of a great rural district" as it assumes "the more complex life brought by mines and manufactures, which belong more directly to the great circulating system of the nation than to the local system to which they have been superadded," and comes "to know the higher pains of a dim political consciousness."[16] A slogan for this novel holds that "there is no private life which has not been determined by a wider public life," and the work's answer to divisive party politics is that the wider public life of the nation can be reformed and reunified through the dedicated local efforts of private individuals (FH 50). Much of this novel's interest is focused on the young Esther, who must refuse her long-desired opportunity to become "queen" of a great house in order to start functioning in focused, pragmatic ways as a moral Queen Esther for the salvation of her people. The novel's charismatic title character, whose cause Esther enlists in, acknowl-

[12] Eliot, *Adam Bede* (1859; Harmondsworth: Penguin, 1980), 8; henceforth AB.

[13] "Incarnate history": from "The Natural History of German Life," *Selected Critical Writings,* 281.

[14] *Silas Marner* (1861; Harmondsworth: Penguin, 1967), 53; henceforth SM.

[15] *Romola* (1863; Harmondsworth: Penguin, 1980), 354, 652, 586, respectively.

[16] *Felix Holt, The Radical* (1866; Harmondsworth: Penguin, 1995), 47, 49; henceforth FH.

edges the presence of vast, unfulfillable ambitions in himself but then devotes himself heart and soul "to make life less bitter for a few within [his] reach" (FH 263), to the achievement of moral benefit in "small things, such as will never be known beyond a few garrets and workshops" (FH 435). The moral imagination animating *Felix Holt* strives for a utopian national unity best described by the evangelical Mr. Lyon as he prepares his sermon on the text from Chronicles, "And all the people said, Amen": "the shout of one nation as of one man, rounded and whole" yet formed by millions of uncoerced individual cries of assent (FH 53). The lessons of *Middlemarch* are carried to London at the close of that novel by Will and Dorothea Ladislaw, where Will promises to inject them into the nation's political life while his wife seconds his efforts with myriad diffusive "unhistoric acts" (M 838); meanwhile, back in Middlemarch, the reformed Fred Vincy and his wife Mary redeem the petrified wasteland of Stone Court by making it a home for love and duty. Seeds of hope are planted in both capital city and provincial "middle." *Daniel Deronda,* of course, contrasts the faithless cosmopolitanism of some of its English characters—first glimpsed passing the "breeding coins of all nations" through their hands at a Continental casino—with the energy-directing nationalism Daniel discovers as his birthright.[17]

A theme of this book has been that the so-called culture-concept of modern times arises only in tandem with the model of the Participant Observer, and that we need to attend to the reciprocal relationship between them if we are to complete our view of *culture's* emergence and of the role English novels played in the process. The idea of discrete cultures ideally coextensive with, though dissociatable from, tribal or state territories brings with it a variety of attempts to represent and conceive of the kind of position one must attain in relation to one of these cultures in order to claim authoritative knowledge of it. In Eliot, to go along with the consistent emphasis on realist thick description and on national frame of reference there also appears the regular and visible project of assessing insider's and outsider's angles of vision on social reality, as well as plentiful signs of the narrator's efforts to reimport into the domain of characters the benefits of the strategically alienated viewpoint I have labeled *insider's outsideness.*

In *Adam Bede,* the arrival of a traveling stranger at the end of the book's first chapter has usually been regarded as a "clumsy" device for obtaining a comprehensive, outsider's view of the rural community that is to be intensively studied in the novel, a device that reduces that community to the status of "something merely seen," rather than known from the inside, as most of the narrative will attempt to know it.[18] It is certainly true that this personage, who first admires the gait and

---

[17] Cf. Amanda Anderson, *The Powers of Distance: Cosmopolitanism and the Cultivation of Detachment* (Princeton: Princeton University Press, 2001), 119–46, for a reading that regards this novel as searching for a productive space *between* "rigid law and traditionalism on the one hand" and "deracinated cosmopolitanism on the other" (139).

[18] Philip Fisher, *Making Up Society: The Novels of George Eliot* (Pittsburgh: University of Pittsburgh Press, 1981), 41. In her fascinating *George Eliot and Nineteenth-Century Science: The Make-Believe of a Beginning* (Cambridge: Cambridge University Press, 1984) Sally Shuttleworth somewhat overplays an opposition between an early "natural historian" narrator, a mere "passive observer of so-

bearing of Adam himself, then takes in the vista of the village and surroundings and stays to listen to the open-air sermon of the Methodist Dinah, offers readers a "traveled" point of view from which the individual characters and unique locations to be dealt with in the novel can appear *typical*—a function vital to the activation of national allegory. Yet the perspective he makes available to us is hardly that of the utterly detached aesthete whose cold capacity for savoring what Eliot later calls "picturesque sentimental wretchedness" (AB 180) made the discourse of picturesqueness so suspect to Victorian commentators;[19] nor does the novel permit him to remain a detached and anonymous observer. At the beginning of chapter 45, the stranger makes a strange and striking return to the sphere of characters, this time acquiring a name ("Colonel Townley" [AB 447]) and performing a small but essential service: the reflective traveler with the "ruminating air" about him turns out to be a magistrate with "power in the prison" where Hetty Sorrell awaits condemnation for the killing of her child, and he arranges to get Dinah admitted to the criminal's cell (AB 446). "I know you have a key to unlock hearts," he tells her, but without his intervention in unlocking the prison door first, Dinah's mission of mercy and the redemptive tears that flow from it cannot commence (AB 447). Precisely enacting the itinerary of the narrator as autoethnographer, the figure who affords readers a view from outside the community does not *remain* outside that community, but returns to take decisive ethical action in it; detachment becomes an indispensable moment in the longer duration of belonging. Adam Bede himself expresses the pleasure and importance of such moments when he remarks, "I like to go to work by a road that'll take me up a bit of a hill, and see the fields for miles round me, and a bridge, or a town, or a bit of a steeple here and there. It makes you feel the world's a big place, and there's other men working in it with their heads and hands besides yourself" (AB 120).

At the outset of *The Mill on the Floss,* the narrator identifies herself as one returning after a long absence to St. Ogg's, her native place as well as her protagonist's. Beginning to lose herself in reminiscences, the narrator testifies to her desire to re-enter the scenes of her acculturation but also exhibits that desire as a dangerous one that might eliminate all further possibilities of productive detachment. She thinks about how the outflowing River Floss is met by "the loving tide [which], rushing to meet it, checks its passage with an impetuous embrace" (MF 53): such language points forward to the fate of the novel's heroine whose drowning in that river is the final defeat of a career spent vainly trying to lift herself out of the current of her time and culture. When the narrator tells us that the scene inspires her to be "in love with moistness" and to "envy the white ducks that are dipping their heads far into the water," the slightly absurd image acquires uncomfortable overtones. This initial chapter stages the question of whether a return to one's culture must take the form of a total re-immersion in it. Are those who re-

---

cial life," and the later "experimental psychologist" who is "an active participant" in the fictive world (1).

[19] Cf. my *The Beaten Track: European Tourism, Literature, and the Ways to "Culture," 1800–1918* (Oxford: Oxford University Press, 1993), 192–216.

turn to their cultures in no better condition than those who never left them—those who flowed along with the current and never lifted their heads above it? Eliot tends to represent her cultural insiders as enjoying the benefits but also exhibiting the limitations of a mainly subrational, animal existence of habit and custom: with the disastrous exceptions of Mr. Tulliver's and Maggie's impetuous unconventionalities, the "emmet-like Dodsons and Tullivers" (MF 363) fit John Stuart Mill's characterization of the person "who lets the world, or his portion of it, choose his plan of life for him" and therefore "has no need of any other faculty than the ape-like one of imitation."[20]

This novel's remarkable opening reflections come to a head in a passage that looks very much like the antithesis of that "autoethnographic uncanny" that I have considered throughout this book: instead of impressing us with the sense that a narrator has come to stand alongside a character in the fictional story-space and has brought the perspective of an achieved insider's outsideness with her, the passage in question appears to bring the intrusive figure of Maggie Tulliver into the *discourse-space,* threatening to inundate that domain of reflection and to obliterate the narrator's separate consciousness. "Now I can turn my eyes towards the mill again," the narrator thinks, "and watch the unresting wheel sending out its diamond jets of water. That little girl is watching it too: she has been standing on just the same spot at the edge of the water ever since I paused on the bridge . . . rapt in its movement. . . . It is time . . . for me to leave off resting my arms on the cold stone of this bridge . . ." (MF 54–55). With that last ellipsis, Eliot's own, the narrator drops off to sleep, leaving Maggie in sole command of the scene. The final paragraph of the chapter then pulls back—as if with a silent "Enough!"—from the pit of overidentification into which the narrator has momentarily tumbled, and the vision of the little girl who shares the narrator's space is dispelled as a dream. "Ah, my arms really are benumbed," writes the narrator: "I have been pressing my elbows on the arms of my chair and dreaming that I was standing on the bridge in front of Dorlcote Mill as it looked one February afternoon many years ago" (MF 55). Only by preserving the boundary between inside and outside can the narrator go on to effect further strategic returns to the story-space, returns that will not negate her power to extricate herself once more. When in the course of the narrative the desperate Maggie comes across the writings of Thomas à Kempis and follows "the quiet hand" of a previous reader of those writings, she learns from it "the possibility of shifting the position from which [to look] at the gratification of her own desires, of taking [a] stand out of herself"—the possibility, in other words, of becoming no one, like a narrator (MF 384). But to the autoethnographic novelist this must not mean achieving "a lasting stand on serene heights above worldly temptation and conflict": she seeks a way of extracting corrective detachment from the Medieval ascetic without giving his self-negating perspective unchecked predominance (MF 451). In the novel's struggle to locate the grounds of an accord between culture and freedom, absolute outsideness cannot be permitted to hold sway any more than unreflective insideness can.

---

[20] Mill, *On Liberty,* ed. Currin V. Shields (1859; New York: Macmillan, 1956), 71.

The traveling stranger's viewpoint is again on display in the fascinating introductory chapter of *Felix Holt,* where we sit atop a stagecoach moving through the landscape thirty-five years before the novel's composition. Eliot's narrator establishes the advantages of this position by contrasting it to both an imagined future form of travel that severs any connection between traveler and traversed territory, on the one hand, and various traveled-past forms of fixity in place and corresponding narrowness of vision, on the other. "Posterity may be shot, like a bullet through a tube, by atmospheric pressure from Winchester to Newcastle," she notes,

> but the slow old-fashioned way of getting from one end of the country to the other is the better thing to have in the memory. The tube-journey can never lend much to picture and narrative; it is as barren as an exclamatory O! Whereas the happy outside passenger seated on the box from dawn to the gloaming gathered enough stories of English life, enough of English labours in town and country, enough aspects of earth and sky, to make episodes for a modern Odyssey. (FH 3)

Glimpsed from the coach-top, the particular localities passed in review yield stories of *English* life and labors: *mere* locality is lifted to the national plane by means of the productive detachment embodied in the traveler. The autoethnographic possibilities of the tale that follows this chapter become apparent when we recognize that it focuses on two latter-day Odysseuses, returnees to the region who are quite schematically opposed to each other as potential reformers: Harold Transome comes back from years at Smyrna to put forward a cynical, divisive "radicalism" and "head the mob" (FH 34); Felix Holt returns from his studies in Glasgow possessed of a vision and a creed that could truly and worthily, or so the novel suggests, set the English Ithaca in order. At a time when political and economic developments are undeniably drawing the small market town of Treby Magna into "the great circulating system of the nation" (FH 47), the creed of Felix Holt arises as a definitively local phenomenon (devoted to intimate, face-to-face reforms) capable of circulating nationally in Eliot's novel.

I have already indicated some ways in which *Middlemarch* introduces the issue of its narrator's position and authority into the domain of the novel's characters. In his botched political speech, Mr. Brooke violates, and helps to define *by* violating, the autoethnographic principle that there is only one thing more important to the aim of knowing one's own culture than departing from it, and that is returning *to* it: he sets off for the wide open sea of Johnsonian, philosophical reflection and generalization but cannot find his way back again, his rambling oratory failing to do what Mr. Brooke is always claiming credit for doing, namely to "pull up" before running away with itself. All this massive novel's many case studies in self-deluding, self-interested interpretation—Dorothea's misreading of Casaubon, Rosamund's of Lydgate (and vice versa), Fred Vincy's of Featherstone's intentions, and so on—give evidence of the need for a position outside the web in which these characters enmesh themselves, a mobile viewpoint that can disrupt each single character's fatal momentum. Mr. Casaubon's Key to All Mythologies, the universal scope and interested thesis of which make it an obvious contrast to Eliot's self-interrupting study of "this particular web," is one "not likely to bruise itself unawares against discoveries," a self-confirming system "as free from interruption as a plan for threading the stars together" (M 478–79).

But the contrast evoked here and throughout the novel is not simply that between distortingly partial and wholly disinterested views: Eliot's narrator figures detachment *as an element of* worthy reattachment or participation in the collective life. The level-headed Mary Garth, who has grasped by a young age "that things were not likely to be arranged for her peculiar satisfaction" and learned "to take life very much as a comedy," does not thereby assume some permanently proto-Nietzschean stance of aesthetic contemplation on the human absurdities played out before her: she makes the "generous resolution not to act the mean or treacherous part" in the drama, recognizing that she "might have become cynical if she had not had parents whom she honoured, and a well of affectionate gratitude within her, which was all the fuller because she had learned to make no unreasonable claims" (M 314). It is not often remarked that Mary and the husband she helps to reform at last, Fred Vincy, become authors at the end of the novel, and that their authorship complements and extends the ethic of quotidian duty they embody as the vitality-restoring tenants of Stone Court: Fred becomes "a theoretic and practical farmer" and pens a work, appropriate to the Waste Land motif in which he participates, on "the *Cultivation of Green Crops and the Economy of Cattle-Feeding;* Mary writes *Stories of Great Men, taken from Plutarch,* for the guidance of her sons.

Dorothea herself struggles toward that famous revelation which not only vouchsafes to her a view of "the largeness of the world and the manifold wakings of men to labour and endurance" but simultaneously makes her feel "a part of that involuntary, palpitating life": she has at her disposal a more "luxurious shelter" to look at life from than Mary Garth enjoys, but no more than for Mary can Dorothea's displacement from the center of things result in the perspective of "a mere spectator" (M 788). Moving outward from narrow self-absorption, Dorothea receives the sympathetic visits of figures that seem to move inward from a position removed from the story-space of her world. In that "blue-green boudoir" that becomes Dorothea's sanctuary in her husband's house, the "pale stag" in the tapestry takes on the look of meaning to say "mutely" to Dorothea, on behalf of the witnessing furniture, "Yes, we know," and "the group of delicately-touched miniatures" hanging on the walls—among them the portrait of Will Ladislaw's wronged mother—make up "an audience as of beings no longer disturbed about their own earthly lot, but still humanly interested" (M 371).[21] This strange moment is comparable to those in Dickens's *Bleak House* when the impersonal narrator appears to have departed the safety of discourse-space and temporarily crossed over into the precinct of characters: like Eliot's narrator, these consoling witnesses are detached from Dorothea's particular web, but not completely or permanently so.

In perhaps the most astounding moment in *Daniel Deronda,* a book not short of

[21] The iconography of the stag, of course, is that of Christ, the suffering and sympathizing god. Cf. Eliot's "Evangelical Teaching: Dr. Cumming," in *Selected Critical Writings,* on "the life and death of Christ as a manifestation of love that constrains"—or interrupts—"the soul" (141).

them, the nineteenth-century English are said to exist in a condition comparable to the diaspora of the Jews. Eliot reaches back to and works through the model of British nation making found not in Scott's *Waverley* but in his *Ivanhoe*. Having learned his ethnicity and acquired his proper destiny, Daniel tells Gwendolen Grandcourt of his plan "of restoring a political existence to [his] people, making them a nation again, giving them a national centre, such as the English have"; and he then adds, in an arresting afterthought, "though they too are scattered over the face of the globe" (DD 803). The passage provocatively likens the supremely powerful nation to the proverbially powerless and unrealized one on the grounds that, though the former possesses capital city, state institutions, and sovereign territory, the lack of any effective check upon its imperial reach has resulted in a *dispersal* of its agents and energies rather than a gathering and focusing of them. Eliot makes her Jewish hero an inside-outsider among the English of the period after the 1857 Indian "mutiny" and immediately after the 1865 Jamaican "rebellion," when, assuming the imperial mantle with a new deliberateness, they were more prone than ever to exalt and export their ways as universalizable Civilization than to regard them as one national culture among others. Daniel's career provides an uncanny mirror for the mentality Eliot diagnoses in her essay "The Modern Hep! Hep! Hep!" when she ventriloquizes her countrymen by writing, "We do not call ourselves a dispersed and a punished people: we are a colonising people, and it is we who have punished others" (ITS 138). This is the mentality Daniel himself dismisses when he quits Cambridge, saying, "I want to be an Englishman, but I want to understand other points of view. And I want to get rid of a merely English attitude in studies" (DD 183).

Yet opposites turn likenesses when we recognize that this ethnocentrism that encourages the English, self-identified as "possessors of the most truth and the most tonnage" (ITS 141–42), to ship their values around the world, parallels the omnidirectional *sympathy* Daniel exhibits in his interactions with others before discovering his parentage. This is the tendency Hans Meyrick refers to when, after Daniel has sacrificed his own prospects at Cambridge in laboring to secure Hans's, he says, "while you are hoisting me you are risking yourself" (DD 182). Daniel provides the imperial English with the admonitory example of a radically centrifugal being whose "half-speculative, half-involuntary identification of himself with the objects he was looking at"—whichever and wherever those might be—had led him to think "how far it might be possible to shift his centre till his own personality would be no less outside him than the landscape" (DD 189). To learn from the story of Daniel's development and self-discovery—which, immediately after the passage I have just quoted, takes its fateful turn as Daniel rescues the despairing Mirah from suicide, and so begins the process by which he, too, might be rescued from his fatal centerlessness—to learn from this story would be to develop a viewpoint like that of Eliot's narrator, designed to recover a positive cultural nationalism for dominant England, a collective "enthusiasm" capable of "keep[ing] unslacked where there is no danger, no challenge" (DD 381), and one whose tendency will somehow be to oppose rather than serve chauvinistic narrowness.

Insofar as the Jewish Daniel is put forward as the kind of charismatic leader England needs—as an anti-Disraeli, in fact—we must take into account that his exemplary "social captainship" (DD 750) is based on the explicit refusal to be simply the transmitter of traditional wisdom or values passed to him from ancestors and teachers. Even when he discovers who he racially is and when he says "my whole being is a consent to the fact" (DD 750), Daniel still pulls up short of going entirely *native*. "I shall call myself a Jew," he determines, "[b]ut I will not say that I shall profess to believe exactly as my fathers have believed" (DD 725). Later he holds the enraptured Mordecai at bay by asking not to be bound by the promise to consider his own soul simply merged in the larger oneness of national being: for Daniel, "what we can't hinder"—who are parents were—"must not make our rule for what we ought to choose" (DD 751). He insists upon remaining loyal to his "spiritual parentage" in English Christianity even as he learns to decipher "the clue of [his] life in the recognition of [his] natural parentage" in Judaism (DD 751). Preserving his Englishness as the check upon his Jewishness, and cultivating his newfound Judaism as a check upon any "merely English attitude," Daniel makes this double allegiance available, in turn, to Gwendolen as the catalyst for *her* rededicated Englishness. Their two irreconcilable narratives intertwine as provocatively and, Eliot seems to intend, perhaps as productively, as do the two incommensurable voices of Dickens's nation-making *Bleak House*.

That Daniel would come to perform this service for Gwendolen was suggested from the start, when he redeemed her father's chain from a Continental pawnbroker's (DD 19–20); it is acknowledged at last when she writes to him, "it shall be better with me because I have known you" (DD 810). In a manner comparable to what we have seen in *Villette* (in chapter 10), Gwendolen's consciousness of Daniel's *different* national consciousness, her incorporation of his positive and irreducibly alien aspirations into her own mentality, decenters her nationalism but also provides the impetus for more valuably recentering it. He functions for her (and for Mordecai, it may be added) the way Eliot's narrator does—an arrangement foreshadowed when Gwendolen thinks, at one point in the novel, "I wish he could know everything about me without my telling him" (DD 430). Like the narrator, Daniel is a device internal to an English mind and an English novel for taking Englishness profitably and not permanently outside itself: he is precisely the kind of "contrivance" John Stuart Mill thought necessary to prevent the routinization of custom in situations where custom has come to enjoy virtually undisputed command of the field.[22] Daniel "dislodge[s]" Gwendolen finally and decisively "from her supremacy in her own world" by giving her "a sense that her horizon was but a dipping onward of an existence with which her own was revolving" (DD 804). As distinct from the domestic English anticulture of Grandcourt, in which intersubjectivity has come to mean forced participation in a series of zero-sum games, Eliot's vision of inter(-national)subjectivity aims at a productive displacement of British self-awareness through genuine recognition of another's national culture.

Eliot's later work places us on the threshold of the twentieth-century global

[22] Cf. Mill, *On Liberty*, 53–54.

mappings enshrined in the League of Nations and later in the United Nations, institutions over whose doors might be inscribed Daniel Deronda's slogan of "separateness with communication" (DD 725). In "The Modern Hep! Hep! Hep!" Eliot suggested raising to the plane of nations Mill's argument, from *On Liberty*, "that from the freedom of individual men to persist in idiosyncracies the world may be enriched" (ITS 155). "Why should we not apply this argument to the idiosyncracy of the nation, and pause in our haste to hoot it down?" she asked. As in Mill's writings, however, this principle could not be universalized in Eliot's: as in Brontë, foreign realms offering productive displacement and then re-placement of English national identity were distinguished from others deemed too distant and different to guarantee returns on English imaginative investment. For Eliot, a possible Jewish nation belonged in the former category because the Jews were a European problem and the people "whose ideas have determined the religion of half the world, and that the more cultivated half" (ITS 140). The Jews were the type rather than the exception for European peoples striving (or who *ought* to be striving) to retrieve their national identities, but they were the type for the nation-*worthy*, while to the rest Eliot could offer only an open-endedly temporizing "not yet."

For the lucky former, the musician Klesmer's composition entitled *Freudvoll, Leidvoll, Gedankenvoll*, in *Daniel Deronda*, described a nation-making dialectic of unreflective at-homeness, displacement, and recovery on a higher plane of consciousness. Jewish homelessness—the suicidal Mirah says, "[t]here was no reason why I should go anywhere" (DD 222)—is bizarrely mimicked in imperial English "world-nausea," the "sick motivelessness" of Gwendolen (DD 272, 274) or the "languor of intention that [comes] over Grandcourt, like a fit of diseased numbness, when an end seem[s] within easy reach" (DD 150), symptoms that arise from having *too many* places to go. The higher national consciousness that promises to heal these ailments would involve (what Walter Benn Michaels has called) the "oxymoron" of "cultural pluralism," but of a strictly nonuniversal variety, not (yet) capable of extension to those vast regions of the world where, as Mill notoriously put it in *On Liberty*, "the despotism of Custom is complete," where traditional mentalities have not suffered the dislodging that may lead to revalidation.[23] Where Mill thought a struggle between custom and reason necessary for genuine historical existence, Eliot thought Klesmer's dialectic necessary for the achievement of genuine cultural existence.

That dialectic of *Freudvoll, Leidvoll, Gedankenvoll*—Joyful, Sorrowful, Thoughtful—is, of course, less Germanic than Wordsworthian, from such poems as "Tintern Abbey" and "Resolution and Independence." Eliot's abiding Wordsworthianism is never more strikingly on display than it is near the start of *Daniel Deronda*, in the famous passage that begins by lamenting Gwendolen's lack of a home "endeared to her by family memories." The passage continues:

> A human life, I think, should be well rooted in some spot of a native land, where it may
> get the love of tender kinship for the face of earth, for the labours men go forth to, for

---

[23] Michaels, *Our America: Nativism, Modernism, and Pluralism* (Durham, N.C.: Duke University Press, 1995), 139; Mill, *On Liberty*, 86.

the sounds and accents that haunt it, for whatever will give that early home a familiar unmistakable difference amidst the future widening of knowledge: a spot where the defi-
niteness of early memories may be inwrought with affection, and kindly acquaintance
with all neighbours, even to the dogs and donkeys, may spread not by sentimental effort
and reflection, but as a sweet habit of the blood. At five years old, mortals are not prepared to be citizens of the world, to be stimulated by abstract nouns, to soar above preference into impartiality. . . . The best introduction to astronomy is to think of the nightly
heavens as a little lot of stars belonging to one's own homestead. (DD 22)

It does not become an element of Eliot's fiction making to worry, as Brontë always
does, about the boundary between circumscribed native locality and native "land"
in the wider national sense; for Eliot, the particular stimuli of a loved childhood
environment simply possess in themselves the capability of being translated into
the features of a national *lieu de memoire,* and no novelist attaches greater significance to such identity-grounding memory-sites than does this premier writer of
the 1860s and 1870s.

But Eliot's Wordsworthianism is as definitively reworked a borrowing as is
Mordecai's romantic idealism or, for that matter, those frequently noted Jane-
Austen-like qualities of the Gwendolen portions of *Daniel Deronda.* The echoes
of Wordsworth and Austen, in fact, serve mainly to indicate the divergence of
1860s England from romantic-era patterns. In a novel dated quite precisely in relation to the Governor Eyre controversy of 1865, Eliot's curious phrase "a sweet
habit of the blood" obviously harks back to Wordsworth's memory of youthful
"sensations sweet, / Felt in the blood," from "Tintern Abbey," but takes on a different valence. While it is true that Daniel Deronda holds out a model of national
belonging that preserves a space for the continuing reassessment and revision of
one's cultural inheritance—for choice, in other words—it remains true as well that
ethnic inheritance is regarded as setting down boundaries beyond which choice is
not to pass. Only in the always already-vanishing traditional rural community do
ethnicity and acculturation—blood and habit—supposedly go hand in hand and
do not even have to be distinguished from one another. Self-consciously mobile
groups, whose members are liable to take up residence among people with different habits and perhaps even to begin adopting some of those habits (recall Brontë's
The Professor and *Villette*), have a greater need to privilege race over culture as
the defining element of group identity. What Daniel teaches Gwendolen and the
other English is that one need not have had any direct experience of the culture
proper to one's ethnicity (as Gwendolen has not) so long as that culture is somehow held in trust, preserved in the collective memory of the race, until the moment
one decides to begin learning how to act like what one is. For Gwendolen, this collective memory is of course troped as her dead father's "chain," not just a piece of
jewelry but an unbreakable bond with the past that the present must not attempt to
discard but must learn how to honor.[24]

---

[24] This reading somewhat complicates Ian Baucom's in *Out of Place: Englishness, Empire, and the
Locations of Identity* (Princeton: Princeton University Press, 1999): though Baucom does not mention
Eliot, her Wordsworthianism would appear to substantiate his claim that, after the colonial uprisings

Eliot's allusions to Austen, also from the early stages of *Daniel Deronda,* have a similarly distorting effect, as for example when Mallinger Grandcourt's entrance into the world of the novel receives the comment, "Some readers of this history will doubtless regard it as incredible that people should construct matrimonial prospects on the mere report that a bachelor of good fortune and possibilities was coming within reach . . . : they will aver that neither they nor their first cousins have minds so unbridled; and that in fact this is not human nature, which would know that such speculations might turn out to be fallacious, and would therefore not entertain them" (DD 91). The celebrated first sentence of *Pride and Prejudice* is here turned inside out, just as the recognizable Austen milieu of three or four "good" families in a rural parish is turned inside out by the casting of a Jew in the leading male role, rather as if those intriguing gypsies from *Emma* had let themselves into Mr. Woodhouse's parlor. F. R. Leavis's notorious suggestion that the novel be bisected so as to preserve the attractive Austenian portions from contamination by the "bad part" focused on Daniel's Zionism represents a reaction, though a hysterical one to be sure, to precisely what Eliot seems to have wanted to provoke a reaction to—the undeniably visible entanglement of the tidy Austen domain in the aspirations and philosophies of aliens.[25]

The *Mansfield Park* situation in which West Indian holdings essential to the maintenance of the English country-house way of life remain discreetly offstage gives way, in *Daniel Deronda,* to a situation in which the "polite pea-shooting" conversation of an English drawing room in November 1865 turns upon "the rinderpest and Jamaica," the latter crowding out all further discussion of parlor games.

> Grandcourt held that the Jamaican negro was a beastly sort of baptist Caliban; Deronda said he had always felt a little with Caliban, who naturally had his own point of view and could sing a good song; Mrs Davilow observed that her father had an estate in Barbadoes, but that she herself had never been in the West Indies; Mrs Torrington was sure she should never sleep in her bed if she lived among blacks; her husband corrected her by saying that the blacks would be manageable enough if it were not for the half-breeds; and Deronda remarked that the whites had to thank themselves for the half-breeds. (DD 331)

As with Eliot's borrowings from Wordsworth, the evocations of Austen help chart the distance between early and later nineteenth-century English relationships of domestic to imperial space. The entanglements and troublesome self-incurred mixtures brought about by earlier, less circumspect modes of colonial rule have become impossible to banish from domestic spaces once treated as sacrosanct, with

---

in India (1857) and Jamaica (1865), "participants in the 'Condition-of-England' debates increasingly identified the British Empire as [a] threat to Englishness and . . . the resonant and memory-enshrining English locale as the one thing that could guard England against an imperial contamination" (36). Yet in *Daniel Deronda,* set against precisely this backdrop, race, not place, is finally the one "secure" determinant of national identity: the novel anticipates the dynamics of nativism and modernism Walter Benn Michaels has studied in *Our America* (cf. 128–29).

[25] Leavis, *The Great Tradition* (New York: New York University Press, 1960), 122.

the result that devices for reimposing essential distinctions among different peoples rise in value. By determining for Daniel and for Gwendolen alike which culture and which nation are properly *theirs,* the category of race would seem to be preparing the way for a "repatriation" of both. Only the stubborn persistence of the intermarried, admirable Klesmers in England—for Herr Klesmer has married the English heiress Catherine Arrowpoint—stands in the way of a recommendation for the wholesale ethnic cleansing of each nation and the clean partitioning of the civilized world into airtight container-nations for the occupation of single races. Readers today may be forgiven for wishing to seize upon the minor interruption in the workings of Eliot's narrative engine provided by Catherine Arrowpoint, who, in defying her parents by marrying the brilliant musician who is a "felicitious combination of the German, the Sclave, and the Semite," may seem to them the true heroine of *Daniel Deronda.*

CHAPTER TWELVE

Ethnography as Interruption: Morris's
News from Nowhere

The question "Where is utopia?" is the same as the question "Where is nowhere?" and the only answer to that question is "Here."
  —Northrop Frye[1]

Art always says, "And yet!" to life.
  —Georg Lukàcs[2]

IF IT SMACKS of perversity to join Eliot, nineteenth-century Britain's leading practitioner of bourgeois realism, with William Morris, its most prominent exponent of Marxist romance, I hope by this point that it will also seem fitting. For, as I suggested in the first chapter of this book, Morris's 1890 utopian tale *News from Nowhere* can be seen as a critical performance of Victorian novelistic self-interruption, affording us a strikingly defamiliarizing view of the romance of culture and authority being carried out in works, including Eliot's, celebrated and often promoted for their unprecedented verisimilitude. The novel's commitment to the "knowable community," and its attempts to imagine England or Britain *as* such a community, were precisely the features identifying its romantic urge, the urge given into with a vengeance in Morris's anti-industrial tale, to attain "a utopian glimpse of an achieved community."[3] Where in Dickens, Brontë, and Eliot, the prospect of such a community is always either deferred (and imagined through allegorical unions) or intimated through its exact, anticultural, opposites, in Morris that prospect is realized in loving detail. But the comprehensive view of the utopia of one's own culture can be had only by establishing the viewer in that position I have called *insider's outsideness.* Like the ethnographic Participant Observer, the Observing Participant of autoethnographic romance crosses the boundary that surrounds "natives" and narrative "characters," laying down and policing that line as he does so, affirming it is there to be crossed.

---

[1] Frye, "Varieties of Literary Utopia," in *The Stubborn Structure: Essays in Criticism and Society* (Ithaca, N.Y.: Cornell University Press, 1970), 134.

[2] Lukàcs, *The Theory of the Novel,* trans. Anna Bostock (Cambridge, Mass.: MIT Press, 1971), 72.

[3] "Knowable community": Raymond Williams, *The Country and the City* (New York: Oxford University Press, 1973), chap. 16; "a utopian glimpse": Fredric Jameson, "Modernism and Imperialism," in Terry Eagleton, Fredric Jameson, and Edward W. Said, *Nationalism, Colonialism, and Literature,* introduction by Seamus Deane (Minneapolis: University of Minnesota Press, 1990), 58.

In *News from Nowhere; or, An Epoch of Rest,* the boundary-work commences with the title. The more we think about this small document in relation to the text it introduces, the more inappropriate do its four nouns appear to become: for, to put it briefly, what Morris's fiction portrays is a future society that is virtually devoid of *news,* that is set in a very particular *somewhere,* that exists in a temporal condition to which the label *an epoch* cannot be applied, and that is characterized, above all else, by constant *work.* Pointedly failing to attach to the utopia itself, each noun in the title has its meaning only in terms of the *relation* between that utopia and the nineteenth-century narrator and readers who desire it. Each noun patrols the border between those desirous Victorian subjects and the future Britain that is their aim and birthright. Consider:

News: In the twenty-second-century communistic Britain that Morris envisions, the whole concept of a finger-on-the-pulse-of-events topical journalism has withered away, along with the major newsmaking, or newspaper-filling, entities familiar to nineteenth-century readers (nation-states, monarchs, Parliaments, courts of law, and so forth). Morris's narrator remarks of his future compatriots that "in default of serious news, . . . they were eager to discuss all the little details of life: the weather, the hay-crop, the last new house, the plenty or lack of such and such birds, and so on; and they talked of these things not in a fatuous and conventional way, but as taking . . . a real interest in them."[4] Their heads and calendars cleared of Victorian ideological dross, the utopians keep abreast of each minute alteration in their environment, manifesting in this attention what their spokesman calls an "intense and overweening love of the very skin and surface of the earth" (News 158).

Nowhere: Since such a love, nurtured by the smallest of details, must be love for a particular *part* of the earth, we are not surprised to learn that the future British, though entirely "free to move about" both on their island and abroad—indeed, freer than even the expanding Victorian empire to go anywhere they like—tend mostly to stay in one place (News 210). "[O]ne gets so pleasantly used to all the detail of life about one; it fits so harmoniously and happily into one's own life," says one of them, "that [relocating and] beginning again, even in a small way, is a kind of pain" (News 210). Attachment to a specific, intensely perceived landscape is also the shaping principle of the text. Outdoing its immediate forerunner, Edward Bellamy's *Looking Backward* (1888), in rendering a particularized utopian terrain, *News from Nowhere* travels between William Morris's two houses, from Hammersmith to Oxfordshire, covering the territory Morris knew best. "I may say that I know every yard of the Thames from Hammersmith to Cricklade," says the narrator (News 204). Much of the last third of the book is occupied with the telling over of well-loved spots along the river, each one slowly savored by the narrator as he rows his way upstream, into the heart of a redeemed Britain.

Epoch: Paddling along the Thames in these late chapters, Morris's narrator begins to adapt himself to the distinctive rhythm of utopian life, the rhythm of a world

---

[4] Morris, *News from Nowhere,* in *News from Nowhere and Other Writings* (Harmondsworth: Penguin, 1993), 193; henceforth News.

in which (he misquotes Tennyson's "Lotos-Eaters") "it is always afternoon" (News 204). As on that river-borne "golden afternoon" of Lewis Carroll, time in Morris's Nowhere seems not to move, everyone becomes a child again forever, and there is no such thing as history. Writing of how anthropology has tended to fix its objects at a temporal remove from their investigators, Johannes Fabian has identified a discursive principle he calls "allochronicity" or "denial of coevalness," a systematic forestalling of the possibility that the object and practitioner of anthropology could be seen as "contemporaneous."[5] The alien temporality inhabited by William Morris's British utopians is that which obtains beyond the historical dialectic, beyond the succession of "epochs"—those bounded blocks of time serving, each in their turn, as the carriers of a teleological, capital-H History. The British, of all people, have largely become (in Eric Wolf's phrase) a People Without History: there *are* no more epochs, eras, ages, or periods (though, atavistically, the Christian calendar is still in use). They are of course the products of history, but they do not live historically.

Rest: The character of Dick, Morris's generic young Briton of the future, "burst[s] out laughing" at the very thought of "people not liking to work!—it's too ridiculous," he says (News 76). Morris's utopians work a great deal; but their labor harmonizes so satisfyingly with their play that the distinction between them is lost (cf. News 160). Their one concern is that there will not be enough tasks to go around, but *this* fear of work-shortage is of course nothing like the one felt by the Victorian working class: it arises out of the need of a free humanity, assured of its means of subsistence, to realize its essence as *homo faber.* Liberated from the need to engage in what Henry Mayhew called "the riot, the struggle, and the scramble for a living" of Victorian Britain, the subjects of *News from Nowhere* nevertheless toil away with a diligence as striking to their visitor as, for instance, the diligence of Trobriand gardeners would be to Malinowski in the Western Pacific of the 1910s.[6] Both Morris's pastoral-communist Britain and Malinowski's Trobriands refute the bourgeois political economists: in both, as Malinowski writes, "work is not carried out on the principle of the least effort. On the contrary, much time and energy is spent on wholly unnecessary effort, that is, from a utilitarian point of view. . . . Work and effort, instead of being merely a means to an end, are in a way an end in themselves."[7] And however much the utopians work, they enjoy a freedom from the clock unimaginable to Victorians. Only the gentle guidance of the seasons keeps them mindful of a changing schedule of obligations—such as haymaking and harvest—and if, when nature calls them to these tasks, they happen to be engrossed in some other "piece of work which interests them" (News 195), they can be sure that enough of their neighbors will be ready and willing to take

---

[5] Cf. Fabian, *Time and the Other: How Anthropology Makes its Object* (New York: Columbia University Press, 1983), esp. 30–32.

[6] Mayhew, *London Labour and the London Poor,* ed. Victor Neuberg (Harmondsworth: Penguin, 1985), 14.

[7] Malinowski, *Argonauts of the Western Pacific* (1922; Prospect Heights, Ill.: Waveland Press, 1984), 60.

on the season's labors. In an unintentionally ironic echo of Adam Smith, an invisible hand seems to align personal wants and social necessities. In short, for Morris as for Malinowski, the Work of the Other is Art, is Play: in the ethnographic field, the distinction between "economy" and "culture" collapses. But that does not mean that the Work of the Other is *Rest*.

The only sense in which Morris's Nowhere offers "an epoch of rest," then, is in the temporary refuge—the almost literally rejuvenating vacation—it offers its nineteenth-century Guest from the conflicted history of his own epoch and the unrewarding labor of Socialist politics. In a manner strangely approximating Einstein's late "thought-experiments" or the later Club Med advertisements, Guest's rate of aging appears to slow the longer he remains in the new spatiotemporal conditions of the future land. The only sense in which *News from Nowhere* brings its readers any *news* is the nonjournalistic sense of *gospel*. First published in the Socialist League paper *Commonweal,* Morris's fiction stood in ironic proximity to news items recounting the late-breaking developments of the class struggle, and it professed the aim of refueling the revolutionary energies of its audience. The only sense in which the future Britain constitutes a "Nowhere" is in relation to the nineteenth-century Britons who have as yet failed to make it into the Somewhere where they live. Whereas Samuel Butler's utopian text *Erewhon* (1874) had used an anagram of "Nowhere" to name a distant and wholly fanciful domain, Morris's work chooses the most familiar territory possible, inviting readers to envision Nowhere as a *Now, Here*. In contravention of anthropological and most utopian practice, it takes up the *least* far-flung, most familiar, most "English" region for its study: the Home Counties, which it makes radiantly *unheimlich* by erasing from them all the mere "machinery" of the nineteenth-century landscape, social relations, and minds. It is worth noting that the comprehensive Ethnographic Survey of the United Kingdom, vainly attempted by the British Association for the Advancement of Science between 1892 and 1899, almost completely ignored these districts, in favor of the North and West, as being too well known to require ethnographic study. To the BAAS, even an "anthropology of ourselves" needed to supply something (comparatively) alien; Morris, on the other hand, applies the modern ethnographer's effort to "salvage" traditional cultures to the very heart of Britain, retrieving from it the countermodern values that might define a British culture saved from history.[8]

News conveys the strong impression that the British utopia is already "there" to be uncovered, could we but excavate beneath the layer of Industrial-era detritus that hides it. The first sign that we have entered this once-and-future Britain comes when Guest, emerging from his baptismal morning plunge into the sparkling Thames near Hammersmith, perceives that "[t]he soap-works with their vomiting chimneys were gone; the engineer's works gone; the lead-works gone"; and the hideous iron bridge has been replaced by one modeled on, but rather better than,

---

[8] Cf. James Urry, "Englishmen, Celts, and Iberians: The Ethnographic Survey of the United Kingdom, 1892–1899," in George W. Stocking Jr., ed., *Functionalism Historicized: Essays on British Social Anthropology* (Madison: University of Wisconsin Press, 1984), 83–105.

the Ponte Vecchio, built from British stones (News 48). Later, he learns that the conurbations of Manchester and Birmingham, so lamentably definitive of his own century, have simply vanished, since they were recognized as lacking all justification for existing save the spurious and obsolete one derived from industrial capitalism (News 102). Twenty-second-century Britain has "dropped the pretension to be the market of the world" (News 101), casting off the White Man's Burden in the same gesture.[9] With the obfuscatory mechanisms of Parliament swept away, such politics as there are take place in pragmatic local communes and Anglo-Saxon-style "motes." On all fronts, the Britain of Morris's dream has scrapped what Louis Althusser called, echoing the antimechanistic language of Carlyle and others, the various "state apparatuses" that held British anticulture together—in bondage.

It is in pursuit of this British culture saved from history that *News* attests to its historicity most plainly, in its relation to anthropology's concurrent, though gradual, move away from an ethnology centered on race and toward an ethnography centered on culture. The transition from Victorian to modern anthropology has often been regarded as the process by which race "vanished as a major concept," giving way to (in Alfred Cort Haddon's words), "the intensive study of limited areas" or "cultures."[10] One can enumerate the ways in which *News from Nowhere* comes nearer to twentieth-century ethnographic concepts than did its official autoethnographic counterpart, the BAAS Survey: it presents us with a single field-worker "immersed" in the visited culture, whereas the Survey employed a team of fact-gatherers; it joins roles of fact-gatherer and synthesizer of data, whereas the Survey divided them; it analyzes the particular customs of a single culture, whereas the Survey attempted a comprehensive account of a region, combining physical anthropology, folklore, linguistics, archaeology, and more; it employs a holistic, parts-for-the-whole approach, whereas the Survey held fast to, and foundered upon, an incremental, positivistic method; it envisions the study of one culture as a relatively autotelic enterprise, whereas the Survey resolutely aimed beyond itself, at a synthetic total science of Man. But for all its foreshadowing of the coming anthropological paradigm, *News* remains committed to the basic assumption of the BAAS Survey, the one idea that pioneers of the new ethnography most needed to jettison: the idea of race as the foundation, limit, and safeguard of human difference.[11] In the course of his much-discussed account of the ways of the twenty-second century and "How the Change Came" from the nineteenth, the utopians' self-appointed archivist Hammond reassures Guest that the future has

---

[9] In one oblique reference to nineteenth-century emigration and colonization, we read that Morris's utopians "have helped to populate other countries—where they were wanted and were called for" (News 106; also 123–26).

[10] Cf. Urry, "Englishmen," 100.

[11] Cf. Walter Benn Michaels, *Our America: Nativism, Modernism, and Pluralism* (Durham, N.C.: Duke University Press, 1995); henceforth Michaels; Kwame Anthony Appiah, *In My Father's House: Africa in the Philosophy of Culture* (New York: Oxford University Press, 1992), chap. 2; Robert J. C. Young, *Colonial Desire: Hybridity in Theory, Culture, and Race* (London: Routledge, 1995), chaps. 1–3.

not witnessed "the obliteration of . . . variety," but that "the different strains of
blood in the world [are now] serviceable and pleasant to each other." "Cross the
water and see," he counsels; "You will find plenty of variety." But this suggestion
works against his explicit renunciation of the "artificial and mechanical groups"
(News 117) called nations, implying that, at least where Britain is concerned, the
frontier between identity and difference is coextensive with the national boundary
that (as Linda Colley puts it) "after 1707 seemed settled once and for all."[12] There
are, to be sure, differences among the future Britons, but the implication is that the
differences that *matter* to the definition of groups are to be sought across the
Channel.

What else but race could underwrite the intense devotion to Britishness that
Morris's utopia and his utopians exhibit? That *News* is intent on preserving, not to
say sacralizing Britishness, is beyond dispute. Its two most important characters
are to be found in quintessentially British locales: Hammond, the old chronicler,
resides in the British Museum, where he dispenses the store of knowledge he and
it contain; Ellen, the muse of Morris's dreamworld, lives at Runnymede, like some
vestal keeper of Magna Carta's flame. What makes these figures choose such
places of abode? More generally, what keeps the ordinary utopians living where
they do and as they do? The stay-at-home preference of these people, who are after
all under no constraint not to follow their fancies at will, works serendipitously toward the preservation of what is at bottom, and for all Morris's repudiations of nationalism, a national culture grounded in race. Just liking to stay put, they will
breed among themselves, reproducing an ethnos that will seem at once wholly op-
tional and powerfully determining, giving identity and direction to individual lives
without requiring either national boundaries or state bureaucracies for the pro-
cessing of citizenship.

Kinship, the modern ethnographer's key to alien cultures, works the same way:
most of Morris's subjects have abandoned the rites and taboos of clan membership, have jettisoned their surnames in diving into a general pool of "neighbor-
ship," yet for some reason "separate ['family'] households are the rule amongst
[them]," and all of them retain a clear view of who is whom in relation to whom
(cf. News 98, 113). It begs the question to say that they do these things because
they prefer to: they prefer to, because they recognize certain ways of acting and
arranging themselves as right for them; they know themselves to have a culture
(involving landscape and a history) that is *theirs*. For all that they enjoy the freedom to pick and choose from other traditions—recall that bridge, modeled on the
Ponte Vecchio—they have clearly retained the conviction that other traditions *are*
other. Culture is functioning for Morris's utopians not as some external ("mechanical") set of constraints upon desire but as an internalized "system *of* desire"
without which desire gets nowhere[13]—and the utopians, as we have seen, cling

---

[12] Colley, *Britons: Forging the Nation, 1707–1837* (New Haven: Yale University Press, 1992), 17.

[13] Christopher Herbert, *Culture and Anomie: Ethnographic Imagination in the Nineteenth Century*
(Chicago: University of Chicago Press, 1991), 51.

with the full force of their "love of the very skin and surface of the earth" to their own delimited section thereof, to their own somewhere.

The adhesive power that attaches ways of doing things, landscapes, and histories to collective identities, that gives culture its affective weight, resides mainly in these figures of Hammond and Ellen, two who bear a special relationship to history and historical consciousness. In Nowhere, the only characters who still "remember" the past (all of it, including those parts they did not personally experience) are the century-old unofficial chroniclers like Hammond and his rural counterpart, Henry Morsom—characters whose retention of surnames marks them (along with "Guest"), in this world where most are on a first-name basis, as still bound to a past that the young are privileged to forget in their Nietzschean strength and joy. Hammond tells Guest that for the vast majority of the younger generation, "the last harvest, the last baby, the last knot of carving in the market-place, is history enough" (News 89). The old sage characterizes himself in a very different way, transforming the metonymic relationship of a man living among books into the synecdochic one of a man who "is" in some sense a vital member of the library's collection, one whose mind contains in its small compass all that the national archive has to tell. Dick says of him, "he looks upon himself as part of the books, or the books as a part of him, I don't know which" (News 86). (Morsom is later referred to as "another edition of old Hammond" [News 198].) This characterization permits Hammond to appear the very embodiment of that well-worn analogy that holds that "history is to the nation . . . as memory is to the individual": his society's history "is" his individual memory. He endows British culture with affect, makes it "an object of pathos," by alchemizing in the cauldron of his mind history (what happened) into memory (what happened to *us*).[14] The imperative underlying such an idea is one both Hammond and Ellen propound: we must never forget what happened to us, which means that we must guide our future actions into courses suitable for one of the "us" to whom it happened. Otherwise we risk enacting a pathetic "fall" away from who we are. Ellen gives voice to this fear in urging the reinstitution of historical study among her compatriots, for, as she says, "Who knows? happy as we are, times may alter; things may seem too wonderful for us to resist, too exciting not to catch at, if we do not know that they are but phases of what has been before; and withal ruinous, deceitful, and sordid" (News 214).

But the utopians are faced with the question, "not *which* past should count as [theirs] but why *any* past should count as t[heirs]" (Michaels 128). None of them, not even Hammond, took part in the events recounted in the "How the Change Came" section, or in the events recountable in any narrative that might be produced of any portion of a past lying beyond all current lifespans. To claim a past

---

[14] "History is . . . ": Arthur M. Schlesinger Jr., *The Disuniting of America: Reflections on a Multicultural Society* (New York: Norton, 1991), 45; "culture as an object of pathos": Walter Benn Michaels, "'You Who Never Was There': Slavery and the New Historicism, Deconstruction and the Holocaust," *Narrative* 4/1 (Jan. 1996), 1–16.

as theirs is to bind themselves, as Walter Benn Michaels puts it, to "the primacy of race," for

> [i]t is only if we think that our culture is not whatever beliefs and practices we actually happen to have but instead the beliefs and practices that should properly go with the sort of people we happen to be that the fact of something belonging to our culture can count as a reason for doing it. But to think this is to appeal to something that must be beyond culture and that cannot be derived from culture precisely because our sense of which culture is properly ours must be derived from it. This has been the function of race. (Michaels 128–29)

In *News from Nowhere,* the acknowledgment of the need for that something other and deeper than culture is never clearer than at the uncanny moment of Guest's recognition that Hammond's face "seemed strangely familiar to me; as if I had seen it before—in a looking-glass, it might be" (News 88). The bridging of the nineteenth-century epoch and the posthistorical utopia is grounded in the suggestion that Hammond is Guest's own grandson, now aged one hundred and five (this makes Dick, as Hammond's great-grandson, Guest's still more distant descendant). In Morris's future no less than in the ethnology of the nineteenth century, blood will out.

In chapter 1, I suggested that Morris's utopian antinovel "opposes its great bourgeois precursors not so much by departing from their methods as by intensifying or radicalizing them," and I situated the work amidst a turn-of-the-century aggregation of texts that, emphasizing the idea of controlled self-alienation, supplied a final step toward the emergence of the anthropological Participant Observer. In this hothouse atmosphere, Victorian-style narrative self-interruption comes "out into the open" as the textual, temporal effect corresponding to the spatial effect of a world seen as "broken up" into separate, mappable cultures. The decisive gesture of withdrawing from narrative, of refusing the lure of the very narrative one has set in motion, takes on masochistic intensity.

In *News,* the desire to imagine and live another kind of life is, of course, the motor of the entire narrative. But across the border, desire and narrative remain possible only if they are strictly delineated from each other, as Morris's text contrives to do in two interrelated ways. For one thing, the future British people whom Morris's narrator meets do sometimes tell stories (cf. News 166), but as a rule they tell them only about things they do not or no longer want, and they do not understand, nor do they *care,* why they tell them: for them, a hankering for narrative is something of a reflex or a throwback, desirous narrative a scandal. (I shall discuss this further below.) In addition, however much the utopian Britain embodies the thwarted nineteenth-century desires of its narrator, that visitor, who invents the name of Guest for himself, must remain in what is finally a spectatorial relation to that world, must restrict his engagement in any personal wish-fulfillment fantasy. A final segment of the book's title—*Being Some Chapters from a Utopian Romance*—suggests the truncated nature of the back-to-the-future dream that Morris permits himself. *News from Nowhere* stakes its authority as the work of a committed, though wavering, socialist upon the guarantee that its narrator's encounter with this other place that is also strangely his own will be temporary, offering only the Participant Observer's "simulated membership," its "membership without commitment to membership" in the visited culture.[15] If, as I argued in chapter 2, narrative is the mode by which the ethnographer conveys his achievement of insideness in that culture, fragmented or disrupted narrative is the mode by which he reassures us he is still himself, one of us. Morris's Guest needs to show—as W. S. Gilbert would say—that

> in spite of all temptations
> To belong to other nations [or to his own of the future],
> He remains an Englishman [of the Victorian age].[16]

The Other of the controlled self-alienation experiment must of course present itself *as* genuinely Other, must never challenge the borderline by being overly amenable or sedulous to the newcomer: that would amount to being "touristy." Emphasizing the aloofness or intransigence of the ethnographic subjects when first met has been an established practice in monographs whose authors claim the prestige of ultimately getting themselves accepted by those unhelpful subjects. At first sight, *News from Nowhere* appears to violate this protocol, for the frank and genial utopians Guest encounters are all too transparently an ethnographer's *dream*. Dick, the very first of the natives Guest meets, volunteers information and guidance with an alacrity that might make a modern anthropologist suspect the authenticity of what he offers. "I should take it as very kind in you if you would allow me to be the showman of our new world to you," Dick proposes (News 50).

Yet his address and actions toward Guest are consistent with the necessity to keep the roles of investigator and objects, outsider and insiders, safely distinguished. It is Dick who assigns Guest his ethnographic task and enforces the relationships appropriate to it. He instantly recognizes that "it won't do to overdose you with information about this place"—every fieldworker's dilemma of being swamped in data—advising instead that Guest "suck it in little by little" (News 50). A little later on, Hammond remarks in a similar vein to Guest, "our life is too complex for me to tell you in detail by means of words how it is arranged; you must find that out by living amongst us" (News 111). Planning to head up river for the hay-harvest, Dick says, "you might go with me, you know, . . . making notes of our ways in Oxfordshire"; and he remonstrates with his comrades who wish to interrogate the visitor,

> Of course you want the guest to be happy and comfortable; and how can that be if he has to trouble himself with answering all sorts of questions when he is still confused with the new customs and people about him? No, no: I am going to take him where he can ask questions himself, and have them answered; that is, to my great-grandfather in Bloomsbury. (News 59)

---

[15] Bernard McGrane, *Beyond Anthropology: Society and the Other* (New York: Columbia University Press, 1989), 125.

[16] From *H. M. S. Pinafore,* in *The Complete Annotated Gilbert & Sullivan,* ed. Ian Bradley (New York: Oxford University Press, 1996), 173.

You ask the questions, you take notes on *us,* he says: his going to such lengths to ensure that Guest preserve a properly ethnographic relation to all he will see is a measure of the anxiety felt about the possibility of Guest's "going native" if not so restrained. Such behavior goes beyond revealing Dick to be one of the conventional guide figures found throughout utopian literature, those native informants who supply visitors with a concentrated tutorial in utopian manners and morals. It hints at how alarmingly liable the visitor is to lose control of the desire that impels the journey, and thereby to relinquish the authority for the sake of which the journey is taken. (In Robert Louis Stevenson's famous tale of the same period, what begins as Jekyll's attempt to turn himself for controlled periods into Hyde winds up as a desperate and eventually futile struggle not even to recover his old identity but simply to impersonate his formerly authoritative self before the world, so that "it seemed only by a great effort as of gymnastics, and only under the immediate stimulation of the drug, that I was able to wear the countenance of Jekyll.")[17]

Interruptions appear throughout the narrative of *News from Nowhere,* and nowhere more strikingly than in its structure. The whole work is an interrupted narrative, clearly divisible into three parts: the arrival and initial discoveries; the encounter with Hammond; and the trip up river to Kelmscott, capped by the always anticipated return to Victorian times. The Hammond section itself is likewise divisible: it begins in the interview mode typical of mid-Victorian works of social analysis, such as the Parliamentary Blue Books or the urban reportage of Edwin Chadwick and Henry Mayhew; it diverges briefly into an approximation of Socratic dialogue; it then shifts into a historical account of the revolution that ended capitalism. It can be read as a valedictory to Whig history, or as a compressed historical novel,[18] contained as a necessary intrusion upon the material of Guest's own narrative, the details of everyday utopian life. Placed as it is within the structure of *News from Nowhere,* Hammond's tale initiates Guest into the successful ethnographer's position of honorary insideness: Guest becomes the privileged possessor of Hammond's inside lore, even as the job of narration passes from Guest to Hammond. Guest's "joining" the utopian society is betokened by the story Hammond tells, which narratively links nineteenth and twenty-second centuries. Guest is, in Vincent Pecora's terms, "the new master of social magic," the anthropologist who "slips into the position of apprentice" to the shaman, who in turn "embodies synecdochically that mastery of culture sought by the anthropologist."[19] We have already noted the biological link and physical resemblance between the two men that set their seal upon this rite of accreditation.

But to be joined to utopia by means of Hammond's history is in another sense to be cut off from it. The shaman's occult wisdom consists not only of the infor-

---

[17] Stevenson, "The Strange Case of Dr. Jekyll and Mr. Hyde," in *Dr. Jekyll and Mr. Hyde and Other Stories* (Harmondsworth: Penguin, 1979), 95.

[18] Cf. Bernard Sharratt, *"News from Nowhere:* Detail and Desire," in Ian Gregor, ed., *Reading the Victorian Novel: Detail into Form* (New York: Barnes & Noble, 1980), 289.

[19] Pecora, "The Sorcerer's Apprentices: Romance, Anthropology, and Literary Theory," *Modern Language Quarterly* 55/4 (Dec. 1994), 356, 354.

mation in his historical narrative but also of the form in which he grasps and trans-
mits it. From his inner sanctum in the British Museum, he dispenses sweeping narrative in the grand Victorian style about that past that nearly every other utopian
ignores. When the likes of Hammond and Morsom finally die—these men so much
identified with the temporal order of language and writing—the last trace of narratable time may go with them, since time for the rest of the utopians is that anthropological time Johannes Fabian describes: an empty, geological medium of
horizonless futurity, "no longer the vehicle of a continuous, meaningful story."[20]
To go there is to enter a temporal condition seemingly anathema to linear narrative, at odds with what Thomas Carlyle, in his 1830 essay "On History," famously
disparaged as the historian's "'chains,' or chainlets, of 'causes and effects,' which
we so assiduously track through certain handbreadths of years and square miles,
when the whole is a broad, deep Immensity, and each atom is 'chained' and complected with all!"[21]

Like Malinowski's Trobrianders, the future Britons inhabit a cyclical order that
does include storytelling in its ritual observances—"exactly as we, when children,
or the peasants of Eastern Europe, will hearken to familiar fairy tales and
Märchen," says Malinowski—but that dispenses with Western narrative logic.[22]
In *News,* a propensity for narrating survives among the younger generations, insofar as it does survive, only as eccentric hobby or childish pastime: there is no
sense that these people will continue either to understand themselves or to express
their longings in narrative form. Their grandiose dustman, appropriately styled
"Boffin," may write "reactionary [historical] novels" (News 60), but the consensus seems to be that sustained narrative itself is what is reactionary. The virtual
elimination of conflict also helps make Morris's future Britain a place inhospitable
to storytelling. Disputes do happen, but they do not "crystallize people into parties permanently hostile to one another" (News 117); exhausted in their separate
occasions, enmities supply no momentum for blood-feud, party politics, or ex-
planatory narrative.

Underpinning the storyless aspect of the future is the notion, economically expressed in Freud's 1908 essay "The Relation of the Poet to Day-Dreaming," that
"happy people never make phantasies, only unsatisfied ones"—the political implication of which is, for Morris, that a just and peaceful society would not require
the compensatory illusions of art.[23] When Guest sleeps in the Britain of tomorrow,
he doesn't dream (cf. News 166). Boffin's curiosity about him derives from the
perception that Guest comes "from some forgotten corner of the earth, where people are unhappy, and consequently interesting to a storyteller" (News 60). And
Ellen rejects the whole idea of fiction as something appropriate to ages "when

---

[20] Fabian, *Time and the Other,* 14.

[21] Carlyle, "On History," in *Selected Writings,* ed. Alan Shelstone (Harmondsworth: Penguin,
1971), 55.

[22] *Argonauts of the Western Pacific,* 248; cf. 258, on native storytelling.

[23] Freud, "The Relation of the Poet to Day-Dreaming," trans. I. F. Grant Duff, in *Character and
Culture* (New York: Macmillan, 1963), 37.

[people] must needs supplement the sordid miseries of their own lives with the imaginations of the lives of other[s]." She points out the window at her world's splendid realities, proclaiming, "*these* are our books . . . !" (News 175). In speculating about the life story that *would* have been hers in Guest's century, Ellen sets forth the kernel of many a Victorian novel:

> My friend, you were saying that you wondered what I should have been if I had lived in those past days of turmoil and oppression. Well, I think I have studied the history of them to know pretty well. I should have been one of the poor, for my father when he was working was a mere tiller of the soil. Well, I could not have borne that; therefore my beauty and cleverness and brightness . . . would have been sold to rich men, and my life would have been wasted indeed; for I know enough of that to know that I should have had no choice, no power of will over my life; and that I should never have bought pleasure from the rich men, or even opportunity of action, whereby I might have won some true excitement. I should have been wrecked and wasted in one way or another, either by penury or by luxury. Is it not so? (News 222–23)

The shades of Hetty Sorrel, Tess of the D'Urbervilles, and others, rise up to confirm her suspicions in silent chorus. The point is that, for the younger generation of Morris's utopians, extended narrative becomes imaginable only when they imagine *themselves* living in their guest's time.

The one remaining fount of discord that might yet give rise to narrative is sexual desire, regarded by the utopians as an unalterable natural force that occasionally produces effects comparable to those of "the earthquake of last year" (News 189). But the various informants Guest hears from appear to take pains to prevent desire from achieving full narrative expression. At several points we hear of clashes that have (invariably) resulted from two men's competition for a woman, but these remain mere fragments of stories, never elaborated. Dick mentions that "only a month ago there was a mishap down by us, that in the end cost the lives of two men and a woman"—but he forecloses on plot development by adding, "Don't ask me about it just now" (News 72). Later we hear, truncatedly, of a man "fairly bitten by love-madness" and recently slain by the rival he attacked (News 189). During Hammond's account of the new society and the history that brought it about, Dick and his estranged wife, Clara, are in an adjoining room offstage, working out a reconciliation—a neat image of the text's partitioning of narrative from desire. A doer and not much of a talker, Dick has told Guest nothing of his past with Clara or of his hopes: it is up to Hammond to supply *this* tale of other people's desires, just as he does for Guest in relating how the Victorian revolutionist's longings have all been realized. Hammond's special power as shamanistic narrator involves his sequestration from desire and from active engagement in the affairs of his world. From his vantage-point, after all, his narrative recounts what has already happened; it cannot be for him, as it is for Guest, a wish-fulfillment dream.

Fresh from his encounter with Hammond, Guest is released back into the utopian world to enjoy life as it is lived and felt by real utopians. His new license to function as an insider is signaled by his unprecedented assumption of active roles during the river journey (he takes the oars for the first time), and by the provision of a new character, Ellen, designed in answer to Guest's keenest and most intimate desire. But Ellen's prominence in the last third of the book helps illustrate the thesis that claimants to the authority of controlled immersion must guarantee *both* the reality of their desire (such as a true participant might feel) *and* the prospective resumption of distance (such as an Observer requires). A notorious passage from Malinowski's *A Diary in the Strict Sense of the Term* (1967) can serve as a model of the dual operation. On 19 April 1918, the ethnographer writes:

> A pretty, finely built [Kiriwinian] girl walked ahead of me. I watched the muscles of her back, her figure, her legs, and the beauty of the body so hidden to us, whites, fascinated me. Probably even with my own wife I'll never have the opportunity to observe the play of back muscles for as long as with this little animal. At moments I was sorry I was not a savage and could not possess this pretty girl.

Admitting controlled desire into the scientific relationship—he is sorry "[a]t moments" that he cannot possess the girl; he is *not* a savage—the fieldworker also tries to preserve some of the naturalist's disinterest regarding his material. The detached language of "observ[ing] the play of back muscles" is echoed later in the same entry, when Malinowski writes of "observ[ing] the play of the fishes among the stones." The episode is worked through in a cycle proceeding from abandonment of control, to revulsion, to reassertion of control. "I pawed a pretty [native] girl," the ethnographer acknowledges; and then, later: "That lousy girl . . . everything fine, but I shouldn't have pawed her. . . . Resolve: absolutely never to touch any Kiriwina whore." And finally: "As a matter of fact, in spite of lapses, I did not succumb to temptations and mastered them, *every one of them in the last instance.*"[24] Having taken the plunge, the anthropologist has resurfaced intact; the cycle recurs throughout his fieldwork.

In *News from Nowhere,* Ellen is set apart from all other characters who function as mere observable specimens of the future British. "[O]f all the persons I had seen in that world renewed," Guest says, "she was the most unfamiliar to me, the most unlike what I could have thought of" (News 203). The assertion of her unfathomable alterity is precisely what guarantees that this is a figure crafted especially to suit the guest's imagination. Ellen is plainly assembled out of the same materials from which emerged the Corinnes, the Glorvinas, the Flora Mac-Ivors of romantic literature, those female figures who embody and speak for some country at once backward and enchanting to modern European men, some cultural heritage those men now claim as their own. In terms well suited to Guest's view of Ellen, Hammond speaks at one point of "the inexplicable desire that comes upon a man of riper years to be the all-in-all to some one woman, whose ordinary human kindness and human beauty he has idealized into superhuman perfection, and made the one object of his desire" (News 91). The book offers her up to the narrator's gaze in the sort of tableau granted to no other character but more than familiar from the United Kingdom National Tale and historical novel of the early nineteenth cen-

---

[24] *A Diary in the Strict Sense of the Term* (1967; Stanford, Calif.: Stanford University Press, 1989), 255–56.

tury: "I looked, and over the low hedge saw Ellen, shading her eyes against the sun as she looked toward the hay-field, a light wind stirring her tawny hair, her eyes like light jewels amidst her sunburnt face, which looked as if the warmth of the sun were yet in it" (News 179). And what Ellen represents above all—as, to her chagrin, she knows—is a powerful magnet for narrative. "[E]ven among us, where there are so many beautiful women," she acknowledges, "I have often troubled men's minds disastrously," such that "they fell to making stories of me—like I know you did, my friend" (News 208). Hers has been a life of repeated decamp-ings and isolations, forced upon her by the need to flee those many men who have fallen sway to her unintended erotic force. When Guest first meets her in Run-nymede, she is virtually in hiding—unsuccessfully: her admirers have been mak-ing pilgrimages there and seem "to find [her] all the more interesting for living alone like that" (News 208)—and she anticipates another journey, away from the south of England "to a place near the Roman wall in Cumberland" (News 210). As the mention of the wall might suggest, Ellen is that element of her culture most in need of protection from contaminating contact, and her most enticing and danger-ous act comes when, about to depart for this deeper British past, she breaks from her usual shunning of men to propose that Guest accompany her and live with her there.

In a manner reminiscent of Scott's *Waverley*, *News from Nowhere* fashions this perfect object of romance for Guest merely in order to be seen to negate her pull. After the tableau of Ellen-in-sunlight quoted above, Dick figuratively shoulders Guest aside, appropriating the young woman for his own tale, that of his and Clara's adventures:

> "Look, guest," said Dick, "doesn't it all look like one of those very stories out of Grimm that we were talking about up in Bloomsbury? Here are two lovers wandering about the world, and we have come to a fairy garden, and there is the very fairy herself amidst of it: I wonder what she will do for us." . . .
>
> We laughed at this [Guest writes]; and I said, "I hope you see that you have left me out of the tale."
>
> "Well," said Dick, "that's true. You had better consider that you have got the cap of dark-ness, and are seeing everything, yourself invisible." (News 179)

These gentle words amount to a self-delivered edict of banishment from the story-space of the narrative. Ellen's repudiation of fictions in which "towards the end of the story we must be contented to see the hero and heroine living happily in an is-land of bliss on other people's troubles" is the guarantee that *News* will be no such story; the troubled other people to whom Guest must return are his nineteenth-century contemporaries (News 175–76). In the end, after he awakes once more in his own dingy era, Morris's narrator ruefully confesses that

> [a]ll along, though those friends were so real to me, I had been feeling as if I had no busi-ness amongst them: as though the time would come when they would reject me, and say, as Ellen's last mournful look seemed to say, "No, it will not do; you cannot be of us; you belong so entirely to the unhappiness of the past that our happiness even would weary you. Go back again." (News 228)

To read *News from Nowhere* as I have tried to do here is to gain a perspective from which the self-interrupting, culture-seeking labors of the midcentury Victorian novel might emerge in *their* fullest utopian dimension, as elements of a counterimperial narrative of English or British identity. It is also to grasp one more way that Morris's text differs from Edward Bellamy's *Looking Backward,* the 1888 tale of perfected life that irritated Morris into producing one of his own. Employing, as Morris's book does, the idea of a dream, Bellamy's work ends with a double-awakening trick: the first time, the narrator returns from his dream of a utopian twentieth century to the gloomy nineteenth; but some pages later, he discovers, as he says, that "my return to the nineteenth century had been the dream, and my presence in the twentieth was the reality." Bellamy's hero actually gets to escape his era and marry the woman who is his nineteenth-century beloved's great-granddaughter. Embracing her, the protagonist of *Looking Backward* cries out, "If I am beside myself, . . . let me remain so!"—and that is precisely what the impossible resolution of the narrative (which Morris despised) permits him to do. Should Morris's Guest be tempted to remain "beside himself," he would pose an unwitting threat to his hosts, reintroducing among them the mostly forgotten habits of modern temporal consciousness and thus acting like an "evil charm" upon their single-minded rapture in the seasonal cycle (News 224–25).

Unlike Bellamy's character but like the modern ethnographer, Guest knows himself an unwilling agent of the forces behind him, the thin end of the wedge of that modernizing process that destroys the traditional culture he cherishes and studies. He must go home again, if for no other reason, so as to limit the damage he may cause in the field. Guest can salvage the culture of the future only by getting out of it. In *News from Nowhere,* of course, it is a fall *back* into modernity that is to be feared, rather than what by the middle of the twentieth century had become the standard ethnographic scenario, a dispiriting vision of cultural entropy involving the dissolution of primitive unities into the modern "monoculture"—the scenario given classic expression in Lévi-Strauss's 1955 *Tristes Tropiques.* This frightful possibility that the boundaries surrounding her posthistorical culture will not hold is what makes Ellen, in other respects so unlike old Hammond, take up the sage's banner and urge her contemporaries to recover the history of the culture that is theirs.

INDEX